OTHER PEOPLE'S MONEY

Other People's Money

The Corporate Mugging of America

Nomi Prins

THE NEW PRESS

NEW YORK
LONDON

Requests for permission to reproduce selections from this book should be mailed to:
Permissions Department, The New Press, 38 Greene Street, New York, NY 10013

Published in the United States by The New Press, New York, 2006
Distributed by W. W. Norton & Company, Inc., New York

LIBRARY OF CONGRESS CATALOGING-IN-PUBLICATION DATA
Prins, Nomi.
  Other people's money : the corporate mugging of America / Nomi Prins.
    p. cm.
  Includes bibliographical references and index.
  ISBN-13 978-1-56584-836-8 (hc.) 978-1-59558-063-4 (pbk)
  ISBN-10 1-56584-836-5 (hc.) 1-59558-063-8 (pbk)
  1. Investment banking—Moral and ethical aspects—United States. 2. Corporations—Moral and ethical
aspects—United States. 3. Corporations—Corrupt practices—United States. 4. Stock Market Bubble,
1995–2000. 5. Capital market—United States—History—20th century.   I. Title.

HG4930.5.P75 2004
330.973'0929—dc22   2004049861

  The New Press was established in 1990 as a not-for-profit alternative
    to the large, commercial publishing houses currently dominating
  the book publishing industry. The New Press operates in the public interest
       rather than for private gain, and is committed to publishing,
    in innovative ways, works of educational, cultural, and community value
         that are often deemed insufficiently profitable.

www.thenewpress.com

Composition by Westchester Book Composition

Printed in the United States of America

2   4   6   8   10   9   7   5   3   1

FOR MY FAMILY

Contents

Preface to the Paperback Edition

It's been almost two years since I put the finishing details on the hard-cover edition of *Other People's Money*, and much has happened in the meantime. Some practices have changed. Many more have remained un-altered. But the main premise of the book—that things can go so obvi-ously wrong, while the causes remain largely unaddressed—has stayed disturbingly the same.

Goldman Sachs threw another gala Christmas party for its senior members at the end of 2004, having missed year-end festivities in 2002 and 2003 due to cost cutting and general market malaise. Held at the newly refurbished Museum of Modern Art, the celebration included white-clothed waiters and tables, a lovely team of violinists . . . but no Bette Midler.

Former Goldman Sachs president and chief operating officer John Thain moved up the street to take the CEO spot at the New York Stock Exchange (no one—certainly no one in Washington—appeared to con-sider it a possible conflict of interest that the new CEO of the exchange still owns about 3.2 million shares of the company that led the world in equity offerings in 2004).

In April 2005, there was an equal lack of regulatory scrutiny—though plenty of competitor grumbling—when Goldman acted as adviser to both the NYSE (the acquirer and private firm wanting to go public) and elec-tronic trading firm Archipelago (the "to-be-acquired" firm in which Goldman owns a 15 percent stake). In only 500 of the 145,000 deals an-nounced since 1982 was that dual position the case. Yet Goldman CEO Hank Paulson, self-professed corporate governance crusader in 2002, wasn't publicly cognizant of that issue. The deal closed and the NYSE became a publicly traded company on March 8, 2006.

We've seen an expensive, ill-conceived, and seemingly unending war rack up hundreds of billions of dollars of U.S. debt and deficit. And, once the public was distracted by the war and the stock market had inched back, the Bush administration resurrected the concocted need to convert the Social Security system into a private mutual fund, one where Wall Street brokerages could get the money and associated fees, and the retiring population—with only verbal assurances of this fund outperforming the old government system—would get no actual protections whatsoever.

On every media outlet, from *Entertainment Tonight* to *Vanity Fair*, we witnessed the "corporate criminal event of the millennium" in full-color-photo journalistic style: we watched Martha Stewart go to jail and then return to serve house arrest, with a book and TV show deal in hand.

As for the real dangerous-to-general-society, white-collar criminals: former CEO and president of WorldCom Bernie Ebbers was convicted of perpetuating America's biggest fraud and sentenced to twenty-five years of prison, pending appeal. His CFO Scott Sullivan, who played ball more expertly with the government, got five years behind bars for the same crime.

Over in energy land, former Enron CEO Ken Lay, indicted on eleven charges of fraud, successfully deferred his trial several times while appearing contrite on shows like *Larry King*. His appearance in court finally began in January 2006. His defense was: that Enron was a victim of a media witchhunt and weak market conditions; that only CFO Andy Fastow committed any crime; and that Enron did not. No CEO involved in any of the proven and documented energy manipulation that brought California to its knees was convicted of anything.

Dick Cheney's former firm, Halliburton, managed to raise the ire of Pentagon auditors for failing to account for $1.8 billion of the $4.2 billion its KBR unit billed the government during the first two years of the Iraq war. (Old habits die hard, or never die.)

Dennis Kozlowski, former head of Tyco, was convicted of looting his company to support his luxury habit, and sentenced to seven years in jail. Richard Scrushy, former head of HealthSouth, a company that committed the largest fraud in the healthcare industry, spent a couple of years PR'ing his defense against eighty-five counts of falsifying books, which included providing moral tips on his Christian cable TV show. His emotionally charged Web site (www.richardscrushy.com) contained six pages of heart-wrenching letters vouching for integrity. He was acquitted of criminal charges in mid-2005.

In telecommunications, former Global Crossing chairman Gary Winnick successfully deflected SEC investigations, maintained his position on the board of the U.S. Chamber of Commerce, and was directed to pay back $50 million of the three-quarters of a billion he banked during the broadband bonanza.

In the fall of 2004, Denver-based Qwest Communications International paid the SEC $250 million to settle civil charges of fraudulently recognizing $3.8 billion in revenues from 1999 to 2002. Former CEO Joseph Nacchio was exonerated of related charges but, in December 2005, was indicted on fresh charges of forty-two counts of insider trading. Qwest went on to engage in a bidding war for MCI, in shades reminiscent of its war with Global Crossing for USWest.

So, if you look at the relationship of media coverage to conviction rates, the score as far as jail-time is concerned is kind of a tie. But if you look at the relationship of legal and regulatory manipulation to conviction rates, it's a bust.

One thing is certain: the CEOs and executives that consistently paid the most homage, money, and attention to Washington—the ones that walked that tightrope between politics and actions most expertly—fared better. Kozlowski, Stewart, and Ebbers were not big friends of Capitol Hill, neither in face-time nor in donations. Winnick, Lay and Scrushy knew what they were doing far better.

However, as I pointed out in the hardcover edition, jail and punishment are not the most crucial components of a system attempting to rectify itself. The larger point is the continued dismantling of a regulatory foundation that, by its very disintegration, invites accounting sleight of hand. While the Wall Street community continues to fund corporate expansions and mergers blurring the lines of numerical integrity, Congress remains an enabler of that status quo. The problem hurts the corporate system itself as much, if not more so, as the individuals personally harmed by the reckless exuberance of the late 1990s and early millennium years.

Meanwhile, golden parachutes not only continued but were upgraded to platinum. With imminent threats of investigation, Frank Raines, former chairman and CEO of FNMA (a government-backed entity controlling 75 percent of single-family mortgages), who ran the company while it bloated financials by $9 billion between the years 2001 and 2004, parted with a $140 million package. Former Disney president in 1995, Michael Ovitz, had his $130 million severance for a fifteen-month term reconfirmed. Morgan Stanley co-president Stephen S. Crawford received a $32 million parting gift four months after joining the firm in March 2005.

As predicted in Chapter 4, the Bush administration ultimately buried the final legal attempts to open Dick Cheney's Energy Policy Commission records for public scrutiny. A few months later, in August 2005, President George W. Bush quietly signed into law energy legislation that destroyed the last vestige of PUHCA under the guise of capping skyrocketing oil prices. They promptly rose further after the signing, and more so in the wake of Hurricane Katrina.

Elsewhere, Arthur Andersen, the company that allegedly inspired the Sarbanes-Oxley Act to split accounting and auditing functions for corporations (and shredded a ton of Enron documentation by its own admission), was let off the hook. That unanimous mid-2005 U.S. Supreme Court decision to overturn the June 2002 obstruction of justice verdict for Arthur Andersen didn't exonerate the former "Big Five" player, but it did signify that the American legal system still hasn't figured out how to define, let alone prosecute, white-collar crime.

The original indictment of the document-shredding activities of Arthur Andersen was not about the crime those documents were hiding. It was not about Enron, nor the conflicted activities of auditors who were also accountants effectively playing both the "hide" and "seek" roles for company balance sheets. It was about whether Arthur Andersen knowingly and "corruptly" destroyed material evidence. The Supreme Court determined that the judge had misled the jury of twelve American citizens by not clarifying that doing something corrupt was not in itself corrupt if it was done unknowingly. (If only corporations could plead innocent by reason of insanity.) In other words, unless Arthur Andersen knowingly acted corruptly, the jury could not find the company guilty of obstructing justice. The decision may have proven the triumph of a legal system following the "letter of the law," but in doing so sadly demonstrated an emptier triumph of language over logic.

In Chapter 2 I addressed the precarious position of car manufacturers at the hands of the banking industry. The predicament worsened.

Former blue-chip, investment-grade goliaths GM and Ford were eventually downgraded to junk-bond status. Soon afterward, in an insidious version of "eat what you kill," Bank of America bid for a hefty chunk of GM's loans. Much like turkey farms fattening up their poultry before Thanksgiving.

When Bank of America bought Fleet Boston in a $47 billion merger, the commercial bank secured its position as the third largest in the United States. At the time, analysts considered the 40 percent premium that CEO Kenneth Lewis paid for Fleet crazy. Since then, Bank of America's stock price accelerated faster than that of its two chief rivals, Citigroup and JPM Chase.

In early July 2005 Lewis bid $35 billion in cash and stock for America's third-largest issuer of credit cards, MBNA, adding $142 billion of credit card receivables to its balance sheet and putting Bank of America on top of the fiercely competitive credit card industry. Now it has a 20.5 percent market share and a spot above former number one, JPMorgan Chase. This continues a wave of domestic credit card consolidations that has the top five credit card companies controlling more than 72 percent of the nation's market share. So, despite a tarnished record of SEC investigations and over $1.5 billion in mutual fund infraction fines and corporate class-action lawsuits, Bank of America continues its lumber to the top. What it doesn't do organically it does by writing big checks. In June 2005 it bought a $3 billion (or 9 percent) stake in China Construction Bank, China's second-largest commercial bank. A month later, Bank of America flexed its asset-building muscle again, getting into the very lucrative car-credit business by agreeing to buy $55 billion worth of GMAC's (General Motors Acceptance Corporation) retail automotive contracts over a five-year period.

But Lewis seems focused on a bigger prize. With competitors concentrating on figuring out his next move, Lewis may well steer Bank of America to become the largest American bank in the not-too-distant future.

There's an old saying that "it takes money to make money." In Corporate America, it also takes money to keep money. This sentiment was aptly demonstrated when mega-wealthy financier and Revlon chairman Ronald O. Perelman was awarded $1.4 billion by a Florida jury for receiving misleading advice from Morgan Stanley regarding Sunbeam back in 1998. Not bad for a man already worth $4.2 billion.

But I didn't quite see it as the "daunting blow" for Morgan Stanley that the *New York Times* identified (though it was bad timing for then-CEO Philip Purcell, who ultimately lost his struggle to keep his job). Perelman recouped the entire value of his investment, something no individual whose investment was destroyed by similar practices was able to achieve. The average person can't afford the multimillion legal fees that Perelman could, nor will they recoup the same percentage on their losses.

During the late-1800s railroad mergers provided a license to untold wealth for railroad barons and their Wall Street bankers. Fast forward 140 years and financial, telecom, and energy mergers became the ticket. As U.S. corporations tallied over 9.4 trillion dollars' worth of mergers during the 1990s, Wall Street raked in over $70 billion in fees.

Citigroup's former chairman and CEO (now just chairman) Sandy Weill was one of the leading architects of the financial system's current conflicted structure. Citigroup paid over $3 billion in fines for recent fraud settlements and subsequently increased their legal reserve to $6.7 billion for pending lawsuits. That didn't mar Citigroup's competitive edge. The firm topped the 2004 and 2005 debt and equity issuance charts.

Though the merger business took a bath after the stock market bust, it was booming again, as were Wall Street compensations, by the end of 2004 and more so in 2005. Leading the record $2 trillion in new corporate consolidation were the usual suspects: the financial, energy, and telecom industries, followed closely by the health care industry. It all proves that nothing erases the memory of fraud and conflicts of interest like a fresh round of cash to float on, and a Congress that refuses to dig beneath the surface.

—Nomi Prins
April 2006, New York City

Preface

I started writing this book about two years after Goldman Sachs's December 2000 holiday event, and six months after I had officially left the banking industry. The economy was withering and the corporate world had experienced a succession of fraud-induced bankruptcies not seen since the Great Depression.

Some people would consider corruption and deliberately orchestrated industrial crime par for capitalism's course, as actions that can sometimes be more blatant, sometimes less, but that are always present. I can't completely disagree with that sentiment, but I do believe that more tightly regulated capitalism provides less opportunity for bending or breaking rules. The fewer the rules, the greater the room for illusory practices and resultant instability, including accounting, tax, and regulatory games—the stuff we thrived on in constructing large deals.

When I left Wall Street, at the height of a wave of scandals uncovering scores of massively destructive deceptions, my choice was based on a very personal sense of right and wrong—what was misleading yet legally acceptable versus what was open and transparent. So, when people who didn't know me very well asked me why I left the banking industry after a fifteen-year climb up the corporate ladder, I answered, "Goldman Sachs."

For it was not until I reached the inner sanctum of this autocratic and hypocritical organization—one too conceited to have its name or logo visible from the sidewalk of its 85 Broad Street headquarters—that I realized I had to get out.

As I said to my then-boss, head of fixed income research, when I resigned in early 2002, "I know exactly what I need to do to be successful here—and I have no desire to do it." It was time to go. The fact that my decision coincided with corporate malfeasance of epic proportions made me realize that it was far more important to use my knowledge to be part of the solution than to continue being part of the problem. I left the firm a week later and haven't looked back since—except to examine how the collaboration among firms like Goldman Sachs, corporate America, and Capitol Hill pumped up and then brought down the economy and people's futures with it.

For years, I had moved between two worlds: the world of high finance, which included international meetings with the central bankers and executives who control the world's financial capital, and the world that was critical of the exploitation of the many for the benefit of the few. As an activist in London, I protested against the World Trade Organization (WTO) at the Jubilee 2000–sponsored rally in Birmingham, England; criticized Shell for its role in the murder of Nigerian author Ken Saro Wiwa; and participated in other similar demonstrations. Then I'd return to my desk at Bear Stearns in Canary Wharf, London's version of New York City's World Financial Center, and produce investment ideas for institutional investors.

While I worked at Goldman Sachs in New York, I was an ardent Ralph Nader supporter and marched in Washington against George W. Bush's Supreme Court–enabled presidency and against World Bank and International Monetary Fund (IMF) control of Third World countries' economic agendas while grappling with Goldman's rhetoric about how globalization was good for its bottom line and the general future of the universe.

After what amounted to a nine-month probe, my acceptance into Goldman's world was sealed. Goldman was notorious for the number of insiders who met new prospects, lengthening the interviewing process considerably. During this period I was repeatedly told, among other things, how important diversity was to them, yet not once was I interviewed by anyone who wasn't a white male. Eighteen months after I started, a group comprised of 85 percent white male partners awarded themselves $250,000 each for their efforts to promote diversity. The head of this committee was Lloyd Blankfein, the white male co-head of my division who has since sped up the Goldman ranks to stand first in line for the CEO throne.

The fact is many investment bankers exist in a cocoon of their own self-worth and entitlement. The same could be said of corporate executives. Appearances and "spin" become far more important than the truth.

Not that there aren't some very smart or decent people in finance—there are. I consider many to be my friends. But the belief that what bankers are doing is extremely valuable pervades the investment banking community: if investment bankers weren't financing expansion and innovation, how would progress occur? If they happen to get paid a lot in the process, it's only because their work is so "critical," or so the thinking goes.

I have been a beneficiary of that system, and when I left it, I left behind more money in unvested (never to be redeemed) stock options than I had accumulated throughout my career. In our more introspective moments, some of my colleagues and I would discuss how we were getting paid way too much for what we did. We were, but in the banking industry, money and position were the two main stamps of validation of your role in the organizational hierarchy. It was similar to the industry of politics, only there money comes in the form of campaign contributions and position in the form of power and influence. Getting paid was a mark of your internal rank, your future potential to make even more money. Although in every single company where I worked it was considered a fireable offense to discuss compensation openly (mostly because it was so subjectively set), everyone was aware of the financial goalposts around them. It was the stuff of hours of office gossip, barely disguised bragging, and a lot of complaining.

Much of the financial industry consists of a bunch of type-A hyper-competitive personalities striving to one-up each other using whatever comparative indicators of success might exemplify their importance. The higher you rise on the corporate ladder, the more external competition and pressures to perform for external quarterly earnings reports collide with internal politics and deceptive maneuvering, making things very ugly—and the stock market bloat of the 1990s and the bust and purge that followed were definitely ugly.

—Nomi Prins
June 2004, New York City

Acknowledgments

During my transition from Wall Street to the world of journalism and writing, I have been extremely fortunate to have received assistance, support, and guidance from a host of truly exceptional people. The ones mentioned here are but a small subset.

First and foremost, I'd like to thank Nicole Luber, my research assistant, without whom this book simply could not have happened. Thanks also to Sarah Fan, my amazing and endlessly patient New Press editor, and to Ted Byfield for creating structure from chaos during the initial editing.

I'm grateful to Colin Robinson at The New Press, my awesome publisher, who took a chance on a first-time author and guided me kindly through every step along the way. Thanks to Maury Botton and the rest of the excellent staff at The New Press for all their work.

Thanks to Doug Henwood for his inspiration and advice. Thanks to Andy Robinson for teaching me how to be a journalist, and to John Dizard for his help from Goldman to writing. Thanks to Andrew Kupfer, my *Fortune* editor, who provided me my first byline on a little story about how Gary Winnick got so rich, and to Julie Creswell, senior writer on that story, one of the best reporters ever. Thanks also to Alleen Barber, my *Newsday* editor, for helping shape my opinions for a wide audience.

Thanks to Tyson Slocum at Public Citizen, who suffered through my countless questions on energy regulation, and to Kate Lee, who took me into her home and connected me with a slew of former WorldCom employees for their stories. Thanks to Jessica Ong for providing Thomson Financial data and to Bill Jones of the Bell Tel Retirees, whose efforts to reform corporate governance are inspirational to so many.

Thanks also to Michael Perelman, David Callahan, Rodney Ward, Eugene Coyle, Michael Pollak, Randall Dodd, Paul Altesman, Andrew Taddei, and Robert Brenner for answers and comments as this book was being shaped, and thanks to all my former colleagues at Goldman Sachs, Bear Stearns, Lehman Brothers, and Chase who shared with me years of experiences and thoughts.

My heartfelt gratitude goes to my best friend, Margaret Bustell, for twenty years of unwavering belief and solid support. Thanks also must go to my dear friends on both sides of "the pond," who have been there throughout my personal and professional transitions: Deborah Dor, Francesca Lieb, Vivian Shelton, Lynne Roberts, Marna Bungers, Jon Davidson, Robin Lentz, Bob Selvaggio, Anant Patel, Tracey McCabe, Laurie Campbell, Paula Dominick, Caroline Chen, Tanya Brady, Gayle Tudisco, Aaron Simon, Matt Suroff, Mark Suroff, Lindsey McMurray, Guy Cross, Barry Nix, Alex Romero, and Natalie Schwartzberg.

Finally, thanks to my family: to my brother, Michael, who provided me his time and accounting knowledge and a critical eye during the detail-intense final stages of editing, to my ultra-fabulous sister, Tami, who made sure I had a life outside the book, to my sister-in-law Marisol for her warmth, to my father, who taught me that numbers tell stories, and to my mother, who taught me to question everything.

Prologue: Midsummer Night's Dream

It isn't every evening that *A Midsummer Night's Dream* coincides with the *Nutcracker Suite*. But, one Saturday night in early December 2000, it happened. Reality was overshadowed by fantasy—temporarily.

It was the Goldman Sachs Managing Directors' Christmas Party of 2000. An exclusive gala in Manhattan for the upper echelons of the firm. The grand finale of the opulent 1990s.

Outside, temperatures were just above freezing and it was raining. With such uncooperative weather, there was nothing left to do but go inside, inside the mammoth glass-and-steel construction that was New York's answer to a King Kong jungle gym: the Jacob K. Javits Convention Center. And so we kept filing in. On the right of the entrance lobby, just beyond the revolving doors, was the coat check. It was staffed by women dressed in black-and-white staff tuxedos. Another man in a tux welcomed us, ushering us over to a table to check in. Even during holiday parties, Santa Claus was keeping his list.

We were directed up any one of the three adjacent escalators leading toward the main reception area for cocktails. At the top of the escalators, the carpet was as green as AstroTurf. Endless lines of mud-brown plastic tree trunks covered with thousands of autumn-colored leaves sprung from the synthetic ground. Beyond the artificial forest were wicker-white gazebos, plucked directly from the set of some English countryside drama, guarded by sparkly swans.

Groups of exceedingly well-dressed but decidedly untrendy managing directors were gathering in cliques under the trees. Hundreds of them. The normally austere, imagination-less space of the convention center had been transformed for the evening. It was like a fairy godmother had stopped by earlier, changing the appearance of everything with the touch of a wand—and the help of expensive caterers. Of course, when the clock struck twelve, everyone would return to his or her regular life: the senior partners back to their penthouses on the Upper East Side, the rest of us scattered to other places in Manhattan, its vicinities, and the suburbs.

We made our way in streams through the main cocktail area, past the gazebos furnished with white wicker chairs and dainty round tables for chatting, past more opulent tables with huge floral centerpieces. I was looking for the bar. Only there wasn't one. Instead, armies of waiters hovered about, extending tidings of pink champagne.

It occurred to me this would be a great place for a dog run. In fact, emptied of all the pretension of festivity—and the people—my dogs would have had a terrific time. Space, trees, and food: what more could any dog ask for? For humans, on the other hand, the place was cold and imposing, merely dressed up to seem otherwise. Upon second glance, the fake tree leaves sparkled as cheaply as fake diamonds. The swan creatures looked like they were made of expensive pipe cleaners. The snow was made of cotton balls shredded into cheap fluff. Everything was as fleeting and insubstantial as the bloated bank balances of since-bankrupt dot-com millionaires.

Later, I found out that, despite what seemed like stellar attendance (which I thought was mandatory), many managing directors avoided this event, or showed up only every other year. One of my colleagues said that once every two years was all she could handle. The prior year's theme had apparently been "Fire and Ice." All the themes were rather reminiscent of prom night. So were the outfits.

There was a noticeable contrast in styles of dress that night. I had bought the only evening gown of my life for the occasion, black velvet and gold trim to fit in with the crowd. The female managing directors (that tiny minority) were dressed fairly conservatively: no backless gowns, and we kept our cleavages in check. But this was less the case for some of the wives and girlfriends, whose clingy or low-cut gowns were designed for maximum trophy display.

Everyone in the crowd was in perma-smile mode. This worked well when the photographer swooped in to immortalize the moment. It wasn't the only such event where Goldman hired photographers. For a company that so prided itself on its secrecy and lack of publicity, Goldman saw to it that many of the large gatherings it compelled employees to attend had photographers on hand. Afterward, the pictures were sent in thick white envelopes via interoffice mail to the featured employees or were used in internal marketing material.

The preceding month, I had been forced to attend a global conference welcoming all new managing directors (MDs). For two straight days, the culture of Goldman Sachs was beaten into the Class of 2000 MDs, complete with skits in which we had to role-play situations such as how to act when your subordinates don't listen to you or when you're privy to some piece of insider information. This event too had had a photographer on hand to snap our glee at having made the MD team—that sacred club—that year. I was seated in the front row of our MD class, just as in elementary school, when the shortest kids were put in front for the class picture.

About an hour into the Christmas party festivities, the CEO of the firm, Henry, aka Hank, Paulson, appeared in the middle of the crowd like Moses parting the Red Sea, looking tall and commanding. A hush fell over the immense space as Goldman MDs and their spouses, significant others, and dates all moved closer to Hank, the better to receive his word.

Hank had risen to the top ranks of Goldman through the investment banking division. He had ousted Jon Corzine from the chairman's seat in 1999 because investment banking ruled over the trading division, where Jon had come from. After losing the battle for Goldman's top spot, Corzine rebounded by securing a U.S. Senate seat from New Jersey after launching the most expensive senate campaign in U.S. history.

Then Hank spoke. He wanted to make sure everybody realized that bonuses would not be what they had been the previous year. Even in its infancy, the market downturn was already being felt, and Hank hadn't gotten as far as he had without reading the signs. He told the spouses to realize that their other halves would not be bringing home as much (in both bonus money and quality time), that we were embarking on tough times and would all be working much harder and longer to get through it all. "Don't even think about extensions for those summer Hampton homes, people."

A waiter came up behind us to offer paper-thin slices of French bread and caviar.

Hank continued to say he expected us all to work a lot harder as the market downturn continued, but that he had great faith in the "people of Goldman Sachs" to persevere. He was right about the market meltdown. The stock market was declining weekly, and this was well before corporation after corporation would collapse under fraud allegations, class-action suits, defaults, and bankruptcies. The corporate decay that would follow the Wall Street–manufactured stock and debt bubble would affect invest-ment banking and stock businesses, areas that counted the most on cheery markets and starry-eyed investor morale.

I looked around me. Everyone's eyes were glued to Hank. I detected nods of understanding, almost a sense of weathering a big storm together, that great team spirit at work.

And then it was over. Moments after the speech, the room transformed itself. Reinforcement armies of waiters joined their comrades, and white-gloved maître d's ushered the crowd toward waiting white-clothed tables. Walls vanished to reveal a ballroom with rows of round tables, a stage, and tons of food. Any kind of food, every kind of food. There were specialty pasta tables, with chefs doling out generous helpings of ravioli, creamy ziti, and wild-mushroom lasagna. There were chefs carving up large sides of strip steak heaped with thick gravy. There were salads galore. Every few tables, all these choices would reappear to allow multiple lines.

Wine was plentiful, though, strangely, it really wasn't a drinking crowd: having fun in front of the senior partners of the firm didn't really make sense. Most of the drinking was being taken care of by the non-Goldman attendees.

Bette Midler had been booked as the evening's performer. For some reason, this had been a colossal secret, as if we wouldn't have showed up unless someone good was entertaining us and they didn't want to take a chance on us not being impressed with the Divine Miss M.

Bette had been given a list of the bad habits of Goldman senior executives from an insider, probably someone from PR, but had spun it her own way—into a caustic, sarcastic swipe at the elite. (I don't believe she was ever asked to perform at another Goldman event.) The rest of her shtick was her own. When she took the stage, her first words were, "I never saw so much money in one place at the same time." That was met with nervous laughter. She contin-ued, wasting no time getting straight to the heart of the irony of the evening. "I never thought I'd be performing at that famous, the magnificent . . . Javits Center. You know, it's just a hop away from the Lincoln Tunnel. Why, in no time I could be doing another gig over the river in beautiful Newark, New Jersey." She sang a biting rendition of "Money"—with its fitting first line, "Money makes the world go round"—and other overly appropriate songs. She stopped short of "You've Got to Pick a Pocket or Two" from the musical *Oliver!*

The night came to a screeching halt soon after Bette left the stage. Corporate gatherings never quite inspire the right atmosphere for sticking around and casually hanging out. Everyone beelined for the coat check, leaving in their wake a trampled and spent fairyland, thoroughly grazed food tables, and capsized swans. We covered up our formal evening wear and headed back into the cold, wet night—to the line of black Lincolns booked to whisk us away. Two weeks later, I received the photos; the person with the plastic smile and fancy gold shawl posing against a background of glitter resembled me but in fact was merely a photo memory of an identity I wanted to shelve.

With the economic downturn intensifying, and all the cost-cutting measures beginning to make their way around the Street, this MD Christmas party was the last of its kind. Afterward, management would be too embarrassed to partake in such open excess. They would focus on the declining market and the business that investment banks were losing steadily to the new supermarket-style commercial-investment bank conglomerates like Citigroup and JP Morgan Chase.

Introduction

> The secret of great wealth with no obvious source is some forgotten crime, forgotten because it was done neatly.
>
> —Balzac, *Old Goriot*

An unbridled air of wall street arrogance prevailed at Goldman Sachs, the most powerful investment bank in the world. It wasn't so much the attitude of the individual employees as much as of the place itself. The very atmosphere oozed smugness. When I joined the firm in March 2000 as a managing director, my arrival coincided with the pinnacle of the bull market, the turning point after which everything headed south. Over the next three years, the NASDAQ shed over 70 percent of its value, over two million jobs were cut, and the unemployment rate rose from 3.9 percent to 6.4 percent. Dreams of comfortable retirement for millions of Americans were shattered.

Over on the other side of the wealth pool, corporate executives did exceedingly well for themselves. According to a *Fortune* magazine study, one thousand corporate executives siphoned off $66 billion between 1998 and 2001, with $23 billion going just to insiders at the top twenty-five firms with the largest amount of cash-outs, a list including names like AOL Time Warner (which returned to its roots as plain old Time Warner by the end of 2003), Yahoo, Global Crossing, and Cisco.[1] Qwest led the Top 25 club with $2.3 billion transferred from the pensions of its workers to the pockets of its leaders. How did that happen? Workers' pensions were invested in their own company's stock. When the senior circles cashed out at the peak just before the crash, they reduced the value of the shares and thus the value of the workers' pensions. The faster chief executive officers (CEOs) cashed out, the faster pensions fell in value. Plus, the overall market got pounded by a combination of factors, including widespread bankruptcies that resulted when corporations were unable to make good on their bond interest payments because their high reported earnings simply weren't real.

Not only did executives manage to grab substantial wealth by exercising their options on company shares at bloated levels as well as by actually selling their shares outright, but CEO pay relative to the average worker shot out of control. This continued a three-decade trend that had spiked in the mid-1990s. The difference in real annual compensation of the top one hundred CEOs rose from $1.3 million in 1970 to $37.5 million in 1999. During the same period, the average annual salary in the United States only rose from $32,522 to $35,864, meaning average worker salaries rose 10 percent while CEO salaries rose 288 percent.[2] Put another way, in 1983 CEOs made forty-two times what the average worker made.[3] That factor today is 1,046 times, and those salaries don't even include stock options or all the ridiculous perks—the $1-million-per-year corporate jets, the $20,000-per-month Manhattan apartments, and the $15,000 umbrella stands.

The years 2001–2003 produced more bankruptcies than any other period in U.S. history. Corporate bankruptcy volume reached over $500 billion in the years following 1980, 75 percent of them occurring in 2001 and 2002. Ninety percent of those were in the energy and telecom industries.[4] Executives of the twenty-five largest bankrupt firms still managed to saunter off with $3.3 billion—before their companies declared bankruptcy.[5]

Total corporate debt in the form of outstanding bonds and loans soared to $8 trillion after 1998, more than triple the amount from 1990 through 1998.[6] Meanwhile, the Federal Reserve lowered rates eleven times in 2001, which only served to make this debt cheaper to accumulate as corporations became desperate to keep their operations going, expanding relentlessly and haphazardly. That's why, in 2001, debt issuance rose even while stock transactions declined. Companies had no choice but to borrow money from investors when they couldn't raise it through the stock market. This excess borrowing made the companies even less healthy and more unstable than their falling earnings alone indicated. It packed their balance sheets with even more debt, leaving them in a precarious financial state.

Meanwhile, systemic accounting fraud—some companies still refer to it as "efficient accounting"—helped boost stock value in the mid- and late-1990s. Then Enron came along. It wasn't the first example of Corporate America's corrupt underbelly—smaller fraudulent telecoms like Exodus,

PSINet, and Winstar had been dropping like flies throughout 2001. It wouldn't be the last, either; WorldCom self-destructed in 2002. Other companies, like AOL Time Warner, Ford, and half the merchant energy industry, continue to suffer fraud investigations and abysmal performance issues.

Regulatory agencies funded by our tax dollars failed to see the train wreck coming or, worse, ignored it completely—because they were partially to blame. Congress lacked the same foresight, not least because they, their corporate sponsors, and even their middle-class constituents were reaping the benefits of the boom. Then, all of a sudden, the party was over and $8 trillion of market value, including stock that had exploded during the boom market on the back of bogus valuations, vanished in two short years.

Although this book concentrates on the U.S. markets, the effects of U.S. corporate disintegration reverberated worldwide as globalization collided with global deregulation throughout the 1990s. Germany closed its equivalent of our NASDAQ stock market index, Neuer Markt, after it lost *all* its value in September 2002. The French telecom giant Vivendi and other European corporations kicked out their leaders in the hopes that their replacements would do better. Only the comparatively strong position of labor groups in Europe insulated workers and jobs there more than in the United States.

What's more astonishing still is that many of the perpetrating companies and executives got away with it. Almost everyone involved in the creation of first the stock bubble and then the wealth, power, and market share—from the corporate executives to the banks to the regulators to Congress to the Oval Office—escaped without admission of responsibility or direct retribution for the jobs and money lost.

EVOLUTION OF THE NEW DEAL

The stock market crash of 1929 put millions of people out of work and wiped out the fortunes of the rich and the poor alike. It also served to illuminate corrupt practices that had falsely inflated stock values and hidden the true nature of corporate and Wall Street business practices.

When the financial scandals of 1929 hit, President Franklin D. Roosevelt's administration, backed by popular support, reacted by installing reform measures. Roosevelt created a group of regulatory bodies to establish some sense of control over a tanking economy and to uphold the public's interest. Major utility sectors were governed by the Federal Communications Commission (FCC) and the Federal Power Commission (FPC). The government sharpened oversight of securities trading by establishing the Securities and Exchange Commission (SEC) "to protect investors and maintain the integrity of the securities markets."[7] Boundaries were established between investment and commercial banks by the Glass-Steagall Act, which was passed amid a whirlwind of fraud committed by the National City Bank (which later became Citibank and then Citigroup). Glass-Steagall, or the Banking Act of 1933, separated investment banking from loan and deposit activities and created important federal rules and regulatory bodies to protect the public from haphazard bank speculation with their money. It established the Federal Deposit Insurance Corporation (FDIC) and gave it authority to regulate and supervise some banks and provide deposit insurance to customers. It prohibited deposit and lending banks from selling securities—in other words, commercial banks could not own brokerages. This idea of separating lending and deposit businesses from securities stemmed from the debacle of speculative investment banking that had egged on mass corruption during the roaring 1920s. Glass-Steagall created an incentive for banks to choose commercial over investment banking by shifting bank-failure risk back to the government via FDIC deposit insurance.

Since then, particularly from the 1970s on, regulatory bodies and the laws they are supposed to enforce have been systematically weakened if not actually nullified by corporations, financial institutions, and their collusive puppet legislators. In early November 1999, Glass-Steagall was repealed by the U.S. Senate in an almost unanimous bipartisan vote. It ushered in a period of mergers between securities firms and commercial banks, further consolidating an already consolidated industry, and enabled the use of insured customer money as carrots in the form of cheap credit for big corporate business. The George W. Bush administration was not just ill-equipped, but also unlikely to regulate the conditions that led to the post-1990s bust; it has too much to gain politically and financially by maintaining the status quo. Even in the aftermath of the dramatic downturn, and at the time of this writing, more deregulation is still under way on the Hill, rendering tough reform talk a joke.

Yet this current market upheaval touched more Americans from an investment and personal wealth standpoint than did the crashes of the

1920s or the late 1890s. The percentage of middle-class households with at least some investment in the stock market tripled from 15 percent in 1983 to 46 percent in 1998, mostly through new types of pension plans—lobbied for by corporations to shift responsibility, and risk of loss, for retirement savings onto employees and away from the corporations themselves. More volatile savings plans like 401(k)s, requiring employees to contribute to their retirement plans generally without being matched by company contributions, and Investment Retirement Accounts (IRAs) replaced more stable benefit pension plans, in which employees were guaranteed a preset monetary award upon retirement.[8] By 1996, such defined benefit plans were the primary retirement savings for only 25 percent of single-employer workers, down from 80 percent in 1980.[9]

The share of households with stock exposure through various schemes quadrupled from 1983 to 1998. Smaller stockholders were more vulnerable to the loss of value in their retirement plans because these investments represented a larger proportion of their overall wealth. Fifteen percent of middle-income households held 8 percent of their wealth indirectly or directly in the stock market, and 12 percent held 17 percent or more in the stock market.[10] If that trend continues, the next time the market falls, it will land on even more Americans.

Some say this boom-and-bust cycle is par for the capitalist course. Look at railroads, look at steel, and look at autos. The robber barons of the 1890s and 1900s were just as crooked as today's unsavory pack of CEOs and made just as much money on the backs of everyone else. But while they share many similarities, there are also glaring differences. For example, the railroad bubble developed slowly over twenty-five years, during which the capacity of railroad tracks doubled the demand; conversely, the telecommunications explosion ballooned and burst in just four years and produced twenty times more capacity than was needed. Also, no one *had* to use railways; no one *had* to buy cars. But everyone *has* to use energy, and over 95 percent of American households own a telephone.[11]

Illicit accounting led to overvaluation of stock, but overvalued assets like fiber-optic networks and profit booked on fake capacity, power, or electricity trades also allowed companies to borrow money without any real source for repayment, causing bankruptcies later on. The growing sophistication of financial tools provided a way (often perfectly legal) for companies to mask their true performance. The lack of regulatory oversight, by design, enabled industries to build on a sand castle of debt, hyper-stock inflation, and deception. The systematic dismantling of New Deal reforms and co-opting of the regulatory bodies created to enforce them culminated in the Clinton era, when major legislation deregulating the telecommunication and energy industries passed in 1996 and legislation deregulating the banking industry passed in 1999. The Bush administration has taken deregulation ever further.

Another difference between the boom-and-bust eras is that in the past, companies merged and acquired other companies with combinations of cash, debt, and stock. For example, in his visionary book *Wall Street*, Doug Henwood explains that 70 percent of all corporate investment between 1952 and 1997 was done with cash.[12] But in the late 1990s, the currency of choice was stock. The more inflated the stock, the more it could buy. Every large merger of that era that ultimately failed was an all-stock-based deal. Investors picked up the tab after driving up stock prices through frenzied, broker-spurred stock buying, which, in turn, caused stock to be overvalued. That same exaggerated stock was used by the acquirer to buy up companies far bigger than itself, like AOL's acquisition of Time Warner. The carcasses of the companies who were most aggressive and least regulated now either litter the floors of bankruptcy courts or are struggling (underneath pitiful revenue streams) and are no match for the debt they incurred or the lawsuits they are facing.

Despite the fact that stock was used as currency and many companies didn't have to put up actual cash, they still incurred megadebt to make questionable acquisitions—and guess what? They're passing that debt load directly onto us: witness the fall of WorldCom, which resulted in a 25 percent increase in the long-distance rates of MCI, its acquisition.[13] In the past, "acquisition" meant that the bigger companies took over the smaller ones, and the result, for better or worse financially, was a larger, stronger company, if not always from a labor perspective. In the 1990s, however, the small took over the big and the two went down together. AOL Time Warner announced an annual loss of $99 billion, the largest in corporate history, on the heels of a mammoth $44 billion goodwill write-down (the amount by which the purchase price exceeds the *net tangible assets* of the acquired company); it booted former AOL chairman Steve Case, and then went back to being just Time Warner after every other department and division there suffered cuts to pay for the value lost when AOL turned out to be worth far less than its evaluations at the height of the bubble had stated.[14]

THE START OF THE DECLINE

It was the hope born of inflated earnings reports that kept the markets up for so long even as real corporate profits were declining. The end of 2000 in particular was a time when many investors wanted to believe in the invincibility of the markets despite mounting evidence to the contrary. Stock market strategists fed this desire by talking up individual company stocks and the overall market. The media feasted on their enthusiasm. Mega-investors such as pension funds bought into the rhetoric with the financial futures of their employees. Meanwhile, corporate executives had anticipated the potential downfall years earlier and were already working over the books.

During the fall of 2000, I spoke at Goldman's Pension Chief Investment Officer (CIO) Conference, to a roomful of portfolio managers representing the retirement plans of companies like IBM and GM. The audience controlled over a trillion dollars, about 60–65 percent in stock and the rest in bonds. Abby Joseph Cohen, "market caller extraordinaire," spoke first. *Fortune* magazine had ranked Abby eighth in their "Most Powerful Women in Business" poll of 2000. But Abby's media coverage and unwavering message of market optimism soon turned unpopular. She dropped to fiftieth place in 2001 and off the chart in 2002, much like the market did.

At the conference, she explained why the current downturn in markets was a temporary blip, claiming that we would see a resurgence of mutual fund investment at the end of the year that would boost the market. Everyone responded with enthusiastic applause when she was finished. They wanted to believe. Abby predicted that the S&P 500 index would hit 1,600 by year's end (it closed the year at 1,320).

I followed Abby, speaking about the changing landscape of the debt market, about how corporate issuance was becoming more dominant as government debt declined, and about the risk that entailed. I got a fairly tepid reaction; no one wanted to see the dangers on the horizon. Robert Schiller of Yale University and *Irrational Exuberance* fame spoke after lunch. His cautionary talk, supported by slides depicting graphs of lowered profitability and other financial health indicators, was challenged by the room. A series of grilling questions poking apart his argument followed. Though Schiller delineated clear reasons why the market was overinflated, no one really wanted to listen.

INTERNAL INVESTMENT BANKING POLITICS

One of the groups I ran at Goldman was called FIRST, which stood for Fixed Income Restructuring and Strategic Transactions (Wall Street is so fond of acronyms). We advised large financial institutions and corporations on ways in which they could use structured securities to take advantage of regulatory, tax, or accounting loopholes and optimize their financial situations. I also ran Goldman's quantitative credit analysis group. We were the geeks who put numbers behind the marketing of credit derivative and corporate bond strategies.

One way to understand derivative trades is to think of a transaction in which what is exchanged is not a commodity but the right to buy or sell that commodity for a specified price, called a "strike price," in the future. Thus, energy derivatives don't involve the actual purchasing or selling of natural gas or jet fuel but, rather, simply the trading of its future expected value, whether real or fabricated. If you thought electricity prices were going to rise in three months, you'd want to lock in a lower price for them now—or buy a derivative giving you the right to buy that electricity at a lower price in the future, even if the prevailing price of electricity turns out to be higher, allowing you to profit by selling electricity at the current higher market price and pocketing the difference.

Credit derivatives involve buying or selling a corporation's chance of defaulting on its debts. The greater the chance of a company defaulting, the more expensive the credit derivative or insurance premium against it is. It's like car insurance: the more accident-prone a driver, the higher the premium he or she will need to pay. Everyone in my division wanted a piece of the credit derivatives product. In fact, for those managing directors prowling for the coveted position of partner—so glowingly depicted in Lisa Endlich's book, *Goldman Sachs: The Culture of Success*—connection to this product showed they knew where the money was. Or, in Goldman terms, they were "commercial."

Hank Paulson, the CEO himself, took credit derivatives on board as his personal pet project. They were hot because they offered a new way to trade the future value of a corporation's ability to repay debt without buying or selling corporate bonds. They were profitable for investment banks because they were new, and like any new financial product, the spread or differential between the buying and selling price was wide, which meant there was more room to extract trading profits or sales commission. Also, because they were new, there was less transparency about how they were priced. Foreign-exchange derivatives and swaps on interest-rate derivatives all started out with wider spreads until the market got accustomed to trading them. Afterward, liquidity increased and spreads tightened accordingly.

ENTER ENRON

My personal introduction to Enron began well before its highly publicized downfall. My credit derivatives strategy group had written a piece on managing credit risk for corporations. It was basically a marketing document outlining strategies for corporations who wanted to hedge their exposure to other corporations in case of default, using credit derivatives traded by Goldman Sachs and other Wall Street firms to do so. Since credit derivatives were among the hottest and fastest-growing products in finance throughout the 1990s, their use grew as corporate debt issuance ballooned.

Enron was one of the market's largest traders, not just of energy derivatives but increasingly of credit derivatives as well. In fact, it was a major competitor with Goldman Sachs and other financial institutions. Until its demise, Enron regularly shared top honors with Goldman Sachs and Morgan Stanley in various categories of the annual Energy Power Risk Management Awards, the industry-wide energy trading honors bestowed by RiskWaters Group beginning in 2000 with the explosion of speculative trading by emerging power marketers and the investment banking community. These two groups would later be at each other's throats; they were trading partners in some transactions but competitors in others, often with the unregulated power marketers going after the investment banks' client base. The result was that investment banks continued to trade with the power companies, but the relationship often took on a tone of hostile silence, rather like a loveless marriage.

Enron wanted to put our publication on its Web site. Why? Because it legitimized the company. Its unregulated credit derivatives trading operation would be rubber-stamped by the mighty Goldman Sachs. Enron was not only trading commodities like electricity, natural gas, and oil—it was trading credit instruments like a bank even though it wasn't regulated like a bank. Enron wasn't even a particularly prominent investment banking client for Goldman, so huge internal debates and numerous phone calls and voice mails ensued about whether or not we should let this sometimes-client always-competitor tout our research. The fear was that they would use it to capture our credit-derivatives clients themselves. In the end, the client part of the relationship won out and Enron did put our research on its Web site. It stayed up there until three months after the company declared bankruptcy.

PERCEPTION VS. REALITY

Goldman announced in April 2002, during the height of the 2002 scandals, that it would separate its equity and investment banking divisions. This was a preemptive move designed to assure customers—and, more important, investors and regulators—of the firm's stance against corruption. Two months later, Hank Paulson addressed the National Press Club in Washington. He used the economic decline and fraud disclosures to underscore this equity/banking distinction, and was hailed by the press as a leader in corporate reform.

Here was the head of one of the world's most prestigious investment banks saying very little and receiving praise for it. He admitted no real culpability for anything, though he did apologize on behalf of Goldman Sachs if, "particularly in the context of the technology and the telecom bubble of the late 1990s, we have not done as good a job as we might have in preserving and protecting the perception of the independence of our analysts."[15]

In reality, the practice of cross-selling debt and equity services continued. Working across divisions to pool client access was also a response to tremendous external competition from the big commercial banks that had, thanks to the Glass-Steagall repeal, been able to buy up investment banks and thus offer both investment banking services and low-cost credit and loans. The opening chapter of this book examines the fights between the different factions of the banking system: between the gold-plated investment banks like Goldman Sachs and Morgan Stanley and the newly evolved "überbanks" like Citigroup and JP Morgan Chase.

It was not simply the hunger of the post–Glass-Steagall banks to win fee business (for which they could charge corporations real up-front cash for their investment banking services) by offering cheap credit, but also the rivalry between investment banks and commercial banks for market supremacy that led to failed IPOs (initial public offerings), skyrocketing debt, and reckless mergers in the fight for corporate business. Banks were too eager to appease their clients and inflate their perceived worth. The more successful their clients were, the more buying power their stock had, which would ensure the next big-ticket transaction. As banks themselves grew through financial mergers (the total volume of mergers in 1998 and 1999 tripled compared to the rest of the decade), competition intensified. Mergers also created ever-bigger corporations, making it all the more necessary for banks to corner their business. Each deal was too lucrative to lose.

This competition and deal mania in turn fueled the bubble. Each institution played to its strengths to capture its piece of the pie: investment banks took advantage of their longterm client relationships, and the über-banks utilized their massive balance sheets to fulfill client appetite for leverage, which included extending loans in conjunction with merger advisory services (loan tying), formerly only investment banking terrain. (Loan tying is a major breach of antitrust law. Therefore, no bank will admit to specifically tying a loan to a deal or maintain any related paper trail. They will deceptively assert they're really just a full-service institution, providing clients credit (on extraordinarily favorable terms) as well as merger, acquisition, and IPO services). At the same time, corporations were happy to hand over some banking business in exchange for loans at better rates. Mutual back-scratching and arm-twisting suited both banks and their corporate clients just fine.

When companies stop paying interest on their loans, those loans become "nonperforming." When companies undergo financial difficulties, the number of loans required to continue operation increase, along with the likelihood of nonperformance. These loans in turn eat into revenues and lower their stock values (meaning more retirement- and pension-fund erosion). Banks make up the difference in part by lowering the interest rates they could be paying on consumer accounts and cutting services such as human tellers.

The überbanks' stock prices tanked as news of these loans and bad performance infiltrated the media in 2002. To counter news of his firm's deteriorating stock performance, William Harrison, CEO of JP Morgan Chase, wrote an editorial for the *Wall Street Journal* depicting his institution as a victim of the deteriorating market, on a par with the rest of the investing public.[16] This stab at confession happened to coincide with an earnings release in which JP Morgan Chase said that, among other things, its telecom loans were not performing. The stock lost 12 percent of its value that day.

COLLECTIVE AMNESIA

Perhaps the most astounding side effect of the eruption of scandals, bankruptcies, and defaults is the collective amnesia that seems to have befallen so many of the chief architects of the boom. Enron's former CEO Kenneth Lay started forgetting things back in early 2001, when he told a group of Wall Street analysts that certain transaction details were simply "above his head."[17] Enron chief financial officer (CFO) Andrew Fastow didn't seem to remember that his loans, backed by his Enron stock (which in turn backed many of the partnerships he opened for Enron) had violated accounting rules. Three other former Enron executives—Fastow's aide Michael Kopper, as well as Richard Buy and Richard Causey—couldn't remember how to speak when they took the Fifth Amendment on February 7, 2002, before the House Energy and Commerce Committee.[18] Former CEO Jeffrey Skilling claimed "no knowledge of intimate details of Enron's financial dealings" when he testified before Congress in February 2002.[19]

Gary Winnick, chairman of the bankrupt Global Crossing, didn't seem to recall the decaying condition of Global Crossing (a company that never produced any dividends for its shareholders) despite daily phone conversations with then-CEO Tom Casey in mid-2001 and the fact that he sold $125 million of his stock and options seven months before the bankruptcy.[20] Jack Grubman, telecom analyst demigod, couldn't seem to remember whether e-mails he'd sent were true or false. Sanford Weill, chairman of Citigroup, didn't remember if he asked Grubman to say nice things about AT&T before an important deal. (In 1999 Weill and Michael Armstrong, chairman of AT&T, sat on each other's boards. Weill has since resigned from AT&T's board; Armstrong remains on Citigroup's.)[21]

Only a handful of people in the Senate, the House, the Oval Office, or any of the major regulatory bodies seemed to remember anything about passing the enabling legislation that further made the accounting and speculative trading rule-bending of the 1990s easier, or the scores of annual reports or 10K filings that might have signaled the oncoming economic crisis yet were never properly examined. That's because political contributions also soared in the late 1990s, alleviating the need for clear focus. Political contributions from 1998 through 2000 more than doubled the amount given in the previous eight years.[22]

The amount of clout the financial sectors wield in Washington can't be underestimated. The FIRE (financial insurance and real estate) sector tops the list of contributions to Washington every year. It has donated over $1.3 billion since 1990, 57 percent to Republicans and 43 percent to Democrats. During the three election cycles that spanned 1998 through 2002, that ratio tilted toward the GOP, who received 60 percent of FIRE's political funds. Goldman Sachs led contributors in the securities and investment subcategory in seven out of eight election cycles. It forked over $7 million in donations during the 2002 and 2004 election cycles and had doled out a grand total of $17 million since 1990. The only year Goldman placed second in its category was 1994, when it gave $957,045, just behind Merrill Lynch's $1.3 million.[23]

Such consistent support undoubtedly paved the way for ex-Goldmanites to take highly visible routes into key government positions; examples include Robert Rubin, Jon Corzine, and Stephen Friedman. Hank Paulson may join their ranks at some point; after all, he began his career working at the Pentagon for the Nixon administration in 1970. Where do you go after you run the most politically influential firm on Wall Street, if not to Washington?

The collective amnesia was still in effect on November 13, 2002, when the FCC approved the largest cable merger ever, between AT&T and Comcast. The deal was originally valued at $29.2 billion. When it was first proposed in December 2001, it was worth $70 billion, yet FCC chairman Michael Powell saw no red flags flying from this new company that would control 30 percent of the unregulated cable market and was starting out with lots of debt, declining stock values, and 1,700 job cuts. AT&T Comcast was another all-stock deal approved in a tattered industry that had already lost 70 percent of its value. The lack of connective reasoning was astonishing. The lack of any kind of accountability was criminal, but not uncharacteristic.

The banks were pretty significant historic figures in that deal. Enter Goldman Sachs and Credit Suisse First Boston (CSFB), financial advisers for AT&T's March 1999 acquisition of the cable company Telecommunications Inc. (TCI), a deal valued at $62 billion and worth $105 million in bank fees. When AT&T sought their financial opinion of the potential acquisition, which was also presented to the FCC for approval, the banks glowingly recommended AT&T's purchase of TCI.

Fast-forward two and a half years to fall 2001, and Goldman Sachs, CSFB, Morgan Stanley, JP Morgan, and Deutsche Bank were giving solid financial reasons why it now made sense to split TCI (now AT&T Broadband) from AT&T, or to "flip" the company. This process of flipping companies for stock rather than cash puffed up the bubble way more than giving CEOs hot shares. When companies were sold in this way, they were sold for a dream, not a reality. The dream moved further away from reality the more the stock prices themselves were overvalued based on exaggerated or misleading expectations of a company's future profit potential. In the AT&T case, the same investment bankers acted as financial advisers again, giving completely different opinions and bagging more fees to undo what they had done earlier. The second time around, deal fees for the five Wall Street banks involved doubled to $221 million.

CORPORATE CORRUPTION AND ITS EFFECTS

Debt in the form of bonds or loans ballooned in the late 1990s—to over $1.2 trillion for the energy sector and $1 trillion for the telecom sector between 1998 and 2002. We knew about the capacity of and networks built by the telecoms because advertising them was a key stock-propping strategy, but it was less clear what the energy sector did with all the money it borrowed. It remains so.

The energy, telecom, and bank sectors all worked together to create the bubble and are thus collectively responsible for its bust. Energy companies were trading broadband while telecom companies swapped capacity with them. Enron was offering financial advice to telecoms. All-stock deals were the rage and endless flows of cheap debt accumulated out of control. It was a recipe for disaster.

Hundreds of thousands of miles of fiber optics were laid or bought by emerging telecom carriers in the mid- to late 1990s in anticipation, or promotion, of an eruption of demand for Internet services. Ninety-six percent of those lines are not in use today. Energy companies began experimenting with fiber-optic networks in the late 1980s, but it took a decade for the concept to spread and for some well-placed rhetoric from UUNet, the precursor to WorldCom, to spur it on.

In the mid-1990s energy companies became speculative trading houses without any thought given to the production or actual distribution of product to consumers (see chapter 4). As a result, California lost over $45 billion when prices spiked to $3,000 per megawatt hour in mid-2001. But it wasn't until a year later that the FERC issued its report stating that energy companies may have manipulated those prices. Today's price is around $40 per megawatt hour.

Williams Companies, one of the big energy companies that gouged California, received a $417 million slap on the wrist payable over three years, the harshest punishment in its sector, but admitted no guilt regarding price manipulation. This was despite the fact that the company systematically closed power generators to increase profits in the ones they left open during the California blackouts. None of the companies involved in manipulating power prices took responsibility for contributing to or creating California's energy crisis. In addition to Enron and Williams, power companies such as Dynegy, El Paso, Duke, Mirant, and Reliant also fell under investigation.

Indeed, everyone is pretty adept at passing blame to everyone else. The U.S. Senate now blames the California energy crisis on FERC for not noticing what Enron was doing. California and power industry officials blame the technology industry for the increased demand that high-tech companies placed on the state's power supplies. California voters blamed former governor Gray Davis and renamed the blackouts "gray-outs," while Davis blamed federal regulators, the Bush administration, and energy providers. Energy companies blame state lawmakers. The Bush-controlled FERC throws the blame back at Davis for not acting more aggressively when the crisis first began to appear a year earlier. Before all that blame throwing, U.S. Senator Dianne Feinstein from California repeatedly found herself ignored by President Bush and pushed off on Vice President Dick Cheney when she asked for help during the blackout crisis.

It's important to note that the "few bad apples" excuse that demonizes Enron is not entirely accurate. The banks didn't create cool new structured products only for single clients. If a strategy was deemed profitable, they'd shop it around. A transaction was never done only once if it could be "leveraged" across the client base and taken to other potential customers. Also, despite the fact that each investment bank thinks it has the corner on the hottest new trade, every bank pretty much peddles the same stuff, which explains why many of the structures that Enron used were equally marketed to and used by all the other energy companies. Many companies performed similar transactions and "flexible" accounting methodology—some just in greater magnitude than others. Some just didn't get caught.

ELIOT SPITZER: THE CRUSADER

New York State Attorney General Eliot Spitzer has spoken about the conflict of interest between the investment banks' research analysts who tout companies and the bankers who garner fees by representing them. Yet neither he nor anyone else in government mentioned the very legal, fully transparent activity of flipping companies for billions of dollars of company assets. The AT&T Comcast deal went through despite the poor track record of prior all-stock megamergers: WorldCom-MCI, Qwest–US West, AOL Time Warner, JP Morgan Chase. They all failed to some degree. The wholes of these combined companies were much less valuable than the sum of their former parts. Many people lost money to these mergers and many lost their jobs, yet the merger beat continues. Still, if it's a conflict of interest for the same firm to provide both audit and accountancy services for the same client, it is definitely a conflict for the same investment bank to merge two companies and then rip them apart within a few years.

Spitzer made it apparent that age-old conflicts exist on Wall Street, but in fact he actually accomplished very little to change them. He did manage to win one small victory when he got the SEC to back a motion—though not a law—to require investment firms to disclose more information about potential conflicts of interest between clients and the banks' research function. But, much as the Surgeon General's warning on cigarette packs doesn't keep people from smoking, disclosing that your firm may have a tight relationship with a client for whom you are also providing research doesn't necessarily provide much of a buffer, and we should recognize this as such.

Investment banks of course research their client companies as well as nonclients. That's the business they are in. Placing a disclosure statement on research reports that "possible relationships may exist"—precisely the wording now used as some pseudocompromise to deflect further regulator or attorney-general interrogations—is completely superfluous. Now, disclosing the actual *depth* of the relationship with a client might go further in enabling an investor to make a more educated decision. For instance, disclosing which senior bank executive resides on which corporate client's board of directors would shed useful light on the real nature of the bank-client relationship. But no one's gone so far as to suggest that.

Disclosing that your client is under SEC investigation might also be illuminating, but no one's suggesting that either. The SEC itself does not even make its investigative activities public until a court action has been filed, unless "some other source discloses this information. . . . As a result, the SEC can neither confirm nor deny the existence of any investigation."[24] The SEC officially recognized in September 2002 that this practice was "frustrating" but explained that, in the event that their investigations don't uncover anything, they are protecting the companies and individuals involved.[25] Of course, allowing companies to plunge from investment-grade status to bankruptcy in the course of a month, taking their stock value to zero in the process with no warnings from the regulatory agency designed to protect investors, isn't particularly protective of that public. But, the SEC ran into its own problems. During the height of the corporate scandal deluge, the commission was left effectively headless for weeks after the 2002 election-night resignation of Harvey Pitt, the Bush appointee who had to recuse himself from twenty-nine SEC fraud cases because of his own conflicts of interest.

ANALYSTS AREN'T THE ONLY CULPRITS

Analysts were just one of Wall Street's tools. Many other modes of collusion, partial-truths, and select media sound bites were used to market the firms and their deal capabilities to the public. "Relationship management" was the big buzz phrase on the Street in 2000 and 2001. Thus in 2001, I found myself on Goldman's marketing committee, which consisted of a bunch of managing directors from all divisions of the firm who convened once a month to talk about how they could maximize the firm's overall "relationship" with its clients. In reality, each division just wanted access to the others' key clients—penetrating the client from all sides, so to speak. Penetration was a key concept, particularly as the market was weakening and any large deal was hard to come by. The question of deal validity rarely came into play. If you could argue that a transaction would be beneficial to a client, your marketing pitch did just that. It was all part of the game, and everyone involved benefited—as long as they could.

Thus, while it is tempting to simply blame the 1990s crisis and scandals on the star stock analysts for their lack of integrity, their bad stock picks, and their ridiculously high compensations (true, Jack Grubman, Henry Blodget, Mary Meeker, and their ilk do bear part of the responsibility for overinflating or exaggerating their recommendations of client corporations), the real culprit is the very nature of a system that has Wall Street funding the corporations, or creating them through mergers, and subsequently marketing and selling the same companies to institutional investors like pension funds, which manage money for individual investors, and to individual investors themselves via brokerage divisions.

So much of Wall Street's 1990s-era communication wasn't captured in e-mails or directly mentioned in meetings. It was implicit—understood without words. If your chairman asked you to take a look at a stock or the head of your division asked you to make a marketing call on a large client about an upcoming deal, you didn't need to be told explicitly what to say or write. It was understood, particularly by the highest paid and most ambitious employees, that you were to comply by lavishing the stock or the deal with positive comments. Even if you voiced your opinion internally about the invalidity of a transaction, you were often ignored by the people in charge.

The conflicts of interest that exist between the institutions that create and trade securities and those that buy them stretches beyond investment banking and into secondary trading activities. An analyst or salesperson "pitching" or "propping" a trade or a security to a client would never say that a trade, which would greatly help the trading desk, was not a good trade—not if she cared about her job. An analyst, who may or may not know better, just wouldn't print anything that would explicitly keep a transaction from going through. It's career suicide.

Additionally, less attention has been paid to the retail brokers at these firms for systematically recommending faulty stocks to the general public—people with smaller brokerage accounts and balances and little investment savvy—just because these stocks were on special company axe sheets (lists of stocks or bonds important to the firm).

Also, no one is commenting on the fact that mutual funds, which individual investors purchase through brokers or asset management companies like Putnam or Fidelity, are comprised of lots of these stocks, and individual investors have no control over the selection, buying, and selling of those stocks.

Change must come from outside the banking industry, but, allowing Merrill Lynch to settle disputes about its conflicts of interest for $100 million, a tiny fraction of its revenues that doesn't even go back to the investors, won't change the system. Salomon Brothers' paying $5 million—only half of 1 percent of the $860 million they made in telecom fees alone—to the National Association of Securities Dealers (NASD) for providing misleading research on one of its clients won't change the system. Just think: Someone steals $860 dollars from you and returns $4.30, and you're supposed to be impressed and satisfied with that resolution? I don't think so. Likewise, CSFB paying $100 million in fines to the SEC and NASD on charges that they were "spinning" hot IPOs (doling out shares in return for promises of future high-fee transactions) without admitting guilt won't change the system. Wall Street, facing about $1.4 billion in total fines, sitting on a pretty comfortable cushion (the top ten firms made over $62 billion in fees since 1998 alone), won't change the system.[26]

THE WALL STREET, CORPORATE AMERICA, AND WASHINGTON TRIANGLE

This book examines the key relationships among members of the 1990s "ruling class"—the collaborations that led to the country's economic downfall and multibillion-dollar cash-outs for calculating executives. It critiques the types of reform that resulted from the scandals of the early 2000s. However, the roles of all the players aren't always clear-cut. In a chameleon-like fashion, these relationships take on different characteristics depending on the market climate. In a rising and strong market, corporations tend to have the upper hand in dictating deal terms and driving speculative expansion, with banks clamoring for their business. That's why Enron, in its prime, could suggest to Merrill Lynch that it fire analysts it didn't like. That's also why Citigroup-Solomon Brothers' "star" telecom analyst, Jack Grubman, changed his recommendation on AT&T for ten minutes and then changed it back once the big deal was agreed upon.

Grubman was the conduit through which influence exerted itself. Corporations lean on banks for good PR, or they will withhold their business by giving it to other, more cooperative banks. That's why Ford can squeeze loans out of its banks at lower rates and play banks off each other for its business when it's sitting on top of the issuance pecking order in corporate good times.

But when things go south, it gets uglier. In a declining market, when money is tight, the banks have more power, and they're not above lending to and suing their corporate customers on the same day. Either way, the personalities involved in creating, maintaining, and exploiting the triangle resurface in multiple ways and multiple times. The triangle effect is explored in greater detail throughout the book, but some examples are worth noting here.

Global Crossing's Gary Winnick's son was a banker at CIBC, the Canadian bank that invested the initial capital in his firm. William Cohen, ex-President Clinton's secretary of defense, was on the board of Global Crossing just before it won a lucrative defense contract. Gary Winnick's private Chase banker, Maria Elena Lagomasino, was on the board of Global Crossing. Gary Winnick is on the board of the U.S. Chamber of Commerce.

It doesn't end there. WorldCom's Operation and Technology Division head Fred Briggs is on the FCC's technology advisory committee and is an ex-army officer; WorldCom ultimately won away the aforementioned defense contract from Global Crossing. WorldCom's former CEO and founder, Bernie Ebbers, raised $8 million for former Senate majority leader Trent Lott in 2000. Lott was the senior senator from Mississippi, where WorldCom is based.

On another front, Enron's Energy Services Division was run for years by Thomas White, who was later appointed Army secretary in the George W. Bush administration. Former Texas Senator Phil Gramm ushered in deregulatory legislation that helped Enron's trading operations flourish without oversight. He was a key architect of the Glass-Steagall repeal that enabled megabanks, which funded these operations, to form. When Gramm left Congress, he landed an executive position at UBS, the big Swiss bank that bought Enron's trading business. There, in the leveraged buyout division, he'll be able to guide UBS to profit by picking up the pieces of the energy market he helped destroy.

Colin Powell, another triangle figure, was on the board of AOL. He resigned on January 11, 2000, the same day the FCC issued its approval of the AOL Time Warner merger, an all-stock deal whose value has only plummeted since it took place. Michael Powell, his son, was an FCC commissioner at the time, and was later appointed FCC chairman by George W. Bush. Michael Powell addressed the 2002 telecom conference of Goldman Sachs, one of the leading telecom investment banks, while Goldman was heavily involved in the telecom merger and acquisition bubble. In effect, the head of the federal agency regulating telecoms was promoting the industry that Goldman and others were banking. Michael Powell was also put on Bush's new window-dressing Fraud Task Force, a group created in the middle of 2002 to supposedly watch over corporate malfeasance, but which has yet to publicize a single action toward that goal.

Another defining 1990s triangle was the bank-to-government-to-bank move that Robert Rubin executed so perfectly in the late 1990s. A cochairman of the executive committee at Goldman Sachs, he became Clinton's secretary of the treasury in 1995 and spent four years in the administration, steering through the Glass-Steagall repeal, which was finally accomplished in November 1999. A month earlier, he landed at his new employer, Citigroup, the mammoth banking conglomerate that benefited mightily from that repeal.

The links go on. All this overlap fosters a system that can't and won't critique itself because there's no external viewpoint; there is no real player outside this network. It is a system in which all the power is inside the triangle and the sides of the triangle are impenetrable. This is precisely why everybody in the government, from Congress to the Oval Office to the regulatory agencies, turned a blind eye to any wrongdoing when the market was going up to its absurd early 2000 heights.

ESCAPED CRIMINALS

The CEOs and CFOs who have resigned, been forced out, or are otherwise hanging on and awaiting indictments are just members of a larger, not fully excavated, group. Indeed, this particular environment of a heightened sense of entitlement combined with unregulated power enabled gross levels of corruption and easy cash-outs. Furthermore, these CEOs and chairmen weren't stupid—maybe reckless, maybe unscrupulous, but not stupid. If they were stupid, then they don't deserve the pay they got; if they deliberately deceived the public, they also don't deserve what they got. Either way, they should be forced to part with their ill-gotten gains, which could then be used as reparation for employees who lost jobs and pensions because of the deception. This should be used to set the stage for an examination of loose laws that enabled corrupt practices to be undertaken so easily.

So far, there have been scores of indictments and few convictions. Of course, there's been a sprinkling of contrition here and there: Gary Winnick of Global Crossing said he'd give back $25 million to help his workers, who lost $275 million and of whom 9,000 were laid off. None received severance pay or continuing health benefits. In the real world, when someone steals a TV, returning the antennae doesn't get him off the hook, but in the world of corporate executive cash-outs, it seems as if an expression of remorse on the Senate floor is all it takes.

The SEC, Corporate America, Wall Street, and Washington are doing everything in their power to deflect attention from corporate rot. The media collude by positioning stories on indictments as if justice is being done; at the same time they do much less to publicize shareholder activism or class-action victories in the face of corruption. Beyond op-eds, the media focus next to nothing on the need to change and strengthen the loose regulations that enable widespread malfeasance to fester. Plus, both banks and corporations continue to lobby for weakening or removing regulations that curtail their more speculative trading activities.

Meanwhile, the federal government, as of this writing, has failed to bring any charges against corporate criminals like Gary Winnick, who pocketed over $735 billion in the fastest rise-and-fall story of the 1990s (Global Crossing's senior executives cashed out $5.2 billion), or Philip Anschutz, who cashed out over $1.5 billion during his reign as chairman of Qwest, or Enron's Ken Lay, who brought California to its knees. These executives pulled off significant corporate scams. (Sure, they sacrificed a couple of people near—but not at—the top. No—those at the top kept their billions and, with the help of some well-placed senators, representatives, the Bush administration, and media commentators, swept the whole thing under the rug like nothing had happened. A couple of people got their wrists slapped; most didn't.)

There have been smatterings of justice, but only the kind that pokes fingers at a few people while leaving the system in which they operated intact. On January 15, 2004, former Enron CFO Andrew Fastow pled guilty to 2 (just 2) of the 98 counts of fraud he was charged with. He was sentenced to ten years in prison and ordered to pay a $23.8 million fine (out of the $37 million he pocketed). WorldCom former CEO and chairman Bernie Ebbers was finally indicted on March 2, 2004. Meanwhile, regulations continue to be obliterated and regulatory bodies remain in a weakened state because of it. Things like defense spending, which will hit almost $400 billion in fiscal year 2005, keep increasing. Corporate defense contracts went up $38 billion in 2002, a 29 percent increase since 2001.[27] In fact, during the first two years of the George W. Bush administration, the Department of Defense doled out $315 billion in contracts, or 48 percent of the defense budget, to private companies.[28] This happened at the same time that the SEC budget was shrinking. Democrats advocated doubling the SEC budget for fiscal year 2003, and even the House Republicans proposed a 77 percent, or $338 million, increase, but President Bush wanted only an additional $100 million to go to the SEC.[29] Such is the sentiment of the man who claims he wants "a stronger SEC—more investigators and more budget."[30] Thus, the imbalance in tax audits, in which lower-income businesses are more frequently audited than higher-income businesses like Enron (and Enron didn't even pay any taxes from 1998 to 2003) remains matched by an imbalance in reviews of 10K, or annual reports to the SEC.

Our tax dollars paid for the federal regulatory oversight bodies that were supposed to be acting in the public interest—our interest. Our votes elected the politicians who never cautioned anyone during the boom and have taken no blame after the bust. Certainly, no one is implementing any real reform of the system that created the catastrophe. It is clear that real change won't occur unless the public demands it.

REFORM

The problem is that more is being done to change the perception of what went wrong than to change the underlying factors that caused the rot. Overriding any one element of reform is the general need for a more tightly regulated system of corporate rules and stiffer penalties for not adhering to them, including, at a minimum, steeper jail sentences and fines and, ideally, dissolution of a corporation's right to exist if it violates those rules. But there are a number of reforms that would have even longer-lasting effects.

Corporations need independent boards of directors—ones with no intertwined client relationships, no ex–government officials on boards of companies that directly benefit from their legislation (and yes, that includes the Carlyle Group, the Washington-based investment company whose board is a *Who's Who* of the political elite). Corporate boards should include public seats as well as representatives from consumers' groups.

Regulations should require retail broker independence, and regulatory bodies should be truly independent. We should demand that the SEC and the FASB work together to find accounting fraud before it leads to enormous bankruptcies, layoffs, and economic instability, instead of allowing them to accept an additional layer of bureaucracy (such as the Public Accounting Oversight Board, which couldn't even sustain honest leadership—its first batter up, William Webster, didn't quite work out—almost a year after its creation).

We should demand retirement money protection, particularly in the face of an increasingly attacked and deteriorating Social Security system, ask for fully insured 401(k) plans, restrictions on company stock participation percentage caps, and elimination of blackout periods in which corporate executives or senior employees can sell stock but regular employees cannot. We should demand defined benefit plans, which are more secure for employees.

Corporations should make Internet access technology available to all citizens, even those residing outside main hub areas. Cable prices should be controlled. Michael Powell's proclamation that cable companies and broadband services are inherently information and not communication technology and thereby exempt from communications regulations is ridiculous.

We should re-regulate energy, particularly wholesale electricity. It would be much easier now anyway; as most of the energy sector has either declared or is hovering near bankruptcy or is suffering from a mixture of extensive debt and fraud investigations. It would be a perfect time to step in and help the state and federal governments regain control of this important utility. Similarly, we should regulate energy derivatives trading and enhance related investment bank disclosure. (Goldman Sachs doesn't itemize any of the profits it makes on energy trading, even though it continually uses its energy-trading accolades to drum up more business.)

Last, and most crucial, Glass-Steagall must be revived. The separation of lending from other investment banking practices was the most important component of New Deal legislation in safeguarding deposits and ensuring overall financial stability. Repeal contributed to the avalanche of poor decisions made by commercial banks in order to capture corporate business, decisions realized with other people's money. The fact that the same brokerage houses have lending and other investment banking relationships with the corporations they tout to their retail customers is a direct and dangerous product of Glass-Steagall repeal.

Fortunately, numerous consumer and public advocacy groups, unions, retiree organizations, and laid-off workers are joining together in their fight against the corporate deception that leads to job and pension losses, higher prices, and fewer product choices. These factions recognize that the immense concentration of wealth, power, and influence has devastated our country. Many have been mobilized for years to do something about it. Still others are rising alongside them.

This is what retirees, consumers, and workers should be most concerned about. At a continuing education class on banking that I addressed in spring 2003, one seventy-eight-year-old retiree told me, "I will never invest in the stock market again. Sure, my mutual fund advertiser says that over any twenty-year period stocks will outperform every other investment. Well, I don't have another twenty years."

Simply excusing the behavior of a few bad CEOs and not tackling the larger systemic problem is reckless. Not acknowledging the regulatory and legislative environment that produced this crisis is negligent. Blaming everything on the "softness" of the economy is lazy. Not holding anyone accountable is criminal. Waging wars to mask lack of reform is unconscionable. It would be a mistake to learn nothing and change little given all that we've witnessed during the first years of the postbubble millennium.

1

The Bank Wars

By the middle of 2001, there was no doubt the stock market was deep in "bear," or negative, territory. Less obvious was the precipitous decline in Goldman Sachs's corporate bond issuance business.[1] The bank blamed the commercial bank conglomerates. Well-known client companies like Ford that had been steady and frequent issuers, or borrowers, in the capital markets for years were leaving their investment banks for the open arms of the commercial banks. Tables were turning at an uncomfortably brisk rate.

Because Goldman Sachs, like other investment banks, didn't have the capacity on its balance sheet to extend the mammoth loans that commercial banks were offering in exchange for issuance business (certainly not at the same prices), corporations began doing business with those supermarket banks now offering services formerly handled exclusively by investment banks, including stock issuance and mergers and acquisitions advisory services. The commercial banks offered an exceedingly important corporate growth tool: cheap credit.

Though this pattern had begun before the repeal of Glass-Steagall, the breakdown of more barriers formerly surrounding the commercial banking business transformed the pace of activity from rapid growth to outright frenetic growth. This change in tide conveniently seemed to coincide with the height of the stock market boom, but, on closer inspection, it became clear that it was actually feeding the boom. With fewer constraints on their activities, supermarket banks were hungry to grow their market share in all types of banking and investment banking activities. Investment banks were equally eager to increase their share. The only way for both types of banks to stay profitable and powerful was for each to create more demand, spurring corporate expansion and consolidation from which they could earn hard fees. Thus, they paved the way for the broadband and Internet revolution, and for power market companies to buy plants and generators across the country. The fire of the boom was ignited by the competitive drive of those companies that financed it and subsequently created and shaped the corporations that acted within it.

Phil Darivoff, head of the investment-grade capital markets desk at Goldman Sachs that raised debt for the highest quality corporate borrowers in the country, such as Ford, IBM, and General Electric, began keeping a record of his area's activities. It included all the bond issuance deals they won from their clients. On the flip side, he reported on the deals they missed, the ones sucked away by the commercial banks. The loan-for-banking business struck at the heart of market share for investment banks. In the past, issuance business had been largely driven by personal relationships and bonding activities like golf games and charity events. All of a sudden, it was now being subsumed by commercial banks that had the capacity to lend money cheaply, regardless of past history. This caused great consternation all the way up the ranks of Goldman Sachs, directly to Hank Paulson.

It was a topic that senior management spent hours belaboring. Every quarter, all the managing directors in the firm would gather to hear the period's performance numbers just ten minutes before they were released to reporters and analysts from other institutions. The main site for these gatherings was a multilevel conference room resembling a mini-arena at Goldman's 32 Old Slip building. These 7:30 A.M. meetings were always well attended, not least because they were preceded by several reminder e-mails to ensure adequate participation. Managing directors starting streaming in around 7:15 A.M., making their way through a set of revolving glass doors into a huge atrium enclosed by glass windows and up a set of escalators marked with a "Managing Directors' Meeting" sign. (During the colder months, there was usually someone around to help put your coat in the closet, avoiding the complication or time it took to do it yourself.) The same arena was used for the divisional meetings (held a week before the firmwide results were released), in which leaders from various departments in each division went over their area's financial results with the requisite colorful graphs and bullet points highlighting the most important transactions and successfully implemented business strategies. Their meetings were more about comparative aggrandizement than forward planning.

The announcement meetings were usually followed by a brief question-and-answer period. At each of these sessions, someone looking

for a compliment on his or her astute read of the business environment
would always ask what "we"—that would be the royal "we"—were doing
about "the banks," referring to the loan-for-fee business strategy that was
getting in "our" way. Of course, the same concerns were being raised at
all the independent investment houses. Sure, loan tying was a violation of
the Sherman Antitrust Act, but only if you could prove it. Commercial
banks were savvy enough not to leave explicit paper trails indicating that
cheap credit or loans had been offered in return for other higher-margin
business, yet the practice underscored a brewing battle between the two
types of banks.

MERGERS AND ACQUISITIONS

Part of the battle involved territorial disputes over the exploding merger
and acquisitions (M&A) business. A merger is when two companies combine to form a completely new company, usually keeping the name (or
some derivation thereof) of the more powerful of the two. An acquisition
is when one company completely takes control of another company. In
both cases the financial statements of the two companies are combined.
In addition to handling mergers and acquisitions, investment banks were
responsible for taking privately-held companies public via the issuance of
new shares of stock through an initial public offering (IPO) of that stock
over a public stock exchange like the New York Stock Exchange (NYSE)
or the NASDAQ.

The right to "bring" potential mergers and acquisitions deals would
be aggressively sought by the top investment banks, with the aid of four-
inch-thick glossy "pitch" books delineating all the reasons a corporation
should do a deal and all the reasons it should do it with the investment
bank presenting that book. Pitch books included an analysis of a corporation's status among its peers and a list of possible combinations of that
corporation with other corporations that would catapult the new entity
into higher profitability and greater market share, making it more "competitive," in free-market terminology.

Debt or loan issuance, or the extension of credit facilities, for corporations would often occur simultaneously with the close of a merger.
Credit facilities are large back-up or emergency lines of credit that corporations can draw upon, but don't need to pay interest on, until necessary.

The idea was that the new, larger entity would be financially healthier than either of its smaller parts, having supposedly gone through streamlining exercises like firing duplicate staff and combining office or building space. The prevailing logic of the markets was that this meant the new corporation could carry more debt to continue expanding its empire. The bigger, the better was the motto that prevailed without, necessarily, any underlying logic.

Historically, investment banks had cornered the market on M&A, landing the merger, stock, and debt issuance all at once and scooping up the associated fees in one lump payment. But the age of überbanks had arrived, and commercial banks now could do it all: advise their clients on investment banking transactions, execute these deals, bring out new issuance, and, most important, extend credit. As the ensuing territorial dispute between the two types of banks became increasingly warlike, no longer was it a foregone conclusion that all these items of business would go to the same financial institution. Corporations would shop around for the best credit terms they could find, regardless of which bank was doing their merger. As time went on, the überbanks cut ever deeper into the merger business that had once belonged exclusively, as per Glass-Steagall, to the investment banks.

Selecting a bond issuer became more like selecting a home mortgage provider. Just as ordinary Americans shop around for the best mortgage rate, corporations shop around for the tightest spread, or the least amount of regular interest or coupon payments they have to pay out, on their bonds. Additionally, choosing a mortgage lender depends upon a more psychological component. In addition to providing the best rate, is the institution stable? Will it stand the test of time or go the way of the bankrupt savings and loan banks of the early 1990s?

It's a similar situation in the debt capital markets, in which corporations (the banks' potential clients) lend money to bond issuers and institutional investors, who buy those bonds in exchange for receiving interest over a number of years. To get the money to issue bonds the corporation must borrow funds. Two things need to come together in the process. First, the borrowing corporation needs to get the best terms—the tightest spread it must pay on its bonds or loans. Second, the corporation must create demand for its bonds: the more demand, the higher its price, the tighter the spread, and the less interest the company will have to pay. In order to land this issuance business, banks must convince clients that their "distribution mechanism"—the way in which they deliver bonds to investors—is the best, meaning the bank can get the bonds to the most clients most efficiently. Excellence in distribution can be achieved through an efficient sales force or a stable of institutional investors, mostly large asset or fund managers or insurance companies with standing demand for certain types of corporate bonds (sometimes referred to as "paper") in advance of an issuance. For example, a client that requires a certain percentage of industrial names (bonds) is almost certain to buy a portion of any industrial that is being offered. Locking down investor clients with regular obligations to purchase bonds is a critical component of a bank's distribution strategy, often rewarded with other favorable treatment to retain the business.

FORGOTTEN HISTORY LESSONS

To understand the financial 1990s, you have to understand what happened during the 1920s. From a regulatory background perspective, the operating rules for banking, energy, and telecommunications sectors were very similar to what we have now—though, in fact, these sectors are even more deregulated now. In other words, regulatory frameworks governing the 1990s were a regression to those of the 1920s, a period during which it had been open season for banks and corporations to raise capital in questionable ways for speculative activities and to hide emerging failures by relying on an environment of nontransparency and little federal regulation. The stock market crash of 1929 and the subsequent depression of the 1930s ushered in a broad series of federal regulation in the New Deal package and the creation of independent regulatory bodies to monitor finance and industry practice. A cornerstone of this new regulation was the Glass-Steagall Act, which imposed strict rules on the banking industry and created walls between corporate-related financial activities and public ones. In turn, it fostered security and stability for decades. In order to understand how far backward regulation went in the 1990s, you have to understand Glass-Steagall—its goals, its structure, its results—and why banks hated it.

Historically, the banking industry has always been at the forefront of both the creation and the destruction of capital. By the 1920s, banks were involved in the deposit and lending of money, the creation of stock and bond securities, and the rounding up of investors to buy these securities. Banks worked in partnership with corporations to create the most efficient means for the corporations to shield all types of financial and equity capital from existing regulations and taxation. In that way, every historical period of excessive borrowing, or "overleverage," of corporations was led by the banking institutions that made it possible. In turn, the banks initiated every period of default and deterioration that followed.

The first major bank casualty after the crash of 1929 was that of the Bank of United States, the fourth-largest U.S. deposit bank, on December 11, 1930.[2] The crash and following deflation caused a spate of over a thousand bank failures in 1930.[3] However, the crash alone did not spur public outrage; it was the "crash examined as a forerunner to depression that did the trick," wrote Ron Chernow in his history of J.P. Morgan.[4]

During the early 1930s, corporate defaults and bankruptcies abounded. In order to try to contain the plummeting value of corporate bonds and stock, short selling (borrowing money to buy and then immediately sell securities in anticipation of a falling market, later buying them back at a lower price and then delivering them as collateral for the original loan, thus closing the loop) was prohibited by President Herbert Hoover, who considered the practice a major factor contributing to the crash.

By the fall of 1932, a nationwide banking crisis was boiling over. Asset or stock collateral used in backing loans had eroded in value—much as today's combination of default, overcapacity (not enough demand to answer the overabundance of supply), and bankruptcies in the highly leveraged telecom and energy industries continues to erode collateral values of hard assets that had previously been overvalued as a result of the vagaries of the market and its constantly fluctuating values.

The congressional hearings that had begun offhandedly in 1930 to examine the fraudulent practices and conflicts of interest that caused the crash continued for years. The hearings were formally known as the Pecora hearings, after Ferdinand Pecora, a scrupulous New York City–based prosecutor. In January 1933, when Franklin D. Roosevelt became president, he formalized those hearings.

The findings of the Pecora hearings led to the Glass-Steagall Act, which separated banks into two categories: those involved in lending credit and those issuing new securities in the form of bonds or stocks.[5] After Glass-Steagall, banks could extend credit in the form of loans to corporate institutions but they could not also bind outside investors to purchase bonds or stock from those same institutions. This meant that a bank would not be able to both market the virtues of their favored corporate customers to individual investors while simultaneously lending those investor deposits to the same institutions. The pre–Glass-Steagall conflicts of interest didn't center on the role of analysts cheerleading malfunctioning companies in conjunction with a receptive media—the major focus of the twenty-first-century witch hunt. Back in the 1930s, it was the media reporters who were directly accused of pumping up stock and taking bribes to hype companies to investors—a cheaper practice than paying hundreds of equity analysts.

The stock market crash of 1929 sparked the Great Depression, and it was almost eleven years before the economy started showing signs of health again. Still, it took four years for the public to get behind the New Deal and its reforms, because it took that long for the full extent of bad corporate and Wall Street practices of the 1920s to be fully understood. The Depression prompted a number of New Deal reforms besides the Glass-Steagall Act. As Paul M. Sweezy wrote in 1953, in *The Present as History: Essays and Reviews on Capitalism and Socialism*, "It shook the structure of the American economy to its very foundation: a policy of reform and concessions, involving greatly increased government activity in the economic sphere, became the only possible way of saving the system itself."[6]

Indeed, it shook the financial structure so soundly that, under the constraints of much-needed regulations, capital was stable for almost fifty years. The next significant stock market crash didn't occur until October 19, 1987, yet even that Black Monday didn't spark a recession because the event was not accompanied by a cocktail of corporate scandal, fraud, and bankruptcy. Plus, individual investor involvement in the stock market was a fraction of what it became in the late 1990s. Black Monday only spurred more speculation, but in the form of more complex investment banking deals and growth in the derivatives market. Mergers accounted for over half of Wall Street profits, and with the subdued trading operations following the crash, that business became more important because of the hard bottom-line fees it brought in.

Black Monday and a weaker dollar ignited the takeover business. Companies became cheaper to raid because their share prices were so low. Even giant Citibank was trading at a historic low of $9 in the fall of 1987. Wall Street, the consummate optimist, exploited the situation by looking for new ways to make money. Craftily led by the more innovative investment banks, it ushered in the takeover heydays that were later brilliantly characterized by Bryan Burrough and John Helyar in *Barbarians at the Gate: The Fall of RJR Nabisco*, a classic business narrative detailing the largest takeover in Wall Street history and the surrounding frenzy on the Street in the fall of 1988.[7] And when Wall Street couldn't find corporate raiders among its clients, it would engineer the raids itself via newly formed merchant banking departments and junk bond syndicates, groups of issuers that would each be responsible for selling a piece of the bond, thereby mitigating the risk of any one issuer getting stuck with the whole bond and no buyers. Merchant banking would in effect be the "principal" in these raids, taking over a company cheaply, then restructuring it in order to break it up into parts for sale at a profit.

The junk bonds of the 1980s reappeared en masse in the mid- to late 1990s as corporate debt ballooned, only this time the Street had a new name for them, "junk" being so negative a term. Now the same inferior corporations would issue bonds classified as "high-yield," a name that masked their speculative nature.

COMMERCIAL VS. INVESTMENT BANKS

During the mid- and late 1980s, investment banks dominated the lucrative leveraged buyouts in which they'd front money to investors to purchase majority interest in a target company in order to subsequently acquire it. In addition, they controlled junk-bond issuance and the emergence of a new asset class called mortgage (or asset)-backed securities (bonds collateralized by pools of residential mortgages, recreational vehicles, trailer homes, and anything else that people borrowed money to purchase). Meanwhile, commercial banks were sidelined and forced to focus on the "volume" businesses that revolved around trading government bonds and foreign exchange rates, providing for marginal commissions in contrast to the heavy fees being generated by the investment banks. This didn't make them happy. Wall Street was, after all, a hypercompetitive place, and the commercial banks were shut out of the more profitable fee-based business becoming monopolized by the investment houses.

I was working at Chase Manhattan Bank, the second-largest U.S. commercial bank, during this carving-out-of-territory period. While the antics of traders at investment banks like Salomon Brothers were the stuff of feature-length movies like Oliver Stone's Oscar-winning film *Wall Street* (1987) and bestsellers like Michael Lewis's *Liar's Poker: Rising Through the Wreckage in Wall Street* (1989) that dove into the humor and horror of the 1980s cutthroat trading mentality, no one bothered filming the more boring and traditional commercial bankers, even those of us in the process of creating some pretty nifty derivative products. Junior traders and analysts mingled with the bond traders down at places like the beer-soaked, wood-floored Jeremy's at the South Street Seaport in the hopes of getting an "in" with the more happening, higher-paying investment banks. That's why I jumped at the offer to become a derivatives strategist with Lehman Brothers in 1991. In that role, I was responsible for sourcing, analyzing, and marketing trading strategies for Lehman and its institutional clients (mostly international central banks) that took advantage of arbitrage, or discrepancies in pricing between cash bond values and their associated future contracts.

In 1987, a group of executives from the commercial banks of Citibank, JP Morgan, and Bankers Trust New York sat Federal Reserve chair Paul Volcker down and demanded the right to sell new, more exciting securities. JP Morgan president Dennis Weatherstone declared that "commercial banks were at a competitive disadvantage relative to investment banks," and demanded Fed approval to get into the complex securities game.[8] Volcker balked because he didn't feel that it was right for commercial banks to enjoy solid FDIC and Federal Reserve protection while getting involved with more speculative products—a luxury not afforded to investment banks. But he was conveniently replaced by Alan Greenspan in August 1987, who, it's rarely noted, was one of Ronald Reagan's 1980 election campaign advisers.[9] Greenspan had also served for ten years on JP Morgan's board of directors. In January 1989, Greenspan's Fed granted permission to commercial banks to float corporate bond issues, and in October 1989, JP Morgan became the first commercial bank to do so since the Great Depression, with the issuance of a $30 million bond for the Savannah Electric and Power Company.[10]

It was precedent-setting in a way; this one bond was an early step in the rampant funding of deregulation that led to the massive downgrading and assumption of debt of the 1990s. Over the next decade, commercial banks would amass billions of dollars of debt and credit on behalf of energy and public utility companies, all of which would be downgraded by the rating agencies as deregulation allowed them to expand too quickly on debt and to morph into diverse trading conglomerates like Enron, which became plagued by debt and fraud problems. In 1997, banks were given permission to go beyond merely issuing corporate bonds like securities; now, commercial banks could buy entire securities firms. This was the first critical factor that later enabled new entities such as JP Morgan Chase, Citigroup, and others to both lend to and underwrite equity and debt issuance for Enron, WorldCom, and other client companies, effectively doing an end run around Glass-Steagall. Because these institutions also owned asset management businesses, they could sell some of the stocks and bonds they issued right into investment portfolios (including pension and retail investor funds) through that asset management business.

In 2002, Citigroup and JP Morgan Chase were sued by WorldCom and other scandal-laden corporate investors for the conflict of interest that arose from the joint activities of lending money to WorldCom and selling its bonds to investors. This scenario was exactly what Glass-Steagall had been established to prevent. The whole point of the financial institution mergers was to allow the supermarket banks to gain access to millions of retail investors. This doesn't mean that the class-action lawsuits filed on behalf of groups of investors against Enron, WorldCom, and other similar companies are not without merit. They absolutely are. There is absolutely a conflict of interest between lending money to and raising money for the same corporation. In fact, these suits make glaringly obvious how bad a move repealing Glass-Steagall actually was.

The various types of banks found themselves on different sides of the Glass-Steagall repeal issue, depending on what suited their business expansion needs at the moment. When the idea of first breaking down the Glass-Steagall barriers was brought up in 1984, Citibank was opposed. At the time, there was no investment bank partner on the horizon and Citibank CEO John Reed knew that an investment-supermarket bank would ultimately have the best shot at market domination. Throughout the 1990s, Greenspan's Fed had been relaxing constraints on the merging of commercial banks and securities or brokerage houses. When Sanford Weill, then CEO of Travelers Group (which also owned Salomon Brothers, the investment bank ultimately bought by Citibank), showed up at John Reed's door, the commercial-investment bank courtship that would transform the nature of American banking began.

In late 1997, Weill and Reed suggested merging their two houses.

The fact that there was no legal precedent yet to do so didn't bother them. A year later, in October 1998, the two companies were combined into one. A year after that, in November 1999, Glass-Steagall was repealed. The mammoth Citicorp-Travelers merger unfolded in a series of succinct steps in which the business of an upscale Wall Street boutique, large retail brokerage network, insurance company, and commercial bank were all merged into one mega-entity.

Amazingly enough, after Citigroup spent fourteen months in the unflattering spotlight cast by investors' class-action suits, fraud investigations, and allegations of IPO-spinning, Weill saw fit to accept a position on the board of the New York Stock Exchange in March 2003.[11] The fact that he was even offered the spot at that time was a clear sign that the leader of the largest commercial bank in the United States would not be held accountable for any of the misleading banking practices that struck the core of corporate America wiping out billions of dollars of employees' retirement funds. Had his appointment been approved by New York State attorney general Eliot Spitzer, Weill would have joined compatriot JP Morgan Chase CEO and chairman Bill Harrison, who, despite suffering similar problems, was still on the NYSE board on which he had served since June 2001.

New York State attorney general Eliot Spitzer was quick to condemn the potential appointment of Weill, stating, "I can think of few people less suited to represent the public interest on the New York Stock Exchange than Sandy Weill."[12] As it turned out, Weill announced his retirement from the banking business, or at least from his post as CEO, a few months later. In hindsight, Spitzer's condemnation simply feathered his corporate vigilance cap, and Weill had other things to do, like remain Citigroup chairman. Still, Weill had long been known for—and successful because of—the chutzpah that marked his acquisitive career. In 1985, he took control of Commercial Credit Corporation, which then acquired Primerica Corporation in 1988. Primerica had already acquired investment firm Salomon Smith Barney. Marching on, Weill bought Travelers Insurance in 1992. Travelers Insurance was the company advertised by the big red umbrella, symbolizing a company that protected its clients from rainy days. A clearer or more cynical eye might view the umbrella as shielding Weill's growing collection of companies from culpability for its practices.

FINANCIAL HOLDING COMPANIES

The repeal of the Glass-Steagall Act goes by a couple of different names, including the Financial Services Modernization Act and the Gramm-Leach-Bliley Act (named for the congressmen who pushed it through) of 1999. Texas senator Phil Gramm (R) was head of the Senate Banking Committee responsible for the repeal. Although the Glass-Steagall repeal is the more well-known ramification of this piece of deregulation, repeal of the Bank Holding Company Act of 1956 was also a significant outcome. The Bank Holding Company Act had limited the types of services a bank could offer clients. In its place, Congress created a new kind of financial services company called the FHC, or financial holding company. As an FHC, a corporation could "affiliate" or combine banks, insurance companies, and securities firms under one FHC umbrella, exactly what Weill had already done in creating and consolidating Citigroup. More than five hundred bank holding companies created FHCs within a year of the Bank Holding Act's repeal.

Financial holding companies got a regulatory green light to own any kind of financial service company as well as investments in companies that had little or nothing to do with finance. They became catchall structures to mask risky investments in nonbank corporations.

Another festering problem created by the Financial Service Modernization Act was so-called functional regulation. The act claimed that each component of these new conglomerate institutions would be regulated by a different government regulatory body. This meant that different federal and state entities had oversight for different components of the same business, yet no body had full oversight for the entire institution's activities as a whole. In other words, the Fed still regulated commercial banking functions, but now the SEC oversaw securities trading, while the state regulators kept an eye on insurance. None of these oversight bodies were compelled to share their slivers of information with each other.

So, functional regulation could more appropriately be called "dysfunctional regulation." If no body was fully accountable for how all the various business units colluded under one financial holding company, it followed that no body was responsible for mitigating internal conflicts of interest or even monitoring any potential fraud that could arise from the ability to hide losses or book profits across different functional divisions within the FHC, much like a balance sheet shell game.

Ultimate approval for bank mergers comes from the Federal Reserve, but Citibank and Travelers had used a loophole under the Bank Holding Company Act to give themselves a two-year review period (by the Federal Reserve—with up to a three year extension—before such mergers must be disallowed) in which to lobby for the Glass-Steagall repeal. Their 1998 merger bringing together Citibank, Travelers, Salomon Smith Barney, and Primerica under one roof, went well beyond the boundaries of existing laws, requiring Weill and Reed to privately obtain temporary approval from Alan Greenspan. That gesture provided the impetus for a heightened lobbying campaign aimed at Congress to repeal Glass-Steagall.[13] The banks listed all sorts of procompetitive reasons, including the fact that in Europe mergers between securities houses and banks were already going on and that U.S. banks shouldn't be shut out. In the meantime, global bank mergers were occurring at a frenetic pace as the barriers to consolidating banking functions were lifted. Between 1960 and 1979, there were 3,404 bank mergers. From 1980 to 1994, the number had swelled to 6,345. But that was nothing compared to the rest of the 1990s. From 1995 to 2000, the number of bank mergers topped 11,100.[14]

POLITICAL MANEUVERING

Former speaker of the U.S. House of Representatives Newt Gingrich and former U.S. senator Alphonse D'Amato (R-NY), then-chairman of the Senate Banking Committee, collaborated to support a 300-page House resolution called HR10, the Financial Services Act of 1998, that eliminated restrictions on the merging of banks and securities houses, effectively setting the stage for the fall of Glass-Steagall. Alan Greenspan lent his powers of deregulatory persuasion to their cause when he testified "to express the [Federal Reserve] Board's strong support for HR10" in June 1998.[15] Resolution HR10 was the corresponding House Act to the Senate's version, the Financial Services Modernization Act.

This resolution was passed by the House the following month, a few months before the marriage of Travelers and Citibank. A chief argument the banks used to support HR10 was that they were losing depositors: from 1969 to 1999, commercial banks lost 55 percent of their customer financial assets to securities firms. It was easier to open brokerage accounts at these firms while maintaining money market or checking accounts there as well, allowing them to buy and sell stocks. As such, depositors moved their money away from banks and toward the brokerage houses that offered them the ability to buy and sell stocks and mutual funds.

D'Amato was always a strong advocate for banking deregulation, since his interests were closely aligned with his key Wall Street constituents. In return, Wall Street was his primary source of political contributions, particularly during the 1998 election. Not coincidentally, D'Amato was also the top Senate fundraiser during 1993–1998, accumulating $19 million—far more than any other senator received during that six-year cycle.[16]

In May 2002, Hank Paulson had discreetly asked Stephen Friedman, former chairman at Goldman Sachs to return to the board. Said Paulson at the time, "Steve . . . is a highly qualified addition to our board of directors."[17] Paulson was politically savvy enough to offer Friedman that board position before Friedman wound up with an influential job in Washington as economic advisor to the White House.

The media greeted President Bush's appointment of Friedman on December 12, 2002, with adulation, describing him as "a serious, honest, honorable, informed, experienced man. A wholly Wall Street man, in fact."[18] Nonetheless, despite all his years at Goldman Sachs and the fact that he was credited with the creation of the entire merger-and-acquisition concept, he was unable to come up with an independent economic plan when he assumed his post. In fact, in his first public speech as the director of the National Economic Council, given at the Federal Reserve Bank of New York on February 21, 2003, he merely promoted the Bush administration's standing plan in its entirety, including dividend tax cuts for the wealthy minority of the population who own stock in companies that hadn't yet deteriorated so badly that they couldn't even pay dividends. He asked that the audience of executives and investors do the same.[19]

The prospect of Glass-Steagall's repeal opened the floodgates for commercial banks' political contributions. Citigroup had donated $13 million since 1990 but topped Goldman's $1.9 million donation in 1998 (the year preceding Glass-Steagall's repeal) with $2.6 million of its own. That year, Bank of America gave the most in its history: $1.9 million, 63 percent to the Republicans.[20] When Clinton signed the Financial Services Modernization Act, critics referred to the legislation as "the Citigroup Authorization Act."[21] Reed and Weill issued a joint statement praising Washington for "liberating our financial companies from an antiquated regulatory structure . . . to ensure global competitiveness."[22]

It was hugs and handshakes all around. Beneath the surface, though, Reed and Weill were having a tough time dealing with each other's controlling personalities. Ultimately, Reed lost and Weill took the helm of the mammoth superbank Citigroup. But Reed didn't do too shabbily in the process: when he was offered the job of nonexecutive chairman, he quit, taking a $30 million retirement package, plus $5 million a year for life, with him.[23] Before that happened, however, the two men considered getting a third person to smooth over the top tier, settling on Robert Rubin.[24]

Robert Rubin provides one of the most glaring examples of our time of the intersection of political and Wall Street interests. His job transitions were always impeccably opportunistic. From Goldman Sachs to the post of Clinton's treasury secretary to the executive vice chairman seat at Citigroup, even considering at one point the possibility of running Citigroup, Rubin executed each move with stunning grace and timing.

Weill wanted him, so he set up a meeting between Rubin and Reed, who were already old friends. Reed's Citicorp had been Goldman Sachs's bank during the period it was co-run by Rubin and Friedman. Convincing Rubin to hop aboard the Citigroup Express didn't take very long. One of Rubin's conditions was that he retain "his own independent involvement in public policy, free to pursue his own interest in politics."[25] In other words, Rubin didn't want to be around the office that much so he could continue with his political ambitions. That arrangement, of course, suited both parties just fine. With Rubin's appointment, Citigroup bought itself political access.

Rubin became a Citigroup director, chairman of the executive committee, and a member of the newly created "office of the chairman"; his initial compensation package was worth around $40 million.[26] He officially took this position on October 25, 1999. Glass-Steagall was repealed ten days later.

Earlier that year, in February, Rubin addressed the House Banking and Financial Services Committee on the topic of banking deregulation. He stated that "the problem our [U.S.] financial services firms face abroad is more one of access than lack of competitiveness."[27] Rubin was referring to the European banks' control of all the distribution channels into the European institutional and retail client base, and the fact that the banks were even stronger because they, unlike U.S. commercial banks, had no restrictions keeping them from buying and teaming up with U.S. investment banks. He was the one who underscored that the bills the

House committee was considering, HR10 and HR665, "take the fundamental actions to modernize our financial system by repealing the Glass-
Steagall Act's prohibition on banks affiliating with securities firms and
repealing the Bank Holding Company Act prohibitions on insurance underwriting [by banks]."[28]

There can be no misconception about where Rubin's loyalties lay.
Whether he knew he'd be joining Citigroup or not, he certainly watched it
become a behemoth organization in late 1998 and he did his own part to
repeal the Glass-Steagall Act. It was obvious from the Citigroup merger
that the institution was more ambitious than regulations constraining commercial banks would allow. So, rather than return to the investment banks
from whence he sprang, or back to Goldman Sachs, Rubin chose the institution that seemed destined to dominate the entire financial industry.

Several days after the Financial Services Modernization Act was
signed into law by President Clinton, a broad coalition of consumer and
community groups called for an ethics investigation into the fact that
Rubin was simultaneously job hunting and lobbying for legislative
changes that would benefit his eventual employer.[29] According to federal
law, retired government officials must not lobby their former agencies on
behalf of their new employers for at least one year after leaving public service. A violation of these lobbying restrictions is considered a federal
criminal offense.[30] But even this brief moratorium proved too long for
Rubin's ambitions. Only four months elapsed between Rubin's resignation as Treasury secretary and appointment to Citigroup's board. Even
though it is lobbying that's specifically prohibited, not employment,
Rubin was walking a fine line. By testifying for deregulation after leaving
the cabinet and before walking into Citigroup, he was lobbying for deregulation that would benefit his new employer, even if his role was not
"strictly defined" as that of a lobbyist. As ex-secretary of the Treasury,
his power to influence was greater than that of a standard lobbyist.

FROM GOLDMAN TO WASHINGTON

The well-traveled Goldman–Washington route dated back to the 1920s,
when a Goldman lawyer was appointed secretary of state.[31] Robert Rubin
and Stephen Friedman, who both followed the path, were appointed co-
chairmen and co-COOs of Goldman Sachs in 1987. Both were lawyers

by training and had grown up at Goldman. Rubin had joined the firm two years after he graduated from Yale Law School in 1966 and became a partner five years later. Friedman joined that same year, and became a partner in 1973.[32]

Rubin was considered calm and methodical; Friedman was intense. "He considered 3 A.M. part of the working day for anyone committed to a career at Goldman," wrote Lisa Endlich in the hagiographic *Goldman Sachs: The Culture of Success.*[33] He created the first M&A department on Wall Street in the mid-1960s as a subsection of investment banking. Goldman eventually became huge in the hostile takeover business, making a name for itself as a defense strategist protecting companies from takeovers. Friedman's message to clients was clear: "Find out what the raider would do and do it yourself."[34] Cleverly, Goldman would thus encourage threatened companies to turn the tables and try to take over the aggressor, booking fees in the process of advising the situation.

Rubin and Friedman became co-CEOs in 1990. By 1991, the two had brought Goldman Sachs to the forefront of investment banking, turning it into a premier firm (in terms of market share) to match its elite reputation. But Rubin's political aspirations were well-known internally, and it was only a matter of time—until the election of a Democrat president, who would be more likely to seek a Democratic treasurer—before Rubin would move on.[35] In 1992, Clinton appointed Rubin as his national economic adviser. (Ten years later, President George W. Bush gave the same job to Stephen Friedman.)

With Rubin gone, it became clear that Friedman wasn't strong enough to go it alone. By 1993, still no successors had been announced, but suitors, all in-house, were angling for an advantage. Finally, Friedman suggested the combination of Jon Corzine, co-head of fixed income, and Hank Paulson, co-head of investment banking. The two became co-CEOs in 1994 when Friedman retired. It looked like the perfect political leadership combination: Corzine was a staunch Democrat who had chaired a presidential commission for Clinton and served on the Borrowing Advisory Committee of the Department of the Treasury; Paulson was a well-connected Republican and Harvard graduate who had served in the Nixon administration.

Rubin by no means left politics when he left Washington in July 1999; He steadfastly maintained his relationships with key legislators.[36] For instance, through his open arrangement with Citigroup, he advised Senate

Majority Leader Tom Daschle on economic policy. A more glaring example of playing both sides of the political and Citigroup fence is when he
became the sounding board for Governor Gray Davis during the California electricity crisis, even though Citigroup was listed as a banker for
almost every energy company involved in manipulating the California
power markets.[37] Bob Woodward may have called his biography of Alan
Greenspan *Maestro*, but, really, Greenspan had nothing on Rubin.

It was Rubin who made the call to Peter R. Fisher, then undersecretary of the treasury for domestic financial markets, to save Enron's credit
rating in November 2001. He told Fisher he thought the energy market
and the public would not be served by Enron's collapse. Of course, neither would Citigroup if Enron defaulted on all of its debts. Rubin suggested Fisher intervene with the presumably independent rating agencies
to keep Enron's rating up. This conversation occurred just three weeks
before Enron declared bankruptcy (a pretty clear sign they were having
problems) and just after they disclosed a $1.2 billion hit to shareholder
equity, equivalent to the net worth of the company.

Rubin was earning millions of dollars as a Citigroup executive (he still
is) at the time that Citigroup was negotiating an Enron-related banking deal.
Telecom analyst Jack Grubman took the very personal heat and received
a $15 million fine for talking up the telecom stocks of favored Citigroup
clients even while they were tanking, but arguably Grubman was doing his
job. After all, he was paid handsomely for getting investment banking fees
into Citigroup.[38] On the other hand, Rubin blatantly abused his position
and political connections with respect to Enron, yet he was ultimately ab-
solved without punishment. He was shielded—in no small part by his
plethora of friends in high places—yet what he did was no different from
analysts making upbeat calls on deadbeat companies: he tried to use his influence to keep the perception of Enron's rating higher than was warranted.
Probably the only difference was that Rubin was more politically astute in
handling his plea on Enron's behalf. He reportedly began his phone call to
Fisher by saying it was probably a "bad idea" for Fisher to pressure the ratings agencies to delay downgrading Enron, and then asked Fisher what he
"thought" of the idea.[39] His language was guarded; his intent was not. Still,
in January 2003, Robert Rubin's role in the Enron affair was deemed legal
and insubstantial by the Senate governmental affairs committee.[40]

To add to his résumé of opportunism, Rubin bagged Citigroup's highest compensation package for 2002. Obviously, political influence was a

very valuable commodity in a year of fraud investigations and lawsuits. The same year that Citigroup's stock value declined 25 percent, its loan losses grew, and it fired hundreds of employees, Rubin's total compensation was $18.4 million, more than double what Weill received that year.[41]

VOLUME BUSINESS

It's not as if the commercial banks didn't get squeezed on fees themselves—after all, following the bust, there was stiff competition for any corporate issuance business. The difference was that they got the higher volume of actual business that was available. If they extended a multibillion-dollar credit facility to a client, it would open the door to increased new issuance business in return, even if that issuance was for lower-than-historic fee levels. Once the prototype was constructed, knockoff deals were cheap and simple to execute. For instance, doing ten different $1 billion issues which netted the bank $4 million each was not a bad take for putting together one simple debt deal and then just changing the deal documentation dates and, maybe, the coupons (interest rates) for the nine other copycat issues.

Meanwhile, at places like Goldman, junior officers continued to dial-for-deals only to be constantly rebuffed. When corporations were executing mergers and acquisitions with investment banks during the mid- and late 1990s, losing just the bond issuance wasn't much of a problem; what corporations needed most between 2001 and 2003 was debt on favorable terms to stay afloat, often repaying old debt with new debt—an increasingly common practice after the stock bubble burst. For the amount of credit required to keep these corporations solvent, only the big commercial banks would suffice. These companies were so big and unwieldy that it seemed like creating more debt was the only way to keep them afloat. This is why supermarket banks are more exposed to the corporate merger downturn than midsized or small banks; they depend upon a booming stock market and endless growth to give them business. The midsized and smaller, mostly regional, banks just didn't have enough deposits on their balance sheets to lend amounts large enough to keep the growing corporate world happy. Ironically, though, these smaller institutions pay a proportionately larger insurance premium to the FDIC to back their investor deposits than do the larger banks, which are more reckless with their individual customers' money.

The ease with which the capital markets officers at Salomon Brothers got deals seemed to be directly related to parent Citigroup's massive balance sheet. As one Goldman Sachs managing director said, "You could have a monkey call up banks and corporations and get issuance deals at Salomon. My cat could do it." With or without animals on the payroll, Citigroup Salomon propelled itself to the top of the corporate bond league tables in 2002 and 2003.

LOAN AND DEBT ISSUANCE

After the 1996 deregulation of the telecom and energy industries, issuances and mergers skyrocketed. And Wall Street egged them on. During the second half of the 1990s, the financial, telecom, and energy industries accumulated more than $4 trillion in bond and loan debt. Debt issuance during 1998–2000, the height of the stock bubble, was on average four times what it had been in 1990–1998 and six times more for the energy and telecom sectors in particular.[42] For that same period, additional debt in the form of short-term and emergency (or "back-up") credit facilities, which isn't publicly disclosed on bank balance sheets because the monies technically have not yet been extended, amounted to approximately $500 billion. The financial sector issued $1.7 trillion in loans to itself.[43] On average, the total volume of debt and credit issuance was eight times the amount issued during the first half of the 1990s.

Loan pricing was based on the corporation's probability of defaulting. The healthier the corporation made its balance sheet appear, the easier it was to bloat it with more debt capital. In general, the lower the credit rating or credit worthiness of an institution, the higher the borrowing costs. Loans that were extended only under emergency circumstances were priced less "scientifically" than other loans since banks are not required to disclose the risk of these undrawn funds. Emergency credit for corporations is like overdraft protection for checking customers. Usually, you overdraw your checking account when there's not enough money in it to pay your bills. Companies draw on their emergency credit funds when they don't have enough money to pay *their* bills. The banks have more room to negotiate these credit interest rates than straightforward commercial loan rates because more is at stake. For example, if an institution wants a $3 billion emergency credit facility, it is charged a certain rate, just like an individual taking out a loan. However, if the institution is committed to paying the bank through other means, such as with M&A, IPO, or derivatives business, the interest on the credit can be negotiated as part of a greater package.

Loan pricing is supposedly transparent, and because more than one bank is frequently involved in the transaction, banks often form a "loan syndicate," working together to extend larger loans to corporations. Thus, banks deny they have room to manipulate loan prices or to tie loans to other business. Plus, no bank wants to admit to violating antitrust law.

In fact, banks dodge the antitrust law violation claim by saying they offer full service to their clients. Good clients are treated better; maybe they get a few perks here and there. Banks say that's the same as a good restaurant giving a valued customer the window table. But once that diner can't pay for his meal one day, the restaurant takes another view. The banks didn't; they continued in many instances to lend good money after bad.

In addition to facing multiple lawsuits, Citigroup and JP Morgan Chase are sitting on billions of dollars of nonperforming loans they offered failing and bankrupt companies since late 2001. Because most of the bankrupt companies, particularly the ones in the telecom sector, own relatively worthless assets—thanks to the immense overcapacity that followed 1996 deregulation—the banks are ever unlikely to ever recoup much on their loans. Nonetheless, given the nature of bankruptcy laws, these creditors still receive what little there is before employees of these firms are compensated for their losses.

It didn't help that supermarket banks developed a habit of bailing out companies whose values were plummeting fast, operating under the philosophy that while these corporations *might* sink even with the extra credit, they would *definitely* sink without it, and banks would lose the entire principal of their loans, not just a couple of interest payments. For instance, JP Morgan Chase was involved in extending $10 billion of lifeline credit facilities just days before bankruptcies were declared by Enron, WorldCom, Adelphia, and Global Crossing. This was a general business practice and not merely a coincidence at work.

The financial institutions that had issued the most loans and therefore had the most exposure, or risk of nonrepayment, were Citigroup and JP Morgan Chase. Both had substantial reductions in their share values due to loan write-downs (and lawsuits), which negatively affected their employees, shareholders, and taxpayers in general. However, since the Fed operates to ensure stability in the banking industry, it generally bails banks out when they get into trouble. The money they use tends to come from Treasury debt and, less directly, from the federal deficit debt that hangs over the heads of every U.S. citizen. Both companies rode the post–Glass-Steagall wave to gain investment banking fees in return for offering corporate loans, and now both count on the government to keep them afloat even as their debtors sink.

And with good reason. In early March 2003, there were market rumors that Standard & Poor's (S&P) was considering downgrading JP Morgan Chase from AAA to A, the lowest-ever credit quality rating for a financial institution of its breadth. That would have meant JP Morgan Chase would have had to pony up more regulatory capital to back their trading positions.

Whether or not someone is a customer of JP Morgan Chase, when money becomes tighter (because it's being used to back up bank activities), rates go up—all rates, mortgages, car loans, etc.—which affects everyone's pockets. If the credit quality of the bank were to be compromised, the Fed and the Treasury would probably be forced to help it fund itself at the higher cost to ensure no abrupt stoppage in services to institutional customers, possibly by lowering interest rates or injecting funds. One Salomon Brother's corporate strategist told me, "If they even thought about [JP Morgan Chase's] downgrade seriously, Bush would be on the phone straight away." Trillions of dollars were at stake, and banks would be forced to refinance all that money at higher interest rate costs to themselves. As it turned out, that downgrade was just a rumor, or perhaps someone at the Fed intervened in time.

RATING AGENCIES

Rating agencies are independent corporations that analyze the debt and corporate structure of public companies and assign a level of creditworthiness to each company based on the company's probability of defaults on its debt. The two biggest rating firms are Moody's and Standard & Poor's. Each employs teams of researchers who focus on specific industry sectors and individual corporations. Ratings range from AAA or Aaa, meaning the most likely to repay debt and thus the most secure, to the poorest grade, D, designating the least likely to repay debt. Junk bond companies are rated at BB and lower.

Companies pay to be rated, but because the agencies rate so many companies, which are effectively a captive market, they manage to maintain a semblance of objectivity. Ratings are assigned by low-paid staffs whose ultimate goals are often to land higher-paying Wall Street jobs.

I don't believe the agencies are as complicit as the banks in corporate deception, just that they are chronically short-staffed and underfunded. Because analysts don't get paid very much at rating agencies, the turnover tends to be very high. Still, the research they put out is generally thorough, to the extent that they have access to appropriate information from the corporations they rate. This is not the case with Wall Street equity analysts, who are just as likely to rate companies based on hype as on the numbers.

Wall Street banks tend to raid rating agencies to hire bright young analysts cheaply. The salaries they have to match to poach these people are far less than what they would have to pay if they plucked the same people from a competitor firm. Young analysts frequently only take jobs at the rating agencies to parlay them into jobs paying bigger money at the investment banks, at least while the market is hot.

BANK ASSETS AND BAD LOANS

Of the $6.6 trillion in assets held by the country's commercial banks, $3.9 trillion, or 60 percent, are loans. Almost $1 trillion, or 25 percent, of loans are commercial and industrial (C&I) loans to large and midsized corporations. Net charge-offs, the collective amount of loans that are no longer likely to be collected and are written off as bad debt expenses (minus recoveries of payments previously charged off),[44] due to bad loan performance totaled $36.5 billion, or 3.7 percent of all loans for 2002.[45] That doesn't sound like a large percentage, but it's more than triple what it was in 2001. What's more, charge-offs occur once a corporation has completely stopped paying interest on its loans.

There are billions of dollars of loans for which interest payments haven't stopped, even though the corporation's credit quality or chance of payment has dramatically decreased, because banks tend to float more loans to troubled companies to prevent them from defaulting. There is no publicly available information on loan deterioration because it's difficult to measure. It is possible, however, to reevaluate loans down each time the ratings of a company are downgraded. But how do you determine that a company currently making its interest payments is nonetheless unlikely to be able to continue paying off its debt? Banks don't have to change their loan evaluations until interest payments are delinquent or stop altogether. The industry's noncurrent rate on C&I loans increased from 2.87 to 3.01 percent during the third quarter of 2002, the first time since the first quarter of 1993 that it had risen above 3 percent.[46] Noncurrent loans are loans for which corporations are behind in payments but on which they haven't yet defaulted. You can try asking any bank what their largest exposures are, and to whom, but you won't get an answer because they are not obligated to disclose that information. C&I loan charge-offs accounted for almost 41 percent of all loan charge-offs in 2002.[47]

On September 18, 2002, JP Morgan Chase CEO William Harrison Jr. launched a plea for understanding of his bank's plight in an editorial in the *Wall Street Journal*, playing the innocent victim in the corporate scandals and credit erosion.[48] Among other things, Harrison said that banks were just "lenders and passive investors" in fraudulent, ailing companies. Placing an op-ed "confession" was certainly a lot more economical than taking out a full-page ad in the same newspaper. It also happened to coincide with the release of JP Morgan Chase's third-quarter earnings figures, which were awful. The bank blamed its miserable performance on faulty loans and poor trading performance. Of course, many of those loans just happened to have been extended to their best investment banking clients. Misunderstood JP Morgan Chase took a beating on its stock that day, which declined 12 percent in value.

Harrison's editorial reeked of desperation to calm investors in JP Morgan Chase's stock and combat any possibility of investment banks using the demise of fraudulent companies to regain the market share that had been taken from them by the commerial banks through easy loans and less-than-transparent practices. Rather than just making the point that JP Morgan Chase was innocent—as opposed to just stupid for not doing better diligence on the loans and credit facilities they extended—Harrison fought back against the public swipes emanating from the investment banks regarding their loan practices. During his luncheon speech in front of the National Press Club in Washington three months earlier, Goldman CEO Hank Paulson had openly targeted überbanks in general and archrival JP Morgan Chase in particular for the lack of full asset and liability disclosure information as part of a larger statement regarding corporate governance reforms.[49]

ACCOUNTING FOR CREDIT RISK

The way in which investment banks and commercial banks account for their credit exposure is very different. Investment banks are subject to fair value accounting (FVA), meaning that all changes to the value of loans and investments have to be reevaluated on a daily basis and reported to the Financial Accounting Standards Board (FASB).[50]

Commercial banks aren't subject to FVA for their loans, supposedly because these loans are long-term and not regularly traded. There's also no FVA for credit facilities either. At Goldman, I worked with a group of strategists and an outside economist on the question of whether or not credit lines should be considered options because they have an implied risk of being drawn down, or depleted, at any point in time, but are never marked or evaluated accordingly. Commercial banks see it differently and don't think they should have to regularly reevaluate their open credit lines, although that matter is still subject to discussion. JP Morgan Chase argued that, because these lines are not "tradable instruments" or commodities (which is true), they don't need to be evaluated as such.

Even in periods of relative corporate financial stability, this is a huge accident waiting to happen. But, as we've witnessed throughout the bankruptcy and scandal period, corporations only draw down on their credit lines in extreme emergencies, like fraud disclosures, executive indictments, and bankruptcies—in other words, at precisely the time when the credit line poses the greatest risk of loss to the extending bank. The risk is ultimately taken on by the Federal Reserve, the last line of bailout defense if dire circumstances require it, and by the taxpayers, as the commercial banks extend credit lines with depositor money insured by the FDIC.

None of this stops banks from extending additional credit to corporations that are obviously in peril. Meanwhile, there is no regulatory mechanism that compels banks to publicly disclose the exact nature of impaired loans—that is, loans for which the ability of debtors to repay has deteriorated but not yet stopped completely. The FDIC compiles a list of banks that have had at least one delinquent payment on any of their loans. But even if a corporation makes good on its loan payments for as long as possible, it could still stop paying at any moment. This is true of anyone, any corporation—that's the nature of risk. But it is not okay for that risk to be protected by the Fed and taxpayer money. Unlike investment banks, commercial banks don't have to reprice loans whose probability of failure to repay is increasing.

C&I loans make up anywhere from 22 to 45 percent of a bank's liabilities.[51] Often, banks shift the worst of these loans off their balance sheets or embed groups of them in portfolios called CLO securities (collateralized loan obligations), which then are purchased by insurance or reinsurance companies or other banks. Only nonperforming loans, which have missed payments or are actually in default, have to be declared. At the end of 2002, 4 percent of all C&I loans were nonperforming.[52] Since loans rank higher in the "waterfall," or order of repayments, of corporations, loan defaults occur after bond defaults. Meanwhile, the number of loan defaults continue to set new historical highs.

MANAGING RELATIONSHIPS AND EXTENDING CREDIT

Managing customer relationships became the cornerstone of many an advertising campaign on the Street. Citigroup, for instance, showcased ads that combined financial advice with therapeutic affirmations like "friendships don't depreciate" and " be independently happy." In July 2002, Tim Carvell examined the phenomenon of Citigroup's "Live Richly" ad campaign in a brilliantly sardonic *Slate* piece entitled "Citi of Fear: What Are Citigroup's Weird Ads Really Saying?" He characterized Citigroup's messages that money isn't all that's important as "not necessarily reassuring from an institution whose sole job is to protect your money."[53] In fact, the money that Citigroup was encouraging its customers to use to "live richly" was being siphoned off to invest in companies like WorldCom.

JP Morgan Chase branches adorned their windows with glossy pictures of smiling multicultural reps beckoning to the customer with the words "The right relationship is everything." It was the very picture of a warm, friendly local bank. But, in practice, what that slogan means, outside of the retail customer realm, is: "Be all things to all clients—as long as they are wealthy and influential."[54]

In reality, JP Morgan Chase was struggling. Their annual loan loss provisions—money set aside by the bank to cover bad loans—shot from $1.38 billion in 2000 and $1.5 billion in 1999 to $3.2 billion in 2001. The bank had a $2.6 billion exposure to Enron on its books, combined with mounting losses from the financial collapse in Argentina.[55] Therefore, Citigroup was willing to go to great measures to keep tanking companies from completely going under. For example, even when Global Crossing stock was trading for pennies, Global Crossing, JP Morgan Chase, and Citigroup met to discuss issuing more credit. With all the other problems on JP Morgan Chase's 2001 balance sheet, the bank was desperate to keep Global Crossing alive until the next calendar year. So, in December 2001, Global Crossing and JP Morgan Chase reached an agreement waiving the right to seek retribution for any future credit violations, which worked out fine for Global Crossing but not so fine for JP Morgan Chase once Global Crossing declared bankruptcy. Exactly two years later, JP Morgan Chase filed a lawsuit against Global Crossing and its former chairman Gary Winnick.[56]

On September 30, 2002, JP Morgan Chase issued profit warnings and a $1.4 billion provision for bad debts, mostly springing from the telecom sector. In late October, they announced that their third-quarter profits were down 91 percent to $40 million. By November 2002, JP Morgan Chase stock had fallen more than 68 percent since March 2000, the biggest periodic decline ever in the Philadelphia KBW index, which is the primary stock index tracking the performance of the nation's twenty-four largest banks.

The growth of "relationship loans" (a euphemism for loan-tying) to capture investment banking business, despite mounting evidence of impending bankruptcies in energy and telecommunications, just keeps getting stronger. Beyond the stupidity of doing business with corporations about to go under (merely another form of loan-tying that is already illegal), these "relationship loans" require closer scrutiny because they are in fact funded by the deposits of millions of Americans. Yet there has been little legislative momentum thus far beyond a few letters, most notably from Representative John Dingell (D-MI), suggesting the practice be monitored. Oversight of lending practices would serve the interests of the investment banks while keeping away from scrutiny behooves the über-banks, and it's these oppositional lobbies that are keeping more stringent legislation from being passed.

Why did banks continue to give loans to Global Crossing even while it was imploding? Why did they give loans to WorldCom? To Enron? To Adelphia? To Dynegy? To El Paso? Again, banks relied upon the convoluted logic that those companies might turn around with lifelines, and would definitely fail without them. So what they're really doing by offering huge last-minute credit lines is protecting their original loan by investing in the well-being of the company. This is not dissimilar from Third World debts, but while Third World countries have to fulfill World Bank and IMF accounting practice requirements to get loans from both of these supranational institutions, corporations are under no obligation to the financial institutions to do so or to change any of their practices.

Banks don't just want lending, issuance, and M&A from corporations— they want all their business, and in 2002 they didn't want regulation stopping them. On September 30, 2002, Bank of America filed a request with FERC for permission to trade wholesale energy, like an investment bank (or Enron).[57] It had already been trading natural gas and oil since 1989, and had even hired power trader Joe Graham from Enron. They wanted FERC to waive the rule preventing them from loaning money to public utilities and acquiring their debt or equity securities at the same time.

Arthur Levitt, SEC head during the Clinton years and author of *Take on the Street*, warned participants at an early 2002 Goldman Sachs conference that the practice of loan tying in the banking industry was getting worse. One year later, during Senate hearings that confirmed his selection to head the SEC, William H. Donaldson swore he would "stamp out tying." He said that loan tying "rivals the use of research to be a handmaiden to investment banking and the securities industry." His words came during the witch hunts for scam research analysts, so the comparison was meant to be a serious promise. To date, Donaldson, has done nothing, however, to catch or curtail the loan-tying activity of banks.[58]

The fact is that the only real remedy for loan tying is what the Glass-Steagall Act did: separate lending business from issuance business. It sounds tautological, but the only way to separate the two businesses is to separate the two businesses. Donaldson is certainly not going to propose a return to that distinction. His own alma mater, Donaldson, Lufkin and Jenrette (DLJ), part of CSFB, the third largest überbank, would have to go back to selling junk bonds on its merits and not on its ability to extend cheap credit lines. Donaldson's speech was really a bunch of empty talk designed to keep the issue at bay by pretending to address it, until it was overwhelmed by a war with Iraq. Meanwhile, equity and investment banking divisions continue to shrink, with banks firing people across the board—but, as always, starting with the analysts.

During 2002, as corporate defaults reached levels last seen in the Great Depression and as scandals piled up, commercial banks tried hard to dodge accusations that they had recklessly tied loans and credit facilities to other issuance and investment banking business. But 2000 and 2001 told a very different story. Following the Glass-Steagall repeal, commercial banks with supermarket aspirations made it clear that they simply weren't going to extend credit without getting anything in return. They were completely up-front about this, but their behavior didn't raise a single eyebrow in Congress. None of the senators who voted to repeal the act appeared to expect a tide of loan tying and the associated debt problems it caused, nor the rush of scandals that tanked companies faster than they could repay much of that debt.

In March 2001, the CEO of Bank One, Jamie Dimon, declared that Bank One would sever relations with customers who only borrowed but didn't use the bank's other services, like cash or portfolio investment management, transactions that entailed complex, and eventually lucrative, combinations of simpler investing or hedging strategies, or debt underwritings.[59] He went on to confirm the strategy at an investors' conference call that quarter, stating, "We will exit low-value relationships." The Chicago-based Bank One was the fourth largest U.S. loan syndicator at the time, in terms of volume.

Bank of America, the second largest arranger of syndicated loans in the United States, had already announced in December 2000 that it would not renew roughly $20 billion of loans that would come due in two years' time without the possibility of those borrowers entering deeper relationships, which many did.[60] To validate that threat, it turned down a request by Wal-Mart, the number-one company in America on the Fortune 500 list, to arrange a $2.25 billion credit line in the summer of 2001, even though it had been the lead underwriter for Wal-Mart since 1995, because Wal-Mart had started to spread its business too thin across the Street.[61]

Ford was a prime example of a corporation that played ball, and Bank of America rewarded their compliance by becoming one of their lead debt underwriters in 2001, after having never even broken into Ford's top-ten list of underwriters before. Long-standing investment bank partners were dropped like yesterday's dot-coms when they wouldn't extend

Ford cheap credit as well. The power lay with the commercial banks, and when Ford followed the terms they set out, they got the cheap credit they wanted. Even wannabe überbanks like Sun Trust Bank, the ninth largest U.S. commercial bank at the beginning of 2001, followed suit, specifically stating it was ending relationships with borrowers unlikely to use it for underwriting debt or equity.

In essence, supermarket banks said, "No credit without banking or issuance business." Corporations responded in kind: "No banking or issuance business from us without credit." Since they were both on the same page, more corporate business went to the überbanks, who in turn issued record loan volumes, loans often collateralized, or backed, by stock in the corporations they were lending to that had been inflated by the media and Wall Street cheerleaders throughout the late 1990s. Corporations borrowed because they had eager lenders. Corporations borrowed because investors were less concerned with their current balance sheets than with future growth possibilities. Corporations borrowed because they could. The debt bubble grew.

THE BANK WARS

If supermarket and investment banks hadn't been fighting over market share, there would have been less deal inflation, less bad debt, and fewer loans. But when they were aggressively competing for league table status, they weren't about to let a few concerns about the likelihood of a client staying afloat get in the way of closing a deal. Nor were they going to stop and think about the real necessity of a deal for a client or its future consequences. There wasn't enough time in the endless quest for financial supremacy.

At the same time, they did their best to discredit each other. JP Morgan Chase openly called Goldman's investment banking tactics needlessly aggressive. Goldman annoyed the banks in return. Around 2000, for example, Goldman arranged an AT&T loan deal. Because Goldman had an excellent, highly ranked loan trading business, it was able to flip, or sell the loans out, to the Street immediately. It was worth breaking even or possibly taking a loss if it could maintain access to AT&T's other business, and Goldman did get a piece of the mega-Comcast and other M&A deals later. So Goldman moved the loan risk out the door at a loss. Meanwhile, the commercial banks whose business was the primary issuance of loans had to pay 100 percent, or $1 on the dollar, for loans that Goldman was selling to clients at a discount, at 99 percent, or 99 cents on the dollar, taking the loss to stay in the business flow.

Fees on convertible bonds, which could be converted to shares of stock if stock prices rose to a certain level, could be 3 to 6 percent of the value of the deal. On straight equity issuance, fees were even higher, between 6 and 7 percent. Goldman was able to do the math: if they could place or distribute a loan in bond form, even at a 1 percent immediate loss, but pick up other, more lucrative business in the process, they would make the loan. The question was, how big a hit could the bank take on a flip to balance out what it would make doing other banking business. For the commercial banks that were typically locked into longer loan-holding periods, this was a problem. Plus, by selling the loans cheaply, Goldman was making the market, or profit, for new issuance of loans by the same corporations less lucrative for banks like Citigroup and JP Morgan Chase.

For banks, extending these loans could be break-even or even negative transactions, but what they really cared about was the amount of capital they had to hold in reserve behind the loan in case of nonrepayment versus using that capital for other investments. If that math worked, they would extend the loan.

Things got downright nasty between investment banks faced with dropping fee business and commercial banks stuck with nonperforming loans and unpaid credit lines. Fights erupted on the pages of major newspapers and in Washington. In an April 2001 letter from Goldman Sachs to the FASB, Goldman stated it was concerned about the way in which commercial banks were using their credit lines, offered at low rates, to lure away customers that it claimed would typically have turned to "Wall Street" expertise to help them raise money through debt and equity issues.[62] But credit lines were more of a problem to overall market stability than outright loans, because banks would be overstretched if too many corporations drew down on credit lines simultaneously.

Goldman claimed that commercial banks had relaxed their underwriting standards to win investment banking (IB) business. The question that must be asked, though, is if that were the case (it was), what was the endgame? The answer was short-term profitability at the expense of disclosure of medium- or longer-term credit problems. Goldman's letter went on to say, "We believe lenders and financial statements will be more representationally faithful of the risks and benefits of lending arrangements if loan commitments are carried at fair value." In other words, if banks were required to periodically reevaluate and disclose the market value of their loans, reflecting the current creditworthiness of their clients, it would force commercial banks to require higher loan premiums, thereby making these loans less attractive to their clients. The risk is that if those banks have outstanding loans that become severely devalued, this will not be immediately transparent on their books. Unlike investment banks that classify loans on their books as "investments" and are therefore mandated to revalue them daily, commercial banks are not obligated to do so.

JP Morgan Chase's rebuttal, through the FASB, was sharp and brief: "We have read Goldman Sachs' letter and do not understand why the information contained therein warrants reopening this issue."[63] In other words: piss off. In yet another letter to the FASB, Goldman countered, "If credit lines are options, they should be accounted for as derivatives."[64] The issue remains under dispute.

FIGHTING BACK CREATIVELY

During 2000 and 2001, Salomon Brothers and Big Daddy Citigroup started stealing business with lightning speed, as previously discussed. But when Bank of America stepped out from behind the curtains to get in on the credit-for-other-business game, it really struck a nerve. A former Goldman Capital Markets associate recalls, "One morning, we were having our regular morning capital markets meeting and Bank of America showed up as a co-adviser on one of our M&A deals. Management freaked out."

"Hey," said one Salomon Brothers banker, "our model works, and we've got the business. Banks that have both strategic and funding relationships win; they have more access to major clients. It's the way it is." Still, he was careful to point out they do not tie loans to business—but this was purely a semantic argument. This banker talks to his clients four to five times a week about issuance at the same time that those clients are doing other business throughout the bank. His Goldman counterpart is lucky if he gets a phone call returned a week later from the same corporations.

By early 2003, the situation propelled Goldman Sachs to link up with Sumitomo Mitsui Financial Group (SMFG). In essence, Goldman would get to use Sumitomo's balance sheet, and be able to mimic what the über-banks were doing by extending credit off-balance sheet for twenty-five years, backed by Sumitomo, who would be supplying that credit when it was needed. Sumitomo would receive fees from Goldman each time it made use of this credit source with its key clients. In effect, Goldman and Sumitomo were replicating the bank supermarket process without undergoing a desta-bilizing merger. It was more like a formal "relationship." The partnership was announced in mid-January 2003, when Goldman purchased $1.27 billion of convertible preferred stock (shares which can be converted to com-mon stock) in SMFG; in return, SMFG would provide Goldman with $1 billion in first-loss protection (cash put up to absorb up to $1 billion of defaults) to "mitigate risks associated with extending credit to Goldman Sachs' investment-grade clients."[65] This was insurance for Goldman in case certain clients defaulted on their credit payments in the future.

But Goldman's solution was risky. Basically, it was using a cheap bal-ance sheet from a third-rate bank in order to fulfill the borrowing demands of its key banking clients. Instead of being exposed to possible defaults spread over an array of clients, Goldman's risk was concentrated in Sumi-tomo. In other words, they exchanged a lot of different, smaller risks for one big risk to gain a balance sheet large enough to support cheaper loans. If Sumitomo went under, Goldman's entire cheap credit business would go under and the bank could kiss its stock investment in SMFG good-bye. Sumitomo didn't exactly have a stable track record: it shut down its own U.S. lending business, firing the entire staff, in 1998. Even the deals in-volving SMFG were landed by piggybacking off the large American banks. It got crumbs of syndicated loan deals because it underpriced its credit en-hancement, or loan insurance, in order to get its name on the deal.

By mid-March 2003, cracks in this strategy had already begun to show. Goldman had to adjust those converts down by $75 million because Sumitomo stock had declined in value. As investment banking business with corporations declined, however, there was always the more specula-tive trading business to count on. In both 2001 and 2002, for instance, Goldman's FICC (fixed income currency and commodities) division set new revenue records.[66] Its trading operations, particularly in commodities, were buzzing. With energy prices running high, volatility sparked by the threat of war with Iraq, and chief competitor corporations either gone, like Enron, or facing fraud suits, like El Paso, commodity trading rose through the roof. Interestingly, Hank Paulson stopped being public about how commercial bank loans should be marked to market around the time Goldman entered into the Sumitomo deal in January 2003.

There were simpler and subtler ways to maintain important client relationships. For instance, one former Goldman Sachs vice president recalled that the co-head of FIG (Financial Institutions Group) banking would write checks to charity events hosted by his banking customers in the hopes of getting on their good side and scraping up some issuance business. "Once with MBNA, Matt* wrote out a $50,000 check for their golf charity event. He wanted me to attend. My whole thing with Matt was: MBNA doesn't issue bonds with us, and my job is working with clients that issue bonds. Not only don't they issue bonds, the likelihood that they ever will is like zero, so for me to waste my time golfing with someone we took off our client list seems useless."

Matt didn't like that answer, but it was true. MBNA had, in fact, stopped locking in its financing, or borrowing requirements, when it closed M&A deals. "You were always at a disadvantage in issuance at Goldman," said the same former Goldman vice president. "All your clients wanted something you couldn't give them, but Goldman didn't care. Vice chairman Bob Hurst had even sent out an internal e-mail when the investment banking environment started deteriorating, telling the whole firm not to worry, we'll do what it takes to protect our important businesses—M&A and equity."

"Kind of made you feel like shit," said one of the vice presidents responsible for bond issuance business.

Goldman wasn't about to bow out of the banking business. They still got the equity offerings and M&A from their premier clients—the chunky stuff that was agreed upon, CEO to CEO. For example, Goldman didn't do a single deal for MBNA for three years, but it happened to land two large equity deals on the strength of old relationship ties.

SPECULATIVE TRADING: INVESTMENT BANKS AS HEDGE FUNDS

By 2002, M&A and equity business was down substantially around the Street, and investment bankers stopped looking so hot. Investment banks

---

*A pseudonym.

with solid trading operations, like Lehman Brothers and Bear Stearns, on the other hand, had great annual results.

Goldman continued to lose market share to the big banks, as feared. While that was happening, though, its FICC trading businesses were reaching record highs. All across the Street, speculative trading business was picking up the slack that investment banking business left behind. Profits were being made by speculating and earning the spread between buying and selling bonds and derivatives, rather than with the more certain, up-front, cash-in-the-door investment banking and issuance business.

Record-breaking trading performance propelled FICC head Lloyd Blankfein up the Goldman ladder just behind Hank Paulson, who had risen to his position from the investment banking division. Today, Goldman's overall business is heavily concentrated on trading profits, a far more speculative enterprise (as Enron's demise revealed) than fee-generated business. Said one former Goldman trader, "Take a look at their investment mix now; I can tell you one thing, they ain't all invested in U.S. treasury bills."

Blankfein will likely take over the Goldman helm one day, given that he's presided over the biggest moneymaking division in the firm. In 2002, Blankfein became the highest-paid Goldman Sachs executive, receiving a total compensation package of $12.6 million. Hank Paulson came in second with a $9.5 million package. The two Johns, Thain and Thornton (occasionally referred to by insiders as Tweedledum and Tweedledee), were paid the same amount: $8.8 million each.[67] Both were co-president and co-chief operating officers. Soon afterward, Thornton announced he was throwing in the towel, resigning from Goldman to teach in China.[68]

But the more that Goldman's revenues are reliant on speculative trading and complex transactions, the more the firm and other investment banks following a similar strategy will begin to resemble large hedge funds: lots of leveraged capital and lots of less regulated and less transparent risk.

DESPERATE TO CLOSE DEALS

Tight external competition gives way to desperation born of illogical business pressures. On the Friday before Christmas 2001, the Street was winding down as many people headed home to their families or off to faraway places for the holidays. In general, volume slumps and at least half the trading floors are vacant during the holidays. The holiday Christmas party for all the employees' kids had already taken place earlier in the week; smells of fresh popcorn had already subsided and for almost the only time during the year, a sense of calm reigned on the Street.

Earlier in the week, I had had a meeting with Patrick*, a former senior partner in the investment banking division who had moved into a hybrid role that involved leveraging the firm's and his own relationships to get strategic or tactical business involving large transactions. One of his clients was an insurance company based in Japan. Like other Japanese insurance companies who wanted to partner with companies in the United States and Canada, it had approached Patrick about investing excess cash (excess that ran to billions of dollars). It was looking for ways to invest the cash in the credit markets, either in straight bonds or derivatives. Patrick called me and a colleague of mine who focused on strategic transactions for insurance companies to discuss what we could do for this client. He wanted it done yesterday.

We put together a chart of different types of investments, listing their pros and cons, and sent it off to his client in Japan. Two days went by; Christmas approached and we had not heard back. Patrick was anxious, but in truth it was unlikely any client would pounce on loading up on credit in an illiquid and uncertain (after Enron's bankruptcy declarations) year-end climate.

I figured we'd wait until after the New Year and regroup. I took off half of the Friday before Christmas, and went to get a haircut. While under the dryer, I didn't hear my cell phone ring. On my way home that evening, the city was full of last-minute shoppers but devoid of suits. I returned to find several messages on my answering machine, all urgent calls from Patrick's secretary. (Only secretaries call for people. During senior partners' ascent through the ranks, their dialing fingers atrophy.)

It was 6 P.M. I talked to Patrick's secretary, got his cell number, and called him. He asked if anything had happened on "the trade," his optimistic euphemism for something that wasn't anywhere close to being a trade. It was simply his opening to a dialogue about a *potential* trade. I told him I had left a message for the client that morning but had not heard back from him. Patrick asked me if I was committed to getting it done.

*A pseudonym.

His tone was somewhere between exasperated and desperate. It was almost the end of the year, and he was grasping at anything that might get the deal done before the books closed on 2001.

The trade never happened, which was unsurprising. It started and ended as a long shot, just one example of the push for closing business becoming the business.

CREDIT SUISSE FIRST BOSTON: WHERE THE ÜBERBANK MODEL FAILS

The model of lending-for-banking-business doesn't work for everyone. CSFB was one of the first major banks to try it out. Swiss-based Credit Suisse had bought U.S. investment bank First Boston back in 1989. In August 2000, Credit Suisse First Boston announced the $11.5 billion acquisition of New York–based investment bank and corporate bond specialists DLJ, operator of a large share-dealing online service called DLJ Direct, a stock deal in which CSFB paid a 22 percent premium for DLJ shares. The acquisition was a move designed to expand CSFB's U.S. presence prior to the repeal of Glass-Steagall. The CSFB grab of DLJ was the second acquisition of a U.S. investment bank by a Swiss bank within a two-month period. In July 2000, CSFB's native rival, the Union Bank of Switzerland (UBS), bought U.S. brokerage firm Paine Webber from General Electric for $10.8 billion.

The CSFB-DLJ merger was heralded as a brilliant move by equity analysts. "In investment banking, you have to have scale to survive," said Bryan Crossley, then a banking analyst at ABN Amro. "This is like a poker game; you have to keep throwing money into the pot to stay at the table."[69]

By 2003, however, CSFB-DLJ was widely perceived as a failed Citigroup. Its stock was trading at five-year lows. CSFB lost $1.2 billion in 2002, paid $70 million in disgorgement (giving back profits) to the U.S. Treasury, and forked over $30 million in civil penalties and fines to the SEC in January 2002 to settle hot IPO-spinning charges without admitting wrongdoing. After the announcement of the December 2002 Wall Street settlement, CSFB had to set aside an additional $600 million against future legal claims. (The DLJ management had been smart: they had cashed out after the sale of their company to CSFB, at the peak of the market. Co-founder William Donaldson had left the firm in 2000 and, of course, eventually became head of the SEC.)

One of Wall Street's highest-profile investment bankers to suffer from the fallout of the late 1990s was CSFB's Frank Quattrone. Quattrone had taken CSFB's technology IPO business from fourteenth place in league tables, or issuer rankings, in 1998 up to number two in 1999 and number three in 2000.[70] Eliot Spitzer started investigating him in the fall of 2001. In March 2003, Quattrone was charged with violating securities rules because of the aggressive strategies he used to land clients. The National Association of Securities Dealers, or NASD, also filed a civil complaint alleging Quattrone had promised that his analysts would provide favorable stock ratings on lucrative IPOs as an enticement to clients considering which bank would do their IPOs.[71]

Regulators claimed Quattrone dispensed hot IPOs to favored clients and spun them back to smaller investors who would get in at higher levels with reduced profit potential on the upside and more risk that the IPO had already attained its highest value and would only go down. By doing so, he made key clients hundreds of millions of dollars right off the bat in companies that later lost smaller investors, who had less access to his insight, hundreds of millions of dollars. He was also charged with the possible destruction of documents key to the NASD investigation. Then he resigned. Quattrone was eventually tried for his crimes. In October 2003, his first trial was declared a mistrial—the second time around, in May 2004, he was convicted on two counts of obstruction of justice, one of witness tampering. Thus, he was convicted of hiding the crime, not the crime itself.

The week that Quattrone resigned was filled with other high-profile bank resignations. David W. Wiley, the CFO of Capital One, also resigned under heat from an SEC investigation into insider trading, prompting another bank to panic. Salomon Brothers, one of Capital One's biggest book runners, or debt distributors, was in the process of closing a deal with the bank when the news broke, even though Wiley had been under formal investigation since the company's July 2002 SEC 8K filings.[72] According to a Salomon Brothers banker, Capital One chose not to mention the investigation to Salomon, and the SEC doesn't make any of its ongoing investigations public. So Capital One simply said, in requisite banker lingo, that the investigation was "not material to the issuance."

All of this has been unexplored territory as far as regulators are concerned, but still an ever-present problem. Insider trading or fraud investigations are clearly material to a company issuing more debt to investors. A possible indictment is something a lender should know, and as soon as possible. Clearly, any kind of information that makes Capital One's stock instantly tank 10 percent and thus lower the price of its bonds is very "material." But there are no regulations requiring that type of disclosure.

FINANCIAL SERVICES CONFERENCES

Several times a year, Wall Street firms take turns sponsoring financial services conferences. Everybody does it. Salomon Brothers and Citigroup hold a joint conference in January. Lehman does two, one in December and one in May. Merrill Lynch has its in September. Goldman's is in May.

The object of these conferences is for each major Wall Street player to extol its virtues to an audience of its peers and investors. These conferences are more important in bad years than good years, when firms are hoping the media or equity analysts covering them will pick up optimistic sound bites. So, from mid-2002 through 2003, almost every Wall Street CEO made sure to put his firm's best foot forward. The events feel something like a family reunion, where squabbling relatives all have to be on their best behavior.

Everyone shows up for these conferences because the audience includes clients of the hosting bank, allowing CEOs access to their competitors' best clients. It's reminiscent of the Westminster Dog Show, except that each bank or investment bank is competing for the coveted titles of "Most Solid Investment" or "Best Partner for a Deal" instead of "Best Toy Dog"— although both the dog and the firm would be more than happy to walk away with the top honor: "Best in Show." The clients are the judges. That's why no matter how many of these things are scheduled per year, they're always well attended. With increased investor scrutiny, they offer any individual bank a prime opportunity to state why it has the best corporate governance, research analyst independence, or plain old solid future.

CITIGROUP'S ENTRY

At the September 2002 Merrill Lynch Financial Services Conference, Citigroup's Sandy Weill went the direct route when he presented his company to Merrill Lynch's group of investors. He started with a bang of a first slide, addressing the issues of corporate governance and responsibility head-on while still managing to brush them aside. The slide was titled "Headline-Driven Environment." The premise was that much of the negativity in the industry had been blown out of proportion by the media. The slide included authentically jagged-edged newspaper clips about "research conflicts," "IPO allocations," "corporate governance," and "integrity of financial reporting."[73] Here was that pesky media running amuck again!

Other slides explained how Citigroup was coping with these "wild" allegations. One slide pointed out that Salomon Smith Barney had been the first firm to adopt the "Spitzer principles" on May 22, 2002, and started to require analysts certify their own research via the SEC's Analyst Certification (AC) on August 1, 2002. Another slide boldly stated that there was *no* evidence of IPO allocations used as quid pro quo for investment banking business.

A slide gloated about Citigroup's standings in the industry, showing that Citigroup ranked number one in global debt and equity issuance, having leapt from number three to number one in global investment grade issuance and leapfrogging several ranks in announced mergers, advancing from number six in 2001 to number three in 2002. Of course, the slide failed to note Citigroup's high share of loan and credit facilities.[74]

Just to review: this was the same bank that had lobbied zealously for the repeal of the Glass-Steagall Act. In fact, its very existence defied the act to begin with. Robert Rubin, one of the key supporters of the Glass-Steagall repeal, was a top executive. Citigroup had no compunction about boasting that it had bested its competition, even though it had helped create the regulation that assured its preeminence, reaping the greatest benefits for its executives at the expense of its shareholders.

SALOMON BROTHERS CONFERENCE, JANUARY 2002

Salomon Brothers' Financial Services Conference was the kickoff conference for 2003. Despite all evidence to the contrary, bankers up and down the Street had high hopes for a much-desired economic turnaround that would allow investment banks to go back to creating bigger companies through renewed merger-and-acquisition activities and more stock and debt issuance.

The weak market of 2002 had continued the pattern of an already weak 2001. The S&P had fallen from 1,395 to 936, an 18 percent drop; the Dow was down 10 percent; and NASDAQ volume was down 35 percent because investors and traders had no clue what to do in this environment. Global equity volume was down 17 percent, IPO issuance was down 11 percent, and investment-grade volume was down 25 percent.

The biggest "down" was in core investment banking business, like M&A. Completed mergers and acquisitions were down a full 47 percent from 2001 to 2002.[75] All the participants in Salomon's January 2003 conference hoped those numbers would go up. That's why they were so pleased to have settled with the SEC and Eliot Spitzer in December: Get it all over with in 2002; start fresh. The reality was that market conditions were nowhere near improving, and corporate governance reforms were not on their way.

JP MORGAN CHASE

When JP Morgan Chase CEO William Harrison took center stage at the Salomon Brothers conference, it was clear from his presentation that JP Morgan Chase was terrified about how it would come across. It was stuck in the middle of melting profits and multiple class-action suits. Rather than tackling research issues or how their loan losses had skyrocketed under the weight of bad telecom and energy debt, he maneuvered around all the difficult issues. He chose to present employee poll results: a whole page of high scores in categories such as cooperation, the quality of the job done by supervisors, and whether employees felt compelled to "put in the extra effort to help JP Morgan Chase succeed." Few employees concerned about keeping their jobs would give a low mark on an employee questionnaire sent out over an internal e-mail system, of course.[76]

If Harrison was going for confidence, it didn't work. He came off looking foolish.

GOLDMAN SACHS

Hank Paulson tried to put the whole situation into a broader perspective than did the other CEOs. He started off by describing the tough business environment, including the long, drawn-out collapse of the 1990s bubble, the Enron debacle, and the WorldCom fraud and bankruptcy.[77] At the same time, the volume of M&As as a percentage of total market cap, or the price of a stock multiplied by the number of shares outstanding, was only 4 percent (adjusted for the falling stock market), well below the long-term average, and a ratio last seen in the beginning of the 1990s, during the savings and loan (S&L) crisis.

Paulson tackled the issue of independent research directly by saying he was looking forward to implementing new research rules and cautioning the audience that regulators were still hovering in the wings. Nonetheless, he predicted a significant increase in banking activity in the midterm future. He had to—Goldman's status as something more prestigious than a bigger version of defunct hedge fund Long Term Capital Management depended on it. He went on to say that most CEOs he'd spoken with were preoccupied with growth and consolidation. U.S. corporate issuance was hitting record highs, while equity underwriting was low because of the stock market. He said there would come a time for the need to deleverage the corporate sector, reducing its debt exposure by not taking on too much new debt.

In both 1973 and 1993, higher equity issuance had directly resulted from that same type of deleveraging; less capital raising via debt gave way to more capital raising via share issuance. Yet defaults and bankruptcies were not nearly as high in either of those years. It would take another $700 billion of new equity issuance to get to the equity-debt ratios of prebubble 1997, but that didn't happen.

Paulson said Goldman Sachs was "relentlessly focused on client relationships, particularly in the Americas, Europe, and Asia, and that the greatest growth opportunities will be from overseas." This was a mantra I heard every year from every firm. He said there was no viable alternative to globalization, a key long-term driver of profitability. "In many ways," said Paulson, "Goldman Sachs operates at the sweet spot of global capitalism."[78] As for the FICC division, he said, "While we have lost market share in investment grade issuance, we have a world-class currency and commodities business." But speculative trading is cyclical. Trading profits are extremely unpredictable even at the best of times. As we witnessed during the late 1990s and early 2000s in particular, stock inflation and subsequent trading profits are predicated on manipulating information and controlling information flow.

MORGAN STANLEY

Chairman and CEO Philip Purcell and CFO Stephen Crawford shared the honor of telling the tale of Morgan Stanley's woes. Of the prestigious investment banks, Morgan Stanley was the most like Goldman Sachs. Morgan Stanley was having the same problems as Goldman, losing out to the big balance sheets of the überbanks, and its industry issuance rankings had also slipped between 2001 and 2002. Revenues were also hit hard. M&A revenues in 2002 for Morgan Stanley were down 32 percent from the prior year; underwriting was down 24 percent.[79]

In early 2003, the SEC began investigating Morgan Stanley's IPO practices. Like Goldman Sachs and JP Morgan Chase, which were also notified of SEC investigations at the same time, the bank was charged with prearranging sales of new stocks at prices higher than the offering price, a clear manipulation of the market. Since its September 2000 peak, its stock had declined 66.5 percent.[80]

CREDIT SUISSE FIRST BOSTON (CSFB)

The CEO of CSFB was the only CEO who didn't bother to show up at Salomon's conference. Maybe he thought it unnecessary since he had a friend at the SEC in DLJ founder William Donaldson. Instead, CSFB sent the co-presidents of institutional securities, who chose not to display its loan rankings to avoid the topic of tying loans to other fee business. But they mentioned other key rankings. In 2002, CSFB placed number four in global M&As, down from number three in 2001. It was number two in global debt issuance—up from number three in 2001—and remained number one in high-yield debt issuance for both years.

Revenues of the ten largest investment banks had reached a record high of $116 billion in 2000 but had fallen to 1997 levels afterward, topping out at $78 billion in 2002. CSFB ominously concluded that revenues might not reach 1999 levels again until 2006.

WARRING BANKS: CORPORATE PREY

Ultimately it was the fight for market share that lead an already aggressive pack of financial institution wolves to fabricate a hyped-up environment from which to extract profits. This precarious situation led to an exaggerated extolling of corporate virtues that inflated quarterly earnings and share prices. It also fostered a lattice of co-dependent and destructive relationships between the banks and corporations. Together, they built the bubble, and separately, they used each other and then blamed each other for its bust as the twenty-first-century fraud disclosures, bankruptcies, asset garage sales, and lawsuits became the ugly norm.

The resulting game of capital accumulation in the form of stock, debt, or acquisitions was predicated on convincing institutional investors that one start-up business plan, or expansion strategy, was better than another—hence the dot-com revolution and tech-stock eruption comprised of companies with no visible income. But highly luring stories were born. Adding to the euphoria, mutual and pension funds bought those overhyped "hot stocks," whose selection wasn't based on corporate fundamentals, in an effort to outperform their competition. This herd mentality further accentuated the stock bubble. The endgame meant executives cashed out at or near the top and resigned before their companies went bankrupt or their indictments hit. It was a particularly fascinating and lucrative game—especially if you don't think about the ramifications of playing fast and loose with other people's money or the consequences for workers, shareholders, and the overall economy.

2

Scratching Backs: Banks and Corporations

POLITICAL POSTURING

Every Friday morning, the secretary working for David Solomon, the fixed-income currency and commodity (FICC) division's former head of credit businesses, e-mailed all the managing directors involved in the credit businesses a reminder about the day's 1:00 meeting. At 1:05, we gathered around a conference table on the twenty-ninth floor for pizza and conversation. David initiated these information-sharing lunches for the leveraged finance, or high-yield credit, department, which provided debt for the more speculative, less financially stable corporations and traded it in the secondary market.[1] The lunch circle had expanded to include the investment-grade, credit analyst, and credit derivatives areas, since David's own involvement extended into all these aspects of the business. Because he was considered a rising partner at the time and sat on the illustrious FICC operating committee, face time with David was a coveted commodity. The gatherings were designed to be, according to David, "relaxed and unstructured: just about informally sharing important business and ideas."

When David was in town and not off meeting with some CEO or in Washington talking with key regulators (as he sometimes boasted), and thus expected to be attending the lunch, all the invited managing directors streamed in, filling the room. There wouldn't be enough room around the sixteen-person conference table to accommodate them, so chairs would be rolled in from the adjacent trading floor. (When David *wasn't* around, about five people showed up, gathered a few slices of pizza, and headed back to their desks.)

During the first half hour of these interludes, stragglers would inevitably stand, clogging the entrance. Then came the face-timers, the ones struggling to grab memory points in David's consciousness. They always rushed in breathless, as if they'd just completed some massive trade, and asked if they could speak immediately because they urgently had to get back to their phone, desk, client, or whatever. Thus they deftly scooped up double "presence" points: first, for knowing how important making it to the meeting was, and second, for knowing what was more important and stressing the need to get back to it. Such tactics worked well. No one seemed particularly suspicious of them. Posturing was an essential survival tactic in banking. Senior management did it with the executive group; the executive group did it with the federal government.

At the well-attended luncheon meetings, the topic of conversation would drift from deal to trade to research recommendations, but one thing that almost always came up was the extent to which the commercial banks were robbing us of business by offering cheap loans from their enormous balance sheets in conjunction with issuance or investment banking business.

As 2001 rolled on, investment banking merger and acquisition business slowed to a trickle. Equity issuance dried up and debt issuance only hung in because Federal Reserve chairman Alan Greenspan had cut rates eleven times, making debt cheap to issue. By the end of the year, investment banking departments throughout the Street shed hundreds of jobs, notably among the junior ranks. At Goldman, analysts who had pulled all-nighters hoping to be noticed by the senior bankers found that they would not be picked up for a third year.

The analyst program generally recruited hires from Ivy League MBA, economics, finance, accounting, or engineering programs. Graduates were given a two-year contract and the option of a third-year extension. In the past, that third year was usually a slam dunk, leading to a career at the firm. In 2001, there were no such assurances. In 2002, prospects were even dimmer, and those who did hold on to their jobs were often doing the work of several people.

INVESTMENT BANKS VS. SUPERMARKET BANKS: GETTING ISSUANCE DEALS

Corporations made it a regular practice to check around the Street, usually with four to five different houses, to get an average swap rate to hedge the debt they were considering issuing. A swap rate protects the issuer from paying higher than current market coupon rates in an environment of falling interest rates and the converse in a rising interest rate environment. The issuer receives the difference between its coupon payments and the higher prevailing rates. Generally, the longer the maturity of the debt, the higher the swap rate, just like the longer someone's mortgage maturity, the greater the rate paid by the mortgage holder to the bank for the mortgage loan. Corporations checked around to verify what each bank posted as its swap rate because the rate could vary slightly—depending on factors like the time of day it was fixed, particularly in choppy markets—just as different banks might offer different mortgage rates. Each corporation wanted to ensure that the banks underwriting their debt did so on the tightest possible terms relative to the swap rate, which meant they would pay the least possible amount of interest to bondholders on their debt.

When the stock market started plummeting, it took down with it the equity issuance business that investment banks counted on. Instead of issuing shares into an unresponsive stock market, corporations had to raise more money through debt to survive, encouraged by rapidly declining interest rates. The commercial banks that extended loans and credit facilities to the corporations who desperately needed them became the same banks that got rewarded with debt issuance business and what was left of other investment bank business, like mergers and acquisitions. Commercial banks themselves were least likely of all corporations to issue via investment banks. That's why the job covering financial institutions at investment banks became an ejection seat out of a banking industry career. Many affected seasoned professionals wound up taking jobs in other areas or leaving finance. Sure, there was pressure from upper management in the investment banks to get other financial institutions to issue through them, but there was just no incentive for commercial banks to do so. After all, they wanted the same cheap credit they were doling out to corporations for fee business.

Sensing opportunity, corporations began playing both sides and pressuring investment banks to lower their fees. Everyone knew corporations could easily go to commercial banks and get equal if not better terms. In some cases, investment banks would capitulate and lower issuance fees in order to hold on to their clients, but that in itself was a money-losing proposition. A former Goldman capital markets vice president said, "We would do some really big deal, like for $1 billion of issuance, but we'd only make $400,000 on it because we'd be cutting our fees back so much just to get it done. In the past we'd have made over $1 million on the same deal."

Citigroup's capital markets team (which was Salomon Brothers' team before the Citi-Salomon merger) tended to fare much better. The conversation at their office might have gone something like this:

> *SB capital markets officer:* "So, the five-year swap spread is pretty tight; this would be a great time to issue."
> *Corporation:* "Sure, I hear you, but we're cutting our budget, so we're not sure we want to issue as large a volume as last time."
> *SB capital markets officer:* "Really? That's a shame. You know, I was just checking that credit facility we gave you. Seems your revolving credit period is almost over. I sure hope we can help you out renewing it."
> *Corporation:* "Uh, you know, maybe we could squeeze out another $500 million on the next deal."
> *SB capital markets officer:* "Excellent. Good idea. Done. How are the kids?"

In real life, it would be a slightly more subtle conversation, of course, held over dinner and not a taped line.

PRIVATE VS. PUBLIC ACTIVITIES

Most of the phone lines on the Street's trading floor are taped. If a trade gets screwed up, you can refer to the backup of conversations surrounding the trade.

The conversations between corporations and banks that lead to debt issuance take place in private; companies do not broadly disclose their intent to issue debt before they are ready to do so. Once they are ready and terms have been agreed upon, the deal gets announced to the public. Before a debt deal is announced, all conversations regarding the nature of the deal are kept on the private side of an artificially constructed concept called the "Chinese wall," which is supposed to keep private and public banking functions separate. After the deal is announced, the information becomes publicly available and jumps over to the public side of the Chinese wall. The new debt is then free to trade as bonds. Conveniently, there is no precise legal definition for the Chinese wall in banking. Chinese walls therefore come with their own lexicon.

"Private" refers to investment banking or debt– or equity–issuance business. "Public" refers to everything that follows, such as distribution and trading of the newly constructed securities, to institutional and retail investors.

While I worked at Chase, Lehman Brothers, and Bear Stearns, I was on the public side of the wall. I analyzed and marketed securities and portfolios to institutional investors. At Goldman, I worked on both sides of the wall depending on the situation. I was in charge of one area that worked with the investment bankers on nonpublic transactions, but I also ran a quantitative credit strategy group, which interacted mostly with the trading desk, salespeople, and institutional customers and which was on the public side. People who worked for me were usually on only one of the two sides, but the public side ones could be "crossed-over" the wall to work on specific private transactions if needed.

The credit floor on which I worked contained private-side capital markets personnel as well as public-side salespeople and traders. During most of my time at Goldman, the trading floor was a completely open environment with no physical walls dividing the two areas. They were housed in separate locations, but they were fully accessible to each other. This changed at the end of 2001, when a door to the capital markets area was installed that required employee ID cards with the proper access code (the same access codes that got you into the investment banking floors) for entry. That physical barrier was rather cosmetic. All you had to do was walk through the shared kitchen area and you could be on the opposite side of the wall without an access code. Still, the door made senior management—and the SEC—feel better.

CREATING AND MOVING CREDIT AND DEBT

There are several different areas that comprise the credit- or corporate debt-oriented function, which are usually situated within the fixed-income division of a bank. Generally, these break down into three main groups: capital markets, sales and trading, and research analytics and structuring. "Fixed income" refers to securities that have fixed payment periods in which investors get some money back on their investment— say, on a quarterly, semiannual, or annual basis. Your mortgage is a fixed-income security for a bank, because the bank counts on you to make payments on a monthly basis—in other words, on a fixed schedule until you pay off your mortgage.

The capital markets area of the fixed-income division raises money for the country's largest corporations through the primary (first-time) issuance of bonds. This department works with corporations to find ways for them to borrow money through the issuance of bonds to various investors.

The second group is sales and trading. The sales force sells corporate bonds, loans, and derivatives to institutional investors such as insurance companies, pension funds, corporate investment portfolios, and asset management companies. The sales force can also buy these securities back if investors want to get rid of them. Traders are the intermediaries who buy and sell securities on the secondary markets (after they've already been issued) with other trading desks or the Street and then through the sales force. They keep positions, or outstanding transactions, in various corporate bonds or derivatives on their trading book based on their views of how a company will perform relative to its ability to repay its debt.

The third group encompasses research and analytics. It includes the credit analysts, who focus on one or more sectors of corporate America, writing reports and speaking with investors about individual companies like Disney or Wal-Mart or McDonald's. It also includes the quantitative credit strategists, which was my group, who analyze the relative value between corporate bonds and derivatives, create complex investment strategies for customers, and quantify the risk of these strategies to the trading desks. Our mandate was more general than that of the company-specific credit analysts.

THE COLLATERALIZED DEBT OBLIGATION (CDO) MARKET

Another component of the third group are structurers, which includes those who combine existing securities or derivatives into new portfolio securities called collateralized debt obligations (CDOs). CDOs were securities comprised of multiple risk levels, backed by groups of bonds, loans, or credit derivatives. In the late 1980s and early 1990s, the advent of packages of mortgage securities called CMOs (collateralized mortgage obligations) allowed a number of different securities or individual mortgage loans to move as one and provide returns to an investor as one. CDOs are the same thing—only instead of consisting of lots of little mortgages, they consist of lots of little corporate bonds, loans, or derivatives.

The CDO market played a key role in the movement of credit risk from issuers and banks to investors, insurance companies, pensions, and various funds. The first collateralized debt obligations started appearing around 1995 as collections of emerging market bonds that were packaged into one portfolio and then sliced up into tranches ("tranche" is French for a slice of cake) of varying degrees of risk.

CDOs promised a way for investors to gain exposure to the emerging markets while distributing the risk of default in such a way that investors who bought AAA tranches had less risk of loss of their investment than equity tranche buyers. CDO equity was effectively a highly leveraged position in the portfolio of underlying credit assets.

Growth of the high-yield (junk-bond) CDO market began in late 1996 and took off between 1997 and 1999 as high-yield debt issuance rose. The first buyers were European insurance companies who were looking for ways to get higher returns because they had 7 percent per year pension contracts to honor while government bonds were only yielding 3 to 4 percent.

CDOs were the perfect homes for junk bonds issued by speculative companies, because they mixed really risky companies with the more conservative ones in one big structure, providing a kind of camouflage. Also, because investment management companies were eager to make their own fees for managing these structures, the more junk bonds they bought in CDOs, the more they could make in fees.

Between 1996 and 2003 over $400 billion worth of CDOs with different types of underlying credit collateral have been issued. According to rating agency, Fitch, seventy individual CDOs held about $570 million of WorldCom debt as of June 2002, before the company defaulted. CDOs considered safe from rating downgrades until 2000 saw downgrades triple in 2002. By then, one-third of telecom junk debt issuers, who featured prominently in these CDOs, had defaulted.

During 1999, $20 billion of high-yield CDO's were issued. That number dropped to less than $1 billion in 2002 because buyers had disappeared as default risk increased. Also, past buyers had gotten burned because of the unexpected lack of liquidity in the market for the lower-quality equity and BB tranches. Investment banks had never really stressed that potential lack of liquidity in their rush to sell this highly lucrative product.

CDOs are generally comprised of one hundred different companies, governed by rules determining the mix. For instance, concentration rules

might indicate that only 10 percent of the bonds can be in any one industry sector, like telecoms, or only 15 percent can be rated less than BB.

Once the CDO is created, it is sliced, or tranched, into different levels
of risk so that different investors can gain access to the portfolio with differ-
ing levels of gain or loss potential on their investment. The AAA investors
have the least downside in terms of risk and therefore the least upside. The
BBB investors have more downside possibility. The equity investors, who
buy the nonrated or highly speculative pieces of the CDO, invest the least
capital but get hit with the "first loss." For example, if 5 percent of the
CDO represents equity risk and each individual security in the CDO loses
5 percent of its value, the equity investors receive nothing on their capital
investment for that period. On the flip side, if the CDO rises in value, investors receive much higher returns for taking on that risk. Equity investors
in the 1990s saw returns as high as 20 percent. The trend reversed in 2002
and 2003, thanks to all the downgrading and defaults suffered by corporations increasingly plagued with scandal and debt.

CDOs provided a quick and easy way for banks to sell a number of
different corporate bonds or loans as a group, thereby enabling banks to
quickly move their risk to a bunch of corporations all at once rather than
one at a time. CDOs grew as the volume of debt issuance grew and were
especially popular methods for getting rid of speculative company risk
and pushing it onto investors or insurers.

Because CDOs are so-called "managed" securities, asset management
companies like Fidelity or Putnam, or hedge funds like the Clinton group,
would receive a relatively high fee based on how the CDOs they were
managing performed. These CDO managers would generally buy and
trade the bonds that comprised the CDO with a particular partner bank
like Goldman Sachs or Bear Stearns. That bank would in turn assist the
asset manager in finding investors for the CDO. The fee for managing the
CDO as one big security was higher than what each asset manager would
receive from simply buying and selling the individual bonds that comprised the CDO as part of a normal bond fund.

INCREASING CORPORATE DEBT

The financial industry underwent record merger volume in the early 1990s.
That amount tripled during the late 1990s, creating bigger institutions with

more balance-sheet might to bestow upon corporate clients.[2] From 1996 through 2000, both corporate debt and earnings shot into the stratosphere, only to plummet in 2001–2003.

Before the late 1990s' frenzy of debt raising, the historic relationship between the issuing corporation and the bank was an important factor in the corporation's selection of bank issuers. History became less significant as corporate profits deteriorated and the need to raise capital as cheaply and quickly as possible took hold. Then it was all about survival of the fittest and getting cheap loans or credit fast. This closed a key chapter in banking history by changing the whole nature of investment banking as past loyalties were set aside for the "commodification" of new relationships that translated into the easiest way to access capital.

Corporations preferred choosing banks that had top-tier underwriters and associated high industry league table positions (or rankings). League tables in banking are like league standings in competitive team sports. For a bank to occupy a top league table position in any product or service category implies it was better at getting business done, or at closing high-volume deals, in that category. The more league table top spots won, the higher the all-around status of the bank in the eyes of its corporate customers. (League tables only rated corporate, not retail customer, business.) As such, they were taken very seriously by banks. The bank's status implied it had "brought" many deals in various sectors or industries "to market" and was thus experienced in selling, or "placing," them with investors. Often corporations negotiate with banks to get copies of investor lists so they can find out how their name (another way of saying their corporate debt) is being distributed or, for example, how many new investors bought the latest Disney bond. If Disney gets the bank's list, it will be less beholden to that same bank the next time it issues for distribution; the governing assumption is that an investor who bought Disney once will buy it again. New investors buying a name for the first time are particularly important. The wider and broader the distribution and the stronger the demand, the better for the corporation, no matter the timing. Primary issuers are contractually obligated to distribute the debt of their corporate clients; if they can't distribute it, they're obligated to hold onto it until they can—which gives them more exposure to downgrade risk.

As an example of this relationship, a week after 9/11, Goldman Sachs managed a $1 billion debt deal for Walt Disney. Despite a rationality plea from the credit research group that the timing was bad, given that most of the country wasn't headed toward large American theme parks just after a terrorist attack, the deal went through. Why? Because that's what Disney and Goldman wanted. The next day, the *New York Times* ran a photograph of Disney World showing a lone father holding the hand of his son in an otherwise empty park. Disney stock fell 18 percent, taking the value of the Disney deal down with it. Goldman, as part of its firm commitment as an underwriter, was obligated to assume full financial responsibility for any unsold portions of the deal and wound up having to hold a large chink of the deal (or the deteriorating issue) on its books because investors weren't interested.

The symbiotic needs of corporations and banks follow two simple axioms: First, corporations raise as much debt as possible, as cheaply and quickly as possible (for growth, acquisitions, inflating share value, global domination, etc.); second, banks book as many fees as possible up front, then worry about any risk afterward. Deregulated high-growth industries, like telecoms and energy, were the perfect targets for Wall Street because of their insatiable need for capital and desire for global expansion. Pension funds and small retail consumers with brokerage accounts at places like Merrill Lynch or investments in mutual funds at Putnam or Fidelity were convenient dumping grounds for pumped-up stock.

When the market was hot, there was plenty of collaboration between corporations and Wall Street. Corporations counted on Wall Street for raising capital, favorable analyst evaluations, and starry-eyed investors. The corporations' power lay in their promise of future success. And the better they could make their balance sheets look, the brighter that future seemed.

By virtue of various balance sheet–altering techniques, including keeping two sets of numbers to reduce tax payments (one for the government, one for investors), offshore mechanisms, and other murky transactions (like loans disguised as other trades), corporations made it look as though they had less debt than they actually did so they could borrow more. Companies were overleveraging while hiding debt and expenses. Banks were looking the other way.

The coercion was mutual. Corporations and banks held each other hostage. After all, banks controlled access to cheap credit in the form of loans of emergency credit lines through their large balance sheets, ripe with customer deposits. They held the necessary money. On the flip side, corporations represented demand for that credit, pitting banks against one another to get it while dangling the carrot of more lucrative follow-up business. Both parties wanted to continue to create debt, while each wanted to ensure that balance sheets continued to appear credit-worthy enough to pile on more. The healthier the balance sheet looked, the more favorable the analysts' opinions and stock prices; the more favorably the corporation was viewed by the rating agencies, and the higher the rating, the cheaper it was to insure the debt.

One capital markets (bond issuance) banker at Salomon Brothers Citigroup told me, "These guys [the corporations] would come to us and say we want loan money. The only way we could keep them was to give it. Not all, but most corporations would come right out and say, 'If you don't give us money, we won't do business with you.' "

An emerging group of these corporate "credit squeezers" was investment-grade, frequent issuers that functioned in many ways as independent finance companies but didn't own nor were owned by a bank. These companies included household names generally not associated in the public eye with the finance industry, such as Ford, General Motors, and General Electric. These companies' business strategies required securing credit lines and debt from banks. At the same time, they acted like banks because they offered their customers financing in the form of extending credit (at much higher rates). Their financial service operations necessitated access to substantial amounts of money.

Wall Street banks counted on these large repeat-issuer corporations for regular fees. Most of the other hard fees that the banks got were related to investment banking, IPO, and stock issuance business. Though they were manufacturing companies per se, they all had significant financing operations to help keep their goods moving out the door. In all, Wall Street has collected over $70 billion in fees from these companies since 1996.[3] Ford, for example, forked over $815 million of those fees. When the market started tanking in 2001, these relationships became increasingly adversarial. Banks gave last-minute bailout credit lines to faulty companies just weeks before getting in line to sue them in bankruptcy court. All of a sudden, the cozy credit-for-fee business relationship turned chilly.

CAR COMPANIES AS BANKS

One of the most ominous consequences of the bubble and debt crisis is the deterioration of historically sound household names. But companies like Ford Motor Credit and GM were always, in a way, banks that sell cars. Like banks, they (with the assistance of banks) finance customers. Like banks, they package these loans into tidy asset-backed securities that consolidate the cash flows coming from customer car loan payments. They sell these securities using the distribution networks of the same banks to institutional investors. It's all part of a multitrillion-dollar asset-backed market.

Like the old-style commercial banks, companies like Ford and GM make money on volume of consumer business. Unlike banks, they don't have access to the same pools of money that banks get from individual and commercial depositors. This is why they rank at the top of the country's borrowers. They are extremely dependent on banks to raise capital necessary for making cars and loaning money to car buyers; they need banks and their credit to survive. Banks need them because they are high-volume repeat borrowers who pay a lot of fees. It's a classic back-scratching relationship.

Überbanks fell over themselves to lend in return for regular helpings of fee issuance business, competing with investment banks to underwrite and find investors for Ford and GM bonds. In the late 1990s, Ford, GM, and others issuing billions of dollars of debt at a time were perfect for institutional investors who required big liquid issues. These bonds were thus very easy to sell.

By the end of 2002, GM and Ford, the number one and number two U.S. car makers respectively, made up 5 percent of all outstanding corporate debt in the United States. Ford's outstanding debt was $162 billion; GM's was $186 billion.[4] The two had blazed a trail up the debt issuance charts and got stuck with large interest payments as a result.

Ford was notable for more than that. Because of the amount of debt- and asset-backed deals it issued and the fees it paid to Wall Street, it was able to extract cheap credit facilities and loans in return for continuing to give their business to a finite cartel of banks. The story changed dramatically when, because of a series of ratings downgrades, it became harder for Ford to borrow debt at attractive rates, and institutional buyers became more hesitant about it.

In fact, Ford's problems were similar to those of Enron's and Global Crossing's, who found themselves unable to pay back the debt that supported their multiproject businesses. The biggest difference was that Ford's balance sheet was easier to understand because it was less involved in unregulated businesses. All of Ford's bravado regarding its ability to play banks off each other to get its business caved in on itself when the leading rating agencies started systematically lowering its ratings. In late October 2002, S&P downgraded Ford's BBB+ rating to BBB–, just one notch above junk status. That's a lot of debt being downgraded.[5]

Ford continued to implode throughout 2003. It possessed a layered business model predicated on borrowing money cheaply to loan to customers to buy their cars. Failures in any of these components reverberated throughout its balance sheet. With a lower rating, borrowing became more expensive. Second, lower stock values translated into less market capital, which made it tougher to have enough cash flow to pay interest on existing debts. Third, people were buying fewer cars. Ford dealerships were stuck with year-old models. Ford desperately tried to put together a "revitalization plan," consisting of creating new products, reducing dividends, cutting costs, and firing staff.[6] In March 2003, Ford announced it was lowering its second-quarter projections of vehicle sales by 17 percent versus the same quarter in 2002. Additionally, it was faced with a global pension shortfall (whereby its defined benefit pension plan didn't have enough money set aside to meet its pension obligations to employees retiring in the future) of $12 billion, 67 percent of its outstanding share value at the time.[7]

By early 2003, Ford had lost over 80 percent of its market value from its mid-1999 highs. Its future prospects were dim and it took to depleting pension funds even further to keep up with its falling financials. At the same time, GM reduced its production by 10 percent and its pension shortfall increased to almost $28 billion—another case of workers taking it on the chin because their employer had declining profits and was swimming in boatloads of debt. So, new corporate pension fund contributions were reduced at the same time that plummeting stock value was shrinking existing pension fund values. GM's rating was lowered from BBB+ to BBB in mid-October 2002.

GOLDMAN SACHS AND FORD

Every blue-chip issuer had a special relationship with some investment bank, but the relationship between Goldman and Ford was fascinating on multiple levels. For years, it embodied the very nature of gentlemen's-agreement investment banking. Goldman Sachs had taken Ford public back in 1956. Sidney Weinberg Sr., then the chairman of Goldman, was the lead banker for the deal. He was also a Ford board member.

As Lisa Endlich explained in her book *Goldman Sachs: The Culture of Success*, "To Weinberg, service on corporate boards was almost a religion."[8] Weinberg thought that it was more important to exert influence over corporate clients than to extract fees from them. He sat on over thirty boards, attending over 250 meetings a year. He remained a board member of Ford until his death at age seventy-seven.

Two generations later, Sidney's grandson John Weinberg sat on Ford's board. A senior partner at Goldman Sachs like his grandfather, John was Goldman's lead investment banker for client Ford. John Weinberg and William (Bill) Clay Ford Jr. were both members of Princeton's class of 1979.[9] There was another important board-level relationship linking Goldman and Ford's board of directors. John Thornton, the president and co-COO of Goldman, had joined Ford's board in March 1996. Thornton had gone to prep school with Bill Ford, and the two men both served as directors at the Brookings Institution.[10] According to a December 23, 2002 *USA Today* article, Ford declined to say whether Bill Ford's acceptance of 400,000 Goldman IPO shares in 1999, when he was non-executive chairman (a convenient title used to give people influence while shielding them from responsibility), violated Ford's policy of restricting gifts over $50 from suppliers to employees.[11] Because he was the non-executive chairman, he supposedly didn't fall under the employee category.[12] As of that article's publication, Ford's Goldman shares were $8 million in the black.

Ford was a busy issuer, particularly during the late 1990s. Adding up its asset-backed securities, bonds backed (collateralized) by Ford's consumer car-loan interest payments, and debt issuance, Ford borrowed $286 billion from 1990 until 2002, 62 percent of it since 1998 alone. The fee it paid the Street over the same period were also eye-popping: over $815 million, with $436 million from 1998 to 2002.[13] Goldman Sachs was the lead book runner (or underwriter) of Ford debt from 1990 until

1997 and was in the top three from 1997 until 2000. Their relationship netted Goldman over $90 million in fees between 1996 and 2002.[14]

CHANGING RELATIONSHIPS

However, when things get too competitive, relationships get chucked out the window. In the hot debt-issuance environment of the late 1990s, Ford flexed its volume muscle and got vocal about demanding that its financial institution partners grant it cheap loans and credit facilities—money, basically—or lose its issuance business. As one of the biggest issuers, it had one of the biggest sticks to wield.

Goldman Sachs resisted—first, because it didn't have a balance sheet comparable to Citigroup or Bank of America, and second, because it thought its deep relationship would suffice to retain its share of business. But it didn't. That year, JP Morgan Chase took the position of lead underwriter for Ford's debt while extending substantial credit facilities to Ford in the process. Goldman Sachs dropped to second.[15]

By 2001, despite a record issuance year, Goldman just couldn't compete with the supermarket banks and their regular transfusions of cheap credit to corporations. Despite decades of close history, Goldman dropped to ninth place in Ford issuance, and Citigroup jumped to number one.[16] Not only were Goldman's John Thornton and John Weinberg on Ford's board, but so was Citigroup's Robert Rubin, who had joined Ford's board in 2000.[17] Bank of America jumped from nowhere into the number two slot in 2001. That was the year the bank went on record saying it would cut customers out of loans and credit facilities unless it was allowed to participate in other banking business, like issuance. By 2002, Goldman was out of the top ten completely.

Even while Goldman was falling down Ford's issuance tables, it was still brought in on the "chunky" deals, like leading a $5 billion convertible bond offering in January 2002. (Citigroup's Robert Rubin had also pushed for that debt deal.) Goldman even took a $5.45 billion charge against 2001 earnings, which included a $1 billion loss on palladium (a metal used in electrical application) trades through its commodity desk, many of which were with Ford. When Ford stopped buying palladium, which it had been stockpiling since early 2000, palladium prices dropped from a peak $1,100 per ounce in January 2001 to $160 in July 2003.[18]

Meanwhile, Bank of America took number one in Ford's business for 2002. That said, the spoils weren't all that lucrative. There was little issuance for Ford that year due to profitability declines and those rating downgrades.

Amid continued scrutiny from the media about the Goldman-Ford relationship, including the December 8, 2002, *New York Times* article, "Ford and Goldman, So Cozy at the Top," Thornton resigned from Ford's auditing committee, a subcommittee of the board of directors in May 2002, though he remained on the board. This was two months before the Sarbanes-Oxley "corporate reform" act was passed in Congress, which required audit committee members to be independent of, and therefore not in the position to collect fees from, the company.[19]

FIGHTING BACK AGAINST LOAN TYING

The dirty-little-secret practice of loan tying ran throughout the banking community even after the corporate debacles and scandals of the beginning of the millennium. It was the stuff of winks and nods, and the rule was: admit nothing, deny everything. The practice is widespread, and regulations against loan tying are not enforced by federal regulators. First, it's hard to capture, and second, it falls somewhere between the cracks of Federal Reserve and SEC jurisdiction, making it easier for both agencies to ignore.

If you were to ask any supermarket banker involved in credit extensions, "So, does your bank give cheap loans or credit in exchange for higher margin business?" the response would range from, "Well, you know how it works," to "Hey, we're just being competitive," to "What do you think?" The official response from senior management circles would be quite different, something like, "We don't tie other business to loans, we simply offer a full set of services to our customers." Still, three years ago, when bad loans weren't piling on top of corporate failures and fallen angel defaults (when companies' ratings dive straight from investment grade to junk without stopping in between), everyone was happy to advertise the practice. Now, everyone is pointing fingers, and the commercial überbanks are quick to defend what was obviously their strongest playing card.

Yet loan tying used to be a great source of pride and power. Though never called loan tying per se, Bank of America, Sun Trust, and Bank One were just a few of the banks that went on record in 2001 that they would cut off corporate customers from their lending facilities if they were not "good customers" of other services offered by the banks.[20] Such a policy blatantly ties the provision of loans to reciprocal fee-banking business, and it led directly to Bank of America's and JP Morgan Chase's rise up the issuance league tables and Citigroup's leap to the top position in high-grade corporate issuance.

Going forward, cheap credit remains a dangerous proposition that flies in the face of overall corporate economic stability. The problem intensifies during periods in which more lucrative fee business like mergers and acquisitions—the rewards for extending cheap credit—declines. In that situation, what was once credit in exchange for higher-fee banking business becomes credit in exchange for the *possibility* of fee banking business in the future.

There are, however, some individual voices in Congress that rose in the wake of Enron and WorldCom to question the practice of loan tying. Representative John Dingell (D-MI), whose father was one of the architects of the original Glass-Steagall Act, has been one of the most vocal opponents of loan tying practices. He has spent years writing to the General Accounting Office and the Federal Reserve, but without receiving any meaningful response to his reservations in reply. Dingell is one of the few people in Congress to recognize that loan tying, among many other deceits, lies at the center of the latest boom-and-bust cycle. Summarizing his concerns in a September 12, 2002, letter to Alan Greenspan and to comptrollers John D. Hawke Jr. of the U.S Treasury Department and David M. Walker of the GAO, he wrote:

> Since tying is understandably never done in written form, do you intend to directly question bank officials about whether they violate formal written policies in verbal communications with corporate borrowers? For example, will you ask them whether, notwithstanding any such policies or procedures, they ever request that a borrower provide investment banking business as a condition of extending or renewing a credit facility?[21]

Dingell was astute. Since it's a major breach of antitrust law, no bank will admit to or have written documents stating they specifically tied a loan to a deal, even though they may have blatant, media-circulated policies requiring customers to utilize other bank services as part of the credit package. And they will lie through their teeth defending their practice with comments like "We're just a 'full service' institution, which provides clients credit [on extraordinarily favorable terms] as well as merger, acquisition and IPO services."

Dingell asked for a specific investigation into any one of the widely publicized reports of loan tying, such as those involving Motorola, Corning, Vivendi, and Lucent's IPO spin-off of Agere Systems, Inc. He also noted that it has been widely reported that Enron's staff systematically linked fee-based business to credit extension.[22]

In the case of Enron, not only was fee-based business related to credit extension, but it was also related to favorable analysts' reports. Thus, when the market is up and investors are eager, the corporations have the upper hand and can squeeze the banks, because they can easily get money and investors from any source. When things go sour, the banks are left with the credit risk but gain the stronger position. Corporations have fewer choices; the bigger banks with the deeper pockets are the most likely sources for ongoing credit.

Dingell also asked, "Do you intend to contact corporate financial executives to inquire as to whether they feel pressure to award investment banking or other services as a condition to obtaining commercial bank participation in loans?"[23] This question gets to the heart of a major conflict of interest. Corporations were not about to say no to loans extended at better rates in return for banking business. Why would they? If someone offered you a mortgage at 6 percent interest and someone else offered you the same mortgage at 4 percent interest, the choice is obvious. And if you were told that you could only have the 4 percent mortgage if you opened a checking account with the bank, wouldn't you do that too?

Greenspan and Hawke responded to Dingell's letter by summarily brushing it aside. They stated that they were "unable to identify any illegal tying of loans to investment banking assignments."[24]

Banks weren't just loaning money to corporations; they were lending directly to the leaders of these companies. But banks don't have to disclose specific loan information any more than they have to publicly disclose in which companies or even which sectors they have the most exposure. Since there are no federal regulations covering this aspect of transparency, many commercial banks further tightened their relationships with corporations by offering their executives cheap loans often backed by the executives' stock in the corporation.

A significant portion of Bank of America's loan charge-offs in 2002, for example, were related to individual executive loans. These included a $44 million loan to ImClone's former CEO, Sam Waksal, collateralized by stock he didn't even own.[25] Bank of America lent $52.1 million to Adelphia's Rigas family and a whopping $3.4 billion to WorldCom's Bernie Ebbers to fund an acquisition in the mid-1990s, in addition to a personal loan backed by his WorldCom stock. WorldCom chose to help Ebbers make good on some of these loans once the margin calls started, diverting cash that might have otherwise helped pay severance to employees or even keep more jobs back at Bank of America.[26]

Bank of America wrote down a total of $1.2 billion in loans in the fourth quarter of 2002, citing weakness in the merchant energy sector rather than bad corporate executive loans. It is also now lobbying FERC to allow it to simultaneously lend money to, underwrite for, and own assets of the same sector. Citigroup loaned Ebbers $134 million as part of a $400 million investment in a company called Joshua Timberlands. In return for the loan extensions, Travelers Insurance, the insurance arm of Citigroup, received a 2.5 percent equity stake. Eight months later, WorldCom chose (Citigroup's) Salomon to be the lead underwriter of $5 billion of debt. It doesn't seem like a coincidence.[27]

INVESTMENT BANKS EXTENDED DUMB CREDIT, TOO

Even though investment banks lacked the balance-sheet heft to support big loans to corporations at the pace and volume of the commercial banks, they were just as enthusiastic about extending credit when their butts, or diminishing business, were on the line. The practice of loan tying was not an antitrust violation for investment banks the way it was for commercial banks, a fact the commercial banks are always quick to point out. Partly, this was because of the assumption that they didn't have the balance sheets to wield that kind of influence.

Take the case of Dutch supermarket Goliath, Ahold N.V., which owns the U.S. Stop and Shop chain. In late February 2003, Ahold joined the increasingly popular Restatement of Earnings Club when it announced it would restate two years of earnings by $500 million, with two immediate results.[28] First, Ahold's stock fell almost 70 percent in one day, and second, a consortium of five banks announced they would extend Ahold a $3.35 billion emergency credit facility—another classic case of pouring money down the drain in the hopes of recouping otherwise greater losses. The group consisted of JP Morgan Chase and three Dutch superbanks: ING, ABN Amro, and Rabobank.

Perhaps the least likely participant was Goldman Sachs, the only investment bank in a group of commercial banks. Although Goldman wouldn't lend to Ford when it was a AAA company, it lent to faltering Ahold. Why? One possible reason was its past business relationship with Ahold. Goldman had advised its 1996 takeover of Stop and Shop, but that in itself wouldn't be enough reason to expose the bank to such a large credit risk in a climate of investor nonconfidence. The more likely reason is that it had massive exposure to Ahold on its trading book. Rumors on the Street that day suggested a possible loss of between $200 and $600 million. Goldman Sachs issued no comment on its exposure. Goldman, JP Morgan Chase, and ABN Amro had been Ahold's top global debt and equity book runners. A bank will throw good money after bad in the hopes of curtailing losses.

IPO SPINNING

An important bartering tool used to extract high-fee corporate business was the giving away of prime pieces in hot IPO deals to an elite and select group of clients via a practice called spinning. Banks offered favored executives percentages of IPOs in the hopes of gleaning business from them in the future. Telecom executives were notorious for getting their share of hot IPO stocks. In September 2002, Eliot Spitzer charged five telecom executives and Salomon Smith Barney with misleading practices related to IPO spinning. His state suit sought repayment of related profits to New York.[29] Salomon Smith Barney had bagged over $277 million in investment banking fees from WorldCom, Qwest, Metromedia Fiber Networks, and McLeodUSA from 1996 to 2002.[30]

In addition to cheap credit, former telecom executives got big personal kickbacks and hot IPO shares as "gifts" from the banks. Ebbers made an $11 million profit on the IPO share he received; Phillip Anschutz of Qwest made almost $5 million; Joseph Nacchio of Qwest wound up with $1 million.[31] Stephen Garofalo of Metromedia personally banked $1.5 million, while Salomon bagged $47 million in banking fees from Metromedia. Clark McLeod made $9.4 million flipping his hot IPO shares, and Salomon made $49 million in fees from McLeodUSA.[32] Every one of these companies except Qwest went bankrupt; every company was placed under investigation. Every executive bailed or got forced out; every executive still has *his* money.

The practice of IPO spinning, or setting aside portions of a corporation's initial public offering for senior management of that corporation, only really works in bull markets, when post-IPO stock values generally rise. In bear markets, there's no such assurance. When the market is going up, providing a means to "get in on the action" via select IPO shares is an effective enticement to capturing other business that executives may be considering. But, when the market is falling, these reinforcements break down. By the time the market turned bearish in mid-2000, corporate executives were bailing from the stock market anyway, as their companies and those they held shares in headed toward financial ruin. That in turn caused further market deterioration.

MONEY FOR NOTHING

Plenty of collusive financial deceptions seemed to have been exposed, mostly by the media (as opposed to the SEC) in the early 2000s, but many of these were mere variations of tried-and-true techniques. Banks would engineer financial strategies for corporations in any given industry to essentially book money up-front, regardless of future profits. Every time banks structured deals to facilitate the appearance of profit for corporations, they got fees from doing the deals themselves and sales commissions on selling the deals to investors or moving them around the Street's trading desks. The actual nature of the business was largely irrelevant—airlines, telecom, energy, clothing, food—since any future cash flow could be reconstructed as present profit.

For instance, two major misleading tricks were variations of the sale and leaseback strategies widely employed by the airline industry throughout the 1980s, wherein long-term liabilities were magically transformed by the wonders of modern financial engineering into short-term assets or cash. For airlines, this meant they were able to buy airplanes, which they would then lease out, sometimes to a subsidiary they owned. They would book the money they collected from the leases up front, which gave the appearance of cash flow, while listing the airplanes on their balance sheet as long-term liabilities (for tax purposes; they could return the planes damaged or worth less than originally estimated).

Similar tricks were employed by the energy and telecom businesses, their subsidiaries, and their bank co-conspirators in the 1990s. These included loan prepays, in which energy companies would receive money for natural gas and other commodities they never transferred and pay it back later with interest, and capacity swaps, in which telecom companies would sell the future use of their networks for money up-front.

Not only did banks extend record loans and credit facilities to companies in the 1990s, they even helped these companies hide the extent of their loans so that they would look healthy enough to borrow more. During a preemptive conference call with investors on September 6, 2002, JP Morgan Chase CEO William Harrison had the nerve to declare, "We have made mistakes, but these have been mistakes of judgment"—not of principle.

ENERGY COMPANIES AS BANKS

Power marketers engaged in long-term natural gas swaps with the banks that were thinly disguised loans. These energy trading companies would agree to deliver a certain amount of natural gas at a certain price on a date—say, five years in the future—to an offshore subsidiary of a bank for a fixed amount paid up-front. For example, Enron agreed to give $394 million of natural gas in five years to Mahonia, a JP Morgan Chase–sponsored special purpose vehicle, which then passed the risk to JP Morgan, which in turn passed the risk back to Enron.[33] In return, JP Morgan Chase agreed to pay Enron $330 million for the same amount of natural gas immediately. No gas actually changed hands in this swap. It was merely a loan disguised as a trade; the underlying commodity never moved. Technically, in five years (if the company hadn't gone bankrupt), Enron would have either delivered the gas it promised, or more likely would transfer a cash payment of $394 million to JP Morgan Chase. That never happened. Once Enron declared bankruptcy, JP Morgan Chase was out that money.

These types of swap transactions resemble taking out a car loan. If you want to buy a car, you might borrow $10,000 from a bank, or from the car company you're buying from, like Ford. Each month you pay roughly 6 percent interest on the loan. In five years, you will have paid back the $10,000 you borrowed, plus five years' worth of interest, for a total of $13,382. You borrow a fixed amount of money, and you pay more back. That's a loan. But in Enron's case, the money wasn't booked by either Enron or JP Morgan Chase as a loan; it was merely booked as two separate trades. Enron booked a $330 million payment for natural gas upfront, pocketing that cash from JP Morgan Chase. It didn't even book the $79 million it would technically have to pay back as interest on borrowing that $330 million. If the transaction were a properly booked loan, Enron and JP Morgan Chase would have shown the principal $330 million upfront, the principal and interest amount of $394 million in five years, and make clear Enron would owe $79 million in interest payments. Instead, Enron just marked an entry stating that in five years it was supposed to give JP Morgan Chase $394 million in natural gas.

Enron and JP Morgan Chase did $5 billion of these "prepays," or disguised loans.[34] After filing for bankruptcy, Enron wasn't planning on paying any of that money back—nor were any of the other companies that engaged in similar faux transactions and then retreated into the cozy world of bankruptcy court. So JP Morgan Chase turned around and sued the insurance companies. JP Morgan Chase had enlisted these insurance companies to back these corporate deals to lessen its risk. Insurance companies received a premium for this role, but the eleven companies argued in Enron's case that they did so under false information. Both JP Morgan Chase and the insurance companies lost out on that maneuver. But the FDIC and the Federal Reserve will always be there to bail out JP Morgan Chase if things get too bad. The FDIC bears the brunt of insuring depositors and the Fed has repeatedly been willing to bail out problem financial institutions, as in the case with the S&Ls in the early 1990s and the Long-Term Capital Management hedge fund debacle in 1998.

Prepays arranged by Citigroup and JP Morgan Chase brought Enron over $8.5 billion in the six years leading up to its demise. From 1997 to 2001, Citigroup made $167 million in fees from Enron for these and other deals, garnering fees from their own loans and other services setting up these transactions.[35] JP Morgan Chase booked $30 million in fees from Enron.[36] If Enron had accounted for all these prepays as the loans they actually were, the amount of outstanding debt on its balance sheet would have been 40 percent more than was shown, totaling $14 billion by 2000 and sending clear warning signals about its true financial state.[37]

JP Morgan Chase didn't actually account for these loans as loans any more than Enron did. The bank logged them as back-to-back separate transactions in its trading book, not as loans on its balance sheet, which would have required it to put up a certain amount of regulatory capital to back them. JP Morgan Chase later ran into extensive lawsuit trouble because of its hidden loan extensions. On July 8, 2002, Chubb Insurance filed a claim against JP Morgan Chase stating that the bank had "surreptitiously lent money to Enron, by way of Mahonia, an offshore English Channel Limited company owned by JP Morgan Chase, and expected to be repaid by Enron with interest." JP Morgan Chase countered that everyone, including insurers, "knew that the [Mahonia] deals were part of a structured finance transaction for Enron's general corporate well being." Citigroup officials have said they believe their prepays were appropriate because they had been reviewed by Arthur Anderson, Enron's accounting firm.[38]

In all, JP Morgan Chase had $2 billion of unsecured loans to Enron; Citigroup had $3 billion. All told, Chase earned over $100 million between 1997 and 2000 from its relationship with Mahonia, arranging natural gas and oil purchases and sales between Enron and Mahonia in which no natural gas or oil was exchanged, and earning arrangement fees without having to pay taxes on offshore profits. Instead, JP Morgan paid up front for energy from Enron and bought protection for its payment from a group of eleven insurance companies. Of course, Enron never delivered any energy to Mahonia.

TELECOM COMPANIES AS BANKS

Telecoms engaged in similarly murky transactions called long-term capacity swaps to book money up-front for future use of their networks. Many later defunct telecom companies sold rights to use capacity on their networks to other carriers for a period of twenty to twenty-five years. They booked the money they received for this future capacity as cash up-front, making their balance sheets appear more cash-rich, increasing their seeming credit worthiness, and thus allowing them to borrow even more cash from banks at a lower rate. Banks played along.

The Telecommunications Act of 1996 started a $1.3 trillion lending avalanche. Telecoms received more loans than any other industry from 1998 through 2001. These loans were sometimes secured by shares of stock. By 2000, the telecom industry had a $60 billion negative cash flow, meaning they owed $60 billion more than they were receiving as net revenue.[39] Often banks neglected to even insure solid collateral against the credit they extended. At one point, Global Crossing had $3.4 billion in stated "revenue" but owed $7.5 billion in debts for which it needed to pay $600 million in interest and $200 million in preferred dividends per year—money it never had.[40] JP Morgan Chase and Citigroup had no lien on Global Crossing's network as collateral in the event of a foreclosure on assets to pay off loans. Meanwhile, the corporation's stock was declining. Even if the banks had been able to seize assets, network values were declining just as fast as the stock prices of their builders were. Still, secured loans win out over bonds because of their higher position in the "corporate waterfall" of creditor hierarchy. Thus, bonds traded at 9 cents on the dollar a few weeks after Global Crossing declared bankruptcy while loans traded at 40 cents on the dollar.

EQUITY ANALYSTS VS. CREDIT ANALYSTS

The market bust and spate of scandals that began in 2001, combined with Eliot Spitzer's crusade to expose the conflicts of interest on Wall Street, thrust equity analysts into a newly negative spotlight. All of a sudden the heroes of the dot-com and technology boom became collaborators in its bust. In the process, they were saddled with a disproportionate amount of blame for all the woes of a deregulated free market. Somewhere along the way, what equity analysts actually *do* got lost.

Equity analysts watch and make recommendations about a company's future stock performance. Credit analysts monitor and make recommendations on a company's debt or bond performance, and their analysis tends to go more into balance sheet depth than equity analysis. Fixed-income analysts generally focus on debt securities as well, but these can include corporate bonds or various kinds of asset-backed bonds or derivative securities. Quantitative analysts or strategists tend to be more involved in the mathematics behind the behavior of securities, derivatives, or portfolios.

One of my former bosses characterized the difference between the 1990s perceptions of an equity analyst and a credit analyst or bond strategist as follows: equity analysts were considered "visionary," while credit analysts and bond quantitative analysts for other fixed incomes were "myopic." Other comparative labels included "Athletes vs. Geeks," "Personas vs. People," and "Rock Stars vs. Backup Band." In the 1980s, the status divisions were even more apparent. Lehman Brothers' Elaine Garzarelli, the famed bear caller of the 1987 crash, used to travel around first-class with her little white poodle while Lehman's fixed-income research geeks traveled coach. Even after all the equity analyst bashing of the last couple years, being a credit analyst is still not in vogue; since the credit analyst's job is to examine upcoming debt problems in corporate balance sheets, it is usually a job of bearing bad news.

For the buy side, every time equity analysts get a piece of news, they call their top investor clients to explain it to them. They are experts in their sectors and possess detailed knowledge of the specific companies they're assigned to cover, usually the ones their employer bank does the most business with (or the ones they would like to do more business with).

Fixed-income analysts first figure out how to help the trading desk internally. It's a well-worn mantra: if your trading desk isn't making money off a trade you suggested, it doesn't matter if a client bought or sold something based on the stellar idea you had, even if the client profits in the end. An ambitious analyst has to ensure a trade is executed through its employer bank, even if it makes better financial sense for it to be transacted "away," creating a more appreciative client for a future trade that would mutually benefit the client *and* that analyst's house.

Additionally, credit analysts had to pass information to their house's trading desk before giving it to their clients. One credit analyst at Lehman Brothers explained: "If you thought, for instance, that Sears was going to implode, you're not about to tell the Street and have them sell Sears short in front of your own trading desk. You tell your desk, to give them the opportunity to trade on that information. You're not about to offer competitors or clients the information first."

It's harder for a high-grade credit or bond analyst to move the entire market than an equity analyst. Equity analysts have that power because they have the ear of the media and because more people understand stocks than bonds. It's largely a matter of access: more people are able to buy stocks than bonds; stocks can be bought and sold in units as small as one share, while bonds require more of an investment. The equity markets are transparent and high-volume, and trades close in nanoseconds. In contrast, the fixed-income markets trade at lower volume and wider spreads, primarily involving institutional clients and not individuals. Thus, news doesn't hit bond prices as fast; stocks are far more sensitive to new information. There are no "star" credit analysts that bonds would "listen" to, plus, the media doesn't get the difference between bonds and stocks.

Post-"reform" companies began firing analysts for talking to their clients before getting permission from their compliance departments, which oversee trading and other activities to ensure that SEC regulations are being followed. The practice merely provided an easy way for investment banks to obey specious reform measures without really protecting investors. For example, Merrill Lynch fired Peter Caruso because he told his clients he'd changed his view on Home Depot—he downgraded it— but hadn't cleared it with compliance before posting his note. That's convoluted. He was actually trying to help his investor clients get out of their positions before Home Depot posted bad news, and he was fired for it.

INSTITUTIONAL INVESTOR (II) RANKINGS

Every year, *Institutional Investor* magazine sends out thousands of surveys to institutional investors across the country asking them to rank analysts in different categories and industry sectors. It's like the *American Idol* of finance, except that actual talent has little to do with the results.

These II rankings have really screwed up the industry. For equity analysts, a high II ranking was the ultimate goal because it meant their banks could tout their expertise and, more important, their popularity with the investing community and thus get more banking and IPO business.

It wasn't the same for credit analysts. Generally, a high II ranking only meant you were perceived to be worth more. "You did it for the bid away," said one analyst. The "bid away" was a Wall Street term for the prize or compensation another potential bank employer would pay to an employee. The term was identical to one used for securities trading: the bid was the prize an investor or other trading desks would pay to buy a security. "No bid" meant no one wanted to buy it, a phrase commonly used while companies like Enron were imploding and no one wanted to buy their bonds.

The period leading up to the announcement of the awards is called

"II season." It is a time when analysts get out on the road and visit people, effectively asking them outright for votes. It is nothing more than a beauty contest, and has nothing to do with objective analytical abilities. One analyst on the fixed-income side was fired from Goldman because the trading desk thought he was useless, sales thought he was useless, and research management thought he was useless. Yet he ranked number one in his category in II. He had spent a lot of time cultivating the relationships that voted him into that spot, but not, it seems, as much time actually doing his job well.

One analyst said he was surprised that the whole SEC/Spitzer investigation didn't create any pressure to get rid of the II system. "It's a total game, a joke," said this analyst, who works for Lehman Brothers. "Why do you need a popularity poll? With all their huge outreach, why not have II use objective criteria, that would rank analysts on their capabilities?" Another person at Lehman said, "Hell, I don't have time to shake hands for votes."

There are lots of opposing views regarding II on the Street. My former boss at Goldman called it a crock (and less polite names) and told us explicitly and often that we'd be paid on profit, not on II rankings. Others believe that rankings are important to customers, and they are very important to investment bankers who give analyst rankings and lists of accomplished deals a prominent placement in their pitch books.

EARNINGS AND REG FD

Another function of equity analysts is to provide views on upcoming corporate earnings announcements. Earnings statements by themselves tend to be an ambiguous tangle of information arranged in the way that a company wants to have information disclosed. The company carefully feeds analysts the information they want to appear in pre-earnings announcement statements. Before a company reveals its true earnings for the past quarter, the equity analyst community provides earnings "guidance," comprised by the array of different earnings guesses. The idea was that investors could use these predictions to assess corporate performance, which would translate into share price movement.

At Goldman Sachs, we used to gather before earnings announcements to hear the CFO, David Viniar, one of the highest paid CFOs in corporate America in 2000, discuss the Street's expectations of Goldman's earnings. Usually the talk was supplemented with a bright blue PowerPoint slide with yellow graphics illustrating analyst estimates from Bear Stearns, Morgan Stanley, Lehman Brothers, and other houses. There was never much difference between the lowest and highest estimates—which made sense, given that all these analysts had already discussed what expectations to give with the CFO of Goldman.

Formulating those expectations is a rather incestuous and circular affair because equity analysts at different firms offer expectations about their competitors' success. The embedded conflict of interest is that these analysts have to provide seemingly objective views while working for companies that want both to outperform their competitors and still have their overall sector do well. Companies meet or beat the consensus of analysts' expectations far more frequently than not. In early 2003, 82 percent of the companies that reported their earnings met or beat the consensus of analyst expectations, the same percentage that held steady throughout the whole of the 1990s.[41] That's because executives want to provide estimates they can meet or beat, and analysts follow their lead. Everyone loves a winner. Even more, everybody admires the person who beats the odds. Even though regulation Fair Disclosure (reg FD for short) stipulates that "when an issuer, or person acting on its behalf, discloses material nonpublic information to certain enumerated persons, it must make public disclosure of that information"—passed by the SEC in October 2000 despite major consternation among the investment banks—it didn't change that percentage.[42] Even after all of Spitzer's attempts to isolate analysts and prevent them from receiving inside information about the companies they cover—with whom they obviously have good relationships (otherwise they wouldn't be covering them)—the ratio of earnings consensus to earnings releases is as high as it was beforehand.

In practice, reg FD just doesn't happen. Analysts have conversations all the time with executives from the companies they cover. That's how the system operates—because it's just possible that in some pre-earnings press release luncheon with a corporate CFO, an analyst will get fed what the CFO wants him or her to use as an earnings estimate. No agency can monitor all conversations between all analysts and all the companies they cover all the time. Before reg FD, 20 percent of companies surveyed by the National Investor Relations Institute claimed they didn't give analysts information about future earnings, meaning that 80 percent did. After reg FD, the percentage went up to only 22 percent.[43]

The whole idea of earnings and preannounced estimates represents a major cornerstone of gaining public information disclosure, but since the status quo works well for corporations, it's unlikely anything will change. If reg FD really worked, you wouldn't need equity analysts discussing their forecasts; more public transparency would be its own information source. This would eliminate another layer of analyst opinions to decipher.

However, because the stock market and general American mentality tends to favor anything that comes "from behind" at the last minute, it benefits companies to hold back information until it can be released and outperformed simultaneously.

On March 20, 2003, Morgan Stanley, Lehman Brothers, and Goldman Sachs all miraculously beat predisclosed consensus (the average of analysts' predictions) earnings estimates, meaning they outdid their own predictions by an average of 22 percent each. Of course, this came as no surprise. Goldman Sachs executives had already "hinted" to analysts in advance that robust trading would fuel a great quarter.[44] Nine months later, the pattern repeated itself when Goldman Sachs announced that its fourth-quarter earnings and its net income of $1.89 a share outperformed Wall Street analyst expectations by 22.7 percent.[45]

TRACKING ANALYSTS

As mid-1990s corporate deregulation spawned tons of new issuance and merger-and-acquisition activities, the role of the equity analyst changed. From the late 1980s through the mid-1990s, the star equity analysts were actually equity market strategists who talked about the overall direction of the stock market—which sector would perform well and why. Then star tech and dot-com equity analysts emerged who focused on individual sectors and touted particular companies within them. The bond with investment banking thus tightened, and despite all claims made during the height of the corporate scandals that equity analysts' compensation was independent from how much associated fee business they brought in, such claims simply weren't true. How much money and other business analysts brought in was *exactly* what determined how much they were paid.

Equity analysts had two ways to make money for their employer: by ensuring the companies they covered did a lot of fee business and by increasing the volume of equity, or stock, they could sell to market investors by creating buzz around certain names. Fees for banking business were simply the more profitable of the two methods. Equity analysts didn't have true control over banking business, but their compensation was tied to it.

In a 1999 memo titled "Managing the Banking Calendar of Internet Research," Merrill Lynch equity analyst Henry Blodget outlined his time as split 85 percent on investment bankers and 15 percent on research (creating and publishing company analysis) for the coming week—so, as an analyst, he spent 85 percent of his time landing IPO or stock bond issuance and 15 percent actually analyzing these companies for investors.[46] Blodget received an e-mail on November 16, 2000, from one of his junior Internet research analysts stating, "The whole idea that research is independent from banking is a big lie." Spitzer later used that e-mail during his investigation of analyst practices. But all this really showed was that investment bankers have the real power—not the analysts, who became the convenient scapegoats of Spitzer's investigation because they were basically safe targets. Focusing on the analysts spared investigators from questioning the larger structural issues of power at banks. In mid-2000, Merrill Lynch circulated a memo to all its equity analysts requesting that they "provide complete details on involvement in investment banking transactions, particularly the degree of [your] research coverage role in origination, execution and follow-up."[47] The explicit request for the direct connection between equity analysts and associated investment banking business directly contradicted the intent of the Chinese wall dissection between equity analysts dealing with public investors (their stated job) and their connection with investment banking (or private) transactions. It essentially admitted the Chinese Wall was a fiction.

The highest-paid analysts drummed up the most investor interest, of which there were two types. First, there was the buy side: the financial services companies and asset management firms, like Fidelity or Putnam, who bought securities underwritten by Wall Street. Second were the corporations on the hunt for new conquests, looking for new companies to buy outright and not simply the debt or equity of those companies. The more interest an analyst could drum up, in other words, the more demand for an issue (or for a full company, in the case of a merger) and the higher the subsequent price for the issuing merged company—all of which translated to greater profit for the bank underwriting the deal. Also, the subsequent stock and bond offerings that would often be attached to an M&A deal would go up as well.

Investment bank equity analysts spent much of their time focused on the volume business in a world where volume was shrinking. At least, it being subsumed by wholesale retailers like Charles Schwab, which allowed customers to transact without using a broker. This led to the inevitable question of how to measure an analyst's worth for compensation purposes.

Different institutions tackled this problem in different ways. Goldman used to track equity analysts electronically. They would have to log in how much time they spent talking to each client and what they said. Management could then go to the client and ask them if they had traded more because of this dialogue with the analyst. But, as one equity analyst complained, "I mean, how does the guy who covers IBM on the equity side make any money? If IBM is trading 84.50–84.51, where's the spread?" There were few other ways to measure performance. "How are we supposed to get paid," he continued, "without being somehow connected to transactions?"

A credit analyst from a major investment bank said, "I ask for the business directly; why shouldn't I? It's no big secret either. If we're axed [or positioned] to do a trade, I'll tell customers, Do the trade with us. The only way I get paid is if business gets transacted." That's why fixed-income credit analysts focus on the secondary markets and trading desks—because that's where the majority of transactions happen.

We were doing a similar thing as Goldman fixed-income strategists, even though I wasn't on the equity side. It was still overt, involving my sending specific e-mails consisting of spreadsheets of information to everyone who reported to me, breaking down the degree to which our work was directly connected to profits (some of which were booked based on complex models of how transactions were expected to perform in the future) rated by number: "1" for very direct, "2" for somewhat, and "3" for an ancillary connection. Toward the end of 2001, we had to submit spreadsheets of all our major "commercial" activities. These were divided into three categories of strategist involvement in completing a transaction: heavy, medium, and light, also rated as 1, 2, and 3. The first category was obviously the most important. Then we had to estimate how much revenue the transactions we listed made and which other groups in the firm (investment banking, trading, sales, etc.) we most directly worked with to pull it off. This served as a cross-check. My manager could then go to the other groups to check whether or not we were exaggerating, an often subjective exercise. That information was used as one component in determining bonus compensation.

I ran the credit quantitative strategies group. The men who ran the foreign exchange, commodity, mortgage, and swaps strategies groups and I would aggregate our spreadsheets into one report delineating strategist contribution to bottom-line revenue. It was a process designed to be subjective, often leading to heated discussions with trading or capital markets desks or investment bankers about how to specifically quantify strategist contribution to profit. Frequently what we thought and what they thought were very different, and we had to ultimately debate and agree upon a profit number which stated our contribution—all of which required exceptional negotiation skills. Some of that profit came from long-term derivative transactions that later deteriorated in value, particularly those deals with some of the now less-solvent corporations. But what really mattered for compensation was revenue for that year and that year alone.

THE SEC AND INVESTMENT BANKS

Following nine months of investigations that began in 2002 into misleading practices involving IPO spinning and equity analysts' lack of independence from investment banking, the Street was tired of all the scrutiny and decided to get more proactive about ending it. In September 2002, the House Financial Services Committee requested e-mails relating to on-going investigations from Goldman Sachs, Credit Suisse First Boston, and Morgan Stanley. This prompted some visits to the SEC. September 27 in particular was a big day for SEC chairman Harvey Pitt and the SEC. Representatives from Salomon met with top members of the enforcement staff of the SEC that day. Minutes of that meeting were not made available, which was unusual. Later that day, Goldman Sachs CEO Hank Paulson paid his own visit to Pitt.

Two months earlier, Paulson had been lauded by the *New York Times* for his role in exposing corporate corruption and "reforming" corporate governance rules. The most interesting thing about the *Times* piece was the characterization of Hank as an insider "corporate reformer." In fact, he was merely trying to spin away from the scrutiny of investment bank practices that had dampened Goldman Sachs stock to his own advantage. It also stated he was "a man who does not relish the spotlight. He prefers fishing alone or bird-watching with his wife to moving and shaking on the New York social scene."[48] In fact, this private guy had appeared on the cover of *Business Week* just three months earlier.[49] In that article, he chanted his favorite refrain: the megabanks are reaping a bitter harvest from profligate loans made to snare investment bank deals. Their losses on bad loans surpass profits made on those deals. On September 27, however, he probably just wanted all the lawsuits and scrutiny to go away.

Paulson's meeting with Pitt took place without any notification to the SEC enforcement staff. Representatives Ed Markey (D-MA) and Dingell both questioned the meeting and its secret nature.[50] According to Markey, "the absence of enforcement staff in these meetings undermines the credibility of the commission." The letter went on to reveal that six months prior, "following a similar episode involving KPMG, Inc., Chairman Pitt assured Reps. Markey and Dingell that he would no longer hold such meetings. . . . In April 2002, Chairman Pitt met with KPMG's CEO while the commission was investigating KPMG for its auditing work at Xerox."[51] If nothing else, Paulson's meeting with Pitt certainly underscored the close relationship between the SEC and Wall Street.[52]

Just three months later, the SEC, Spitzer, and Wall Street reached a settlement, sweeping the scandals under the carpet. No bank admitted any guilt in misleading practices. No bank lost much money out of pocket, though they all put aside some extra reserves just in case future lawsuits got ugly. No bank fundamentally changed any of its practices; they all just buried them deeper into the system's infrastructure, officially transforming good equity analysts into investment bankers, and good credit analysts into salespeople, thus bypassing any already-weak reforms supposedly revamping research departments. So, a credit analyst–turned-salesperson could now tell his or her clients anything about a bond without having to call it research as such. Basically, the same information is going out even more blatantly to close transactions. Banks are getting around research analyst scrutiny by changing research analysts' titles, not their practices. Hence, if a former credit analyst proved as persuasive as a salesperson, the deal would still close, but the information that salespeople disseminated about it wouldn't even have to undergo the scrutiny or pretense of being checked for conflict of interest or integrity. It pushes the investor into the role of accepting or rejecting information the salesperson is giving, but because the salesperson *was* an analyst, the analyst's aura of knowledgeable authority still entices the potential investor.

Financial engineering, or structuring, always finds ways around regulations if potential profit or deals are involved.

THE MEDIA'S RESPONSE

The media played an undeniable role in boosting the market and pumping air into the stock bubble. They also were responsible in part for exposing the scandals that followed. Some financial companies, like Wachovia/Prudential Financial Advisors, LLC, now majority-owned by Wachovia, prohibited their analysts from even talking to the press. Many other large firms, like Goldman Sachs, Morgan Stanley, and CSFB, are restricting press access, saying all contact must be cleared through the PR department. And it's not just the banks controlling what information gets out; government regulatory bodies are following suit.[53]

The *Wall Street Journal* applauded efforts by the NYSE, SEC, and National Association of Securities Dealers (NASD) to compel analysts to disclose the full scope of their firms' relationships to the companies they cover. Such disclosures are hardly full, however, since numbers, like fee revenues, are never mentioned. All the fanfare around so-called new equity analyst disclosure rules is meaningless because the disclosures themselves are meaningless. The rules imposed restrictions on what analysts could say to reporters: "When analysts talk to journalists about a stock, they would have to disclose whether they own that stock or whether their firms do business for that company."[54] The *Wall Street Journal* went on to say, "But decisions as to what information to include in articles lie with reporters and editors."[55] In other words: Say whatever you want, we'll print whatever we want. None of this acknowledges the fact that the real conflicts lie between the clients and the bankers, not between clients and analysts. Bankers actually close the deals. The 2002 rally for disclosure was largely met with a resounding cry of "business as usual" in 2003.

Following the settlement, little changed in media coverage. The newswires and TV shows still focus on the retail investors, the so-called mom and pops. Fixed-income analysts mostly focus on institutional investors. CNN, CNBC, and MSNBC continue to put equity analysts on their shows. When they quote analysts, they're still quoting equity, not credit, analysts, even though credit analysts have more detailed knowledge of a company's ability to pay its debt, useful information during the ongoing slew of bankruptcies. But the general public doesn't own debt; they own stock, so that's the side the media cover.

The networks still open their business and market stories with the words "Analysts think" or "Analysts say." They are light-years away from presenting alternative voices, even ones that were proven right in their past skepticism—like the Communications Workers of America (CWA), whose brilliant early-1998 report about why the WorldCom/MCI merger would lead to disaster was ignored by the mainstream media (and federal regulators). Part of this is because the CWA is a union, not a company formally involved in financial services. The larger point, though, is that restricting the flow of information about corporations and banks creates too much of an incestuous vacuum, a feedback loop where those corporations and banks that have the most to gain by harnessing and controlling the output and flow of information are the ones that control the reporting media. In fact, outside perspective from institutions without profit to gain from airing their opinions should be involved and their recommendations reported in order for true evaluations to emerge.

CORPORATE VS. TREASURY ISSUANCE

As the economy limps along and we all discover that Bush's tax cuts won't necessarily open the floodgates of consumer spending or create jobs, the Treasury Department continues to increase the supply of debt. The projected deficit reached $521 billion during the presidency of George W. Bush after a Clinton administration surplus. That surplus had allowed the Treasury Department to get rid of the thirty-year bond auction and pare back issuance along the yield curve, which shows the relationship between *yields* and *maturity dates* for a set of similar *bonds*, usually *treasuries*, at a given point in time. This in turn allowed issuers like Ford to fill in the gap for investors (pension funds in particular) who required long-dated investments to be able to pay out their liabilities, or amounts they owe pensioners.

Even before the war with Iraq began on March 19, 2003, the Bush administration was backtracking on borrowing requirements. In February

2003, Treasury announced it expected it would borrow $110 billion by the end of the first quarter of 2003, up $26 billion from a previous estimate of $84 billion. Meanwhile, the supply of investment-grade bonds was already decreasing as companies running into downgrades cut back on new debt issuance.

In 1995, U.S. treasuries, or government bonds, made up 46 percent of all U.S. public debt and corporate debt accounted for just 17 percent. By 2001, treasuries had declined to 20 percent and corporates had risen to 28 percent.[56] By early 2003, treasuries were at 22 percent and corporates at 26 percent, thanks to an increase in Treasury Department issuance and the fact that any corporates that hadn't defaulted or declared bankruptcy were nonetheless tapped out with interest-rate payments on their debt.

In general, capital is always searching for the next "great investment opportunity." The leveraged buyouts and the junk-bond markets in the late 1980s later found a home in emerging markets, mostly the Latin American countries. Following Mexico's peso crisis in 1994, after the Asian "Tiger" markets were in vogue, crisis sent capital packing once more; in its eternal search for a new home, it found corporate bonds—specifically, the technology and telecom sectors that were embarking on a historic issuance path.

Some claim that if the deficit increases and more treasuries are issued, it will push up treasury yields, or interest rates, making it more expensive for corporations to raise debt. Others say with equal vehemence that an increase in treasury supply (increasing the deficit and issuing more treasuries), driving up yields, would close the gap between corporate and Treasury Department bond yields, pushing up the value or price of corporate bonds by default. Neither argument takes into account the lack of profitability or the declining cash flow of once-eager borrowers to make good on new debt payments. But even with more Treasury debt, corporate debt will continue to show signs of weakness because fundamental conditions surrounding its profitability have not changed. In other words, even though companies cut costs, jobs, and restructured debt in the early part of the millennium, they didn't dramatically alter their business strategies. Going forward, that fact, plus a heavy debt burden, will still make it hard to prosper. If the market takes another significant plunge, there won't be any fat left to cut.

WHERE DID ALL THE CREDIT RISK GO?

The growth of the credit derivative or credit default swap market in the late 1990s was partly due to the inability of financial institutions to go short, or sell on the expectation of future declines, corporate bonds. In other words, it was difficult to borrow money in order to buy corporate bonds and then sell them back to the market because the market for loaning money collateralized by corporate bonds wasn't as mature as it was for loans backed by treasury bonds.

Mostly, this was because there were too many variables that went into the evaluation of corporate bonds, whereas treasury bonds issued by the U.S. government were far more transparently priced and liquid.

Credit default swaps (CDSs) offered a way to "short" corporate bonds, or bet on them to decline in value, without paying high borrowing costs for money to actually purchase and then sell them. Moreover, they provided a way to buy and sell the value of the perceived credit risk of a corporation without actually exchanging the underlying corporate bonds. The pricing of CDSs is based on and linked to specific bonds, but what is exchanged is the likelihood of those bonds defaulting, and not the value of the bonds themselves. You could buy a CDS on a company like Ford, and that would mean that if Ford defaulted, you would receive full value, or par, back on some Ford reference bond (the bond the default swap price was based on). In return for that security, you pay an annual premium, a kind of insurance covering bond defaults in the event of corporate fraud or bankruptcy. If you thought Ford would never default, you could sell a Ford-linked CDS and take the other side of the trade and receive that regular premium instead. But if Ford did default, you'd be stuck paying the CDS buyer the full value of Ford bonds, even if the market value of those bonds was zero. As with any other securities, though, you planned to be out of that position before it bit you from behind.

Banks worldwide are currently exposed to $2 trillion of CDSs, double the $1 trillion CDS market at the end of 2001. Billionaire investor and free-market guru Warren Buffett called these credit default swaps "a time bomb."[57] Yet, his company, Berkshire Hathaway Insurance Group, is the nation's number two property and casualty company and one of the largest owner of credit risk in the form of bonds and CDSs.

Banks used the CDS market to remove risk from their balance sheet, thereby reducing the regulatory capital they were required to put up to back that risk. European banks started the practice in 1997. By removing risk, they could proceed to use their balance sheets to extend further credit to corporations, or for other, more speculative enterprises. As such, these banks were net sellers of more dated credit risk and buyers of new risk.

Insurance companies were the biggest institutional buyers of corporate bonds and sellers of CDSs, giving them double exposure to credit risk. Through their net short default swap strategies, they would take in premiums to insure that corporate bonds would not default. The exposure of bond insurers to credit derivatives was zero in the mid-1990s but swelled to 18 percent by the end of 2002. Financial guaranty companies, generally rated AAA, were net sellers of $222 billion of protection ($166 billion in CDSs and $56 billion of CDOs).[58]

If all this seems unclear to you, you're not alone. A few months before I left Goldman, the partner in charge of swaps on the liability side (for issuers, or corporate clients) called to ask if I'd have a meeting with him and one of the senior partners in investment banking. The topic was credit derivatives, and he wanted to discuss not when to use them or with which customers, but just what the hell were they.

For two years, senior investment banking division (IBD) partners had lined up behind Hank Paulson to extol the virtues of this unregulated credit product, which was booking so much profit for the rival fixed-income, currency, and commission (FICC) division, but if you had asked any of them what the product actually was, in any kind of detail, none of them would have been able to answer. Following my meeting with the partners, it was decided that we should have an educational powwow with the investment bankers. The M&A business had gone down the drain, and they were desperate to find ways to make money. Conversely, they were extraordinarily good at making it look like they were insanely busy and productive even while they were just scrambling for business and something substantial to do.

After another slew of boring logistical meetings, we chose a day for FICC to educate IBD—a momentous occasion. All the senior IBD partners had thought the meeting was a fantastic idea, but not a single one of them showed up for their day of education. They couldn't be bothered, saying they were too busy doing deals. Since the M&A market at the time was almost nonexistent, they were simply unwilling to learn or admit to needing to learn. There we were, ready with slides, handouts, and piles of sandwiches, potato chip bags, and soda cans in the back corner of one of the conference rooms, and only ten IBD folks had come, all junior bankers who had no pull, power, or client interaction.

By early 2003, the insurance industry had sold more than a net $238 billion of credit default protection. Banks had bought a net $97 billion of that, transferring that amount of risk off their books.[59] These figures come from an extensive survey by the Fitch rating agency, to which 147 of 200 institutions responded.[60] Interestingly, the ones that didn't respond were primarily insurers and reinsurers (who insure insurance companies), which had the largest exposure to the deteriorating credit markets. Most of the significant credit exposure was rated below BBB. The top three counterparties involved in the credit derivatives market were JP Morgan Chase, Merrill Lynch, and Deutsche Bank. The three most actively traded credit references, or corporations, were Ford, GM, and GE, also the three largest bond issuers.

One of the reasons credit derivatives were so attractive to insurance companies was the lax regulatory environment. Insurance companies are the biggest owners or holders of credit risk, yet they don't generally evaluate much of that risk, nor do they regularly disclose it in financial statements. That's partly because murkily worded insurance contracts and policies help disguise risk, making it hard for regulators to trace though the FASB.

Just like an auto insurance policy means that an insurance company should pay your repair bills in the event of a car crash, a credit default policy means that an insurance company pays in a "credit event" such as a corporate default (the equivalent of a corporate bond crash). But the company doesn't have to disclose the possibility of any payouts that *might* occur, no matter their size. Even if a company like WorldCom undergoes four downgrades in two months, its insurance company's balance sheet will not indicate that a default might be on the horizon.

The monoline insurers, like the Financial Services Authority (FSA) and Municipal Bond Insurance Association Insurance Corporation (MBIAIC), are companies whose business is to insure the risk of other insurance companies and banks. While reinsurers insure insurance companies, monolines are paid to provide enough insurance to certain risky assets of any financial institution and to convert the rating of portfolios of those assets to AAA. As such, they are the "backstop" (think doorstop) preventing the insurance companies' risk from spiraling out of control—making them the biggest potential losers. Yet these insurers of both the banks and the insurance companies don't have to disclose their risk exposure either. The picture will only worsen when they start admitting their losses and value declines, which they are not obligated to disclose during their fall, but only when they hit bottom. In the meantime, the skeletons pile up in the insurance company market.

CREDIT DERIVATIVES CONFLICTS OF INTEREST

A brewing area of conflict of interest for the supermarket banks is their use of credit derivatives. A bank's CDS trading activity tends to noticeably increase just before the bank brings a big issue of debt for that company to market. In other words, as with insider trading, in which knowledge of future information that can impact market value is used by a select few, banks could conceivably use knowledge of future credit problems to profit from trading in the parallel CDS.

For instance, just before Ahold—a multi-national food retail company and owner of Stop & Shop—announced its $500 million of misstated earnings in March 2003, there was a sharp increase in activity in Ahold CDSs during the Wednesday through Friday of the week before the news hit. It was rumored that one large bank involved in the deal had made an easy $15 million on its knowledge of an emergency credit facility in the offering. Banks don't put emergency credit facilities together without knowing that something bad is about to happen.

The bankers that had put together the rescue package had gone "over the wall"—the Chinese wall—meaning they used "nonpublic material information" to create the emergency credit. They used that insider knowledge to hedge their position in another public but unregulated market: credit derivatives. Other participants in that market did not have access to that same information at the time. Alan Greenspan might say that was a good use of the credit derivatives market to limit bank risk. He was a big fan of complex instruments, even after seeing enormous stock market losses and massive deceptive balance sheet practices, some of which utilized derivatives. On May 8, 2003, he stated, "Although the benefits and costs of derivatives remain the subject of spirited debate, the performance of the financial industry and the financial system in recent years suggests that those benefits have materially exceeded the costs." Warren

Buffett, on the other hand, saw "derivatives as financial weapons of mass destruction."[61] Either way, it remains a form of unregulated insider trading. As a direct result, banks profited at the expense of the rest of the public, particularly the investors who owned Ahold.

According to one Lehman analyst, the Street rumor surrounding Ahold was that when JP Morgan Chase bought $80 million of CDSs between Thursday and Friday, the bank knew it was creating the rescue package it then announced the following Monday. Buying credit protection by trading on inside information is a way for banks to steal from investors without access to that information, and the practice is unhampered by regulations. Tyson Foods, Inc., was another food company that traded heavily in the CDS market before it announced big negative news. Still another was UnumProvident, an umbrella company for a number of insurance companies. Just before the stock of UnumProvident had plunged from $60 in January 1999 to $6 in early March 2003 and its bonds fell 800 basis points (basis points are equivalent to one-hundredth of a percent), credit defaults swaps in UnumProvident went up dramatically.

The list goes on and on and will surely continue to grow as the credit derivatives market expands. So far, there are no legislators or regulators looking to establish stricter rules to curtail this serious and growing conflict of interest.

3

Deregulation and Creating Instability

Money was so easy to get. The public was so eager to buy equities and pieces of
paper [bonds] that money was . . . pressed upon domestic corporations. . . .
—Otto Kahn, 1929, quoted in Matthew Josephson's *Money Lords*

MY LIFE AS A WALL STREET BANKER HAD ALMOST nothing to do with the
government bodies that set and monitor the rules of corporate behavior.
I constructed investment portfolios for multinational institutions and the
central banks that set monetary policy throughout the world on a regular
basis. I never stopped to consider what capping electricity rates had to do
with getting a deal done. While we were structuring some newfangled type
of security, it never occurred to me or my colleagues to question who was
winning the battles for Internet access market share, unregulated cable
companies, or the only slightly more regulated local telephone companies,
nor did we wonder how these struggles for control would ultimately affect
a broad section of the economy.

I can count on one hand the number of times that nonfinancial regulatory bodies (i.e., those other than the NASD, the SEC, and the FASB)
actually affected my work. But, in fact, the government organizations that
oversee communication and energy, the FCC and FERC, more deeply affected my life—really, all of our lives.

As a banker, I spent over a decade designing financial analytical tools
and strategies for the companies that provide services that fall under the jurisdiction of the FCC and FERC. I marketed their bonds to institutional
investors, and the sale of those bonds allowed them to expand their empires. Without help from the banks, none of those corporations could
have attained the stock heights they reached or bloated their balance sheets
with the debt they borrowed. Financial engineers (or structurers) at these
banks, including me, created ways to make balance sheets appear healthier, much as cosmetic surgeons falsify youth for aging faces. I personally
constructed and marketed financial securities and investment strategies to

familiar financial institutions like the Bank of New York, Bank of America, and MetLife. That's why I understand how and why banks invest their money, which is really your money, in the form of *your* deposits.

Years ago, my first job on Wall Street consisted of programming financial models that banks used to hedge against risky strategies. Back on October 19, 1987, when the stock market crashed, I was busy protecting my employer, Chase Manhattan, from customers who had stock-linked deposit accounts. I had helped design a financial product that linked interest rates on savings accounts with the S&P 500. If stocks went up, Chase would pay out more interest. If stocks went down, Chase guaranteed a preset minimum interest rate. Of course, when the market fell beneath expectations on that Black Monday, Chase lost money making good on that promise. As a result, I was called into all sorts of "strategy" meetings on how to mitigate Chase's losses, mostly to the big corporate clients, who were offered the same deal as smaller customers but on a far greater scale.

It wasn't that bank scientists were somehow coming up with innovative ways to move and hide debt that only affected huge corporations. These banks pawned off the results of this creativity on the public via the calculated destruction of a host of public protections that had formerly forced banks to operate according to the Glass-Steagall Act. Today, you can invest in the stock market through your bank, or bank through your brokerage firm (Merrill Lynch wants to offer checking to its customers, just like JP Morgan Chase does). From the outside, grouping together various financial activities may appear to be a public convenience, but it also opens up a host of ways for institutions to extract less-than-transparent fees from customers and escape the mindful (and, unfortunately, often *un*mindful) watch of regulatory bodies.

Within a banking career, even while you're working on transactions with federally regulated corporations, you don't necessarily spend time contemplating these regulations. Your main goal is to ensure the transaction meets the standards of accounting law—although, as we'll see, there are plenty of ways to maneuver around those too. Beyond that, you want to make sure the deal can close and sell. Period. In fact, most bankers couldn't tell you what the letters FCC and FERC stand for. The exceptions work at the most senior levels, where federal regulation of client corporations is seen as an impediment to dismantle. Yet it was, and continues to be, these bodies that blessed the mergers that bring in investment banking fees, debt or loan issuance, and stock offerings, and facilitate trading volume.

Corporate deregulation meant more opportunities for mergers, issuance, and selling. Much as when your parents went away for the weekend, it was the perfect chance to throw a party. You invited some friends to come over, but inevitably word would get out pretty fast that your parents were away—in other words, there would be no enforcement of house regulations. What would begin as a forty-person get-together could quickly balloon into an all-out keg party. While the 1990s stock and debt bubble frenzy was in full swing, the cops never came to break up the party; instead, the SEC just drove past as on some routine neighborhood run.

GLOBAL BANKING CONSOLIDATION

When I first started working at Bear Stearns in early 1993, the investment bank was the only occupant in the fifty-story Canada Square building in Canary Wharf, London's answer to New York's World Financial Center. During my seven years at Bear, Canada Square and Canary Wharf became overcrowded with company residents. We used to play "Guess the Merger" a lot during the late-1990s. The game usually started after some big merger was announced. And since we were in banking in the London branch of a U.S. investment bank, the mergers we cared about involved European banks taking over U.S. investment banks. These bank consolidations preceded some of the biggest mergers ever (notably in the communications industry) that would take place a few years later.

We discussed bank pairings as if we were matchmakers, ranking their chances of succeeding the same way we would debate whether or not someone's latest love interest was going to lead to a solid relationship, marriage or catastrophe. At the same time, we watched for signs of Bear to be taken over. For instance, fixed-income (and later firmwide) chief Warren Spector was once seen getting out of a plane in Frankfurt in 1999. We concluded that we were doomed to merge with WestDeustcheLandesbank. That didn't happen.

Meanwhile, Deutsche Bank gobbled up Bankers Trust (BT) in November 1999, one of many Deustche mergers that involved the old British bank Morgan Grenfell, once part of the great House of Morgan.

We predicted disaster. It's not as if we cared about how the move toward focusing on investment over consumer banking would affect Deutsche Bank's retail customers. Frankly, customers—the quality of their service, the safety of their deposits, or how they would be used as a receptacle for convoluted securities that Deutsche Bank would create and distribute— never entered our minds. We just felt sorry for all our friends at BT.

BT's identity as an intelligent derivatives trading shop would be lost, replaced by a monolithic bureaucratic giant. Any BT trader or analyst with brains got a job somewhere else. The buzz about Deutsche Bank was that you went there for the two-year plan. Because Deutsche, like all commercial banks, was noted for being big, dumb, and slow, only good compensation packages could have enticed people to work there. Both the Street and Deutsche knew that. In fact, Deutsche could double what you were making elsewhere during the mid- and late 1990s; not only that, they gave you a two-year guarantee, which in practice meant you didn't have to do very much for two years because your bonus was a sure thing. After collecting your money, you could then leave to go to a better firm. Likewise, two-year incentive bonuses sprung up at several telecommunication companies, like Global Crossing and WorldCom, in the late 1990s.

The biggest mergers in the United States followed the biggest ones in Europe. There was no way U.S. banks wanted to get stuck behind their European competitors, not when distribution of securities was expanding globally. To maximize profits, you needed a bigger distribution base. Additionally, you need dollar product to distribute. As a result, the European banks began buying boutique U.S. investment houses that could create and market complex dollar securities, like Donaldson Lufkin & Jenrette, Inc. (DLJ), which specialized in high-yield corporate bonds.

Fear of European domination was precisely the main argument for the demolition of the 1933 Glass-Steagall Act. If the European commercial banks could buy up investment houses, how could U.S. banks not be allowed the same competitive advantage? This reasoning worked with the U.S. Federal Reserve and the Senate Banking Committee.

By the time Credit Suisse First Boston (CSFB) grabbed DLJ in August 2000, Glass-Steagall was already enough of a dim memory that CSFB proudly ran praise for its new number three full-service bank status, citing seven different media sources across its company Web site. As of this writing, the blurbs are still there.

When George W. Bush announced in November 2002 that William

Donaldson was going to rectify the problems that the SEC had experienced under Harvey Pitt's leadership, the media swallowed whole the story about Donaldson founding DLJ forty years ago as a respectable, research-oriented firm. The press concluded that Donaldson was thus a good choice to lead the SEC's crusade against the research analysts on Wall Street who had talked up bad stocks throughout the 1990s.

That was far from DLJ's reputation on the Street. I understood its reputation to be that of a cutthroat leveraged finance (junk bond) organization. It bottom-fished for corporations of lower credit quality, whose borrowing spreads—or interest rates they'd have to pay to get people to buy their bonds—were wide enough to drive a truck through, and which would pay substantial fees.

WAVES OF BANKING CONSOLIDATION

The waves of global banking consolidation that took place throughout the twentieth century created larger, more powerful institutions along the way. But, as we've seen, it was the frenzied and global financial industry mergers in the early to mid-1990s, coupled with the deregulation of key corporate client industries, particularly in the telecom and energy sectors, that created a dangerous and unstable overaccumulation of companies, debt, and bloated stock values. This set the stage for disaster.

From the late 1980s through the mid-1990s, European banks went on a shopping spree. First they bought other European insurance companies, then they moved on to other European equity houses, and finally they went after U.S. investment banks. There were no regulations restricting them from doing so. A European commercial bank could own a U.S. investment bank, but a U.S. commercial bank could not, because the Glass-Steagall Act prohibited deposit and lending institutions from owning securities firms. As a result, the European banks hooked up with U.S. investment banks—product-generating machines that created U.S. denominated securities—which they then sold to European institutional and individual investors. In this way, European-led bank mergers were taking away market share from the United States.

This didn't sit well with U.S. commercial banks, which were angling to stay on top of the global banking pecking order but were losing territory fast to the likes of Union Bank of Switzerland (UBS), Deutsche

Bank, and Credit Suisse. They wanted to buy up some U.S. investment banks of their own, but first, they had to lobby for two kinds of banking deregulation. One would allow investment banks and insurance companies to merge, which Sandy Weill did when he combined Travelers Insurance and Salomon Smith Barney in 1997. The second permitted commercial banks to buy securities firms, or investment banks. So the commercial banks lobbied Congress, with the aid of secretary of the treasury and former investment banker Robert Rubin and the support of supreme deregulator and former Texas senator Phil Gramm, to allow them to do what the European banks were doing.

When U.S. banks finally broke down the barriers that Glass-Steagall had put into place, U.S. bank mergers began to surpass European ones, though both were increasing steadily throughout the mid- to late 1990s. The number of players in the game was declining, as the remaining players themselves were bulking up. Even though the size of the banking business pie remained the same, every time one bank lost business to another, it lost a larger percentage of overall market share. This would put it on worse footing when it had to present its market prowess to its corporate clients in its bid for the next deal.

To retain supremacy, banks had to prey upon their existing and emerging corporate clients to increase the banking business they were doing. This meant they had to aggressively and deliberately increase the number of M&A, debt, loan, stock, and IPO deals they did. It was more than just a thirst for fees or profitability; it was a drive for survival and dominant market share in a limited banking space.

Citigroup was able to capitalize on its size by offering its old commercial banking balance sheet (backed by billions of dollars of FDIC-insured customer bank accounts) in the form of cheap loans to corporations in return for more lucrative investment banking merger and issuance business armed with Salomon Brothers' expertise and client list. Chase Manhattan was able to do the same after it merged with JP Morgan at the end of 2000, combining the number one corporate loan provider with a middling investment bank.

In the rush to capture the kind of business that used to belong to the pure investment banks like Goldman Sachs, Lehman Brothers, and Morgan Stanley, these banks were less careful about due diligence, or full background analysis, on their corporate customers—it wasted time. The late 1990s were the Internet years—all about speed, not patience.

The fact that these superbanks were getting business the investment banks used to count on forced the investment banks to gear up several notches, relying on a strategy of full relationship management for their best corporate clients. This meant providing equity and debt-deals packaged alongside private wealth services for the executives, and even buying up some of the structured debts or assets themselves to increase appearance of demand. Banks went into sales overdrive to close merger deals, leading to enormous debt and loan issuance. The most convenient corporate targets were the most deregulated industries since they had their own incentives to expand and dominate their newly opened markets. As a result, telecom and energy mergers topped bank mergers starting in 1998. These industries worked directly with the banks in creating record debt-level issuance supposedly to fund their expansions, but often to support and hide mounting losses.

OTHER INDUSTRY DEREGULATION

Other industries underwent waves of deregulation beginning in the 1970s under former president Jimmy Carter, who buckled under pressure from the airline and trucking industries. Airlines were deregulated in 1978. While airfares did fall, as promised, so did service: fewer connections, more delays, overbooked flights, and lower safety standards. Proponents of deregulation touted the lowered fares as evidence of policy success, but, in fact, the price declines were merely equivalent to those already in motion prior to the 1978 deregulation.[1]

Then Ronald Reagan took office. Congress subsequently deregulated lending standards in 1980 and 1982, allowing savings and loan institutions (S&Ls) to offer new products like checking and commercial loans, and doubling FDIC insurance for S&Ls at the same time. By offering federal deposit insurance from the FDIC only to commercial banks, Glass-Steagall created an incentive for banks to choose commercial over investment banking because it shifted bank-failure risk back to the government. Deregulation of those lending standards was a major contributing factor of the S&L crisis of the early 1990s, the biggest banking emergency since the Great Depression and "a massive public policy failure," according to the FDIC's 1997 analysis.[2]

Cable rates were deregulated by the FCC in 1984, reregulated in

1992, and then deregulated again in 1996. Deregulated cable rates have risen 47 percent since 1996. Nonetheless, deregulation's cheerleaders claim that this has led to a spate of new networks, offering more choice to viewers. Yet fifteen of the top twenty cable networks, including CNN and C-SPAN, were launched during regulation, not afterward.[3]

The deregulation of the 1990s drove broad corporate consolidation across a number of industry lines, much as it had in the 1920s. Across the country and the world, energy companies became part-telecoms. Every single energy company that either confronted the brink of failure or simply severe deterioration in value, including Dynegy, El Paso, Duke, Williams, and Reliant, had taken advantage of telecom deregulation to raise debt to finance fiber-optic networks. Energy companies became trading companies. Enron didn't just expand into broadband; it traded everything with a cash flow—weather, newspaper advertising space, earthquake risk. Investment banks became speculative energy traders, trading energy commodities and derivatives. They bought energy assets, oil drilling sites, and equipment. Telecoms loaned each other money and swapped future capacity with each other the same way banks swapped long-term derivative structures. None of this had anything to do with servicing the bulk of the American public, yet they wound up the unlucky ones who paid for it with their jobs, retirement savings, and general financial stability, all while incurring higher prices for poorer electricity, phone, cable, and banking service.

The removal of the rules that limited corporations to concentrating on a finite number of core businesses wasn't just a U.S. phenomenon. Paris, France–based Vivendi, known in some circles as a media giant and the parent of Universal Pictures, raises most of its revenues from water privatization. Movies mixed with water, electricity with broadband, owning oil wells with trading securities portfolios—all of these combinations came courtesy of the deregulated 1990s.

FACTORS LEADING TO THE NEW DEAL

Stepping back to a time when regulation was the order of the day, the New Deal of the 1930s ushered in a period of federal scrutiny. It was a time when regulatory bodies and rules were installed to monitor banks and corporations. It followed a period of unbridled corruption and fraud that culminated in the great stock market crash of 1929.

There were many unregulated industries growing quickly in the 1920s as the country underwent a hot stock market and corporate consolidations. The unregulated banking system (then as now) was involved in the issuance of substantial debt to already highly leveraged companies, and public utilities companies were in search of ways to expand beyond their core businesses, building internal layer after layer to obscure their true business intents.

There were some differences between the 1920s and the 1990s, of course, but the regulatory environments surrounding the most capital-intensive industries and the banking systems that fed them during these decades were more similar than not. In the 1920s, however, banks didn't have research analysts acting as public intermediaries between the investors and the issuers. Bankers simply went directly to the media to tout opportunities.

Between 1927 and 1931, Morgan Bank participated in more than fifty stock pools that the New Deal would later outlaw. Other shady stock practices included syndicates, or groups of elite banks and individuals, openly manipulating stock prices and bribing reporters to "talk up" stocks. Additionally, by October 1929, more than a hundred stocks were being openly rigged by colluding market operators.[4]

In early 1929, brokerage houses like Goldman Sachs used murky devices like the "holding company," which was a paper entity that could own a number of other companies, to hide its true risks and ventures. (A "bank holding company" is any company that owns two or more banks. It is required to register with the governors of the Federal Reserve System.)[5] Building a holding company in the 1920s meant taking over many smaller operating companies, then using the dividends that had been paid by the takeover companies to pay off their bondholders, who had financed the takeovers of the small companies in the first place. This permitted an often imperceptible circle of financing in which it was frequently difficult to tell which component of the chain owed what to whom.

HOW THE NEW DEAL WAS PASSED

History has given most of the credit for the creation of the Glass-Steagall Act in 1933 to Franklin Delano Roosevelt. In reality, he simply possessed the guts and political acumen to push through a measure that had been circulating since March 1929.

As the market was reaching dizzying heights in 1929, Republican president Herbert Hoover started to get a bit concerned and took a trip to the New York Stock Exchange to ask if they wouldn't mind curtailing speculation. His request was ignored. In addition to blaming the NYSE, Hoover also blamed the Fed for lowering interest rates, which led to growing bank reserves that the banks could then use as collateral for financing various activities on margin (or borrowed) funds. While he never talked to the Fed directly, Hoover was worried about the increasing number of stock mergers and questioned whether the government should take actions to stop Wall Street speculation since the NYSE refused to cooperate. Hoover's chief Wall Street adviser told him not to worry, paying homage to the self-correcting nature of the marketplace, not unlike Alan Greenspan's mantras seventy years later.

Then came the crash. Over a two-day period, the stock market lost 25 percent of its value, devastating not just investors who owned stock but also the banks, which had had so many loans out to corporations backed by stock as collateral. The House of Morgan, for example, had $100 million in outstanding stock-backed loans.[6]

Just after the crash, bankers became popularly known as "banksters," a term of derision reflecting a perception that bankers' activities fell somewhere between a banker's and a gangster's, stealing money from smaller investors or the public. Yet bankers and speculators wanted to believe the worst was over. (They always do—bankers are great optimists.) In fact, Thomas Lamont, who was a partner at J.P. Morgan & Company from 1911 to 1940, said in late 1929, "I cannot help but feel that it may after all be a valuable lesson and the experience gained may be turned to our future advantage. . . ."[7] Unfortunately, that lesson lasted only four years despite the ruinous effects. It threw 13 million Americans (over 10 percent of a total population of 125 million) out of jobs. Between 1929 and 1932, Morgan's asset value dropped 37 percent.[8] In contrast, between January 2001 and January 2003, überbank JP Morgan Chase, one of the latest incarnations that stemmed from the original JP Morgan & Company, dropped a full 67 percent in value.

Senator Carter Glass (D-VA) formally introduced the idea of separating lending and deposit businesses from more speculative investment banking activities, which had coexisted at Morgan Bank, in a 1930 banking bill, which later formed part of the Democratic Party corporate platform in 1932. During the 1932 presidential campaign, FDR openly blamed

Hoover for the speculation and resultant defaults that had run rampant during his administration.

Then came the birth of the Glass-Steagall, or Banking, Act of 1933. The act established the FDIC initially as a temporary corporation with the authority to regulate and supervise some banks, provide deposit insurance to banks, and prohibit banks from selling securities. The second Banking Act, of 1935, established the FDIC as a permanent government agency.

In 1933, Ferdinand Pecora, a former assistant district attorney from New York boasting an 80 percent conviction rate, took over the Senate's Wall Street probe. The current New York district attorney (as of this writing), Eliot Spitzer, could have modeled himself after this feisty Italian-American progressive Democrat. Pecora aggressively pushed for Senate hearings in late February 1933.[9] In his investigation, he uncovered risky loans that potentially endangered depositors' money, such as the $12 million loan Morgan extended to enable National City's (the predecessor to Citibank) merger with the Corn Exchange Bank, an amount representing an excessively high percentage (at least 5 percent) of Morgan's total net worth. He also exposed another scandal that would be echoed by the host of executive loans banks offered during the 1990s. Bank officers had borrowed $2.4 million, interest-free, from a special "morale loan fund," which never required repayment of loans.[10] Pecora's investigation lasted until May 1934. Its findings showed how interlocked Morgan was with its clients.

Pecora pointed out that Morgan partners held 126 directorships in 89 corporations. He referred to it as "incomparably the greatest reach of power in private hands in our entire history."[11]

The logic that underpinned the Glass-Steagall Act has now been forgotten. At the time, there was concern that banks could take bad loans, repackage them as bonds, and sell them off to investors. (Today, collateralized debt obligations, or CDOs, do that trick.) National City had done exactly that with Latin American loans. Such practices engendered an intrinsic conflict of interest. Banks were both issuing "iffy" debt and lending money to investors to buy that debt in the form of bonds. Then, the Federal Reserve system had to stand behind both depositors and speculators, who were doing business with different departments of the same bank. If a securities affiliate, or trading division, failed, the Fed might need to rescue it to protect the parent bank. In other words, the government might have to protect speculators to save depositors.

Regulatory overhaul in the New Deal formed a cornerstone of rules that not only calmed an incredibly volatile economic and employment environment, but also served to maintain stability for decades afterward. Not surprisingly, the popular response to the New Deal at the November 1934 midterm elections led to a sweeping victory for the Democrats—a historical fact lost on today's politicians. They picked up thirteen seats in the House and a whopping nine seats in the Senate. It was, as historian Charles A. Beard declared, a "thunder on the left."[12]

The New Deal was the answer to years of fraud, business collapses, and investigations. Was it perfect? No, but it not only created a much-needed social program structure, it also made it far more difficult for the companies controlling economic production to operate in a nontransparent manner. It's high time for a similar revamping of the system.

Today's economic environment isn't quite as weak as it was then. Only 2.7 million payroll jobs were lost between the bust's peak in February 2001 and August 2003, due to speculative growth (frequently based on deceptive corporate practices) out of a total population of 292 million Americans, compared to 25 percent of the working population during the Great Depression.[13] However, given that the deregulation and lack of federal regulatory oversight that caused the 1990s stock bubble aren't being corrected and are in fact worsening, it's likely that the economic weakness following the 2001 stock market bust will stick around at least as long as the Great Depression. As I write this book, we are unfortunately halfway there. Though the stock market itself rebounded slightly in 2003, the sectors that deflated the most, energy and telecom, underperformed dramatically. By the end of 2003 and start of 2004, the financial services firms, particularly mutual funds and banks, were undergoing a fresh round of scandals and fraud discoveries.

THE SECURITIES AND EXCHANGE COMMISSION

The New Deal sought to create regulatory bodies to protect public interests, particularly in industries like banking, energy, and communications that were intrinsic to daily life. It was meant to stop the type of nontransparent and speculative operations companies and banks engaged in throughout the 1920s that proved so dangerous to the country as a whole. One of the most important New Deal contributions arising from the fraudulent corporate and Wall Street practices of the 1920s was the establishment of the

SEC to oversee the stock exchanges and regulate the integrity of securities issued by public companies. It is the SEC's job to validate the integrity of a firm's financial statements and determine whether there is anything intentionally misleading on its balance sheet that can confuse or mislead investors. The SEC failed miserably in that task during the latter half of the 1990s.

The SEC had an operating budget of $413 million in 2001.[14] It took in $44 million in penalties, $478 million in disgorgements (money retrieved from ill-gotten profits), and $2 billion in fees. *Fortune* called it a "moneymaking machine."[15] Of course, it doesn't keep all the money: the U.S. Treasury gets fees and penalties, and fraud victims get their share of disgorgements funds.

Many members of Congress have taken swipes at the SEC over the years, weakening its mission and reach. For instance, Phil Gramm, then-chairman of the Senate banking committee, was downright hostile to proposals to increase the budget of the SEC in 2000. According to him, "We are collecting more than three times as much money as we need to run the Securities and Exchange Commission. This amounts to a general government tax on businesses that are trying to get capital to create jobs. . . . It is my objective as chairman of the Senate Banking Committee to end this situation."[16]

THE FEDERAL COMMUNICATIONS COMMISSION

Another New Deal commission created to protect public interests was the FCC. Until the New Deal, all federal regulation of communications fell under the joint watch of the Department of Commerce and the Interstate Commerce Commission (ICC). In June 1934, under pressure to consolidate telecom regulations for wire (phones) and wireless (radio wave) services under one government body, FDR passed the Communications Act of 1934, which established the FCC.[17] This act laid out three important provisions: first, the airwaves are public property; second, commercial broadcasters must be licensed to use them; and finally, the main condition for airwave use was that the broadcaster served "the public interest, convenience, and necessity." The FCC is charged with regulating interstate and international communications by radio, television, wire, satellite, and cable. Its jurisdiction spans the fifty United States, including the District of Columbia and U.S. possessions.[18] It is also the FCC's job to bless or kill those industries' mergers based on its assessment of a proposed merger's adherence to a measure of competition and public interest. The FCC has fueled the telecom flame with its increasingly deregulatory stance, having rejected only one megamerger in the past thirty-five years.

The FCC answers directly to Congress, which sets overall regulatory policy based on its recommendations. Communications policy, however, tends to be up for sale, as in other industries. The media and telecom sectors are particularly generous political donors. Since 1990—primarily since the 1996 deregulation—they have contributed over $491 million in political donations to Congress and over $1 billion to lobbyists. Those amounts are second only to the financial industry for total political contributions.[19]

THE FEDERAL ENERGY REGULATORY COMMISSION

The third pillar of the New Deal that regulated a crucial public good was the establishment of the organization (or Federal Power Commission) that ultimately became the FERC, the independent regulatory agency now within the Department of Energy that, among other things, monitors the transmission of natural gas for resale, the transmission of oil by pipelines, and the transmission of wholesale electricity between states. Like the FCC, it is responsible for approving or rejecting mergers within the industry it regulates.

FERC is supposed to consist of five commissioners, but despite a $45 billion California energy crisis in the middle of 2000, there were only three standing commissioners from August 2001, until another joined in November, 2003. Underscoring the importance the last couple of administrations have placed on energy regulation, FERC has been streamlining its oversight operations and has cut about 307 jobs, or 25 percent of its staff, since 1991. At the same time, as of this writing we are experiencing a historically high energy merger period, not to mention the current crisis in the industry. The lack of leadership pushing for more stringent enforcement via an increased budget and more personnel reinforces FERC's lack of interest in effecting positive change in the industry by reregulating. As at the FCC, even more deregulation is in the cards. The Bush administration, headed by two former oil CEOs in President Bush and Vice President Cheney, and peppered with figures like former Chevron director

Condoleezza Rice, certainly isn't about to advocate more rules to govern its buddies in the energy industry.

Texas oil makes a strong bond linking its regulators, politicians, and executives; the current head of FERC's framework, Pat Wood III, was appointed by George W. Bush.[20] Wood had been recommended for the state energy watchdog post of chief of the Public Utilities Commission in Texas in 1994 by none other than Enron's former CEO, Ken Lay.[21] Bush was governor of Texas at the time.

THE PUBLIC HOLDING COMPANY ACT OF 1933 (PUHCA)

In addition to establishing FERC, the New Deal created the Public Utility Holding Company Act (PUHCA) in response to a tide of energy company fraud in the 1920s, similar to Enron of the 1990s. At the time, the Federal Trade Commission (FTC) called holding companies a "menace to investors or consumers or both."[22]

The behavior of Enron, El Paso, Williams, Dynegy, and others is startling but is not without some historical precedent. In the 1920s, energy companies also used massive debt associated with profits from noncore activities to create convoluted empires and businesses spanning well beyond their stated purposes. Likewise, the energy companies of the 1990s spawned broadband units and commodity trading operations. The holding companies that sat on top of these scores of diverse businesses were thus able to engage in millions of dollars (billions in today's terms) of sham transactions in the 1920s, as they would in the 1990s.

The fact that there were so many layers of companies within one holding company allowed those companies to transmit profits and expenses back and forth and cloud true revenues. Energy companies of the 1990s effected the same obfuscation—some through the use of special-purpose entities or off-balance sheet companies that were generally more obscure and paid less or no domestic tax compared to companies or subsidiaries clearly included on a corporate balance sheet, and others by creating new types of holding companies that finagled exemptions to PUHCA.

In the 1920s, these holding companies owned controlling stock percentages in local electric utilities across the country, making state regulation incredibly difficult. Utility failures of companies that had reached beyond their local customer bases helped contribute to the 1929 crash, and when the market did crash, many other companies folded under fraud or debt.

PUHCA, enforced by the SEC, was designed to eliminate the stacking of companies within one holding company framework and create greater transparency. It outlawed more than three tiers of subsidiary companies. (Enron's special-purpose entities were exempt from PUHCA because Enron itself was and formed far more than three tiers in which to move money and assets around.) After the implementation of PUHCA, the U.S. electric utility industry was run primarily as a state-regulated monopoly. State utilities could sell in specific service regions at regulated prices, and they engaged in all aspects of their business, generating electricity and distributing it locally and over longer hauls. From a corporate stability perspective, state utilities were solidly rated AAA, the highest credit rating attainable, until the 1996 energy deregulation.

PUHCA further requires that electric, natural gas, and water utilities reinvest money collected from ratepayers into "integrated systems," or utilities designed to operate in an efficient single, coordinated, and transparent system. Until 1992, PUCHA prohibited holding companies from investing ratepayer money into any assets that wouldn't directly result in lower bills or better services for customers, which kept utilities from straying from their core services. This enforced security led to a stable dividend stream and the highest quality ratings for utility companies.

Energy and utility companies launched a massive campaign against PUHCA in 1999. Since then, they have given $150 million in political donations and to lobbyists for PUHCA's repeal. Seventy-two percent of the soft money has gone to the GOP. At the top of the donors' list were American Electric Power, Duke Energy, CMS Energy, and Mirant, all of which are under investigation for fraud and which lost significant market value throughout 2002 yet continue to seek abolishment of government oversight of their activities.[23] Their claim is that PUHCA inhibits them from making sound investments. Of course, they considered broadband sound in the late 1990s, but given the types of debt burdens they have and the bad decisions they've made, it would be far more stable for the long term to concentrate on a more conservative business strategy than piling on more leverage.

Despite (1) blatant collusion among energy power marketers that led to energy market price manipulations in the West, (2) fabricated revenues from wash trades ("when one firm sells energy to another and then the second firm simultaneously sells the same amount of energy back to the first company at exactly the same price. No commodity ever changes hands. But when done on an exchange, these transactions send a price signal to the market and they artificially boost revenue for the company," as California senator Dianne Feinstein defined them) between broad subsidiaries of the same companies, and (3) the continuing decline of the energy industry, Congress effectively indicated intent to repeal PUHCA in 2003.[24] That legislation was proposed under the latest version of the Senate energy bill (S2095) as of early 2004, championed by Senate Majority Leader Bill Frist (R-TN) and House Majority Leader Tom DeLay (R-TX).

DEREGULATION OF THE BANKING INDUSTRY

Regulations established with the New Deal have been systematically dismantled since the 1970s, beginning after Nixon and Ford left office, gaining momentum during the mid-1980s under Reagan, and accelerating in the 1990s with George H.W. Bush and Bill Clinton. Many holding company regulations put in place as part of the New Deal were dismantled in the 1980s and 1990s, allowing banks once again to own shares with associated voting rights, for financial and nonfinancial ventures at the holding company level.

As soon as the Glass-Steagall Act started regulating the banking industry, Wall Street banks began looking for ways to deregulate it. The Bank Holding Company Act of 1984 was one such swipe at regulation. Relaxation of rules governing merchant banking allowed banks to be able to hold entire companies as if they were a portfolio of investments, even if these corporations don't perform banking-related functions, all under their merchant bank license. For example, they could hold interest in an energy company like Alleghany or Enron. At the holding company level, which is the top tier and central trunk of a corporation from which all other subsidiaries emanate, a bank can technically own anything; the subsidiaries don't have to be financially oriented.

Since the high inflation of the 1970s, the walls that divided securities from lending firms have been systematically weakened, culminating in Glass-Steagall's repeal. While all this was going on, the swap market, started only in the early 1980s, grew to a $45 trillion market by 2002. Besides the banks, the biggest customers of swaps were the corporations that generally hedged their own interest-rate exposure on their debt with swaps, usually in connection with a new debt-issuance deal.

There was always a battle going on between the swaps and capital markets desks at banks. The fight revolved around determining who was really responsible for bringing in the corporate business: those underwriting the debt or those hedging it. Who should get the biggest bonuses at the end of the year for their efforts?

The eruption of financial industry mergers began in 1995 and only gained momentum through 1997–2000. It was the initial burst of banking mergers and banks aggressively looking for customers that predated both 1996 deregulation and the flood of related corporate mergers. The biggest telecom merger year was 1999, when almost half a trillion dollars worth of deals took place, a year after the biggest banking merger year.

The more consolidated the banking industry got, the more it needed to keep corporate business going. Debt and loan issuance reached a peak in 2001, after the stock market burst, because banks still had to find a way to get business done, and rates were so low that corporations could issue debt more cheaply even as they were becoming more leveraged and heading toward bankruptcy.

The biggest bank merger of the bubble period was Citigroup's acquisition of Travelers, which closed in October 1998 and was valued at $37 billion. Other notable bank consolidations occurred around the same time. NationsBank took over Bank of America in late 1998. Bank One took over First Chicago in September 1998. The burst of the bubble slowed down merger pace somewhat, but it picked up again in 2003. Bank of America announced their $48 billion takeover of FleetBoston Financial Corporation on October 27, 2003. The deal was approved by the Fed on March 8, 2003. Not to be outdone by Bank of America, JP Morgan Chase announced its own $58 billion acquisition of Bank One on January 14, 2004. Every time one of these mergers happened, banks got a "free" period in which they could write down a portion of bad loans. Normally this meant selling nonperforming loans (on which corporations had ceased interest payments) mixed with "good" loans to an investment bank that securitized defaulted companies. The banks then sold these prepackaged loans off to insurance companies or pension funds, who were eager to buy these products, which generally came with a lot of spread.

GLASS-STEAGALL REPEAL

On November 4, 1999, the United States Senate officially killed Glass-Steagall. It voted 90–8 to approve S900, the Gramm-Leach-Bliley Act, which severed all barriers preventing banking, insurance, and securities firms from combining their services under one umbrella. On that day, Phil Gramm issued the following statement: "I believe we have passed what will prove to be the most important banking bill in sixty years. The Gramm-Leach-Bliley Act strikes down these walls and opens up new competition."[25] Gramm was right—just not for the reasons he thought.

In addition to allowing the legal merger of securities firms and commercial banks, Gramm-Leach-Bliley created a new "financial holding company" clause in the Bank Holding Company Act. The clause allowed for a financial corporation to create a separate financial holding company that could engage in a broad variety of financial activities, regardless of the larger corporation's main functions. These activities ran the gamut from insurance and securities underwriting to merchant banking and insurance company portfolio investment activities. It also authorized dabbling in nonfinancial activities that are "complementary to a financial activity and not posing a substantial risk to the safety or soundness of depository institutions or the financial system generally."[26]

After the act was passed, former Senate majority leader Trent Lott was full of gratitude. Most of it was reserved for Phil Gramm in particular, but Lott also thanked "all those involved . . . obviously Secretary [Robert] Rubin; Alan Greenspan . . . [Treasury] Secretary [Lawrence] Summers . . . leaders in both the House and the Senate (and others) who worked to make this happen." Despite all this government involvement, Gramm told the House, when they passed the companion Financial Services Modernization Act on November 4, 1999, that "Glass-Steagall, in the midst of the Great Depression, thought government was the answer. In this period of economic growth and prosperity, we believe freedom is the answer."[27] Unfortunately, those conditions of growth and prosperity were drastically diminished by a three-year bear market and corresponding recession. Deregulation actually played a major role in inducing the bear market and economic recession by allowing companies to expand on debt into areas in which they had no historic expertise without an overarching plan for logical and sustainable growth or expansion.

WHY NO UPROAR OVER THE GLASS-STEAGALL REPEAL?

Given how much money and market share was at stake between investment banks and supermarket banks, it was remarkable that more investment banks didn't lobby harder against the repeal of Glass-Steagall. They didn't because, quite simply, things were too good. With unprecedented stock market growth, mergers and acquisitions closing left and right, and IPOs making instant millionaires of those with good timing and inside access, there seemed to be plenty of new issuance business, both equity and bond, to go around.

Although investment bankers realized they would lose issuance market share to the supermarket banks, they believed, armed with solid corporate arrogance and ego, that they would maintain most issuance business because of their skill and experience in advising mergers and acquisitions. In other words, they expected their knowledge and past relationships, on the average, to outweigh the temptation of cheap credit from the superbanks. Investment banks were making too much fee money doing mergers and acquisitions for corporations to care much about the less profitable issuance business now open to the überbanks. Investment bankers believed the boom was going to last forever. If they lost some debt deals—which brought in fewer fees than M&A business, after all—so be it.

Ironically, had the markets been less euphoric in the late 1990s during the time of the most intense congressional debates regarding breaking down the barriers Glass-Steagall had erected between lending and issuing institutions, there would have been a clear battle on Capitol Hill between the investment and commercial banks. For, if there had been less business—or the expectation of less business—to go around, the investment banks would have fought much harder to keep the commercial banks from encroaching on their territory.

TELECOM DEREGULATION

The telecom industry has gone through numerous phases of deregulation since the early 1980s. The various players that comprise today's telecom business were each formed by distinct stages of deregulation, each of which, in turn, cut jobs and helped destabilize the economy. First, there was AT&T, providing the country with both local and long-distance telephone service. For the most part, American Telephone and Telegraph operated as a monopoly under U.S. government and FCC regulation until 1984. Competing with AT&T prior to 1984 were long-distance companies like MCI and United Telecommunications (the predecessor to Sprint). Much as banks were given the choice whether to operate in the deposit-and-lending or securities businesses back in 1933, in 1984 AT&T was given the choice between providing local or long-distance service. It chose long-distance, a move which led to a twelve-year turf war between AT&T and its offspring.

The backwash caused by those internecine feuds led to the 1996 Telecommunications Act, the largest legislative overhaul of the communications industry since FDR established the FCC. It passed with overwhelming bipartisan support in both the House (416–16) and the Senate (91–5) and was signed by President Clinton on February 8, 1996.

The 1996 act promised open competition, like every other act of deregulation. Bells or "Baby Bells," the name given to the U.S. regional telephone companies that emerged from the breakup of the AT&T (or Ma Bell) empire in 1984, would get long-distance business in return for offering wire access to smaller local companies or new entrants (new telecoms). Additionally, they were expected to compete with each other, driving down the prices of local calls and driving up the number and quality of services offered. It was also assumed that new, superior technology would spawn demand. But the general public never fared as well as Congress and the FCC promised they would. Although long-distance rates have fallen 50 percent since 1984, they barely budged after 1996, and those declining rates disproportionately benefited business and bulk users. Plus, the reductions were mostly due to regulated cuts to line access charges, not deregulation. Not only that, declining business rates were effectively subsidized by less frequent users (generally lower on the economic totem pole), whose rates have increased 20 percent since 1984. Since 2002, long-distance rates have crept upward for everyone, from an average of 7 cents a minute in 2002 to 22.5 cents a minute in 2003.[28]

In 1996, the Bells serviced 48 percent of the country's phone lines. Today, the four remaining Bells (Verizon, SBC, Bellsouth, and Qwest) control 94 percent. Local rates have risen by 17 percent. Competitors, or CLECs (competitive local exchange carriers), failed in droves and blamed the Bells for restricting access. But the CLECs are tiny political contributors, and no one really cared.

The 1996 act provided the perfect marketing opportunity for companies wanting to get in on the nascent Internet wave: local lines were begging to be utilized for the online revolution. Upstart companies had a shot at dominating the Internet by muscling into these existing lines, but they needed loans to fund themselves. To back these loans, they needed newly minted stock. To keep up the currency, or acquisition value, of that stock, they needed praise from analysts. Wall Street complied eagerly, meeting all these needs. Then these predators, whose existence was contingent on inflating stocks to use as currency to buy up smaller existing and established companies and take over their businesses, went on a shopping spree, gobbling up companies or networks to create their sand-castle empires. That's how WorldCom acquired MCI, Global Crossing acquired Frontier, and Qwest acquired US West. The result was a fee-fest on Wall Street as banks fell over themselves to raise the $1.5 trillion of debt the sector demanded. Wall Street has pocketed $15 billion in telecom fees since the 1996 deregulation, far more than the mere $3 billion they received after the 1984 deregulation.

Domestic deregulation in 1996 was followed by global telecom liberalization blessed by the World Trade Organization (WTO) in February 1998, and entities like Global Crossing, 360networks, Winstar, PSInet, Exodus, and other doomed novelties were spawned across oceans as U.S. companies moved into foreign markets and new, similar telecoms started up overseas. Their goal was to build global fiber-optic networks that would meet all future communication needs, real and imagined. Sixty-nine countries committed to reducing communication barriers to market access and foreign investment and removing national restrictions at WTO. As a result, a slew of international mergers and negotiations for acquisitions took place. The practice of tax dodging by distributing revenues into countries with the most favorable regulatory environments, like Ireland, became even more widespread. By early 2001, in a period of only five years, telecoms had built over twenty times more capacity than demanded. The "Capacity Glut," as it was dubbed by the American press, could not have reached such mammoth proportions (enough fiber miles to circle the globe 11,000 times) if not for the massive global deregulation that accompanied U.S. deregulation. In many ways, the telecom disaster is the biggest industry disaster of corporate globalization. This sector raised the most debt, enjoyed the highest fabricated stock values and subsequently ate through the most debt, stock values, and millions of jobs worldwide.

Large carriers and Internet providers muscled their way into the local phone line market mostly by buying up existing companies and feeding on the revenue bases of the firms they acquired. Because more customers failed to materialize, the companies turned to accounting fraud to make it look like there was demand. When telecom executives discovered they didn't have enough revenue to pay off their debt, they did two things. First, they fabricated earnings to keep the appearance of the fiber-optic dream alive. Second, they escaped with the dough. The executives of the bankrupt telecoms alone siphoned off $2.2 billion from stock and option sales.

In October 2002, the NASDAQ telecom index fell 93 percent from its March 2000 highs. By the end of 2003, it was still down 86 percent off those highs.[29] Smaller carriers that had failed to get a slice of the acquisition pie were the first to go under as overcapacity swelled. The next to go were the new local-service companies that had sprung out of the 1996 deregulation. Those Internet carriers and local-service companies accounted for most of the telecom sector's sixty-plus bankruptcies. Then, starting in 2001, midsize Internet-based telecom companies dropped like flies, including 360networks, Winstar, Exodus, and a host of others. By 2002, giants like WorldCom, Global Crossing, and Adelphia had followed suit. That's not to mention Qwest, Lucent, Nortel, and others still flirting with financial failure.

The public interest was hardly served by a $1.8 trillion merger spree in a deregulated broadband-based market mania in which a half a million people lost jobs, 92 percent of the market value of telecoms eroded in the stock markets, and eleven of the top twenty-five U.S. bankruptcies of all time (six of which were under SEC investigation for fraud) were produced. The sector's implosion occurred after telecommunication executives walked away with a total of $18 billion.[30] Workers were forced to pay for the executives' greed and poor and corrupt management with lost pensions and jobs, while consumers paid with increased rates and worse service. Competition does not equal choice if mergers wipe companies away before they can take root and establish their services. It's not even logical to assume it would. There seems to be a willful failure to recognize the interrelationship of deregulation and the mergers of both companies and banks.

ENERGY DEREGULATION

Deregulation of the energy industry took place in four main stages over the past twenty-five years. The oil industry strongly lobbied for each one. Rather than opening the door to what was dubbed "further competition," these deregulatory steps were in fact a systematic dissolution of what had once been a stable sector. The four stages were: passage of the Public Utility Regulatory Policies Act (PURPA) in 1978, a series of competitive bidding processes to build new power plants in the 1980s, the passage of Energy Policy Act of 1992, and the implementation of Order 888 in 1996 leading to state-by-state deregulation.

PURPA opened the door for independent power producers (like Enron) who were not affiliated with regulated utility industries to get into the energy business. Such companies had no allegiance or responsibility to their retail consumers because they were not obligated to be located near their core customer bases; thus, their activities were not regulated and could not be monitored by the regulatory commissions of the states where they operated. It was enacted at the height of the 1970s energy crisis, during the rise of OPEC and the oil embargo, and required utilities to buy power from these independent power producers instead of producing energy themselves.

The competitive bidding required between 1984 and 1996 meant that existing U.S. electric utilities had to request bids from independent producers for energy. When the practice was initiated, utilities received bids up to eleven times the amount of necessary energy capacity from independent power producers, a sure sign of future instability to come. It was also a sign that, given the chance, these independent producers would create a capacity surplus, which they did, ultimately fueling a larger disintegration of the sector in general. Independent producers built half of all new generating capacity in the United States between 1985 and 1995, and in the process acquired a whole lot of debt.

The Energy Policy Act came about because independent power producers, like Enron, were annoyed that they couldn't move their electricity when they wanted to whomever they wanted. Buckling to demands from Enron, AEP, Duke, CMS, and other independent power marketers, Congress removed that obstacle with the 1992 act.[31] The act required electric utilities to allow open access to their transmission lines, much as the 1996

Telecommunications Act required the regional Bell phone companies to open their phone lines to independent network builders, which sometimes included energy companies.

FERC realized that if larger corporate customers left the public utility services to get independent services at cheaper prices—and let's face it, Enron wasn't in the business of supplying electricity to Grandma's house down the road—then smaller consumers would have to pick up the tab with increased costs. So, under Order 888, FERC required wholesale corporate customers to pay a minor charge to cover their share of these leftover costs from switching services. As of February 2003, twenty-four states and the District of Columbia had either deregulated or were in the process of deregulating, allowing open access to their transmission lines.[32]

Right away, the new independent power companies had a competitive advantage over the incumbent utilities, much as the new emerging Internet carriers, like Global Crossing, had had an advantage over local phone companies. They had no debt or stranded costs left over from previous deregulation (like unrecovered capital investment following the 1978 regulation), which public utility companies largely passed on to their customers in the form of higher locked-in rates. Since it typically takes thirty to forty years for a regulated electric utility to recover its power plan investments, part of that investment would never be returned if markets were open to competition before the investment was paid back through formerly predictable rates. Other costs included contracts to purchase electricity in the future at above-market, or unregulated, rates as well as power plant overhead.[33]

In 1996, California became the first state to restructure its electric utility industry and was soon followed by twenty other states that year.[34] The states that deregulated first have suffered the most in terms of price and market manipulations. Consumers bore the highest costs while the utility industry converted from a stable state- and government-controlled monopoly to a free-for-all speculative arena of independent power producers. The twenty-one states that deregulated in 1996 have suffered and continue to suffer the greatest losses and highest volatility of prices.

Energy merger deals reached their peak in 1998, including British Petroleum's takeover of Amoco in December. The all-time biggest, however, remains Exxon's takeover of Mobil in late 1999, an $87 billion deal at the time of its December 1998 announcement. Advisers on the biggest energy deals tended to be the same banks who worked on the biggest telecom mergers: Goldman Sachs, Morgan Stanley, Salomon Brothers, Merrill Lynch, and JP Morgan Chase, among others. By 2000, the top ten utilities owned half of the capacity in the country, up from one-third before the 1992 Energy Policy Act.

Energy deregulation paved the path for power marketers to swoop in and buy and trade transmission lines for profit. They then advertised substantial savings for existing state utility customers if they switched to new providers. But electricity prices were not positively affected by deregulation, as its proponents would have us believe. In fact, they have stayed the same or declined in thirty-three of the last forty regulated years.[35] Pennsylvania had the greatest number of consumers switch to competing suppliers—530,000 out of 5 million residential consumers by April 2002. However, 180,000 eventually switched back due to poor or discontinued service.

The energy sector suffered a slower meltdown than the telecom sector, but that was largely because not all of the states in the country deregulated simultaneously. Still, it produced some gem bankruptcies. El Paso, for example, which placed second (just behind Enron) in energy trading volume and first in electricity trading volume in 2001, had $25 billion in debt and suffered a five-notch downgrade in ratings in early February 2003. Its CEO, William Wise, stepped down at the end of 2003 without a replacement in sight; El Paso merely stated it was in the midst of its "CEO transition process."[36]

The underlying values of energy company stock and assets have been depreciating substantially. Eight of the top ten energy companies that became all-purpose trading and independent power companies after 1992's and then 1996's deregulation lost, on average, 80 to 90 percent of their market value over 2002.[37]

MERGER MAYHEM

The merger mania wave of the 1980s, fueled by corporate raiders swooping in and acquiring companies through leveraged buyouts in which they garnered a big enough percentage of outstanding shares to take over these companies, was certainly spectacular. It paled, however, in comparison to the late 1990s post-deregulation run of mergers financed through inflated stock as currency. Bank mergers further ignited telecom and energy mergers resulting from the deregulation wave of legislation such as the 1996 Telecom Act and the Electric Consumers' Power to Choose Act of 1996. Coinciding with Glass-Steagall repeal, investment banks found themselves in a quandary as the stakes got higher and the number of corporations to gobble up declined. Competitor supermarket banks could offer all kinds of credit in the form of loans in exchange for, or in addition to, investment banking services. Investment banks had to resort to beefing up "added value business" like mergers and acquisitions, structured finance, and credit derivatives.

Teams of investment bankers hit the road with glossy pitch books and aggressively pushed customers to do more business with them; more business meant more money and ferreting it out was the only way to stay competitive with the commercial banks. Meanwhile, commercial bankers convinced corporations that bigger and broader was better than smaller and smarter. This worked well while the stock markets were humming along and rendering every corporate decision ingenious.

While banks were adapting their strategies to the new competition, the telecom and energy industries were undergoing the biggest wave of deregulation seen since the New Deal. With the regulatory handcuffs off, companies could go on an acquisition binge, merging with or acquiring whatever they saw fit. The market was wide open. They didn't even have to go through the clunky old leveraged-buyout mechanisms of the 1980s Michael Milken days, which entailed purchasing enough stock in target companies to gain majority control in them and then execute a hostile takeover.

Since 1990, U.S. corporations underwent 9.4 trillion dollars' worth of mergers, in a staggering 201,712 separate deals. Over half of these took place after 1999. Similarly, non-U.S. corporations led over $8.7 trillion of merger volume, or 117,727 deals. In the process, Wall Street firms raked in over $70 billion in fees for consolidating these companies, raising debt in multiple currencies, and issuing stock on various global exchanges. The fastest pace of consolidation came from the industries undergoing the most deregulation, and they had lobbied hard for the privilege. Since 1990, the financial, energy, and telecom sectors combined gave Washington over $2 billion in soft- and hard-money contributions.

The 1990s method of buying companies was so much easier: all you had to do was make sure your stock was propped up high enough and then use it as currency. You could even get all the management and employees in the target company excited about the prospect of owning your skyrocketing stock. In the communications industry, this created a gold rush mentality as new predator carrier companies scrambled to build, or piece together through buying, parts of fiber-optic networks. Likewise, energy companies went on a generator grab that ultimately led to mass market manipulation of the most deregulated states, like California, Nevada, Oregon, and Washington. The fact that energy companies also became trading houses free of any of the restrictive disclosure requirements assigned to the energy trading operations of banks meant they could profit by trading the same energy they controlled and distributed simply by redirecting or withholding it when they wanted.

The late 1990s were all about the next merger being grander than the last. The highest volume of mergers and debt issuance occurred after the most sweeping deregulation. Over 91 percent of energy mergers since 1990, worth $1 trillion, occurred after 1996. Likewise, over 93 percent of telecom mergers, worth $1.8 trillion, occurred after 1990. The financial sector recorded $1.7 trillion of its own mergers since 1990, 81 percent of which occurred after these client industries deregulated. Yet, because of the 1980s residue of sharklike takeovers (like the notorious RJR-Nabisco deal documented in *Barbarians at the Gate*), the word "acquisition" was almost erased from merger language. Instead, the public descriptions of these transactions were friendly, proconsumer, procompetition: the "target" company got rising stock, the acquirer got synergy.

It is nearly impossible to identify any merger that turned out to be net beneficial from an economic or consumer standpoint. In particular, the merger-happy telecom industry, over-betting on the Internet, created a series of megamergers that each failed to some degree, whether manifested as fraud, layoffs, salary reductions, bankruptcy, or poor service.

In each case, merger applicants had to convince the FCC and the Department of Justice that their merger was procompetitive, synergistic, and in the best interests of the public. The top ten telecom mergers of all time began with WorldCom-MCI, then the biggest, which closed in September 1998. When the deal was announced in October 1997, the value of the combined WorldCom-MCI was $42 billion. By the time it closed a year later, it was worth $37 billion. Soon after the merger, WorldCom stock reached its high of $64. By July 2002, it was bankrupt and its stock traded at 9 cents. By February 2002, the company's value had declined to $415 million.

The AOL Time Warner merger was announced at a staggering $165 billion value. When it closed, the value had shrunk to $105 billion. Today, the company is valued at $47 billion and declining. As the market fell throughout 2001, the pace of mergers slowed and the difference between their announced and closing values widened. For example, AT&T and Comcast's merger was announced in July 2001 at a value of $72 billion. By the time it closed, in November 2002, it was worth $29 billion, a 64 percent deterioration.[38] That's astonishing, especially when you consider that AT&T-Comcast consisted mostly of the failed AT&T-TCI merger, which had been worth $46 billion in November 2000. The Qwest-US West merger had a combined market value of $56 billion when it was announced in June 1999. Today, the entity is valued at $2 billion.

Yet corporations continue to pour hundreds of millions of dollars into lobbying for further "freedoms" that merely mask their true businesses, earnings, and intents. Greater maneuverability in the 1990s translated into gross instability and losses. Bank commercial loan losses doubled each year since 2000. Corporate default volumes achieved record highs. Noncurrent loan balances at banks doubled in 2002 as corporate loan payments became increasingly delinquent.

Many corporations, like Lucent, Nortel, Dynegy, Qwest, Mirant, El Paso, and CMS Energy, continue to struggle to meet their debt obligations, barely keeping out of default or bankruptcy. While much of the air has been let out of the stock market balloon, debt investors still have yet to feel the same pain. This is because bonds and loans can go through multiple restructurings to extend payment schedules without actually erasing the debt altogether.

The insurance industry in the United States bought most of the corporate bonds and loans that the banks issued either in pure, derivative, or packaged form. More frightening is the fact that many of these insurance companies own or are owned by the very banks that created the debt to begin with, thanks to holding company deregulation and the repeal of Glass-Steagall. Current accounting law does not require them to disclose credit losses, which means they could be sitting on a several-trillion-dollar powder keg of debt that the banks and their accumulation-hungry corporate customers created.

Deregulation leads directly to mergers; mergers lead to more debt accumulation. Since 1996, the financial, telecom, energy, manufacturing, and health-care sectors issued a total of $7 trillion of debt. Additionally, loan volume from 1996 to 2002 was four times what it had been during the first half of the 1990s. More debt leads to bankruptcy. Fraud, corruption, and defaults come along the way. This pattern repeats every time there's an unregulated speculative expansion, and it will continue until appropriate regulation curtails it. Yet, there is no indication that anyone in Congress has a clue about the connection between a bad regulatory environment and irresponsible, criminal corporate behavior. That means that the only thing that's keeping mergers, stock inflation, and debt issuance suppressed at the moment is the poor state of the economy, coupled with a small measure of investor skepticism, and a few toothless reforms. These are merely temporary deterrents.

From a regulatory perspective, the country is almost right back to the point where it was before Glass-Steagall, PUHCA, and other protective legislation was put in place to recover from the landslide depression of the 1930s. Everything remains in place for a continued downward slide or a repeat performance of the millennium bubble-and-bust—if we ever manage to really dig ourselves out.

4

Enron, Energy, and Entropy

I'm upbeat about America, I truly am. I think this is a country that is going to
show the rest of the world how to deal wisely with energy.

—President George W. Bush, May 16, 2001

Enron is moving so fast that sometimes others have trouble defining us.

—1999 Enron annual report

ENRON, THE GOLDMAN SACHS OF MERCHANT ENERGY

WHEN MY HEADHUNTER INFORMED ME GOLDMAN SACHS WAS INTERESTED
in me, I was flattered. It wasn't the first time a headhunter had approached me with some stunning job offer, but this was the first time the
offer had come from Goldman Sachs. Jaded as I had become about the industry, after thirteen years, it was an ego-inflating last hurrah.

I wasn't even certain that I wanted to leave Bear Stearns, my employer at
the time. Of all the places I had worked, around the Street and around the
world, I still had a soft spot for Bear after seven years. I grew up there as a
person, as a professional, as a banker. Bear wasn't the most prestigious
of firms; in fact there were clients, particularly in Europe, who openly
snubbed us. They thought we were blatant money-grubbing crooks compared to our higher-budgeted, top-tier competitors, who were more subtle
in the art of gouging clients. Still, we enjoyed a certain underdog status and
very colorful management. Bear chairman Alan "Ace" Greenberg was a
Wall Street legend, a millionaire who did magic tricks on the trading floor.
He was known for his economically prudent wisdom, particularly his famous mantra: never use paper clips. Paper clips were a waste. More expensive, less solid, and less permanent than staples. Why bother? But paper
clips were nothing compared to the excesses born of falseness that characterized the 1990s boom.

Despite my affection for Bear Stearns, I took the Goldman Sachs offer.
I joined the research department. There, one of my major responsibilities

was managing the credit derivatives strategy group. It was in commodity and credit derivatives trading that companies like Enron collided with companies like Goldman.

At its pinnacle, power marketer Enron was the Goldman Sachs of the energy sector: prestigious, aggressive, and envied. It was the new economy, "asset-light, trading-heavy" crème de la crème of corporate America. It was a place where excellence was rewarded with huge salaries and bonuses even though, as on Wall Street, praise was often as fleeting as one's last big trade. So, it was no accident that Enron started accumulating award after award, year after year, for Most Creative this and Most Original that. It was the most highly skilled energy company when it came to designing complex financial instruments and transactions. It was equally adept at lobbying to destroy old regulatory boundaries in order to trade around them. If you couldn't be a hotshot top-tier Wall Street trader, you could come in a close second by joining Enron's rapidly expanding team, with ambitions no less grandiose than to dominate the world's power trading business.

Enron's former chairman and CEO Ken Lay perpetuated the superstar status that epitomized the "culturization" of Enron employees. He acknowledged in numerous internal e-mails and memos that every individual on the Enron team was a unique contributor to the prestigious whole, and therefore possessed the power to change the economy, the flow of trade, the way the world did business. Everyone was supposed to be a visionary. Unencumbered with things like real assets, Enron shot to the top of everyone's corporate A-list, particularly among investors and lenders. It enjoyed its own special glory, even as dot-coms became the temporary new world order. In the process, Wall Street began ever so slightly to lose its edge to Enron and other emerging corporate trading companies that were unhampered by the financial rules that even the most creative Wall Street teams had to observe.

It was that sense of self-importance, that deeply ingrained exceptionalness that propelled Enron's striving to concoct the most intricate of deals. For it wasn't that Enron was simply looking to dominate its own industry; it wanted to take on Wall Street at its own game. So it took advantage of the intersection of three major loopholes that fell between the cracks of various aspects of deregulation. These spanned accounting, financial trading, and energy trading. It effectively transformed itself into a corporate trading god, while at the same time masking its escalating weaknesses, losses, and debt accumulation.

When Enron finally fell to earth, the journey was fast and the impact was hard. But, while it was up on top, it left its corporate competition in the dust with the sheer intricacy and volume of its financial engineering. It wasn't that any one Enron deal was more complicated than any other energy corporation's or even that it was unique; they all engaged in the same kind of financial maneuvering in conjunction with the same set of banks. It was the comparative difficulty of connecting the dots between all the Enron-established special-purpose vehicles and pseudo-operations, which Enron had designed to be impossibly complicated. Ultimately, the examination of Enron's activities revealed a slew of other market manipulations and deceptions. These prevailed across the entire energy industry, were aided by an identical set of Wall Street co-conspirators, and went largely ignored by Washington.

THE POWER ENERGY SECTOR BUILD-UP AND MELTDOWN

In order to fully appreciate the intricacies and impact of energy deregulation, political maneuvering, Wall Street's role, Enron, and the rest of the power energy marketers, it is important to understand that none of the relationships are linear. Indeed, dissecting all the reasons and methods behind the 1990s stock inflation, debt accumulation, and subsequent deceit, fraud, and economic deterioration can seem inordinately complicated. The common link was simple; it was money. And every activity undertaken by corporations that involved money also involved banks.

Power marketer or "merchant" energy companies took advantage of deregulation to build and acquire power-generating plants. As a group, they ran a close second to telecoms for debt collection, stock inflation, asset write-downs, downgrades, and bankruptcy. They not only controlled the creation and distribution of energy, but engaged in a host of speculative financial pursuits designed to inflate profits and screw consumers and shareholders. Without government scrutiny or any semblance of transparency, they traded everything: natural gas, electricity, bandwidth, the risk of earthquakes, the amount of rainfall per season, the number of advertising pages newspapers could count on during economic downturns. There were no liquid or price-regulated markets for these transactions because many of them were traded in derivative form or designed for very particular and limited uses. There was no objective evaluation for them.

This, in effect, gave Enron and others the license to simply make up values and book them as profits.

Even though Enron's frauds captured a disproportionate share of the media and congressional spotlight, its actions were not unique. Every other merchant energy company benefited from a dismantling of regulations—both of the energy industry itself and of its ability to trade its own products for profit. The SEC or FERC will be investigating flailing energy companies for years. Many of these companies staved off bankruptcies only by significant debt restructurings that merely prolong the inevitable. It is a sector that for five years (from 1996 to 2001) paid more attention to numbers on balance sheets and manipulative trading practices than the actual distribution of the energy it created. When the party was over, the sector was in shambles. It had vaporized half a trillion dollars of stock market value, tens of thousands of jobs, and hundreds of billions of dollars of pension money.[1]

THE GRAMMS

The manipulation of regulatory procedure, the susceptibility of regulators to the whims of electoral politics, and the fact that the energy sector was deemed so arcane had dire consequences. It allowed experts to freely switch job alliances between public and private sectors. This set the stage for energy deregulation to wreak as much havoc as it did.

Deregulation paved the way to fewer corporate competitors and political operators exerting greater power and influence over the public. Rarely does it lead to anything but temporarily increased competition. This is quickly mitigated as soon as mergers increase, leaving fewer companies controlling more market share. A handful of people in both the public and private sectors took advantage of this situation to "personalize" structural changes and maximize the benefits to their companies. In the energy sector, and for Enron in particular, these changes came via a self-interested network of politicians and their appointees.

The political abetting of intensely harmful and fraud-enabling deregulation was personified in the duo of Phil and Wendy Gramm in the early 1990s. The couple—he a Texas senator, she the chair of the Commodity Futures Trading Commission (CFTC)—were leaders in removing the rules that would have forced companies like Enron to be more transparent through closely monitored activities and well-defined boundaries.[2]

On November 16, 1992, a fledgling Enron (but one that already enjoyed strong ties between its CEO Ken Lay and then-president, George H. W. Bush) requested that Wendy Gramm exempt Enron's energy derivatives and swap trading businesses from government oversight and disclosure.

Shortly thereafter, Ms. Gramm happily obliged, but she selected her moment very wisely. She chose a lame-duck, lost-between-elections period to make her move. George H. W. Bush had decisively lost the presidential election to upstart Democrat Bill Clinton. As a last minute procorporate maneuver, the week before Clinton's inauguration on January 20, 1993, Wendy Gramm initiated the rule-making process that eventually led to removal of Enron's financial oversight. Her exemption rules would ultimately be approved by the Senate Banking Committee (chaired by Phil Gramm) in the middle of 1993, during the beginning of the Clinton presidency.

Six days after the exemption was put into practice under Wendy Gramm's rationale that it would be "too complicated" for shareholders of nonfinancial corporations to be bothered with going through the details of their financial trading activities, she resigned from her CFTC post.[3] About five weeks later, she was elected to Enron's board of directors, where she served for nine years.[4] Wendy Gramm did well at Enron: from 1993 to 2001 her salary, attendance fees, stock option sales, and dividends totaled between $915,000 and $1.85 million.[5] Her stock options swelled from $15,000 in 1995 to approximately $500,000 by 2000.

Not only was she on Enron's board, but Wendy Gramm was also on the board's audit committee. (Her pal George W. Bush had served on a similar committee during his time on the board at Harken Energy Corporation.) She therefore would have been privy to inside knowledge of Enron's financial make-up that was not available to average shareholders. In that audit capacity, she should have known about the 874 tax-haven subsidiaries that allowed Enron to funnel billions of dollars to offshore accounts.[6]

Her husband Phil was also the beneficiary of Enron's generosity; he was the second largest congressional recipient of Enron campaign contributions, receiving $97,350 since 1989.[7] The two influential Texans, Gramm and Lay, were close allies.

By the end of 2000, Phil Gramm had a prime opportunity to repay Enron. He led an effort to bury key commodity deregulation legislation

(S3283, Commodity Futures Modernization Act) by hiding it in an unrelated appropriations bill. At the same time, the Supreme Court was otherwise engaged with issuing a ruling that catapulted George W. Bush into the White House, despite a popular vote victory from his challenger Al Gore.[8] The Commodity Futures Modernization Act had first been introduced earlier that year, in June 2000, and if it had passed as it was originally worded, it would have placed tighter regulations on Enron's energy trading activities. But, that month, Enron's political action committee went into high gear and contributed $220,000 in soft money to both the Republican and Democratic parties. They also lobbied heavily for exemptions to various kinds of derivative trading—their forte—to be added to the act.[9] Eventually, they got what they wanted: a critical exemption. When the appropriations bill passed in December 15, 2000, that exemption became known as the "Enron exclusion."

The bill was signed into law by President Clinton on December 21, 2000. Just days after the bill took effect, California was plunged into a monthlong nightmare of rolling blackouts. Combined with California's electricity deregulation legislation, the commodity-trading deregulation law enabled Enron to operate beyond public or federal scrutiny. It also enabled other Texas power marketers like Dynegy and El Paso to get away with smaller versions of Enron-esque maneuvers.

In addition, the exemption rubber-stamped Enron's operation of its nascent but growing online energy trading business.[10] Enron had been running Enron Online (EOL) since 1999, and its trade revenues accounted for 90 percent of Enron's overall revenue that year.[11] EOL was supposedly designed to enable Enron to trade with its own counterparties or to hedge its positions, meaning Enron would always be on one side of each transaction. Instead, it morphed into an online system that enabled Enron to act as a regular financial broker.

After the passage of Gramm's oversight removal bill, the EOL trading system was legally transformed from a counterparty into a corporate, commodity, and derivatives trading intermediary, or an investment bank of sorts involved in transactions between corporations. It was able to officially act as a brokerage house just like any other Wall Street brokerage, but without the associated regulations to inhibit its activities. Operating an online, unregulated, unmonitored commodities exchange trading business, Enron garnered even more market share than before Gramm's legislation was passed.

ENERGY TRADING DEREGULATION

It was in the interest of investment banks to promote the deregulation of financial activities of their corporate clients. The fewer rules governing the derivative transactions that nonfinancial corporations engaged in, the more money Wall Street could extract by structuring and trading them with these firms. Thus, it was unsurprising that the kingpins of bank deregulation, such as Robert Rubin, former Clinton treasury secretary, former co-chairman of Goldman Sachs, and then vice chairman of Citigroup, were heavily involved in ensuring the financial activities between corporations, and banks would be, at best, loosely monitored.

In April 1998, a meeting took place between Rubin and Brooksley Born, the new head of the CFTC who had replaced Mary L. Schapiro, who chaired the commission in 1994–1996.[12] In stark contrast to Wendy Gramm, Born actually attempted to *create* regulation. In particular, Born wanted more regulation of the over-the-counter (OTC) derivatives market, which had quintupled in size to $29 trillion in the six years since regulation of financial commodity instruments had last undergone serious debate. OTC derivatives are a bit like over-the-counter drugs because you don't need any special paperwork or permission to use or sell them.[13]

Born was understandably worried about leaving this massive market unregulated and nontransparent. Unfortunately, she was up against some major deregulation heavyweights. Rubin was not about to piss Wall Street off by making a large portion of its corporate customer base disclose the exact nature of the highly lucrative derivative instruments Wall Street was selling them or advising them to construct. In June 1998, in response to Born's plight to regulate the OTC derivative market, Robert Rubin, Alan Greenspan, and Arthur Levitt issued an unprecedented joint statement. In it, they attacked a May 1998 release by the CFTC arguing that it was necessary to reevaluate a 1993 swaps exemption to the Commodity Exchange Act. The letter stated, "We believe that it was not Congress's intent when it enacted the Future Trading Practices Act of 1992 to allow the CFTC to impose unilaterally a comprehensive regulatory scheme for the OTC derivatives market."[14]

Chase Manhattan lobbied Congress to block the CFTC's study on regulation in early May 1998.[15] That pretty much shut down the conversation. Greenspan still maintains that these unregulated derivatives somehow made markets safer and insulated flailing companies from worse fates, even though the corporations most heavily involved in the OTC derivatives market had the biggest fraud disclosures and losses.

DEREGULATING ENERGY VIA WASHINGTON

Through political contributions, focused lobbying, and cozy relationships, Enron paid to have federal rules dismantled; Ken Lay personally gave $772,850 in political contributions during the 2000 election.[16] But it wasn't the only company to do so. Since 1990, the energy sector donated over $320 million to politicians, 69 percent to Republicans and 31 percent to Democrats.[17] Industry lobbying and deregulation went hand in hand in the 1990s, though this certainly was not unique to the energy sector. The money and influence which characterized Enron's business strategy had the effect of helping its compatriots as well. Dynegy (lobbying via its parent, Chevron-Texaco), El Paso, Williams, Reliant, and others all counted on the same deregulation to allow them to expand their corporations out of the creation and into the trading of energy. Their most significant profits would come from control and manipulation of commodity prices and markets—particularly as states restructured their electricity frameworks in 1999 (the year in which deregulation was put into effect, following its establishment on 1996)—not through service and customer satisfaction.

During an early 1996 House Commerce Committee meeting, Lay discounted all arguments made in opposition to deregulation, citing his experience with natural gas deregulation. He layered this with a time-honored conservative excuse for deregulation: the more open the market playing field, the more companies will fill in the space and the more choices consumers will have. "I still remember some of the protests against 'open access' competition for the interstate gas market a decade ago," Lay said. "Too risky; bad for consumers; reliability will suffer; it won't work."[18] In fact, the interstate gas market Lay mentioned suffered a slew of problems. Deregulation spurred an increase in consolidation, causing less competition between wholesale and interstate distribution. Leading up to the California electricity crisis, the lack of interstate boundaries caused an increase in the competition between parent and affiliates of the same company, not between different companies.

The first year Enron broke into the top-ten energy political contributors list was 1994. That year, the number one contributor was Atlantic

Richfield, run by Lodwrick Cook, an old friend of George H. W. Bush who wound up on the board of Global Crossing three years later. Campaign contributions bought legislation. Thus, Enron and Lay had a strong hand in shaping energy policy. In March 2002, it was reported that Enron had spent $2.46 million, up from an originally stated $825,000, to influence energy policy decisions.[19] The total of their political donations was eventually disclosed as $3.5 million. In addition, $6.7 million was spent in federal lobbying for the 1998 and 2000 election cycles.[20]

Enron's core strategy was to turn electricity into a speculative commodity and escape government oversight. Deregulation of financial activities for corporations spurred revenues at Enron Gas Services to jump substantially by April 2000.[21] Enron's "wholesale service" revenues leapt from $12 billion in the first quarter of 2000 to $48.4 billion in the first quarter of 2001.[22] Along, the way, about 600 employees deemed "critical to Enron's operations" bagged more than $100 million in bonuses in November 2000.[23] Enron's revenues rose astronomically, increasing over $70 billion from the previous year.[24] A host of other power companies benefited from a playing field without rules and a president and vice president who didn't care.

It was the height of California's electricity crisis that coincided with the pinnacle of Enron Wholesale Services' revenues, which topped $96 billion for the first half of 2001, a 350 percent increase over the same period in 2000.[25] Churning California kept Enron afloat despite mounting debt and real losses which were beginning to surface in areas of the Enron empire not involved in trading electricity. Meanwhile, its top executives cashed more than $1 billion out of the company. Manipulation of California's electricity markets and related trading was the piggy bank that kept the entire sector profitable well past the bull market's peak. The NASDAQ, which listed technology, telecoms, and all the dot-com upstarts, reached its peak in March 2000 and then began its dramatic three-year descent. Energy companies didn't start to really falter until the middle of 2001. Manipulating prices and power in California kept them going longer.

ENRON'S RISE

Enron wasn't the first major energy collapse of the twenty-first century, nor the last—just the most famous (so far). Before Enron's massive fraud disclosure and bankruptcy in December 2001, California Pacific Gas & Electric (PG&E) became the first major post–energy deregulation tragedy, going bankrupt with $21 billion in assets on April 6, 2001.[26] Another major California utility, Southern California Edison, one of the largest electric utilities in the United States, remains hampered by heavy expenses and debt. The difference between PG&E and Enron was that PG&E collapsed amid economic decline largely caused by unregulated power marketers poaching its territory, not scandal and fraud.

Right up until its bankruptcy, Enron's timing and political and financial prowess were unmatched in its sector. Its ability to reinvent itself as a trading dynamo from its roots as a small pipeline company sprang from the very worst political incest, deregulation, and market and financial instruments manipulation.

Enron began in 1985 as a merger between two natural gas pipeline companies, Houston Natural Gas and InterNorth. Over the years it mutated from a regulated energy company focused on distributing gas from producers to power plants and then to customers into a deregulated energy trading powerhouse. It then moved as quickly as possible into commodities trading, stepping up from trading gas in 1989 to trading electrons in 1994. Still, even by 1997, 60 percent of Enron's revenues were coming from regulated pipeline activities.[27]

In 1999, having added bandwidth trading, as well as pulp and paper, plastics, and metals trading to its repertoire, the trading operation became Enron's largest moneymaker. This was in no small part due to the profit it extracted by being a highly knowledgeable middleman for its growing list of corporate clients. In that sense, the banks from which it began to steal clients had created their very own monster, a partner and competitor all in one. Enron dominated energy trading and, at the same time, created markets for trading all sorts of esoteric derivatives. By 1999, the business revenues makeup had morphed to 90 percent trading revenue and just 10 percent pipeline business.[28] Enron's annual report that year stated, "We are satisfied with nothing less than the very best in everything we do. We will continue to raise the bar for everyone. The great fun here will be for all of us to discover just how good we can really be."[29] And discover they did. In 2000, on the back of heavy trading volumes, Enron's overall business revenues soared by 87 percent.

ENRON DECEPTIONS

During its years of operation, Enron created 2,832 subsidiaries, 31 percent of them offshore. Most were so multilayered and purposely convoluted, in terms of their construction and relationship to Enron, that no one at the SEC bothered to question them. In addition, Enron created a series of trading strategies that served to increase their trading revenues at the expense of California energy consumers by manipulating prices and passing the fallout to consumers. Their own subsidiaries executed their strategy with fellow merchant energy companies and with Wall Street trading desks.

It took five months after Enron declared bankruptcy for an investigative report into its trading activities to hit the mainstream press. The FERC report described how traders were "creating," and then "relieving," phantom congestion. When price caps were in effect in California but not in neighboring states, Enron bought power cheaply in California and then resold it out of state at a higher price. They then bought it back at still higher prices and resold it to California, explaining they had to purchase it more expensively, and must be compensated accordingly, thereby circumventing price caps and getting paid handsomely for doing so.[30] Because they had access to all price levels and trading via their online trading platform, they were well positioned to take advantage of the information and move power—and money—accordingly.

Under one strategy employed during December 2000, Enron bought power from state-run exchanges for $250 a megawatt hour, the maximum allowed under the existing price cap (one megawatt hour runs 1,000 air conditioners for one hour). It then resold it outside California for five times that, or $1,250 a megawatt hour. Another strategy, charmingly called Death Star, involved Enron getting paid "for moving energy to relieve congestion without moving energy or relieving congestion."[31] Enron knew the energy supply plans of their competitors (mostly because of the online system they operated from which these details could be garnered). Therefore, it could intentionally overschedule energy supply by telling the system operator it had plans to deliver an amount it knew was greater than what the system could handle. California would be obligated to pay Enron to deliver that excess elsewhere so as not to overload the system. Often Enron didn't even bother to get the energy before promising to sell it. Therefore, it didn't even have to put up any money up front. To execute this rather elegant strategy only required Enron to lie about the power it was going to supply without actually having to generate it. A May 2002 *New York Times* article described the "Load Shift" strategy that enabled Enron to profit $30 million in 2000 by creating "the appearance of congestion through deliberate overstatement of power to be delivered."[32]

These trading strategies were largely reported separately from the multitude of Enron partnerships, but both the trade strategies and the existence of those partnerships coalesced to form an intricate lattice of profit creation and loss and tax mitigation. Central to these operations were the shell games Enron played with its numerous special-purpose vehicles, or partnerships, in moving those profits around, making tracking them even more difficult. These off–balance sheet entities would promise exaggerated returns to investors or state commissions. Their returns were loosely based on claims of future profit that often emanated from a chain of other off–balance sheet entities. For example, Public Utility Commission president Loretta Lynch testified on April 11, 2002, before the U.S. Senate Commerce, Science and Transportation Committee, that 30 percent of trades by Enron affiliates and subs were among themselves.[33] The special-purpose entity LJM2 (named by Chief Financial Officer Andrew Fastow after the initials of his wife, Lea, and their two children) was just one such partnership that advertised higher than likely expected returns on the projects it represented. In one 1999 deal, Enron sold a site for a power plant in Oregon through LJM2. On August 14, 2000, Enron testified before the Oregon Public Utility Commission that the return on the proceeds from that project would be 15 percent, yet LMJ2's internal documents showed a 22 percent return on this investment.[34] This was just one illumination of the inconsistency between what the parent Enron said and what its special purpose entity, LJM2, recorded as profit.

ACCOUNTING AND PARTNERSHIPS, ENRON STYLE

Enron prided itself on hiring the "best and brightest" traders and financial engineers and won accolades galore for their creativity. The 1999 "Vision and Values" section of its Web site reads, "Enron is a laboratory for innovation."

Concurrent with the deregulation of the energy business itself, Enron began bending some—and breaking other—financial trading and accounting rules. Because of the murky nature of those rules, lawyers will probably be debating for years the exact point at which Enron's tactics were specifically illegal. Under existing rules and regulations, many of Enron's trading and accounting tactics actually were legal, albeit highly unethical. Then again, Enron helped shape the rules it later bent or broke.

The financial engineering techniques used by Enron to make its balance sheet appear stronger were pretty standard, in one form or another, among most of the world's corporations. None of them could work without some Wall Street bank either helping with the financial engineering or raising capital through its investor base. Unfortunately, abuse of such techniques became widespread.

The brilliance of all of Enron's accounting-related maneuvers was that they showed a remarkable affinity for the complex scope (in sheer numbers) and the convoluted relationships among them. Enron wasn't content simply to have special-purpose entities dotting the Caymans; each of its entities had to have numerous and nontransparent ties with each other. Some of Enron's financial activities displayed true genius in terms of mapping out tangled cash flows that hid asset and liability values when necessary. But central to its activities was the fact that Enron simply chose to ignore standard accounting practice and didn't consolidate the performances of its partnerships onto a new balance sheet. (To this day, no investigatory body in Washington seems to be able to make a criminal case stick to the corporation itself.)

If a parent company owns greater than a 3 percent interest in a business entity, then that entity must be included in the parent's consolidated financial statements, according to the FASB. Enron repeatedly violated that rule with respect to its special-purpose entities (SPEs) or partnerships. However, despite the fact that former CFO Andrew Fastow was indicted for personally violating that rule, Enron was not found guilty or fined as a corporation. This was despite the fact that its board would have had to sign off on the integrity of its SPEs. Two qualities make prosecuting Enron tricky: (a) the stuff it created was complex, and (b) that complexity requires more time and focus by regulators and prosecutors to understand before meting out corporate punishment. For the purpose of prosecuting future deception, complete transparency would be utopian. Though there's probably no such thing, more transparency is definitely needed; minimally all SPEs should be reported on the consolidated balance sheet regardless of the parent's ownership interest. That way, at least their presence is made transparent on the company's financial statement.

Enron's stock was used to back many of its special-purpose entities and as margin collateral to keep its trading businesses alive, and when it began to plummet, the game was nearly over. Enron's stock value peaked at $90.56 in August 2000; by May 5, 2001, it was down to $59.78; on August 16, 2001, it was $36.88; and by November 26, 2001, it was at $4.01. It hovered below a dollar the day before Enron declared bankruptcy.[35] Because many larger special-purpose vehicles were capitalized, or backed, by Enron stock, when the value of Enron stock fell, the SPEs required more shares (at lower prices) to make up the same capital amount to continue to function. The downward cascade of Enron stock value accelerated the company's implosion. It caused margin calls on trading positions to escalate and trigger levels for special-purpose vehicles to be hit. Consequently, a greater injection of cash, or more shares at lower values, would have been necessary to keep the operation afloat.

FASTOW, SUBSIDIARIES, AND SPECIAL-PURPOSE ENTITIES

Enron created a web of interlocking subsidiaries and special purpose entities to mask actual profits and losses, including New Power Company, Enron Energy Services, Enron Power Marketing, and Portland General Electricity. Portland General Electricity alone traded 12 million megawatt hours of electricity at prices ranging from 5 cents to $3,322 an hour during the height of the California crisis. Before deregulation, that electricity sold for $30 a megawatt hour. By booking the same trade (with one of its own subsidiaries) multiple times, Enron managed to inflate its balance sheet substantially (as did other energy companies). This in turn enabled it to raise more debt via the capital markets than any other merchant energy company. By hiding debt in off–balance sheet special-purpose entities, Enron gave the appearance of being more solvent than it actually was, a factor that contributed to its investment-grade credit ratings.

In all, Enron created almost 3,000 SPEs (filling sixty-one pages of its 2000 annual SEC filing), and had over 20,000 large and small creditors. Enron also set up a web of limited partnerships to invest in offshore entities, like LJM1 and LJM2, Raptor, the Joint Energy Development Investments, L.P. (or Jedi, for short), and Chewco Investments, L.P. (usually just Chewco). Obscuring transparency as much as possible, these partnerships had controlling interests in each other. This made it difficult to gauge the extent of interaction among them all.

Enron used the tools of law and accounting but dispensed with the ethics incumbent on those fields. Its offshore partnerships and SPEs served both as tax havens and ways to mask risk by relocating real and artificially inflated assets. Furthermore, Enron's abuse of standard financial instruments and derivative structuring took place with the aid of the investment banking community. The Cayman Islands became the company's offshore haven of choice. There, it established a complex multidimensional network of these special-purpose vehicles to hide losses and debt with help from JP Morgan Chase, Merrill Lynch, DLJ, and others.

As CFO, Andrew Fastow's job was to create financing alternatives that would allow Enron to buy and sell assets without carrying debt on its books or impairing its credit ratings. He was also a Wall Street liaison who touted the company's prospects to investors and coerced analysts to sing along.

One Enron partnership, Chewco, became an investor in another partnership, Jedi. Enron itself was also an investor in Jedi, whose activities should have been consolidated into Enron's overall financial statement in November 1997. That integration didn't happen until the first quarter of 2001. Another Enron subsidiary, LJM1, regularly traded derivatives with its parent company. It also wasn't consolidated onto the main balance sheet. The consolidation of Jedi, Chewco, and LJM1 had been reported as $2.6 billion in net income from 1997 to 2000. Proper reporting would have revealed a $396 million loss. Chewco should have been consolidated with Enron in 1997 because it failed the accounting criteria required for it to qualify as an independent special-purpose entity. LJM1 should have been consolidated when it first failed similar capitalization criteria in 1999.[36]

Then there was LJM2. This was Enron's fiber-optic entity, the one that dabbled in broadband and had its own stake in the Internet boom. It purchased dark fiber-optic cable from Enron for $100 million in June 2000, prompting a ridiculously complex set of fiber trades both with other industry participants and to another special-purpose entity of Enron's.

LJM2 also invested in New Power Holdings, a subsidiary of Enron which became a public company in October 2000. LJM1 and LJM2 together made $191 million in equity investments in five other SPEs, of which three (Raptor I, II, and IV) were also capitalized by Enron stock and stock options. Enron further paid LJM2 management fees to keep track of its investments, receiving $319 million back for effectively servicing itself.

A number of factors contributed to Enron's demise and fraud, including the leveraging of its balance sheets discreetly via SPEs and loans disguised as trades, trading in esoteric derivatives contracts, and the shredding of incriminating documents by auditor/accountant Arthur Andersen amid its investigation. But an equally important factor was when the FASB provided Enron and other corporations that 3-percent independence loophole to begin with, making special-purpose vehicles particularly attractive.

Andrew Fastow and members of his family owned portions of Enron's various off–balance sheet entities using, among other things, personal loans backed by Enron shares. The use of Enron shares to buy these stakes compromised the independent ownership requirement as set by the FASB. That independence rule requires that at least 3 percent of a special-purpose entity be owned by a third party in order to keep it off the parent's consolidated financial statements. This is an arbitrary percentage to begin with, yet one that Fastow and others took advantage of. As the value of Enron stock fell, these entities could only continue to function if they were replenished with more shares at those lower prices. This created a downward spiral as Enron stock prices went into free-fall that translated into collapsing SPEs across the board. It further caused the company itself and Arthur Andersen to finally alert the public to the problem, but it was much too late. That the SEC never checked up on these entities or pushed for disclosure from corporations on their makeup was gross negligence on its part.

While reading through Enron's original and impressively twisted SEC filings (many of which the SEC disregarded), there's really no way to avoid a massive headache. Enron ultimately issued an explanatory statement on its Web site that miraculously managed to be more convoluted that the transactions themselves.[37] Unfortunately, reading the explanation of its actions, furnished under federal request, you get the same headache. Enron counted on a lot of headaches hampering investigations when they created their paper labyrinth in the first place. And it counts on it them still, as thousands of investigation documents and hours pile up. It counts on people giving up.

MERRILL LYNCH

Merrill Lynch and JP Morgan Chase, among other Wall Street firms, helped establish these offshore vehicles. However, they were not stringent enough about checking who backed them and how. Certainly they didn't relay the information to investors as openly as they could have. Merrill Lynch was initially afraid to play ball with Fastow. In Sherron Watkins's memo to Ken Lay, she said that Fastow had threatened the institutions, telling Merrill that "if you don't invest in LJM, Enron will not use you as a banker or an investment banker again."[38] Under Fastow's threat to end Enron's banking relationships and fee-generation machine, Merrill buckled. Later, Merrill found itself in the media spotlight for relaying inside information, consisting of false Fastow-fed promises, to their investors in order to scrounge up equity capital backing for Enron's partnerships.[39] It was also charged with conspiracy to commit wire fraud, falsifying books and records, and perjury.[40]

It is a breach of fiduciary responsibility to invest discretionary money—money that investors have trusted an asset management company to use in the best interests of their financial goals, and in a prudent manner—if it is known that the investment may be questionable. But, according to the SEC, Merrill Lynch violated that mandate when it helped create a false sale in 1999. The "sale" was of three barges and was only designed to look like a sale, but it was, in reality, a loan. The supposed sale helped Enron meet its profit target for the last quarter of 1999. The transaction was an "asset parking" arrangement. Merrill bought an interest in a number of Nigerian barges from Enron with the understanding that it would be paid back with interest within six months.[41] The effect was of a bridge, or temporary loan, for which the SEC claimed Merrill Lynch and four of its executives knew Enron would record $28 million in revenue and $12 million in pretax income from the trade.[42] In 2000, Enron removed Merrill's interest in those barges. Merrill Lynch also extracted an $8.5 million structuring fee (down from an originally estimated $17 million fee) for another deceptive deal undertaken to inflate Enron's income by approximately $50 million, through two complex energy option trades in late December 1999.

On March 17, 2003, Merrill Lynch paid the SEC an $80 million fine on Enron-related federal investigations.[43] According to Merrill, that resolution "concluded the SEC's investigation into Enron-related matters with respect to the company."[44] Merrill neither admitted nor denied wrongdoing and consented to an injunction barring it from violating federal securities laws. In other words, they had to promise not to do it again.

THE ENRON/DYNEGY SAGA AND BANKRUPTCY

Energy and /financial deregulation allowed Enron to become one of the most powerful corporations in the world. They enabled it to escape price regulations and trading oversight, both key factors in the company's meteoric, 1,750 percent increase in revenues throughout the 1990s.[45] When federal regulators finally reregulated the entire Western market, including California, through temporary price caps on June 19, 2001, it had a very negative impact on Enron. All of a sudden Enron was unable to churn (excessively trade) to increase the appearance of profit and demand, as well as to control prices. The company plunged into bankruptcy less than six months later.[46] Two months after that, in August 2001, Jeff Skilling stepped down as CEO of Enron after only six months at the helm, a move that failed to incite enough suspicion at the time. Lay emerged from his luxurious retirement to resume his spot at the top of the Enron empire.

In September 2001, Phil Gramm announced he would not seek reelection to the Senate. The Union Bank of Switzerland (UBS) proudly announced in October that Gramm was joining its team.[47] UBS eventually bought Enron's trading businesses in January 2002. It has since been at the forefront of lobbying for commercial banks to trade and own energy assets.[48]

Enron ultimately plunged much faster than it rose. On October 16, 2001, Enron first officially posted a $681 million third-quarter loss and a $1.2 billion hit to shareholders equity, partly due to Fastow's flailing partnerships and special-purpose entities. On October 28, 2001, Enron announced it had eaten through its $3.3 billion credit facility.[49] It's always a sign of doom when a company runs through its credit facility.

When Enron disclosed that $1.2 billion hit in their third-quarter 2001 earnings statement, it took most of Wall Street by surprise. After 9/11, the atmosphere was jittery for far more important reasons, but when that mega-adjustment was announced, it overshadowed other conversation, at least temporarily. It was especially awesome for those of us who worked in credit derivatives, capturing our attention and capacity for gossip much the way seeing a car crash would. Before that, the host of 2001 stock declines was blamed on the "overall market" or "economy." The financial community was unprepared for the darling of derivatives to be facing the abyss. So, when even beloved Enron started going down, spreads for other merchant energy companies started to blow out. Corporate bond and credit derivatives traders started getting very nervous as bids for energy companies vanished from the market.

Up until Enron's last desperate prebankruptcy moments, Lay and other senior Enron executives were sending e-mails to their staff urging them to hold onto their stock even while the company was slipping. This was in addition to the fact that Enron 401(k) plans actually prevented their employees from selling stock except during certain prespecified periods. Holding onto the disintegrating remains of a sinking ship, more than 15,000 Enron workers lost $1.3 billion, 62 percent of the $2.1 billion in Enron's 401(k) plan in 2001.[50]

Just before Enron tanked completely, a group of bankers from JP Morgan Chase and Citigroup hightailed it to Houston to try to fashion a last-minute, high-stakes merger deal with Dynegy. As part of the deal, Dynegy would buy Enron for $9 billion.[51] It would even give Enron $1.5 billion cash up-front to help Enron survive until the close of the deal, which was collateralized by Enron's Northern Natural Gas pipeline.

The same day that Dynegy had originally targeted for its $9 billion Enron acquisition, the merger announcement was suddenly deferred, giving Robert Rubin, Michael Carper (head of Citigroup's investment banking unit), JP Morgan Chase CEO Bill Harrison, and JP Morgan's vice chairman and former head of investment banking Jimmy Lee enough time to keep Enron's rating up long enough to close the deal. They flew into action despite the seriousness of Enron's already drawing down its $3 billion credit line.[52] Those four guys wielded some pretty heavy firepower. Debra Perry, senior managing director for corporate finance at Moody's, told a Senate committee that she had "never been contacted by such high-level bank officials with respect to the ratings of any other entity" before.[53]

The November 2001 gamble meant that if Enron could stay afloat long enough for Dynegy to acquire it, a number of big banks would do very well: first, through merger fees, and second, by not having to take a hit on billions of dollars of defaulting debt. But it didn't turn out that way. Enron was sinking into a quicksand of plummeting stock values hitting all sorts of triggers and facing huge margin calls.

A month later, on December 1, 2001, Dynegy bailed. A Chase banker involved in the deal told me, "We were trying to get Dynegy to understand just what they were in for buying Enron, but we still wanted to get the deal done. Enron would show us one set of books with certain information; then they'd show us another set of books where that same information had completely different numbers." Enron was nonetheless extended an emergency bank credit line of $1.5 billion, led by JP Morgan Chase and Citigroup; the collateral for Chase's credit included the Northern Natural Gas pipeline again. Not only did Enron have a double set of books, but it also doubly collateralized loans. Dynegy's termination of the merger still sealed their purchase of Enron's pipeline for that $1.5 billion in cash, per the original deal agreement.

Enron filed for bankruptcy the next day, on December 2, 2001, citing $63.4 billion of assets, and thus became the country's largest bankruptcy ever. Earlier that day, in desperation, it had filed a $10 billion lawsuit against Dynegy for breach of contract.[54] The nasty legal dispute between Enron and Dynegy over the matter was eventually settled for $25 million on August 21, 2002.[55] Desperate for survival cash of its own, Dynegy turned around and sold the pipeline to Mid-American Energy for $928 million, a loss of half a billion dollars, in July 2002.[56] Dynegy got the Northern Natural Gas Company (NNG) in February 2002.

Enron's original Chapter 11 filing documents listed fourteen affiliated entities of the firm, including Enron Power Marketing, Inc., Enron Broadband Services, and Enron Energy Services. The twenty largest creditors listed included the Chase Manhattan Bank at approximately $2 billion, Citibank at $3 billion, the Bank of New York at about $2 billion, and Arthur Andersen, which closed down for its role in Enron's fraud after suffering a $500,000 fine, at $2 million.[57] Both AXA Financial, Inc., and Janus Capital Corporation were listed as more than 5 percent holders of voting securities, and 6.4 million shares of common stock were reserved against an option held by Bank of America, with nearly one billion shares of additional stock in the form of outstanding shares or reserved against options for shares.[58]

Even while Enron was propped up by extensive last-minute credit extensions from the überbanks, the Wall Street investment banking community was largely content to watch the Enron car wreck smolder from the sidelines. Their behavior was in stark contrast to their frenzied efforts to preserve Long Term Capital Management in 1998. At the time, all of

Wall Street heavily lobbied Alan Greenspan to protect Long Term Capital because their own trading positions would be affected. They had loaned Long Term billions of dollars, and many prominent Wall Street executives had their own personal wealth tied up in Long Term. They were too entangled to give up without a fight.

But, despite the hundreds of millions in fees that Wall Street firms were content to make from Enron, its trading operations actually competed with their own. Plus, Enron had been prowling around, looking to take corporate derivatives customers away from them. So investment banks neither demanded that the Fed help launch a bailout nor organized one among themselves. Beyond chief creditors, the rest of Wall Street was content to let Enron slide into oblivion, just as they had been content to let Drexel, Burnham, Lambert, a once-ferocious competitor, declare bankruptcy. Enron was simply better friends with Washington than with Wall Street.

RATING AGENCIES AND ROBERT RUBIN

The rating agency Standard & Poor's reported that Enron and its consolidated entities had $13 billion of on-balance sheet debt when it filed for Chapter 11 protection from its creditors. Enron's prior quarterly report, released September 30, 2001, just before it had first disclosed the $1.2 billion shareholder hit that prompted its quick demise, showed more than $19 billion of liabilities on derivatives contracts: energy, power, and other commodity trades, as well as swaps and options held by a wide variety of financial institutions.

Enron's fall in ratings was even more dramatic and far quicker than its revenue climb on the back of unregulated trading and a roaring, unchecked stock market. Enron was still an investment-grade company in May 2001. Its senior (most likely to get repaid) debt was rated Baa1 until mid-October 2001; on October 29, it dropped to Baa2; on November 3, it changed to Baa3; on November 28, it fell to B2; and on December 3, it had fallen to Ca. Enron didn't just bring down its own ratings either; few public utility companies are now rated above single A. The downgrades of once-solid AAA companies began just after 1996 deregulation, and the companies were never upgraded once they fell. During Enron's ratings fall, Robert Rubin warned the rating agencies that downgrading Enron to junk "might wreak havoc in the markets" just three weeks before Enron's bankruptcy and just after they disclosed their $1.2 billion shareholder equity hit. At the time, of course, Rubin's employer, Citigroup, was negotiating the failed Dynegy/Enron merger and extending a boatload of lifetime credit to them in the process.

Rubin's attempt to exert his influence on a debt rating situation, when Enron holdings were scattered throughout the country (including state pension funds), is obscene. It is no different from investment bankers or CEOs urging analysts to maintain upbeat calls on deadbeat companies. In fact, given his powerful position and connections with Washington, it's far worse than an executive or an analyst trying to tilt opinion in his favor, yet Rubin received no punishment.[59] Investigations by the U.S. Senate Committee on Governmental Affairs were closed on January 3, 2003, after it concluded Rubin did not violate any federal law or regulation by calling a top treasury official on behalf of troubled Enron Corp in early November 2001.

It wasn't until later that night—after the team of bank lenders, including Citigroup, had agreed to provide additional financing and secure changes to the terms of the proposed acquisition of Enron by Dynegy, Inc., at better rates, based on the current ratings—that Moody's officials lowered Enron's rating. And even then, they kept it above investment grade, until just before Enron went bankrupt.[60]

BUSH ADMINISTRATION ENERGY SECTOR TIES

Many members of the second Bush administration enjoyed a revolving door into the energy sector, notably (but not exclusively) George W. Bush, Vice President Dick Cheney, and Thomas White. Even without a direct career path to and from Washington, executives in the industry continued to get high-paying jobs at competitors, sometimes resigning from one firm amid a cloud of fraud investigations only to join another.

A disproportionate number of people in Bush's entourage were connected to Enron in particular. Bush's political adviser, Karl Rove, owned Enron stock (worth between $100,000 and $250,000).[61] His first economic adviser, Lawrence Lindsey, was on the company's consulting payroll. Marc F. Racicot was an Enron lobbyist before becoming chair of the Republican National Committee. Ken Lay's political contributions during the 2000 election went exclusively to Republican candidates, particularly those who were close to Bush.[62]

It's no wonder then that energy companies are a popular investment of choice for top officials. The Bush administration has made those choices a cornerstone of its corporate policy, however. Indeed, the majority of the financial holdings of the top hundred Bush administration appointees were in the energy sector: approximately 221 separate investments valued around $144.6 million. They had 32 investments in the metal and mineral industries, worth no more than $102 million, and 367 investments in financial companies, worth $82.8 million.[63]

Both President George W. Bush and Vice President Dick Cheney have backgrounds in the energy industry—via Harken and Halliburton, respectively—as do six other members of the administration, including Commerce Secretary Donald Evans and Undersecretary Kathleen Cooper, who both went straight from the energy industry to Washington.[64]

George W. Bush's ties to energy companies and associated scandals dates back to 1990, when he was a director of the Houston-based energy firm Harken and his dad was president. That year he sold his Harken stock for $848,560.[65] But Bush didn't just sell his Harken stock; he also sold shares in four other companies that were worth $700,000, most of which went toward paying off a 1989 bank loan Bush had taken out to buy a stake in the Texas Rangers baseball team. (In 1998, Bush sold that stake for $16 million.)[66] Harken's stock soon went sharply downhill.

A well-publicized SEC investigation followed in 1991 to determine whether Bush had had any insider information that propelled him to sell the stock right before Harken's shares plummeted, and to find out why he had failed to disclose the transaction to the SEC in a timely fashion, a violation of federal law. Normally, this crime would have at least engendered a fine—but not if you're a Bush, or your father is president, or both. Bush failed to disclose three other transactions as well. An internal SEC memo prepared at the time of its investigation noted that Bush had filed his Form 4's (reports that company insiders are required to submit to disclose stock purchases and sales by the tenth day of the month after the transaction), involving over $1 million of Harken stock sales, thirty-four weeks late. When Bush sold that $848,560 of stock on June 22, 1990, it was trading at $30.48 a share. The next quarterly report was released a few weeks later and revealed a $23 million loss for the company, causing the stock to close the year at around $9.24 a share.[67]

The $23 million loss would have been higher if not for a concocted $10 million "sale" of a Harken subsidiary to Harken insiders.[68] That sale was merely a parent-to-subsidiary transfer designed to reduce the reported losses. It was really a deceptive accounting maneuver. According to general accounting principles, intercompany sales are excluded from the parent's consolidated income statements. In Harken's case, the intercompany sale was used to avoid a fall in the stock price, inflating sales revenue for that reporting period. The infamous accounting firm Arthur Andersen blessed the sale at the time.[69]

Under unwelcome public and media scrutiny, the Bush administration was quick to point out any number of reasons why Bush did nothing illegal on a host of right-wing talk shows over the summer of 2002. One excuse offered was that Bush didn't know that Smith Barney consultants hired by the audit committee had discovered that Harken was $150 million deeper in debt than previously known, when he sold his shares.[70] Given that Bush was not only a member of Harken's board but of its audit committee as well, the only way that excuse would be remotely valid would be if Bush were an unaware moron who had slept through every meeting. Although logic doesn't permit ruling out that possibility entirely, Bush did seem to have enough wits about him to sell his stock before the loss announcement.

With friends in the SEC and a dad in the Oval Office, Bush saw the SEC investigations find their way into a convenient black hole. Richard Breedan, appointed by President George H. W. Bush to run the SEC, quickly closed the case on George W.'s transgressions.[71] But even the best political insulation doesn't ensure corporate stability. By the middle of July 2003, Harken stock was trading at $0.39, and George W. Bush's former company was flirting with bankruptcy, though by that time he had no stake left in the company.

HALLIBURTON

The number two man in the Bush White House, Vice President Dick Cheney, had a much deeper and longer connection to Halliburton than President Bush had with Harken. Founded in 1919, Halliburton is the world's second largest oil services provider, headquartered in Houston, the oil-and-dodge capital of the country. Cheney was its chairman and CEO from 1995 through his election campaign until August 2000. An intricate component of Halliburton was its Kellogg Brown and Root (formerly Brown and Root) energy and construction division, purchased in 1962 and dependent upon government contracts even back in the 1930s. Brown and Root also performed work for U.S.-declared terrorists like Libya's Mohammar Gadhafi.[72] Although Cheney wasn't leading Halliburton when these Gadhafi sales started, subsidiaries' sales to Libya continued throughout his tenure. According to the *Baltimore Sun*, Brown and Root was fined $3.8 million by the government for violating Libyan sanctions.[73]

Prior to joining Halliburton, Cheney was a longtime Washington insider. He showed his political deftness over a quarter-century ago when Gerald Ford appointed him to be the youngest-ever White House chief of staff in 1975, alongside Donald Rumsfeld, the youngest secretary of defense. He later served as a member of the House of Representatives from 1979 to 1989. Then, as secretary of defense under George H. W. Bush from 1989 until 1993, he commanded the armed forces during the first Gulf War. In an elegant revolving political-corporate door maneuver, Cheney became chairman of the board and CEO of Halliburton two years after his position with Bush came to an end.[74]

In the five years prior to Cheney's arrival at Halliburton, Brown and Root received about $100 million in loans and guarantees from the Export-Import Bank and the Overseas Private Investment Corporation (OPIC), headed by a formal Bechtel executive. After Cheney came on board, Kellogg Brown and Root's cut from the government increased to $1.5 billion,[75] and Cheney's connections didn't hurt prospects for even more government contracts.[76] When he joined Halliburton, the company did less than $300 million a year of business with the defense department, 98 percent of which went to Kellogg Brown and Root. During his reign, that absolute figure increased by 60 percent, while the split with Kellogg remained roughly unchanged. Since Cheney joined the second Bush White House, Halliburton's government generated revenue began running a backlog (or series of government IOU's), going up 40 percent in the fourth quarter of 2002 alone from what it made in 2001.[77] Cheney did more to drive up Halliburton's stock price with his connections than with stay-at-home workaday business acumen. He spent countless days on the road, using his contacts to court key business players around the world, especially in the Middle East.[78] "Clearly one of his abilities was to get doors open," former secretary of state and then-Halliburton board member Lawrence Eagleburger told the *Dallas Morning News*.[79]

Cheney was equally skilled at accumulating accounting irregularities, amounting to a 7 percent inflation of after-tax profits. In 1998, Halliburton was inclined to switch accounting methodologies to book revenue up front from construction customers, but not fully disclose it appropriately in the footnotes to the financial statements required under generally accepted accounting principles (GAAP). The SEC finally opened an investigation into Halliburton's practices in July 2002, but no guilt was found and no fine levied, as of the publication of this book, the investigation continues.

In December 1998, Cheney elected to defer 1999 compensation for five years of fixed installments plus interest, thereby remaining linked to Halliburton throughout his tenure as George W. Bush's vice president.[80] In 2002, he received $163,000 from this plan—after receiving $1.6 million in bonus and deferred compensation from Halliburton in 2001.[81]

Cheney retired from Halliburton on August 16, 2000, only three months before the election in which the Supreme Court would give him a vice presidency.[82] On his way out, he sold 660,000 Halliburton common shares, valued at about $35 million.[83] Upon his departure, the CEO seat shifted to David Lesar, who had come to Halliburton via a senior position at Arthur Andersen, the company's auditor. After the Enron scandal caused Arthur Andersen to close its doors, Halliburton hired KPMG to do its accounting. KPMG had its own problems. In April 2002, Xerox paid $10 million to settle SEC charges that it manipulated its earnings from 1997 to 2000; KPMG, Xerox's auditor at the time, and four of its partners were charged by the SEC with fraud in January 2003.[84] On March 10, 2003, KPMG agreed to pay $200 million to settle charges stemming from its faulty auditing of Rite-Aid Corporation.[85] KPMG later renamed itself Bearing Point to distance itself from past scandals.

THE NINE LIVES OF CHENEY AND THE ENERGY POLICY BOARD

The U.S. General Accounting Office (GAO) considers itself the primary watchdog agency within Washington. At the top of its list of responsibilities is its commitment "to support the Congress in meeting its Constitutional responsibilities and to help improve the performance and ensure the accountability of the federal government for the American people." It is not just overall government integrity the GAO is supposed to ensure;

the GAO is the body tasked with "financial audits, program reviews and evaluations, analyses, investigations, and other services."[86] In addition to government oversight, the GAO was also in charge of investigating Cheney's role as head of the Energy Policy Committee from January until May 2001. The Energy Policy Committee was created by an executive branch order establishing it as a White House committee, with Cheney as its head, comprised of the corporate heads of energy companies like Enron. Had it been created by Congress, it would be subject to FOIA (Freedom of Information Act) jurisdiction and its records would have been made public. But, according to Cheney, it was solely serving the White House and therefore exempt from the GAO investigation or the necessity of public disclosure.[87]

On January 31, 2002, Senator Barbara Boxer (D-CA) cited a memo from Bush and Cheney's Energy Policy Task Force in which former Enron CEO Kenneth Lay urged Cheney to reject the wholesale electricity price caps that California governor Gray Davis and other state officials were desperately seeking.[88] She recognized that the memo potentially detailed evidence of Washington and corporate maneuvering that directly and harmfully impacted California during its energy crisis. In a letter to FERC chairman Patrick Wood, she stated, "This connection between influence and policy relating to the California electricity crisis is quite disturbing."[89] In fact, the link bordered on the incestuous. Ken Lay had met with Cheney and other task force members five times from February 2001 through October 2001 to dictate the language of the Bush administration's National Energy Policy proposal.[90] In spite of such concerns, the GAO concluded that Cheney be allowed to keep all records of those meetings a secret.

Though the GAO is supposed to be independent and nonpartisan, pressure from the Bush White House and congressional Republicans, on top of the threat of a $440 million budget cut, pushed comptroller David Walker to drop the pending lawsuit against Cheney on February 7, 2003.[91] As a result, all records of those energy policy discussions were spared public disclosure, despite FERC's detailed report of California market manipulation during the months the committee met.[92]

Even prior to Walker's decision, U.S. district court judge John Bates had announced in December 2002 that Walker lacked sufficient grounds to compel Cheney to disclose the nature of the White House Energy Policy Task Force he headed during the California blackouts and energy company market manipulations. Walker had originally filed the suit in February 2002, two months after Enron's bankruptcy. It was the first time in its eighty-one-year history that the GAO had sued a member of the executive branch for withholding information.[93]

On July 8, 2003, a federal appeals court overturned that decision and decided 2–1 that the government had no right to ask an appeals court to block the ruling requiring Cheney to disclose energy policy board information. The White House had previously overturned trial judge Emmet G. Sullivan's ruling that some of the information that Cheney shared with senior energy executives had to be disclosed.[94]

The White House went into defensive mode, starting at the federal appeals court ruling all the way up to the Supreme Court. Given the Supreme Court's predisposition to help the Bush administration out, this interim victory might be just that. Fortunately, in a separate case, filed under the Freedom of Information Act, federal judge Paul L. Friedman ruled in April 2004 that they would have to release thousands of pages of documents related to the White House Energy Task Force activities.[95] The FOIA angle focused not on the task force itself but was cleverly centered around the government agencies that provided officials to work on that task force. This just upped the ante for the administration; since even if it won the Supreme Court case, it would still face challenges related to the FOIA. No matter what the outcome, the Bush cartel seems determined to keep those files a secret.

THOMAS WHITE

Then there was Thomas White. For years, White played a prominent role in building up the most manipulative and crooked of Enron's subsidiaries as vice chairman of Enron Energy Services (EES) from March 1998 until May 2001. While at EES he invoked a number of questionable bookkeeping practices to inflate long-term energy contracts profits, which boosted revenues from $1 billion in 1998 to $4.6 billion in 2000. Most of those profits were booked at the same time that the Bush administration was openly advocating against price controls. Without such controls or caps, Enron had more room to jack up prices through trading and market manipulation. Though President Clinton was in office from 1998 until 2000, it wasn't until the Bush administration came to power in 2000 that the most extreme profits were booked, even though those profits could have drawn upon practices from the preceding years. The accounting manipulation actually coincided with the height of the California crisis, which happened while Bush was in office and Cheney was heading the Energy Policy Task Force.

After having directed Energy Services at Enron and its subsidiaries for eleven years, White was appointed army secretary by George W. Bush in May 2001—the height of public utility price hikes and rolling blackouts. Enron Energy Services, under White's leadership, traded 11 million megawatts of electricity in California; 98 percent of those trades were with other Enron divisions. All that internal churning caused prices to shoot from $340 a megawatt hour to over $2,500 a megawatt hour.[96]

Although he was sitting comfortably in his Pentagon seat, White's ties with Enron executives didn't come to an end. In October 2001, just prior to his sale of 200,000 Enron shares and a month before Enron declared bankruptcy, White phoned his former Enron colleagues a total of thirteen times.[97] Those calls were in addition to the twenty-nine he had initially disclosed to the committee in January 2002.

They coincided with the start of an informal SEC inquiry into Enron's fraud that began on October 22, 2001. That day White and Ken Lay engaged in a failed game of phone tag.[98] Two days later, White sold 121,663 shares of stock at $16 a share after a call to Enron board member John Duncan.[99] The same day, Enron CFO Andrew Fastow resigned. (Five months afterward, the House Government Reform Committee received further information that White had made forty-four calls to Enron colleagues since assuming his Bush administration post.)

Five days after Fastow's resignation, White held a meeting with John Carr, an executive at Enron Energy Services. The next day he called Jude Rolfes, an Enron vice president, and sold another 86,709 shares at $12.86 a share.[100] According to Rolfes, they didn't discuss the financial state of Enron; instead, he characterized their conversation as being "mainly about golf and racquetball"—a rather lighthearted conversation, given the unraveling of the country's biggest fraud at the time.[101] Though his share values had gone down significantly from their highs because Enron's stock price was falling so precipitously, White did manage to pocket a total of $12.1 million from his Enron stock sales.

The next day, Enron publicly announced that the SEC's inquiry had become a full-scale formal investigation. But White's involvement with the company didn't cease. On November 1, 2001, White called Clifford Baxter, former chairman of Enron North America. Baxter, who had intimate knowledge of Enron's accounting schemes, was subsequently found dead of an apparent suicide three months later, on January 25, 2002.[102] As with many Enron matters, Baxter's suicide brought its own set of questions. The police on the scene immediately declared the death a suicide without benefit of an autopsy. Later, an autopsy did take place, suspiciously quickly, and its results were sealed with equal haste. Baxter's death occurred just days after Ken Lay resigned from Enron and Arthur Andersen executives started appearing before Congress.[103] According to Brian Cruver, author of *Anatomy of Greed,* "Many believed he was a key figure in the investigation; he was even mentioned in Sherron Watkins's memo to Ken Lay: 'Cliff Baxter complained mightily to Skilling and all who would listen about the inappropriateness of our transactions with LJM.' As the hearings were beginning, the timing of his death was significant."[104]

Clifford Baxter wasn't the only senior Houston-based energy insider to meet an untimely death. Four months later, on June 1, 2002, El Paso senior vice president and treasurer Charles Dana Rice was also found dead. Rice, forty-seven, had been employed by El Paso for twenty-five years. Houston policewoman Sylvia Trevino told CNN that Rice died of a gunshot wound at his Houston home; El Paso chairman William Wise called Rice's death "tragic." The company slashed its earnings guidance for the next two years and disclosed plans to cut its energy trading business significantly a week before Rice's death.[105]

On May 8, 2002, Public Citizen called for Army Secretary Thomas White's resignation in conjunction with documents released earlier that week by FERC disclosing that White earned tens of millions of dollars during his tenure at Enron, including $5.5 million in salary and bonuses in the year preceding his May 2001 Senate confirmation to serve as army secretary.[106]

According to Public Citizen president Joan Claybrook, the FERC documents showed "manipulation and deception so extreme that it borders on maniacal."[107] Yet it took over a year after those documents surfaced for White to be booted from his post as head of the army. He was finally removed in March 2002, at the beginning of the U.S.-led war with Iraq—but that was only due to personal conflicts of style with Secretary of Defense Donald Rumsfeld and not because White helped gouge California consumers for billions of dollars before being plucked to preside over the army and its more than $90 billion budget.

BATTLING FOR TRADING LEFTOVERS

More than merely providing an opportunity to share power lines and plants, deregulation of the power industry created a means to control both production and distribution. This was also the case for the investment banks that traded energy and owned or had large stakes in the underlying assets, including pipelines and storage facilities, and that's why these banks lobbied right alongside the energy companies for deregulation. Since Enron, commercial banks like Bank of America have intensified lobbying efforts with FERC to get more deeply involved in the energy trading game. In September 2002, the Bank of America filed a petition with FERC to allow them to trade wholesale electricity, the very act that power marketers engaged in to defraud California, after receiving permission to trade derivatives in June.[108]

Energy related financial deregulation benefited nonenergy companies as well. For instance, Global Crossing, Qwest, GE, Williams, Tyco, WorldCom, and Lucent all benefited from the fact that corporations were subject to different accounting rules regarding trading disclosure than financial institutions were. Power energy and commodity traders like Goldman Sachs, Morgan Stanley, and UBS were more than happy to take up the space in the energy trading market left behind by their former energy clients and trading partners. Moreover, since investment banks don't have to disclose itemized commodity derivatives transactions, their trading operations in commodities and energy derivatives remain murky. Thus, Goldman Sachs' online, "nonregulated, nonaudited, . . . manipulation and fraud entity" (in the words of California senator Dianne Feinstein), the Intercontinental Exchange (ICE) commodity trading system, wound up replacing Enron Online as the highest volume online trading system after Enron went under.[109]

Every year, the top energy trading awards are split between Wall Street and energy companies. Enron was named Energy Derivatives Trading House of the Year in 2001 by the Energy Power Risk Management Awards—the most prestigious financial/energy award in the energy trading business. Goldman Sachs gladly took over their position in 2002. Additionally, Enron was Natural Gas Trader of the Year in 2001, a position El Paso assumed, barely missing a beat, in 2002. El Paso denied any California market manipulation, yet had some of the largest trading positions in California besides Enron in 2001, which nonetheless led to a 30 percent growth in their earnings that year. It was deliberately difficult to track the exact impact of El Paso's trading that year to its role in California market manipulation because energy traders file power marketers' quarterly reports, which are not required to be especially transparent. But the timing of their earnings ascent implies a strong correlation. That year, North Carolina–based Duke Energy Corporation, one of the country's largest utility owners, won the electricity trading award.

Energy companies manipulated the electricity market in California—and in Oregon, Nevada, Montana, and Washington—for trading gains. They also admitted to billions of dollars of wash trades. Round-trip or wash trades occur when companies buy and sell a commodity or security just to make it seem as if there is heavy volume or demand for it. They can then book the difference between the sale and the buy price as profit. Beyond that, such trades serve no real business or economic purpose. But you can't trade without trading partners, even if you hold all the information, as Enron did via Enron Online, which captured much of it electronically. Because Enron wasn't a bank, it wasn't required to publish its trading results in as detailed a format as the banks had to; if it had, the growth of the company would have looked far less impressive.

Meanwhile, superbanks like the Bank of America were lobbying the FERC to allow them to own and trade actual energy assets, not just financial instruments, to compete with the investment banks, like Goldman Sachs, who were buying up power plants and trading power.[110] Indeed, in Bank of America's headquarter's town, Charlotte, North Carolina, Goldman Sachs bought Cogentrix Energy, Inc. for $2.4 billion in late 2003, adding 26 plants to its power portfolio.

MERGERS, DEBT AND DOWNGRADES

During the 1990s, oil prices declined. Lowered oil prices have been credited as a major factor in powering the general U.S. economic boom. However, it also caused many oil and energy companies to go on a mad scramble to diversify their businesses after finding themselves flush with currency in the form of artificially inflated stock, yet generating fewer revenues from oil than they had been. The core business plan changed from making sure people could turn on the lights to trading anything and everything to generate quarterly earnings. Deregulation prompted a record amount of high-profile mergers, like Exxon-Mobil, as well as scores of medium-sized ones, within the United States and across the globe. Merger volume reached almost $900 billion in the latter half of the 1990s, 9.47 times the amount from 1990 to 1996.[111] This meant that fewer companies dominated the market, which effectively made up for any shortfall in prices.

Moreover, deregulation of holding companies enabled companies that were involved in energy and oil but weren't state utilities (i.e., Enron) to transform as fast as they could into trading powerhouses. In Texas, Enron, El Paso, Dynegy (26 percent of which was owned by Chevron-Texaco; Texaco still ranks as one of the country's top ten bankruptcies), Halliburton, and others rapidly broke through traditional business boundaries to go into commodities trading and other financial activities. They entered completely new industries, like telecommunications and broadband, hoping to ride the Internet wave alongside emerging telecom companies. Most of the power-marketer companies, for instance, put down fiber-optic networks alongside the beds of old pipelines, or even unused train tracks (a throwback to the days when pipeline routes followed train routes), to take advantage of the Internet boom. Meanwhile, hyperinflated stock prices presented the picture of pink-cheeked corporate health before the revelations of systemic fraud and manipulation cast their deadly pall. Those discoveries, coupled with high debt ratios, took the diversified energy sector down in market value by 80–85 percent from its late 1990s highs.[112]

After the 1996 energy deregulation, energy debt issuance took off. During 1996–2001 alone, the sector, with the aid of the Wall Street community, raised more than $1.2 trillion, $800 billion through bank loans and credit facilities and $400 billion through bond issuance. Though those figures are lower than the telecom sector's debt rampage, there are also fewer companies in the energy sector; comparatively, the amount of debt per company is staggering. As the sector faltered amid fraudulent balance sheets, overcapacity, and plummeting stock prices, that debt was a ticking bomb whose timer was extended only by a wave of desperate refinancings in 2003. (According to an April 2003 Standard & Poor's report over $80 billion of debt is due to be repaid by 2007.)[113] That massive debt went toward four main endeavors, none of which had anything to do with the quality of consumer services.

First, it was used to capitalize highly leveraged, massive speculative trading operations (like those at Enron, Dynegy, El Paso, CMS Energy, and Reliant) that then pissed away the money and had to close shop for various reasons. Investment banks quickly moved in to fill the void such failed operations left behind. Commercial banks that had bought pieces of old power marketer trading operations increased efforts to lobby the FERC for greater trading latitude. Of course, no financial institute is under any obligation to ensure a stable supply of electricity to American customers, unlike traditional utility companies. Hence, deregulation of energy trading means that players with no vested interest in public protection get in the game, their profit motive entirely unchecked.

Second, debt was tucked away in plant, property, equipment, or goodwill slots on corporate balance sheets. During 2002 and 2003, the top power marketing companies as a group lost over 85 percent of their value. Once-prominent investment-grade merchant companies such as Dynegy, Reliant Resources, El Paso, Mirant, Calpine, CMS, Aquila, and Allegheny were downgraded to junk and subjected to fraud investigations. Their stocks subsequently took up to 95 percent plunges from past highs.[114]

Even though power-marketing companies shed assets at fire-sale prices and aggressively refinanced, they still posted an average of 20 percent declines in revenues through 2003.

Third, companies used debt to purchase old plants and generators so they could buy and then extend old utility contracts, taking advantage of deregulation that had opened utility contracts for sale to the highest bidder. Prior to deregulation, the same companies both produced and distributed the electricity promised by those contracts. Now power marketers could purchase or even trade those contracts without having to worry about servicing customers by distributing electricity when needed or maintaining well-functioning grids. Merchant energy companies bought entire power companies or constructed new natural gas–fired power plants with credit. As part of the bargain, they securitized the cash flows from those utility contracts and used them as collateral to borrow more.

Finally, like in telecoms, billions of dollars of debt were used by these unregulated energy companies to acquire nonenergy companies. Over $856 billion in energy merger volume was transacted from the 1996 deregulation through 2002, a full 9.5 times the volume over the first half of the 1990s.[115] As with the telecoms, some of the debt was used to build fiber-optic networks that nobody needed. Yes, energy companies were going broadband.

The deluge of energy-sector debt after deregulation, coupled with the sector's poor performance, fraud, and closure of formerly highly profitable trading operations, sparked a slew of ratings downgrades throughout 2002 and 2003. On June 28, 2002, Moody's downgraded Dynegy's more than $8 billion of debt to junk status. El Paso's $25 billion debt was cut to junk status by Moody's in late November 2002, prompting a share price drop to $2.05, down 81 percent for the year. Reliant Resources, Mirant Corporation, and Williams Company were all downgraded from investment grade to junk.[116] In addition to being downgraded, energy companies had to find ways to keep making payments on their old debt. Restructuring debt to extend its maturity was one option. Making a severe lack of cash situation worse, borrowing slowed down overall because the lowered ratings made it so much more expensive a prospect.

Reliant Resources, which had a debt ratio (debt capital divided by total assets, a figure that tells you how much the company relies on debt to finance assets) of 52 percent, had to refinance almost $6 billion by February 2003; CMS had $4 billion in debt coming due at the same time with a debt ratio of 70 percent; and Calpine owed $7.3 billion and carries a debt ratio of 72 percent, just to name a few examples.[117]

Williams Company, the Oklahoma-based power marketing firm, was so desperate for cash to furnish its debt that it struck the equivalent of a loan-shark deal with Lehman Brothers and Warren Buffett's Berkshire Hathaway in July 2002 at worse terms than an Überbank would ever extend. At the time, the big commercial banks were suffering a very temporary case of cold credit-extension feet. The banks were still reeling from an enormous amount of telecom exposure in mid-2002, and they tried to keep their energy exposure as low-profile as possible, even while scores of those refinancing discussions were taking place. JP Morgan Chase, which had acknowledged lots of bad telecom and cable loans, admitted at least another $2.2 billion in exposure to merchant energy companies on September 30, 2002.[118]

Dynegy needed money fast, and it would have taken too much time to convince an Überbank, given its struggling status. The company hadn't been a big historical fee generator for banks, so it had fewer "friends" on Wall Street ready to help out. In return for a one-year, $900 million loan with a staggering 30 percent interest rate, the company had to pledge $26 million in assets as additional collateral.[119] Not only were many of the once-prominent high-flying energy companies being downgraded to junk, but the havoc they wreaked on California's economy which caused the state's debt to be downgraded by S&P in January 2001 and Moody's in May 2001. This left California's state government with the worst credit rating in the country.

By the third quarter of 2002, flailing energy companies that needed cash to make good on debt-interest payments were selling any assets they could. El Paso put $3.7 billion in assets on the block on November 27, 2002.[120] During June 2000, El Paso Electric sold 527 megawatts of power to California, charging $750 per megawatt hour for power it bought at an average price of $52.50.[121] On September 25, 2002, Duke Energy announced that it would sell shares to raise almost $1 billion to repay an unsecured short-term loan from the acquisition of Westcoast Energy, Inc. In mid-July 2003, Maryland-based Allegheny Energy filed an emergency request with the SEC to borrow $2.2 billion. Missouri-based Aquila Inc. begged Colorado's public utility commission to allow it to use utility assets as collateral just to maintain daily operations.[122] Aquila's request was granted, and the state wound up subsidizing Aquila for its bad investment and business decisions by allowing it to use more stable assets to pay for speculative losses. In other words, it granted Aquila the use of utility assets, like ratepayer money, to fund or fix speculative decisions. But Missouri had little choice. If it hadn't allowed Aquila the use of those assets as collateral, bankrupting Aquila, it would have been Missouri customers hurt by a potential decline in electricity provision.

TANKING JOBS AND TRADING DESKS

As the energy sector tanked, it cut its workforce and closed its fraudulent, speculative trading operations. The fall was made particularly harsh, given the accompanying loss of pension money. Enron's 2001 collapse had provoked an estimated 20,000 job cuts in the U.S. merchant energy business as of November 2002.[123] Dynegy laid off 18 percent of its workforce, or 1,000 workers, in November 2002, while facing $1.6 billion in debt payments.[124] Duke Energy cut 2,000 jobs as its profits plunged 71 percent during the third quarter of 2002 and it was being issued a subpoena by the

CFTC for its energy trading activities.[125] Both Mirant Corporation and Aquila, Inc.—who had jumped to a second-place ranking in power marketing in early 2002—shed workers and completely pulled out of speculative trading activities.[126]

Energy company trading operations that had flourished during the age of Enron found themselves in the precarious position of closing down and unwinding positions at huge losses. Enron was first, selling its trading operation to UBS on January 21, 2002. Dynegy shut down its online trading system, Dynegy Direct, on June 20, 2002, and Aquila followed suit, shutting its energy trading operations on July 8, 2002.[127] El Paso announced plans to close its energy trading business in early November 2002 and a $600 million charge against fourth-quarter earnings at the same time.

It would be wishful thinking to presume that the trading operations of the power-marketing energy companies were shuttered because speculative trading of the underlying commodities was drying up, or that public or regulatory scrutiny was somehow affecting profit potential, although that argument was certainly popular with the media publications and conservatives. The only problem was that it couldn't be further from the truth. Trading operations ceased for three reasons. One, under massive debt and liquidity crunch problems, companies simply couldn't afford to pony up the capital required to back trading businesses. Secondly, trading just wasn't profitable anymore. Third, traders weren't cheap, even when kept on for scaled-back trading operations. The good ones got swallowed up by Wall Street commodity-trading operations; the less-stellar candidates are still searching for jobs.

REVOLVING ENERGY CEOS

Whenever an energy company began experiencing fraud allegations, exceptional losses, and/or debt payment problems, the CEO would be ousted. But there would always be another one willing to take over the top spot. Four months after Dynegy founder and CEO Chuck Watson resigned with a comfy $33 million golden parachute on May 28, 2002, the company announced another energy CEO would take his place: Bruce Williamson, a former Duke Energy executive. News of Williamson's appointment came on October 23, 2002, right after Dynegy cut 780 jobs.

Four days before Watson's resignation, William McCormick Jr. left his position as chairman and CEO of CMS Energy Corporation after it became public that federal regulators were investigating allegations that Dynegy and CMS had engaged in "round-trip" wash trades with each other.[128]

Dynegy had a tough time getting a CEO to stick around, however. Their first hire to replace Watson actually was Glenn Tilton, then the vice-chairman of Chevron-Texaco (a 26.5 percent stakeholder in Dynegy). But Tilton left shortly thereafter to become chairman, president, and CEO of United Airlines. Just three months after Tilton's arrival, on December 9, 2002, United filed for Chapter 11 with $25 billion in assets, muscling its way onto the highly competitive list of the nation's top ten bankruptcies.[129]

Over at El Paso, William A. Wise resigned as CEO on February 11, 2003. While announcing his departure, Wise insisted, "We are focused on creating value for our shareholders by generating stable earnings and cash flow in our core businesses, strengthening and simplifying our balance sheet, maximizing liquidity, reducing our debt, and resolving our other outstanding issues. I intend to continue to implement this plan while assisting the board in achieving a smooth and successful transition."[130] Though Wise had previously told the press that El Paso did nothing wrong vis-à-vis California, two days after his announcement, on February 13, 2003, El Paso was slapped with a $15.5 million fine payable to California's Electric Power Fund.[131] Other energy CEOs merely got ousted by boards or resigned amid fraud investigations, usually taking millions of dollars of severance pay on the way out the door, such as in the case former Reliant Resources CEO, Steve Letbetter, who collected a $7.6 million package as he left the company in April 2003 in scandal.

ENERGY, ELECTRICITY, AND BROADBAND

One of the causes of the 1990s stock bubble was broadband mania. Taking a key supporting role alongside the more famous dot-com and high-tech companies, almost every energy company had decided to go broadband by the late 1990s. Broadband was a hot new area completely unhampered by regulation, and any company wanting to raise money to get into that business was fawned over by Wall Street and investors.

Goldman Sachs, for example, transformed Montana Power into Touch

America, pocketing a $20 million investment banking fee in the process. Montana Power was an "old-economy" energy utility company, and Touch America was its telecommunications subsidiary. In March 2000, Montana Power sold its energy operations and became solely a telecommunications firm. It wasn't long before deregulated electricity prices soared through the roof and Montana Power/Touch America shed all its assets. Touch America filed for Chapter 11 bankruptcy protection on June 19, 2003.[132] 360networks, bankrupt in 2001, back in 2002, acquired Touch America's assets in early 2004.

Other examples of the energy-broadband grab included Dynegy, El Paso, and Duke. In fact, it became much harder to find an energy company that hadn't embraced the broadband bullet than one that had. Dynegy created Dynegy Broadband Services in August 2000, laying 16,000 fiber-optic miles.[133] El Paso created El Paso Global Networks, a wholly owned subsidiary of El Paso's Energy Corporation and signed an agreement with Broadwing Communications on July 17, 2000, to put down 17,000 fiber-optic miles of its own.[134] Duke Energy created Duke Net Communications and 16,000 new fiber-optic miles in the southeast United States. Mirant created Phoenix Broadband. Reliant created Reliant Broadband (Grande Communication) in September 2000.[135]

Energy companies used broadband and not energy plans to augment their appeal to investors at large. Not surprisingly, Enron's 2000 annual report exaggerated its potential broadband profitability: "Data storage is a $30 billion-per-year business, and we know customers would like to purchase it on an as-needed basis."[136] On the back of that, Enron announced the formation of subsidiary Enron Broadband Services, Inc. in July 2000, capable of 18,000 fiber-optic miles of transmission.[137] They partnered up with Rice University, garnering academic legitimacy from the relationship, which Ken Lay said would "bring tremendous benefits to Enron from a recruiting and business perspective." He added, "The broadband services alliance with Rice also should serve as a launching pad for similar initiatives with other universities."[138] There were no other such combinations, however, and Enron's broadband subsidiary never achieved the profit heights Lay predicted. In fact, it followed its parent into bankruptcy court, filing for Chapter 11 on January 17, 2002.[139]

On April 22, 2002, Williams Communication, the broadband arm of the Williams Company Incorporated, became the second energy broadband spin-off to file for bankruptcy protection.[140] Energy companies not only fueled corporate debt volumes, they contributed to already-skyrocketing overcapacity in the telecom sector by piling on more and more unused fiber miles. Many broadband arms of energy companies avoided the same fate by being sold off to broadband companies, often post–Chapter 11 themselves; for example, 360networks also got Dynergy's communications business in 2003.

OTHER ENERGY COMPANY INVESTIGATIONS

Criminal practices abounded throughout the power sector. The FERC opened investigations into "Enronian" practices at other key energy companies in February 2002.[141]

In July 2002, Duke Energy confessed to twenty-three round-trip trades totaling $126 million. Duke said those trades were intended to raise volume on the electronic trading platform ICE, run by Goldman Sachs and others.[142] A month later, Duke further admitted that they had booked $1.1 billion in wash trades since 1999, reporting sixty-six "improper" energy trades to the SEC, which had informally (and "non-publicly") requested information on round-trip or wash trades.[143] On May 21, 2002, Reliant admitted to booking $1.2 billion, or 14 percent of their 2001 revenues, in wash trades.[144] CEO Steve Letbetter resigned nearly a year later, on April 13, 2003, conveniently a week before the FERC released documents depicting how Reliant manipulated energy prices during the California crisis.[145] CMS Energy booked $5.3 billion, or 23 percent of its revenues from wash trades during 2000 and 2001.[146] 80 percent of its trades in 2001 alone were round-trips.[147]

By August 2002, El Paso, Avista Corporation, Avista Energy Corp., and three Enron corporate affiliates were also under investigation.[148] By early November 2002, Reliant Resources, Duke Energy, Williams, Mirant, and Advanced Energy Systems had all received federal subpoenas relating to market manipulation in California during its crisis.[149] The subpoenas' charges included misreporting of prices to energy data publishers, withholding of power generation, and wash trading.[150]

Through deception, the core corporate energy cartel manipulating California's electricity market bagged an average of 15 percent of their annual revenues from round-tripping, virtually concocting trade values and revenues from thin air, while booking paper profits. And that percentage only accounts for the round tripping that was confirmed by corporations to lower their fines. Dynegy, Duke Energy, El Paso, Reliant Resources, CMS Energy, and Williams Company all admitted to engaging in some false "round-trip" or "wash" trades. Their fines were not entirely commensurate with their fake trading activities.[151]

In addition to booking false trades, the energy companies were reporting false prices to industry publications, which they used to pump up trade profits. On December 5, 2002, Todd Geiger, former vice president at El Paso Merchant Energy who oversaw its Canadian natural gas trading desk, was charged with wire fraud and filing a false report for allegedly releasing prices for forty-eight natural gas trades that he never transacted in order to boost prices and subsequent profits to a trade publication. Six weeks later, Michelle Marie Valencia, a former Dynegy senior energy trader, was arrested on charges that she reported fictitious natural gas prices to another industry publication.

In all, the power sector engaged in and admitted to billions of dollars of imaginary transactions and evaluations, and booked their fake profits as a significant portion of their revenues. Including the cost of price manipulation in California and neighboring states and the money lost to energy companies' post-deregulation looting spree, the real cost of their faux-business comes to approximately $60 billion. Adding in the values lost through other means of balance-sheet fraud and bankruptcies, the sector lied about or ate through over $126 billion. The culprit corporations and executives paid back less than $1 billion in cash fines—less than one percent of the total damage.

RELIANT RESOURCES

On July 8, 2002, two months after FERC began an investigation into its trading practices in May 2002, Reliant Resources, another independent energy producer, admitted to almost $8 billion of sham energy trades and accounting tricks in the period from 1999 through 2001.[152] It took almost a year later for FERC to release documents that specifically explained how Reliant traders and plant operators manipulated energy prices during the California crisis. At the time, FERC, attempting a show of power, even threatened to revoke Reliant's right to do business in wholesale power markets—amazingly, the first time it had ever threatened a company in such a manner.[153] But it didn't make good on the threat. Meanwhile, Reliant escaped bankruptcy, thanks to last-minute debt restructuring.

FERC's case focused on three main incidents. The first was a series of December 2000 gas trades between Reliant and Enron that drove up West Coast natural gas prices by $1.15 billion by "churning," or buying and selling quickly, creating more power than was actually needed.[154] The second consisted of two faked electricity deals between British Petroleum (BP Energy) and Reliant that artificially increased power prices. More than 10 percent of Reliant's fourth-quarter 2000 income, or $23.4 million, came from those two little tricks.[155] Finally, the documents revealed that Reliant deliberately shut down power plants to hike up prices for two days in June 2000.[156] On January 31, 2003 Reliant agreed to pay $13.8 million to California for shutting down its plants, a mere slap on the wrist considering the evidence of clear and convincing fraud.[157] A revised settlement in October 2003 added another $250 million in fines to be extracted from Reliant's auctioning of generation capacity.

EL PASO AND ITS PARTNERSHIPS

Deregulation of power plants was key to El Paso's and others' ability to transform power producing into power trading. The accounting rules allowed for long-term contract profit to be booked up front, regardless of when that money would actually be received, or if it would ever be received.

While Enron was busy with its own convoluted partnerships, El Paso, with the help of Ralph Eads, an investment banker at DLJ, was creating a few of its own.[158] To avoid the appearance of more debt on its balance sheet, DLJ and El Paso formed an off–balance sheet partnership called Chaparral Investors, LLC in 1999. It eventually raised $1 billion to acquire a bunch of old power plants.[159] El Paso and DLJ sold its old power plants to Chaparral for $900 million, and then negotiated contracts with those same plants in a venture called Project Electron. El Paso thus managed to trade the future income from long-term contracts with utilities at high fixed prices for money up front, which they immediately booked as current profit.[160] It was later disclosed that DLJ had a 95 percent share in common stock and a 100 percent share in preferred stock interest in the sale, a conflict of interest based on a compromise of DLJ's position as both an advisor and almost sole beneficiary of its clients activities.[161]

El Paso had set up a new merchant energy division for gas and power trading to take care of that and similar transactions, like the purchase of power plants. The old power contracts would be negotiated and transformed into longer-term contracts with utility companies, then collateralized to raise more debt. Thus, El Paso played the same partnership games as Enron. Off–balance sheet, it booked millions of dollars of profits and hid billions of dollars of debt by restructuring a portfolio of old power supply contracts in the wake of energy deregulation.[162] The partnerships were vaguely alluded to in its 2001 annual report, but their effect on boosting profits and decreasing the appearance of debt was not mentioned at all.[163] In addition to booking profits, the partnerships also collected "management fees" to ensure the contracts held by them were paid as promised. El Paso generated $330 million just from that little bait-and-switch ploy between 2000 and 2001, by shifting management expenses off its consolidated income statement and booking them as profit to its partnership, a win-win scenario from a tax perspective for the company.

In addition to creating special-purpose entities to raise debt backed by long-term contracts, El Paso, through its El Paso Natural Gas pipeline subsidiary, withheld at least 10 percent of the capacity on its pipeline between the Southwest gas fields to California from November 2000 to March 2001.[164] California regulators alleged El Paso used its dominance of the Southern California market to inflate gas prices there by $3.7 billion.[165]

El Paso thought otherwise, stating, "The evidence in this case demonstrates that, at all times, El Paso Natural Gas operated its system to maximize the amount of capacity available in California."[166] Six months later, El Paso received a $15.5 million fine, most of which they were not required to be paid in cash, but in renegotiated contracts.[167]

It wasn't until October 2003 that the SEC finally launched an investigation into El Paso's accounting. Their inquiry focused on August 2002 changes to a power supply contract with Pacific Gas and Electric, a California state utility company and a unit of the Public Service Enterprise Group of Newark. Restructuring of that contract led to a one-time gain of 70 percent for El Paso's first quarter 2002 operating income.[168]

CALIFORNIA MARKET MANIPULATION

Conservatives blamed California price hikes on "bad deregulation," not deregulation itself, a distinction designed to justify the removal of even more rules: it was all California's fault, not the result of a corporate manipulation free-for-all.[169] That kind of twisted logic set the stage for Arnold Schwarzenegger, California movie icon and the man involved in the two-time bankruptcy of Planet Hollywood International Inc., to boot Governor Gray Davis out and take over the governorship. But it was Senator Dianne Feinstein who had desperately tried to make the true situation clear, and it was Feinstein who pointed out that the practices that led to California's price manipulations were far more widespread than just Enron's quest for profit. She said, "The market abuse was not limited to a few rogue traders at one firm, but was a widespread series of schemes perpetuated by many employees across most companies that supplied and traded in the West."[170]

California's energy system operates by something called a reverse auction process. In this process, traders and producers offer up supplies, and an independent agency, called an Independent Systems Operator (ISO), buys enough power to cover the day's expected demand. The ISO chooses as many plants as it needs to keep the lights on, selecting the lowest bids first, then the next lowest, and so on. Once it has met its power demand, the highest bid accepted becomes the price every generator receives.

The reason electricity prices are so easy to manipulate is simple: people and businesses need electricity. They have no choice but to pay for it, no matter the cost. In economic terms, this is referred to as a low-elasticity market. As demand reached the limits of supply, producers knew they could receive any price they asked for; all they had to do was game the system in their favor to create a veritable chokehold and reap the benefits of a captive consumer base. The risk of suppliers not being chosen was negligible in California, especially during the summer months.

Energy suppliers who had become power plant owners thanks to deregulation could keep prices high on days when demand was particularly low simply by creating false emergencies: such as closing down their generators (a favorite ploy of Williams Company Inc.) and thereby extracting high bids. On November 11, 2002, Williams Company was fined $417 million for intentionally closing some plants in April 2000, illegally pricing energy, in the process.[171]

Companies never acted alone. They used their own subsidiaries or other companies as trading partners. Traders at Williams conspired with AES Energy plant operators to withhold power from the system and drive prices up, a move that could be easily be considered an antitrust violation. On April 27, 2000, Williams outage coordinator Rhonda Morgan had the following conversation with Eric Pendergraft, a high-ranking AES employee, to extend one plant outage and provide inconsistent reasons for idling another because the California grid operator was paying "a premium" for power at the time.

> *Pendergraft:* "You guys were saying that it might not be such a bad thing if it took us a little while longer to do our work?"
> *Morgan:* "I don't want to do something underhanded, but if there's work you can continue to do . . ."
> *Pendergraft:* "I understand. You don't have to talk anymore."[172]

Though that was the end of the conversation, it wasn't the end of power manipulation.

California was fighting a losing battle against the power manipulators. In fact, to combat price spikes, the state attempted to put price caps in place when the crisis began in mid-2000. But traders found a way around that by selling power to neighboring states that didn't have any caps and then reselling that power back to California, effectively circumventing California's caps. It was not until regional caps were finally put in place, per a June 2001 FERC initiative that the crisis eased.

By late February 2003, in the wake of enormous evidence of widespread malfeasance, Senator Feinstein, who is a member of the Energy and Natural Resources Committee, proposed adding the Energy Market Oversight Amendment to an energy bill in order to establish basic ground rules and disclosure requirements for energy trading.[173] Though the overall cost of energy in California had risen from $8 billion to $28 billion in 2000 alone, a 400 percent increase, the amendment failed to pass.[174]

The amended energy bill failed again when it went up for vote on June 25, 2003, despite the fact that by then additional damning conversations at Reliant Resources had been revealed. The following conversation took place in June 2000:

> *Reliant Operations Manager 1:* . . . tomorrow we will have all the units at Coolwater off.

Reliant Plant Operator 2: Really?

Reliant Operations Manager 1: Potentially. Even number four. More due to some market manipulation attempts on our part.

Reliant Plant Operator 2: Trying to shorten the supply, huh? That way the price on demand goes up.

Reliant Operations Manager 1: Well, we'll see.

Reliant Plant Operator 2: I can understand. That's cool.

Reliant Operations Manager 1: We've got some term positions that, you know, that would benefit. So, we'll see what happens. So you're scheduled tomorrow on two and four probably initially at least. I know two will be off and the initial schedule will say four is off. . . .[175]

It doesn't get clearer than that. The larger question is why Reliant is still allowed to operate or, more importantly, why the FERC didn't flex its proverbial muscle to protect the public by shutting Reliant down.

GETTING BUSH TO RESPOND

While California power prices were exploding, Senator Feinstein tried again and again to discuss the crisis with President Bush. She was unable to get his attention, however, and was shunted aside into "group meetings" on March 27, 2001 and June 12, 2001 with Vice President Dick Cheney, head of the Energy Task Force Committee, which led nowhere. According to the *New York Times*, Feinstein said she tried "three or four times" to speak with Bush about the state's crisis but the president refused to see her. The two brief meetings she did receive were with Cheney, but only in the context of larger meetings. "Their attitude was laissez-faire, let the market do what the market does, but it was a broken market," she told the *Times*. Feinstein's continuing efforts to highlight price manipulation examples as they were unfolding for President Bush were always ignored. She said, "This is one of the things I tried to see the President about, but he wouldn't see me. . . . I had hoped if I could give this information to the President of the United States at that time that he might look into it and we might have prevented some of what happened in the western energy markets. Unfortunately—and I wrote three letters—he refused to see me on this subject."[176] During California's electricity crisis,

Cheney helpfully remarked that he "never saw price regulations [he'd] felt good about."[177]

In May 2001, four months after he took office and two months after dissing Senator Feinstein (for the first time), Bush held a press conference on national energy policy with cabinet members following a national energy policy development group presentation. Regarding California's rolling blackouts, Bush made it crystal clear just how in touch he was with the state's pain, stating, "I'm upbeat about America, I truly am. I think this is a country that is going to show the rest of the world how to deal wisely with energy." Demonstrating his commitment to California's plight, he announced that he would "call on the Federal Trade Commission to make sure nobody in America gets illegally charged. And . . . to make sure FERC will monitor electricity suppliers to make sure that they charge rates that are fair and reasonable." He concluded with the promise that "the Attorney General and I will work with the FTC."[178] That prompted a rather ominous question-and-answer period with the press in which Bush demonstrated his inability to understand—and lack of desire to do anything about—the price manipulation running rampant in California.

> Q: Mr. President, let me make it clearer. Are you calling on an FTC and FERC investigation, or are you plainly restating their obligations under the law already?
>
> THE PRESIDENT: I am calling on the FTC to take appropriate action any time there is a complaint against illegal pricing.
>
> Q: Is there any evidence, to your mind, that there is illegal pricing now? Is there a reason for an investigation?
>
> THE PRESIDENT: None whatsoever. But should somebody have a complaint, it is the appropriate role of the FTC to look into that complaint.
>
> Q: And you feel the same on FERC, sir? None whatsoever?
>
> THE PRESIDENT: Yes, sir, I do.[179]

In summary, President Bush had this to say: "We're deeply concerned about the state of California, as we are with the rest of the nation. But we haven't had an energy policy."[180] Unfortunately, that statement was all too true.

THE INCULPABLE FERC

Instead of stepping up and showing some leadership and understanding, or at least asserting their federally-mandated control over power companies, the FERC did the opposite. In 2003, it allowed contracts worth $13 billion that California signed during the height of the electricity market crisis to stand. It was tantamount to a truly criminal act: locking in the fraudulent contract values for California for years to come. California is stuck paying inflated rates on twenty year contracts. Thus, the contracted energy companies will benefit over and over from their past price manipulations. At the very least, the FERC should have allowed California out of the 2000–2001 contracts with energy companies that were shown to have perpetrated price manipulation, and let the state negotiate those contracts anew—a more equitable solution. Yet FERC Chairman Patrick Wood III and FERC commissioner Nora Brownell (both Bush Jr. appointees and Republicans) voted two-to-one against any such redress, making the FERC a partisan accessory to the deceit rather than a protector of the public. This didn't come as that big a surprise: in addition to writing Bush, Feinstein had also written repeatedly to Wood to request public access to information that the FERC and Energy Policy Commission had uncovered regarding market manipulation in the Western states. Her February 6, 2003, letter was ignored. So was the one she sent on March 3, 2003.

The FERC's refusal meant that, although energy companies deliberately spiked prices, their inaction effectively translates into future profit for the same companies. In the course of that same decision, the FERC made an example of Enron, and revoked its right to trade. Given that Enron's trading operations had long since ceased, however, that act of punishment seemed hollow and merely cosmetic.[181]

A few days after that FERC decision, Tyson Slocum, research director for Public Citizen's Energy Program, commented to me on the decision to uphold California's long-term energy contracts: "On the one hand, they're effectively saying to Enron 'We are revoking your rights for contract-based trading because you manipulated prices.' On the other hand, they're saying 'But we're still going to keep all those contracts and their prices in place for everyone else.' It's completely outrageous."[182]

Ironically, the best California could hope for is if any of these energy companies defaults, California will be forced to find energy elsewhere, perhaps at more reasonable rates.

The FERC's dodge successfully allowed energy companies under fraud investigation, with serious evidence of market manipulation and admitted wash trades, to overbook future revenue based on their past crimes. Senator Feinstein stated, "FERC has already found that energy companies had deliberately manipulated the electricity and natural gas markets, and it is incomprehensible to me that FERC would not allow California to open up long-term contracts signed at the height of the crisis."[183] As those remaining energy companies continue to reap gains, California consumers will be paying for their deceit for years to come.

MONTANA'S LAWSUIT AND STATES' ACTIONS

States had to sue the companies that federal regulators let off the hook with tiny fines and no reform. Joining California, Montana launched a lawsuit of its own on July 1, 2003. It was against Portland General Electric (PGE) and eleven other companies.[184] Their complaint accused these companies of causing related spikes in Montana's energy prices due to their manipulation of the California energy market for both residential and industrial customers. It sought refunds and cancellations of licenses from the culprit companies.

The Texas Public Utility Commission (PUC) opened its own investigation into price manipulation in March 2003, a full fourteen months after Enron went bankrupt. Taking advantage of congestion in the power line system caused prices to rise unnaturally even in Houston, cradle of Enron, Halliburton, and El Paso. An eighteen-fold price spike in electricity prices in late February 2003 had pushed Texas Commercial Energy (TCE) into Chapter 11 bankruptcy protection and triggered the state utility regulators to launch their own investigation into potential trading abuses.

Power prices at the Electric Reliability Council of Texas (ERCOT) spiked to $990 per megawatt hour between February 24 and 25, 2003, as frigid temperatures, rising natural gas prices, and technical plant problems created a temporary supply squeeze, driving up prices. The Texas PUC said it would look into the activity of so-called hockey stick bidding, which occurs when a trader submits a small portion of its bid at an extremely high price, driving up the market; the PUC said the practice was a major factor in those price hikes.[185] Pat Wood used to run that agency. He had been appointed by then-governor George W. Bush in February

1995.[186] If the lessons Wood took from the Texas PUC to the federal level can be viewed as a reliable barometer, though, Texans are in trouble, and price manipulation will continue.

What's even more distressing than the evidence of mass market manipulation by the largest energy companies in the country throughout 2000 and 2001 is the lack of an effective response from FERC, whose only actions have consisted of minor fees and no regulatory changes.

Par for the non-culpability course, no energy company ever admitted any wrongdoing regarding fraud or electricity market manipulation to anybody. Williams Company wound up paying a $417 million fine even though they systematically closed down their power plants to squeeze profits. When the fine was announced, Williams declared that investigations were a "distraction" to its business. To minimize similar distractions, Dynegy paid $3 million to the SEC for committing round-trip trades, but without formally admitting guilt. Reliant paid a $13.8 million fine in early 2003 and later agreed to $50 million more. El Paso and Duke Energy both stated the SEC investigations were "a nuisance" to their business in 2003. By 2004, the bad news was still coming regularly from the power marketers. In early March of that year, Reliant announced that they were facing criminal indictments for shutting down California power plants.[187] The same month, El Paso announced they'd be late filing their fourth-quarter 2003 reports. It seems they had inflated the value of their natural gas and oil reserves by 41 percent, or over $1 billion. Old habits die hard.

As for Enron, two and a half years and nineteen indictments after Enron's collapse, Ken Lay had yet to be indicted. On January 14, 2004, former CFO Andrew Fastow became the highest-ranking Enron official to plead guilty to any wrongdoing. His trial was initially scheduled for April 2004, but was postponed, as was his sentencing, indefinitely (as of the writing of this book). Under the agreement reached with prosecutors, Fastow pled guilty to two of the ninety-eight counts of fraud and other crimes in connection with Enron he'd been charged with. In exchange, he received a ten-year prison sentence and $23.8 million fine. His wife, Lea Fastow, ultimately pled guilty to a misdemeanor tax charge, instead of an initial six-count felony charge. On May 6, 2004 she was sentenced to one year in prison. Former Enron CEO, Jeff Skilling, was indicted on thirty-six felony charges of insider trading, securities fraud, wire fraud, and manipulating earnings, on February 18, 2004.[188] He immediately pleaded innocent.

Just before its 2003 summer recess, the Senate passed a Democrat-drafted deregulatory energy bill first proposed in 2002. The bill effectively repealed PUHCA, the last vestige of New Deal electricity and energy company regulation. It did not establish punishments or safeguards against the myriad power market and electricity price manipulations. (Amendments implementing those changes had been proposed, only to be voted down by the Republican majority Senate.)

Then came the Great Northeast Blackout of August 2003. That power outage, the largest in North American history, was ironically, not caused by a lack of power, but a lack of rules. Deregulation had created a situation where the companies that produced the power were not responsible for ensuring it actually got across properly maintained grids to the paying customers. That wasn't for lack of money, since the energy sector had raised over $1.2 trillion in capital. It was due to an absence of regulations that would have imposed corporate responsibility for how some of that money was spent, for example, to maintain high quality functional power grids.

While deregulation spawned immense power overcapacity in the United States, as power marketers built generators without thinking twice about how that power would get transmitted to end users, creating the potential for unstable electricity supply. In response to the blackouts, Energy Secretary Spencer Abraham argued that increasing the (still-regulated) returns utilities receive for the transmitting of electricity was a good idea. He argued that a revenue boost would somehow spur Wall Street investment. He suggested this might lead to a feeding frenzy of utilities and power marketers buying up the lines they all had sold off during the preceding few years and upgrading them. Unfortunately, this is unlikely to happen because most of the potential profitability in the energy sector centers around power generation (due to deregulation), not transmission.

Indeed, FERC was equally hopeless and negligent in fulfilling any semblance of public responsibility—their mandated but ignored job—by failing to fine power marketers in proportion to their proven manipulation, upholding California power contracts signed during the height of the worst exploitation, and advocating more, not less deregulation of

power. The fact that individual states had to sue fraudulent and manipulative companies and banks, alongside scores of investor and employee-led
class-action suits, underscores the severe lack of accountability and leadership at the federal level. Meanwhile, most of the companies that perpetuated the frauds remain standing, albeit weaker through their own
recklessness and deceptions. The ones that went bankrupt, including the
mighty Enron and less notable Mirant, will emerge with less debt and go
about their business for round two. With the exception of Jeffrey Skilling,
none of the CEOs who ran any of these companies were indicted or even
fined. Only a total overhaul of the power and energy sector requiring all
corporate players to share accountability for the creation and transmission
of power, supported by concerted oversight of both federal and state regulators, can make a real difference.

5

Telecom Implosion

Quite simply, we know how big business does business.
                                    —2000 Global Crossing annual report

We continue to believe that WorldCom, with its high quality revenue mix and
the best set of assets on the planet . . . is the best-positioned company in this
industry.
                    —Salomon Brothers telecom analyst Jack Grubman, July 1, 1999

THE PRESENCE INSTINCT

EVERY CORPORATION, EVERY DEPARTMENT, EVERY GROUP HAS A HARVEY. A
Harvey states the obvious with conviction. A Harvey listens intently to
what his boss just said, and then registers agreement by regurgitating ver-
batim what he heard, or responds with an earnest "That's exactly what I
was thinking." A Harvey never pays the slightest attention to what his
subordinates or peers think but hangs on his bosses' every syllable. A
Harvey absolutely believes his ascent up the corporate ladder is based on
his superior abilities, though the only one that really counts is his ability
to reinforce the status quo to his advantage.

A Harvey is in love with the sound of his own voice and has a keen
"presence instinct"—he instinctively knows when the chairman is about
to emerge from the men's room, or when the division head is about to get
into a car to the airport, and positions himself accordingly. He gets an
apartment in the same Upper East Side building as his boss's boss. On
the surface and to peers, it might seem like Harvey is merely a talentless
ass kisser, yet in fact he's a very effective cross between a businessman and
a politician. Some combination of these two characteristics can usually be
found in the fastest rising corporate executives. A Harvey always knows
where he needs to be and what he needs to do to maximize his exposure,
his influence, and his power. A Harvey uses a speakerphone as much as

possible—it perpetuates power in the "I am so busy and important I cannot even physically pick up the phone!" sort of way.

Former chairman of Global Crossing Gary Winnick was a Harvey before he hit the big time, brownnosing his way up the corporate ladder. His ambition ultimately placed him in position to extract more money out of the telecom bubble than any other individual. It was a task made easier by absentee federal oversight and the Wall Street–fed media fanfare that surrounded the late 1990s on-paper broadband boom.

A combination of power, politics, and control defined the giant telecom companies that grew out of rational proportion following the 1996 telecom deregulation. Many subsequently crashed or lost significant market value between 2001 and 2002. The most noticeable failures were WorldCom and Global Crossing. During their rise, their very monikers, showcasing the words "World" and "Global," symbolized the ominous desire for unbridled expansion and total dominance of the Internet economy. These two companies exemplified two dangerous styles of deception, one personified by the shady political opportunism of Gary Winnick and the other by the control tactics of Bernie Ebbers. These firms housed more intricate deceptions and misleading finances than any CEO or CFO could concoct individually. Their deceptions were made possible because of the relaxed regulatory controls surrounding their industry, and they were pumped up by predator Wall Street banks who seized on a fantastic method of growing their fee businesses by making stars out of their broadband clients, then later, sucking them dry.

Telecoms comprised more than 25 percent of the $15 billion of fees that Wall Street raked in during the 1990s.[1] In just four years, Global Crossing's contribution was over $420 million, almost 3 percent of that total, and WorldCom's share was $400 million. Wall Street greatly revered these companies, which paid the biggest fees and were the best clients for mergers and acquisitions, IPOs, and debt issuance.[2]

In addition to boosting Wall Street to great profit during the 1990s (particularly the second half), the telecom industry spent a fair chunk of its inflated stock money on buying politicians and federal policy. The communications industry is second only to the financial industry in giving the most money to Washington. Political donations since 1990 topped $491 million, 71 percent of which came after 1996 deregulation, demonstrating just how much deregulation raised the influence stakes. In addition, lobbying money from the sector topped $734 million during its fastest postderegulation growth spurt from 1997 through 2000.[3]

GLOBAL CROSSING AND GARY WINNICK

I don't subscribe to the "bad apples" theory. The web of corporate corruption was far more complicated than a few CEOs going morally or ethically astray. It was mass industry deregulation, combined with the thirst for accumulating market share and short-term personal wealth that created a heightened period of unsustainable and irrational growth, fraud, and destruction. Nonetheless, in the case of the Global Crossing saga, Gary Winnick should be singled out as a particularly insidious figure. There is no individual from that time period that better personified the ability to influence the system for his own benefit. He manipulated the financial and political sectors faster than any robber baron or stock market king to emerge from the late 1990s market bubble. When he was done, after cashing out over $734 million, he returned to his well-honed sales skills. He sold his "lack of knowledge" about the company's deteriorating condition to a House investigations committee in October 2002, in order to escape culpability for its fraudulent acts and subsequent collapse. The government bought it. Two months later, Attorney General John Ashcroft exonerated him completely. Winnick and all his collaborators ultimately emerged from the wreck of their company not only unscathed but much richer.

Like many luminaries of the corporate scandals, Winnick began life humbly. He went to high school in a small Long Island, New York, town. He attended a local university, C.W. Post, from which he graduated with a degree in business and economics. His father was a furniture salesman who died of a heart attack at the age of fifty-two. Following in his father's footsteps, Winnick joined the furniture business, which provided his initial sales training. His real rags-to-riches all-American dream story began in 1972. Winnick joined Burnham and Co. as a trainee broker. He rose to become a top aide to junk bond king Michael Milken at what became Drexel Burnham Lambert. In 1985, he decided to start his own business, so he left his position as a bond salesman and created a small financial investment company in California called Pacific Capital Group (PCG) with start-up capital from his former Drexel buddies. For eleven years, Winnick ran

PCG and remained largely unknown to the public. Then the 1996 telecom deregulation arrived. At the time, PCG was in talks with AT&T about raising financing for PCG's network when Winnick decided he'd do it himself. As fits his banking background, he acted as if the telecom industry revolved around raising capital, not creating inventions or providing customer service.

Winnick knew better than any other telecom executive how to work the Wall Street system to get credit, huge debt issues, and favorable stock recommendations. That was the world he had come from. His Wall Street education took place during the mid-1980s, a time dominated by junk bonds and leveraged buyouts; he had worked alongside Milken at a time when junk bonds, or debt for highly leveraged and speculative companies, ruled the Street. (Milken later pleaded guilty to securities fraud and was sentenced to ten years in prison and a $500 million fine. He was released after two years.) As a longtime student of leveraged finance, Winnick also knew that if he put some of his own money up first, more would follow.

Since financial loyalty was a buyable commodity, Winnick didn't attempt to make banks compete with each other on price. He knew that if he didn't spread his business around too thinly, he and his company would get more attention from the banks, which were deferential to significant fees and size. Plus, the larger the issue, the more liquid the bonds would be considered and the more confident the firm issuing them. So Global Crossing issued $1 billion blocks of bonds—anything short of that would have failed to receive the appropriate attention, or financial respect, from the banks or the investors. Additionally, Winnick was willing to pay generous fees by market standards for those issues. He was never known to haggle over a basis point (tiny fraction of price) here or there. This was in contrast to companies like Ford, notorious for talking down fees or squeezing banks. Winnick's tactics enabled Global Crossing to establish a reputation, albeit briefly, as the next blue chip of telecoms; even with its junk bond credit rating, people talked about it like the next AT&T. By the end of 2001, Global Crossing's bonds accounted for 2 percent of the entire corporate high-yield bond market and 16 percent of the wire line sector.

Winnick knew how to spin an idea. Global Crossing's grand underlying concept was as deceptively simple as its balance sheet was complex: to create the first fully connected global fiber-optic network, crisscrossing the world to transmit data and other communications at Internet speed.

It was difficult for investors to resist the heady concept of total global connectivity for all fiber-optic systems and state-of-the-art networks that covered the planet. In 1999, as other carriers were feverishly building or acquiring new networks, Global Crossing boasted of getting 80 percent of all the world's businesses connected to its network.[4] Money followed that dream. As such, Global Crossing's ascent took Winnick far from those Long Island roots. It put him in the big time, hobnobbing with the power elite. It landed him in Beverly Hills, the capital of show, and in a $95 million mansion called Casa Enchanta on Stone Canyon Drive, just off Sunset Boulevard. By the time Winnick exited the fiber-optic network business, he was almost $1 billion wealthier. In contrast, his 9,000 laid-off employees were $325 million poorer.

To start it all off, Winnick put up $15 million of his own money and convinced a few of his PCG partners and a Canadian bank, Canadian Imperial Bank of Commerce (CIBC), to back him. He then launched a little private telecom company called Global Telesystems, which was renamed Global Crossing in March 1997. Global Crossing later rewarded CIBC's early support with $55 million in fees, and the bank received a $1.7 billion return on its $41 million investment, as well as five seats on the board.[5] (CIBC also happened to employ Gary Winnick's son.) Winnick was in search of a power base as much as a business coup; if he could latch onto the "new economy" with first-mover advantage and the ability to garner a broad international and domestic market share, he could achieve the kind of status that, coupled with riches, could corner influence and political power in one fell swoop.

The private Global Crossing was transformed into the public company Global Crossing Limited, courtesy of a 1998 IPO managed by Salomon Brothers and Merrill Lynch, who were each paid $30 million for the privilege. The following year, on April 19, 1999, Winnick broke the "speed to wealth" barrier, outpacing John D. Rockefeller, Henry Ford, and Bill Gates to his first billion. It only took him eighteen months to get there, at a rate of $100 million a month. He was rewarded with a *Forbes* cover story.[6]

Winnick had created PCG Telecom Services a year earlier. This faux consulting company copied one of Enron's maneuvers discussed in chapter 4, shifting income back and forth between the parent company and related offshoots. PCG Telecom Services charged Winnick's other company, Global Crossing, consulting fees. The $142 million in consulting revenue thus reverted back to maestro Winnick, who was effectively consulting to himself. In addition, those fees covered his start-up risk completely.[7] Winnick also got Global Crossing to pony up the annual $400,000 rent and $7.5 million in renovations for another of his companies, North Crescent Realty, a real estate firm that happened to own Global Crossing's headquarters building.[8] For years, Winnick sucked cash out of Global Crossing and into various other companies owned or partially owned by PCG, a firm he, as of the writing of this book, still runs.

POLITICS AND THE ROYAL COOK

The political intricacies of Global Crossing were astonishing, given its five-year history (compared to Enron's seventeen years). Winnick worked the political arena with a vengeance, filling the pockets and stroking the egos of Republicans and Democrats alike. Winnick booked George H.W. Bush to address an international Global Crossing conference in Tokyo in April 1998 for an $80,000 fee, paid in 100,000 shares of pre-IPO stock, which Bush cashed out for $4.5 million in 1999 and 2000.[9]

Winnick also gave Bill Clinton's library foundation $1 million following a 1999 golf game with Clinton. Clinton's former aide Terry McAuliffe, now head of the Democratic National Committee, had scheduled the game. Two years earlier, Winnick had gotten McAuliffe a Global Crossing consultancy spot, which McAuliffe happily accepted, along with $100,000 in pre-IPO stock. That stock ultimately ballooned to an $18 million windfall.[10] As McAuliffe later told Fox News, "I invested in many companies, and I'm happy this one worked. This is capitalism. You invest in stock, it goes up, it goes down. You know, if you don't like capitalism, you don't like making money with stock, move to Cuba or China."

Winnick asked the well-connected Republican Lodwrick Cook to join PCG in September 1997 as vice chairman and managing director, and later appointed Cook co-chairman of Global Crossing, where he remained from 1998 to 2003. Cook, an old oil buddy of George H.W. Bush and a major donor to the Republican Party, was already doing pretty well in the power influence arena before he met Gary, but he didn't mind pocketing another $35 million in Global Crossing stock sales to boost his bank account.[11]

Prior to joining Global Crossing, Cook enjoyed a thirty-nine-year career at Atlantic Richfield Company (ARCO), which was the seventh largest U.S. oil company before it merged with BP and Amoco. He became chairman and CEO of the firm in January 1986 and chairman emeritus upon retiring in June 1995.[12] In addition, he chaired the Owners' Committee of the Trans-Alaska Pipeline System. ARCO was the leading U.S. oil-drilling company in Alaska.

In one of many overlaps between the energy and telecommunications industries, Cook shared one particular distinction with Ken Lay: both were recipients of the John Roger Award for Energy Law. The award is presented annually by the Center for American and International Law's Institute for Energy Law to a person associated with the petroleum industry in recognition of extraordinary professional and civic achievement. Cook won in 1991. Lay won in 2001.[13]

During the 1988 election, Cook was a member of George Bush's Team 100, a group of executives and other members of the wealthy elite who formed the core financial support for Bush's campaign, with all hundred donating at least $100,000.[14] When Bush reached the Oval Office, his inner circle was rewarded with favorable legislation. In Cook's case, his $862,000 donation bought ARCO a reformulated gas provision in Bush's clean air proposal and a White House push for more Alaska oil drilling. In fact, just before his 1989 inauguration, George Bush publicly commented on his ties to his oil comrades. "They got a president of the United States that came out of the oil and gas industry, that knows it and knows it well," said Bush in reference to the political good fortune of his friends in the oil business.[15] Cook's other ties to the Bush/Reagan era included a trusteeship of the George Bush Presidential Library Foundation (alongside fellow trustee Gary Winnick), and a former chairmanship and directorship of the Ronald Reagan Presidential Foundation. In February 2001, Cook was presented with the George Bush Corporate Leadership Award, created by the Points of Light Foundation in 2000 to "honor a corporate leader who supports the involvement of his or her company's employees as volunteers and demonstrates the importance of service through personal example" for his role in corporate citizenship.[16] A year later, employees of the corporation he co-chaired watched their 401(k) retirement plans dwindle to nothing, frozen into five-year lockout periods that prohibited stock sales for regular employees but not for senior executives.

Cook's influence wasn't restricted to the United States, he spread it around Europe, particularly in the United Kingdom, where he was a member of the Chancellor's Court of Benefactors of Oxford University.

In November 1994, he was appointed an honorary Knight Commander of the Most Excellent Order of the British Empire (KBE) by the Queen of England.[17]

It was Cook's knighthood that paved the way for Global Crossing's entry into the UK market. Out of nowhere and despite plenty of local competition, the company started getting prestigious contracts galore in Britain. In 1999, it won a $33 million contract to become the Royal Mail network provider. Global Crossing also provided the Royal Air Force (RAF) with messaging and directory services for 55,000 users at 70 sites.[18] A year later, it was awarded a ten-year contract by the Foreign and Commonwealth Office (FCO) to implement and support the FCO Telecommunications Network (FTN).[19] The contract was for providing voice, data, and messaging services to 240 British embassies, consulates, and high commissions worldwide, covering 85 percent of FCO overseas staff.

As chairman of Global Crossing's board, Cook turned his sharply honed political ties and influence from energy to telecommunications. "If we're going to compete, we've got to be heard," said Cook at a conference in 1999; "I don't apologize for access"—or for his success in exploiting it, apparently.[20]

Global Crossing *was* heard, loud and clear. The company convinced the FCC to streamline its permit process for laying undersea fiber-optic cable, its central business. Republican senator John McCain helped out. In March 1999, he wrote a letter urging the FCC to encourage the development of the company's cables. That month, McCain's presidential campaign got a $23,000 boost from Cook, Winnick, and other donors with ties to Global Crossing.[21]

POLITICAL CONTRIBUTIONS AS INSURANCE

Global Crossing's political relationships served it well both while it grew and when it disintegrated. As telecom profits and stock values plummeted, lobbying and campaign donations increased. Global Crossing outpaced Enron in political contributions from 1999 through 2001, seeing and raising Enron's $2.9 million bid with $3.6 million of its own (not including a $4 million annual lobbying budget).[22] The subsidiary Global Crossing Development gave $1.33 million in political contributions between 1998 and 2001.[23] In the 2000 election alone, Global Crossing donated $2.4 million to

Washington politicians, leading the telecom services and equipment sector—a category that included big spenders Qwest, Lucent, and Level 3. In the 2002 election, despite great financial difficulties (including bankruptcy), the executives of Global Crossing still managed to come in second in this group, coughing up $1.2 million.[24]

These donations were carefully targeted. For example, Global Crossing in 2000 contributed $20,000 to New York's Democratic state comptroller Carl H. McCall, the sole trustee of New York State's pension fund, which held retirement money for all state civil workers. The comptroller invested money from the state public-employee pension fund in Global Crossing in 2001. The fund wound up losing $63 million on Global Crossing investments, and McCall later filed a lawsuit against the company. That same year, Global Crossing proved it was equally comfortable on both sides of the partisan fence by contributing $22,000 to Republican governor George Pataki's reelection committee.

ROTATING CEOS

The fact that Gary Winnick kept his CEOs for remarkably brief periods, often less than a year, was a way for him to retain power over his company and information flow. CEOs were shoved aside when they were done meeting some short-term goal, and no one was there long enough to develop his own independent, longer-term vision of the company. In addition, just as Winnick paid generous fees to Wall Street, he made sure his CEOs received generous sign-on and departure packages for their stints. In all, Global Crossing's CEOs made over $85.4 million in stock sales and $19.5 million in salary and compensation. Other senior executives pocketed more that $580 million courtesy of Winnick's generosity illuminating the blatant inequity in executive vs. employee pay.

Stock ownership of the company was held in large proportion by the top executives, making a CEO slot at Global Crossing mighty attractive. In June 1999, Global Crossing insiders—including initial investors at CIBC, David Lee and Barry Porter from PCG, Winnick, and others— owned a staggering 68 percent of the company.[25] Six months later, after the Frontier deal was completed, their stake was down to 41 percent.[26] Three months after that, it was down to 25 percent.[27] By the end of the year 2000, their share fell to 15 percent.[28] Executives and insiders were scooping up candy from the Global Crossing piñata for almost two years before it hit bankruptcy by selling off their stake in the company.

The parade of CEOs (five in four years) all had their own ideas about how to run the company, but of course no one stuck around long enough to implement anything, or to challenge Winnick. Instead, they just got things started: business plans changed every six months, promoting a continual sense of instability among employees.

Senior Motorola executive Jack Scanlon became the first CEO in April 1998. His reign was short-lived but profitable—he was CEO when Global Crossing went public. In February 1999, Gary Winnick decided to bag a bigger name and garner some instant legitimacy. Scanlon was bumped to a newly created vice chairman position, concentrating on international development, and in walked Robert Annunziata with a $10 million signing bonus and lots of stock options.

Annunziata had come from a long career at AT&T. At Global Crossing, he was the CEO responsible for engineering the $11.4 billion acquisition of the Rochester-based local telephone company Frontier Communications Corporation in March 1999, which wound up giving Global Crossing its only semblance of stable (or real) revenue. Global Crossing, a two-year-old company with 200 employees, took over a hundred-year-old company with 12,000 employees.[29] It was a case of the tiny and strong taking over the large and weak (in stock price terms), and then destroying it.

Until November 1999, Leo Hindery was president and CEO of AT&T Broadband. From December 1999 until January 2001, he was Chairman and CEO of GlobalCenter, Inc., the Internet services subsidiary of Global Crossing Ltd. While still serving in that capacity, he served a seven-month stint as CEO of Global Crossing beginning in March 2000. He was rumored to be all about lattes and Hermes ties.[30] Some former Global Crossing employees referred to him as "the ultimate empty suit." But that attitude didn't dampen his attention-grabbing exploits. The few times he visited Rochester—Frontier's headquarters had become Global Crossing's headquarters—he transformed the town. He hired all the limos available to cart him and his entourage around.

In a page right out of the McKinsey management consulting book on leadership, Hindery was a strong advocate of team-building exercises and diversity measures. Both Global Crossing and Frontier had appalling diversity conditions among its executives. As Michael Nighan, former head of regulatory affairs for Global Crossing, told me, "You could count senior vice president minorities and women on one hand." That's still the case. Global Crossing's leadership committee is completely male, as is its board of directors.[31]

Hindery's team spirit didn't extend past his severance contract with Global Crossing, though. In October 2002, Hindery's lawyers asked the bankruptcy court to have Global Crossing pony up more than $708,000 in back pay and another $100,000 as part of a two-year severance agreement, which included rental of a sumptuous Manhattan apartment. Hindery's severance package also included a $2 million two-year consulting contract. Laid-off workers, on the other hand, got nothing.[32]

Next in line to lead Global Crossing was Tom Casey, who became CEO number four in November 2000. Casey already had a cozy relationship with Global Crossing and Gary Winnick; he had been partner and co-head of the worldwide telecom/media legal practice of Skadden, Arps, Slate, Meagher and Flom, the law firm involved in the Frontier merger and most of Global Crossing's other significant deals. He had also served as co-head of Merrill Lynch's global telecom banking group. Casey presided over Global Crossing's most creative period—in accounting, that is—yet he escaped any indictments whatsoever. Casey played the pointless upbeat CEO, bordering on the manipulative as he attempted to boost employee and investor perceptions of the firm while it sped toward bankruptcy. He declared "Global Crossing business plans to be fully funded," despite the fact that its stock price was already tanking and its debt burden was substantial. Wall Street helped him out with his PR campaign. Analysts at Merrill Lynch said, "Unlike many other competitive carriers, Global Crossing has proved able to pass through the peak of its funding needs."[33]

CEO number five was John Legere, who had been running Asia Global Crossing when he was tapped to take over the top spot, receiving a $3.5 million signing bonus (even though he already worked for the firm); he also had a $10 million corporate loan forgiven. It was Legere who presided over the bankruptcy and attempted to talk up the value of the bankrupt company above the initial $750 million that Hong Kong–based Hutchison Whampoa and Singapore Technologies Telemedia first offered when news of the bankruptcy hit.

In the end, the veterans of Global Crossing were Gary Winnick, Lodwrick Cook, and Joseph Perrone. Perrone had jettisoned into the Global Crossing circle from his very nearby post at Arthur Andersen, where he had directed the firm's work for Global Crossing's IPO in 1998.[34] He also happened to have worked for a number of the companies with which Global Crossing traded capacity swaps; the most noteworthy of Arthur Andersen's former telecom clients were WorldCom and Qwest. In May 2000, Perrone joined Global Crossing as senior vice president of finance, arriving with a sign-on bonus of $2.5 million, a $400,000 salary with an anticipated 100 percent bonus, and five hundred thousand stock options.[35] In the summer of 2000, the SEC got around to questioning whether Arthur Andersen was truly an independent auditor of Global Crossing in light of Perrone's connections to his former employer, but it reached no negative conclusions. Global Crossing spokesman Dan Coulter said that the SEC's questions were routine and that the commission was satisfied with the company's answers.[36] Perrone remains at the company as of this writing.

BUILDING THE SAND CASTLE COMPANY

Global Crossing didn't do very much acquiring during its short life; it was more intent on raising debt to expand, which suited Wall Street just fine. What little it did buy, mostly in 1999 and early 2000, it quickly broke up into pieces and sold cheaply to raise cash from mid-2000 through the end of 2001, while insiders and executives went on their own stock and options selling spree. Still, a few acquisitions proved key. The most notable, and the only reason it stayed afloat long enough for executives to cash out, was the domestic network and local phone company Frontier Communications. (Frontier had bought local phone company Rochester Telephone Corporation as part of its own merger spree.) Another company, Global Marine, was part of that deal. The rest of the Global Crossing network was built from scratch and funded by debt. Its balance sheet was bloated through swapping its future network capacity with other carriers and booking the money up-front, regardless of whether or not it was ever received.

In April 1997, Global Crossing received the first of four legs, or phases, of financing for its first network, Atlantic Crossing, or AC-1, a transatlantic system connected by high bandwidth and fiber-optic cable.[37] It received a type of financing called project financing, a more specialized form of raising capital than simply borrowing money by issuing bonds. In project finance, a particular undertaking requires capital. The $482 million needed to build AC-1 was financed by CIBC and Deutsche Bank.

A year later, Global Crossing and partners Marubeni and KDD-SCS received $800 million to finance the first high-capacity undersea fiber-optic network between the United States and Japan. Financing for the project was again provided by CIBC, as well by as Deutsche Morgan Grenfell and newcomer to the Global Crossing party, Goldman Sachs. Pacific Crossing (PC-1) was the second major Global Crossing undertaking. Collateral for the credit was partly comprised of a borrowed $50 million "bridge loan"— a temporary loan that a bank extends to a corporation before issuing a longer-term loan—from CIBC and guaranteed by a promissory note, a document signed by a borrower promising to repay a loan under agreed-upon terms, from Global Crossing. Afterward, Chase or Salomon Brothers extended most of Global Crossing's credit in some form. Jimmy Lee, head of Chase's investment banking division, "jumped in with both feet and angled strenuously to pick up business," recalled a former Goldman Sachs telecom banker in an interview with me.

The Chase/Global Crossing relationship, which began in 1998, gave Winnick the chance to hobnob with the likes of David Rockefeller. Winnick returned the favor by making Maria Elena Lagomasino, co-head of Chase's private banking unit, his personal banker in early 2000. He put her on Global Crossing's board of directors in April 2001, where she stayed for six months. More broadly, he also rewarded Chase with lucrative fee business. The timing of Chase's involvement with Global Crossing was fortuitous. Once the company's capital requirements progressed past the project finance stage with its first two networks, it was necessary to adopt a broader corporate funding model and secure credit facilities from larger banks. Chase was the leading U.S. syndicated commercial loan provider.

In August 1998, Salomon Smith Barney and Merrill Lynch took Global Crossing public, and $399 million of shares began trading on the NASDAQ, the largest non-U.S. (the company was headquartered in Bermuda) IPO up to that point. Already, Global Crossing had an agreement with Qwest to exchange capacity between Europe and the United States utilizing both companies' networks, and a $371 million deal with Worldport Communications to carry signals in the United States and Europe.

As with many network-based companies in the 1990s, though, Global Crossing's boasts about its profitability were primarily for show. When it became a publicly traded company, Global Crossing had yet to turn any profit. The company was steeped in debt and indicated it would need substantial further capital to pursue its global network development. From its gestation until its second-quarter 1999 report, Global Crossing incurred a net loss of $167 million for its common shareholders. It never turned a profit. Yet that didn't stop it from piling on debt. Billions of dollars of syndicated loans and credit facilities poured in from the likes of CIBC, JP Morgan Chase, and Citigroup. All told, Global Crossing accumulated $20 billion of debt to construct the undersea network, using new debt to repay old debt, and went bankrupt owing $12.4 billion to creditors.

THE MERGER WITH FRONTIER COMMUNICATIONS

It was after a bitter battle with Qwest—a long distance telecom attempting to reinvent itself as a "new economy" Internet-oriented firm that was angling to expand its empire—that Global Crossing acquired local telecom Frontier Communications. The 1996 deregulation allowed Global Crossing to acquire Frontier in an $11.4 billion all-stock deal that closed September 28, 1999. The fight leading to that acquisition also included a nasty tug-of-war with Qwest over another former Bell company, US West. Any company that had a revenue stream or lines already in place was up for grabs. Ultimately, Qwest decided it could pay for only one and chose US West, its Denver neighbor, leaving Frontier to Global Crossing. Eventually, Qwest won US West and paid $214 million to Global Crossing for luring it away since Global Crossing had seen it first. As part of that deal, Qwest also agreed to acquire capacity on Global's network for $140 million over two years.[38] Capacity junkies made friends of even fierce competitors.

At the time of the merger, most Frontier employees were ecstatic. They overwhelmingly approved the deal at an internal meeting held at the Crowne Plaza Hotel in Rochester, although some had reservations about the speed of the late 1990s grab for local telecoms. They were concerned that too many new corporate chiefs and only short-term strategy would impact their job stability, which turned out to be the case.[39] Global Crossing's stock was trading at $26.25, surpassing Frontier's stock value of $20. Global Crossing felt confident enough to pay two-for-one—two shares of Global Crossing stock for each share of Frontier stock. The combined company, under the umbrella of Global Crossing Holdings Limited, saw its share value shoot to $64 six months later.

As part of the merger, Chase managed a $3 billion credit facility. Though they later denied this credit was extended to get the merger business, the dates indicate otherwise. The facility happened to close on July 2, 1999, and the Frontier acquisition closed afterward, on September 28, 1999.[40] This chronology certainly implied the credit line sealed the merger deal.

Global Crossing went on to buy Racal Electronics in the United Kingdom for $1.65 billion in November 1999, a deal led by Goldman Sachs International. Finally, Global Crossing/Frontier acquired IXnet and its parent, IPC Communications, for $3.8 billion of stock in a March 2000 deal advised by Chase and Salomon Brothers.[41] That was the end of the acquisitions. From then on, it was all about struggling to raise money to keep the operation afloat, via the willing aid of Wall Street and the ongoing sale of pieces of the company.

By the end of 2000, the company claimed 85,000 miles of its planned 101,000-mile network were in service, though many former Global Crossing engineers say that the network never worked very well.[42] In 2000, Global Crossing raised an additional $5 billion in financing, a $1 billion bond in January 2001 (which was guaranteed by Global Crossing itself) and $3 billion of cash and bank facilities on its balance sheet. But things were deteriorating quickly—debt was piling up much faster than revenues were coming in, while operating losses were escalating.

In October 2000, Asia Global Crossing (AGC) went public and began trading on the NASDAQ. Its underwriting team was led by Goldman Sachs, Salomon Smith Barney, and Merrill Lynch.[43] AGC attracted some pretty prestigious investors: Microsoft and Softbank. As part of their joint venture, both corporations agreed to purchase $200 million worth of capacity on the not-yet-built Asian network as well as paying $150 million in cash.

INTERLOCKING TELECOM RELATIONSHIPS

Many of the Internet companies spawned after 1996 deregulation had some trading arrangement with Global Crossing, whose 2000 annual report listed ties with over a hundred other telecoms. Whether it was PSInet, Exodus, NextWave, 360networks, Qwest, Enron, Tyco, or almost any other energy or telecom company that either filed for bankruptcy protection or is currently under fraud investigation, all were involved with Global Crossing somehow, at some point.

For example, in March 1999, Global Crossing established a contract valued at $700 million with Tyco Submarine Systems Ltd. (TSSL) to build an undersea cable to South America. The contract included a clause in which TSSL agreed to notify Global Crossing if it ever engaged in competing construction prior to February 2000. Yet TSSL agreed to build a similar cable, SAM-1, for Spanish telecom giant Telefonica in May 1999. This set off a bitter dispute, and Global Crossing filed a $1 billion lawsuit against TSSL in March 2000, alleging violation of that noncompete clause.[44] As a result, the construction project was never completed. Another telecom, Lucent, provided financing to Global Crossing—despite its own financial struggles—for two of its networks in mid-1999. In February 2000, Global Crossing had over $2 billion of in-capacity agreements owed it by such struggling customers as Level 3, WorldCom, and Exodus.[45] Though at the time these companies were supposedly doing well, they just weren't paying their bills. Meanwhile, Global Crossing agreed to provide capacity to Deutsche Tel and to build high-capacity fiber-optic cable with debt-laden Level 3. The company made an equity investment in (later) bankrupt NextWave Tel, and entered into another agreement with (later) bankrupt Telergy to acquire ninety-six strands of New York fiber.

Global Crossing even sought to enter capacity trading deals with energy companies to pump up its balance sheet and meet Wall Street earnings expectations. In June 2001, Winnick sent an e-mail message to then-CEO Tom Casey about an unspecified deal with none other than power marketer Enron, saying, "I spoke with Jeff Skilling and there are 3 people vying for the business—we're one of them. They too are looking to do something here by quarter end."[46] The quarter end of the year coincided with a steep decline in Global Crossing's revenues. In one August 2001 internal Global Crossing e-mail, Winnick was listed as having assisted in brokering a deal with the infamous WorldCom.[47] Every place there was a deal to be done, Global Crossing was involved or angling to get involved.

THE DEPARTMENT OF DEFENSE

Government contracts were an important source of recurring revenue, so it was important for Global Crossing to wield its political influence not just for favorable legislation but for much-needed contracts that politicians could help the company obtain. It thus appeared particularly strategic of Global Crossing to appoint former U.S. secretary of defense William S. Cohen to the board of directors on April 16, 2001.[48] Two months after Cohen's arrival, Global Crossing Government Markets, a unit of Global Crossing Ltd., announced it had been selected by the U.S. Department of Defense (DOD) to provide an advanced wide-area network for its Defenses Research and Engineering Network (DREN).[49] The three-year contract, valued at $400 million, required Global Crossing to design virtual private networks throughout the United States, Guam, Puerto Rico, and other U.S. territories.

Telecom lobbying is a competitive process full of backstabbing among an array of separate interests, including the "old economy" Baby Bells and long-distance companies and the "new economy" Internet and broadband ones. Two months after the DOD granted the DREN contract to Global Crossing, following bitter protest from losing bidders AT&T, Sprint, Qwest, and WorldCom, the Defense Information Systems Agency revoked Global Crossing's contract, citing its technical deficiencies. WorldCom eventually won the contract in April 2002 while under an SEC fraud investigation.

"Global Crossing was set up by bean counters and financial lawyers, not people who cared about the regulatory issues of what they were doing. They set up a series of shell companies across Europe to evade American regulations," said Michael Nighan in a conversation with me in February 2003. "This became problematic when they bid for the DOD contract. They never should have been able to get to that point, because they weren't even based in the U.S., but in Bermuda. Officers of the company needed to have certain security clearance that they didn't have."

Even though the contract was pulled back by the DOD and rebids were planned, Global Crossing refused to be a loser. Instead, it retrenched and strengthened its efforts. It enlisted another Washington insider, retired army general John M. (Mike) McDuffie, to serve as president of Global Crossing Government Markets beginning in November 2001. McDuffie was to be based in the Washington, D.C., office, according to

Global Crossing.[50] Only "there was no such company," says Nighan. "I built that company so the general could be president of the whole thing." Nighan was laid off by Global Crossing in October 2001 and McDuffie left shortly after that.

TAX SCHEMES AND LEGAL MACHINATIONS

It would be easier to list the areas in which Global Crossing did *not* take advantage of tax manipulation strategies than those where it did, but that wouldn't fill one page. Global Crossing played the tax dodge game in almost every way imaginable. It took advantage of tax havens in Ireland to book tax-free revenues. Winnick also bought a 13.4 percent stake in a venture-capital firm, K1 Ventures Ltd., in less-regulated Singapore, partnering with Steven Green, Clinton's old ambassador to Singapore. The company was controlled by another Asian firm, Temasek Holdings Ltd., that, in turn, backed Hutchison Global Crossing.

But Global Crossing's most important tax-dodge decision was its first. Started as an offshore company, Global Crossing Limited is one of many U.S. corporations technically headquartered in Bermuda, an island whose yellow pages are a Who's Who of international corporations. Like so many other "limited" companies, it has no employees there. Winnick incorporated Global Crossing Limited and many of its 200 subsidiaries in Bermuda to avoid paying U.S. taxes. The non-U.S. status has the added property of making it even more difficult for U.S. regulators, shareholders, and laid-off Global Crossing employees to press criminal charges against the firm.

Global Telesystems, Winnick's original incarnation of Global Crossing, had also been incorporated offshore, in the Cayman Islands, in the beginning of 1997. The majority of what's left of Global Crossing's staff postbankruptcy is located in New Jersey, New York, and California. If you track the original PCG clan's money, including Winnick's, you'll find it located in offshore accounts, hedge funds, or reinsurance companies.

By the time of its merger with Global Crossing, Frontier already had about a hundred subsidiary companies of its own, but these were distinct, regulated companies that filed reports with state commissions. Chiefly a local company, Frontier was regulated by the state, which provided an external check on its activities. Onshore, the Frontier portion of Global

Crossing remained a regulated phone company, but offshore it was an unregulated shell game.

The setup created a situation where 300 companies could sell and book profits from services to each other. Some internal transactions went through five different companies. Goods and services passed through many different tax jurisdictions and regulatory environments creating a worldwide tax evasion scheme. This aspect of the firm's deceit was never fully investigated by the SEC. One would have to scrutinize every entry to determine where money entered and left the company and the corresponding tax laws that should have governed each of those transactions in order to gauge the whole picture. The consolidated numbers would only provide a fraction of the full story.

Global Crossing also evaded taxes through the creation of master contracts with its corporate customers in which many services were consolidated into one invoice. Having one master contract for all services is atypical in telecoms. Customers saw frequent modifications to their two-inch-thick master contracts, changing which entity of Global Crossing they actually had a contract with. Winnick had decided that it would be "easier" to have all customers sign one master agreement for all services provided by Global Crossing, as opposed to a set of separate, more specific agreements that concentrated on a particular service. In that way, Global Crossing made it very difficult for any auditor or regulator looking at its contracts to determine just which component of Global Crossing was actually selling a service or booking a profit. With respect to internal accounting procedures, it was equally unclear who bought what from whom, allowing Global Crossing to easily move dollars around the balance sheet.

The Irish Bundling scam was another tax dodge. Ireland-based corporations did not have to pay taxes on their capital gains or on their derivative (or swap) gains. That is why Dublin grew quickly in the late 1990s as a place for international banks to relocate derivatives operations that had previously been housed in the UK. Bundled contracts allowed revenues coming from America to Britain and continental Europe to be booked through Irish companies, making true cash flows impossible to detect. Compare it to Volkswagen entering a communications contract in Germany for phone traffic between its U.S. distributors. Global Crossing could book the contract between Ireland and Germany, keeping as much revenue as possible hidden from U.S. regulators—not that anyone was looking very closely or asking any questions.

CAPACITY SWAPS OR TRADING AIR

Global Crossing and other telecoms regularly traded capacity on their networks through financial instruments called indefeasible rights of use (IRUs) for bandwidth needs fifteen to twenty-five years in the future. Telecoms employed a series of bandwidth trades designed to "expand its network," which frequently merely inflated their balance sheets. Global Crossing bought and sold unused fiber-optic capacity with other telecommunications companies, including 360networks, which went bankrupt, and Qwest, which stills totters under the weight of $25 billion of debt and SEC investigations.

The capacity that these companies traded with each other could be used to pump up balance sheets, since associated revenues could be booked up front, even for identical or very similar fiber-optic lines. In other words, if Global Crossing owned line A to B, and Qwest owned line B to A, effectively both lines connected the same points. So, there would be no need to trade them to augment each company's network. However, if a capacity trade between the companies enhanced each one's up-front income, they would have reason to engage in that trade, a practice the House investigations committee ultimately investigated.

The fact that certain capacity might have been redundant or increasingly worthless didn't stop Global Crossing from booking the money it received as quick cash to make their financial statements appear healthier to investors. The need to meet quarterly earnings expectations also led Global Crossing to continually alter its accounting methodology, changing the names of entries to confuse and convolute losses. For instance, an entry called "revenue" later became "recurring revenue" and then "reported recurring revenue."

Not only was building networks unregulated; trading capacity back and forth was as well. No one at the SEC or the FASB was examining the true value underlying those swaps. If they had, they would have noticed a major disconnect between the revenues that were booked and actual network prices. If the networks themselves lost their value when a glut of similar networks had to compete for the same information paths, long-term contracts involving the use of those networks lost more. In that way, the whole business of capacity swapping popped the telecom and Internet bubble far quicker than building excessive capacity did.

Derivatives trades and their integrity fall under the purview of the

SEC, and the FASB sets the accounting rules for them. Arthur Andersen, in addition to having worked with Enron, Tyco, Qwest, Dynegy, and other energy and telecom companies, was a pioneer in the accounting treatment for capacity swaps. Their UK division wrote a full marketing brochure on the topic back in 1999.

There are fairly clear-cut ways to differentiate between capacity swaps and determine which ones are potentially fraudulent. First, you have to look beyond just the dates of the swaps; it's a problem if numbers are moving around just before quarterly reports are due. Second, it's important to examine what's actually being swapped. For example, if Global Crossing and Qwest swap parts of their networks that are similar, the swap is in all likelihood purely an accounting ploy—not necessarily illegal, but certainly misleading, even if the dates differ.

You can compare capacity swaps to two development companies wanting to build houses on the same street. There are only two lots available, so they each buy one and build a house on it. The houses stand on separate lots but are otherwise identical, although they were built by two separate companies. Each company sells its house to a waiting buyer, pocketing the profit from the deal. End of story, right? Not in capacity swap land, where the story would continue. Let's say one company also sells the other company the future profit on the resale of its house ten years later so that the second company gets the profit from the resale of the first company's house in ten years and vice versa. You may be wondering about the people who bought the house. Well, you can pretend they don't matter, or that they wanted the house so badly that they agreed to give up future profits on its sale. Of course, this wouldn't happen in real life. That's part of what makes capacity swaps so bizarre.

In this scenario, both developers have pocketed money from the actual house sales and from selling the resale profits in ten years (the values for which are unknown but estimated). They also both have paid a small amount of money to each other up front to secure the deal. But what if no more buyers ever come to the neighborhood again? What if the first buyers of the houses decide after five years to stay there forever, pass it on to their kids, etc.? Then those resale rights are rendered worthless. The money each company paid to secure a future profit is irrelevant because the ten-year estimate is nothing more than an arbitrary parameter that both parties agree upon.

Yet the development companies don't have to acknowledge that possible scenario. Instead, based on the profits they make from selling the houses and the future profits on them, they are able to show prospective buyers a profitable operation. They can work a few more years doing the same thing in other locations, or cash out and head for the beach. Thus, there would be no one left to check on the contract's execution, such as when companies go bankrupt and erase their obligations as part of bankruptcy court proceedings.

In the case of capacity swaps, the fact that capacity becomes worthless does not mean that the sellers of that capacity retroactively subtract the difference between the original and the current values from their balance sheets. Accounting law doesn't require that. When capacity values are at their lowest, telecoms won't profit from selling capacity at deflated rates. Instead, they should adjust downward revenues booked from the future sales of that capacity as a result. Nonetheless, they do not have to account for that loss under current accounting law.

THE WHISTLE-BLOWER

Global Crossing grew so fast that it took some time before an employee cried foul, but on August 6, 2001, Roy Olofson, a vice president in Global Crossing's finance department, finally did.[51] He wrote a letter to James Gorton, the company's chief ethics officer and general legal counsel, describing deceptive accounting practices, mostly involving swaps of capacity between Global Crossing's own carriers conveniently recorded right before quarterly earnings announcements. Olofson's background had given him the skills to notice when balance sheets were going wrong. Prior to becoming Global Crossing's fortieth employee, he had enjoyed a long career in accounting; his former jobs included being the CFO of FedCo Inc. and a CPA at Price Waterhouse.[52] At Global Crossing, his primary product focus was the sale of capacity. When Joseph Perrone, former senior partner at Arthur Andersen, was hired in May 2000, he took over Olofson's role and all accounting and financial reporting functions.[53]

In February 2001, Olofson was diagnosed with lung cancer. While on medical leave, he learned of Global Crossing's financial difficulties in trying to meet the Street's first quarter projections. As it turned out, Global Crossing did manage to make those projections, but only after some fancy numerical maneuvering involving network capacity trading.

When he returned to work in early May 2001, Olofson listened to that first quarter Global Crossing earnings announcement. When asked by a Wall Street analyst, CEO Tom Casey unequivocally stated that no swaps had taken place that quarter.[54] Olofson disagreed, pointing out a last-minute swap with 360networks in which Global Crossing booked $150 million in cash revenue just before the books closed for the quarter, even though it hadn't actually received any cash yet.[55] In exchange, Global Crossing was supposed to pay $200 million to 360networks for the use of its capacity, but Global Crossing was nervous that if it went ahead and paid the full $200 million to 360networks, it might never get the money back; 360networks had filed for Chapter 11 protection just three months later. So Global Crossing didn't pay out the $200 million at all; it kept its $200 million *and* booked an incoming $150 million. (Global Crossing hasn't made good on most of its commitments with other carriers since filing its own bankruptcy, not to mention severance owed laid-off employees.)

According to Olofson, "When I walked into [CFO] Dan Cohrs's office, he was working on a press release for the next quarter. I asked whether the press release was to reduce guidance [projections] for the rest of the year. Cohrs stated, 'I would like to, but the chairman just sold ten million shares of stock.' "[56] Cohrs also told Olfoson that the company had decided to in-directly guarantee loans made to certain officers, and he hoped the price of Global Crossing's stock would increase soon because these loan guarantees would have to be disclosed in the next proxy statement.[57]

Olofson told the House Energy and Commerce Subcommittee on Oversight and Investigations during their hearings on the potential sham nature of Global Crossing and Qwest capacity swaps, "During June and July, I received a copy of a document indicating that approximately thir-teen of the largest eighteen IRU deals completed in the second quarter were last-minute swaps where identical or substantially identical amounts of money were being exchanged along with the underlying capacity. I didn't understand why they weren't accounted for as like-kind exchange of similar business or investment assets, on which gains may be tax-deferred." As Timothy Lucas, head of the FASB Emerging Issues Task Force, said, "An exchange of similar network capacity is the equivalent of trading a blue truck for a red truck; it shouldn't boost a company's rev-enues."[58] But in fact it did boost Global Crossing's second-quarter 2001 earnings (though they still reported a $1.2 billion operating loss) six months before the company declared bankruptcy.

On August 2, 2001, Olofson listened to the company's second-quarter earnings conference call with financial analysts. Again, Tom Casey stated there were no swaps in that quarter. What's odder is that, by the third-quarter earnings announcements, Global Crossing claimed a huge decrease in revenues precisely because they had booked fewer IRU swaps than the previous quarter.[59]

Placed on administrative leave within a few weeks of writing his letter to Gorton, Olofson was eventually fired in November 2001. Global Crossing's justification for his dismissal was that he was laid off, along with 1,200 others, in a restructuring.[60] Gorton left the company three days afterward. Olofson's claims led to the opening of the FBI and SEC investigation on February 4, 2002, and hearty denials and character assassination attempts from Global Crossing. According to an internal study completed in mid-2001, most of the IRUs Global Crossing received through its capacity swap transactions were worthless because counterparties had either declared bankruptcy or were close to it.

DUMPING STOCK AND FIRE SALES

Global Crossing executives and insiders began selling the company off and dumping their stock in early 2000—not just stock, but whole pieces of the company, and not pieces like fingers and toes, but pieces like arms and legs. In order to make marginal revenue targets, Global Crossing had to keep selling its network capacity, ultimately at rock-bottom prices.

Frontier, the only legitimate company from a revenue perspective that Global Crossing ever bought, was cut up as Global Crossing began eliminating activities it considered noncore. Just six months after the merger, its local phone service business was sold to Citizen Communications for $3.65 billion, well below what it was worth, in order to raise cash. The deal took almost a year to close because of the deteriorating financial climate.[61]

It was the same with the January 2001 sale of Global Center to Exodus Communications for stock. Global Crossing put it on the chopping block soon after the $6 billion merger, and settled for $1.9 billion worth of Exodus common stock. Leo Hindery had engineered the deal back in October 2000, when it was worth $6.5 billion in Exodus stock. Nine months later, Exodus filed a $3.9 billion bankruptcy, rendering that deal nearly worthless. The same month, Global Crossing started to defer planned construction, like that of its Caribbean system, to save millions in cash commitments.

While Global Center was being dismembered, insiders and executives were selling their stock. The capacity swaps that had been used to boost declining revenue became almost an afterthought while people scrambled to get out with as much as they could. But even after the glorious Frontier merger, the company reported only $214 million of cash on their first-quarter 1999 earnings report, whereas goodwill, which is not a tangible item, was valued at an unsubstantiated $10 billion—not too stable a situation. That is what formed the backdrop for all the sales and cash-outs, not the declining economy. The mismatch between cash-on-hand and goodwill should have raised the red flag over at the SEC, but it didn't.

The middle of 2001 brought a tidal wave of telecommunications bankruptcies, including Winstar Communications with $4.98 billion in April, PSInet with a $4.5 billion bankruptcy in May, and 360networks (headquartered in Canada and run by former Microsoft CFO Greg Maffei) with $5.6 billion in assets in June 2001.[62] Global Crossing's customers were going bankrupt while it struggled to meet or make up its own revenues. It didn't help matters that the company stopped making timely payments to its troubled customers and vendors. The thinking was, "They're going down anyway, why let them take our money with them?" and it was prevalent throughout the telecom industry. Concurrent with its failure to pay what it owed, Global Crossing booked over $1 billion in revenue from IRU capacity swaps. According to a lawyer for Roy Olofson, Global Crossing spent $1.3 billion buying and $1.6 billion selling IRUs during 2001.[63] In November 2001, desperate for capital, Global Crossing sold its IPC Trading System units to an investment group led by Goldman Sachs Capital Partners 2000 (GSCP) for $360 million in cash, a steep drop from its original value of $1.6 billion.

The fact that Global Crossing was able to convince so many investors to finance or buy capacity in its network for up-front cash makes it so much more unbelievable that they sank so fast. It also became increasingly apparent that extraction of that money by insiders was like removing the foundation of a house of cards.

CHAPTER 11

On January 28, 2002, Global Crossing became the fourth largest U.S.—and the largest telecom—bankruptcy in history, filing for Chapter 11 with $22.2 billion of assets and $12.4 billion of debt. (It retained number one status until WorldCom usurped it six months later.) During Global Crossing's reign as the hottest thing to come out of the new economy, the company had used the Wall Street machine with impressive efficiency. As part of its fast expansion plan, it got Jack Grubman at Salomon Brothers to drive up its stock price with extravagant praise, Chase to scrounge up sizable credit lines, and Goldman Sachs to scare up mega-investors like Microsoft for its Asian expansion. Before it crashed, Global Crossing insiders and execs walked off with $5.2 billion, vastly more than the $1 billion Enron executives pocketed.[64]

In the five years of its existence, Global Crossing accumulated an immense pile of debt. Investors, with the help of Wall Street underwriters, happily financed its quest to dominate the world's fiber-optic networks. It became a great success, the youngest firm ever to qualify for a NASDAQ listing. From the time it was first issued to its pinnacle, Global Crossing's market value shot from zero to $47 billion—all floated on a $20 billion mountain of debt. When Global Crossing filed for Chapter 11 bankruptcy, its once-$64 stock was worth 28 cents. Former darling of the "grown-up" NASDAQ main board, it fell as low as 1.5 cents on NASDAQ's "pink sheets" quotes.

Global Crossing investors included state pension funds like Pennsylvania Commonwealth, Texas Teachers, New York State Common Retirement Fund (which filed a lawsuit over its $63 million loss), Colorado Public Employees, New Mexico Employee Retirement Association, Missouri State Employee Retirement Association, Wisconsin State Investment Board, Ohio State Teachers Retirement and Public Employee Funds, Florida State Pension, and the California Public Employees' Retirement System (Calpers). Lenders included JP Morgan Chase, Merrill Lynch, Citigroup, and, of course, CIBC, the bank that started it off and even bought back its original bonds when the market wouldn't. These financial institutions featured prominently in the creation of Global Crossing's empire yet admitted no responsibility for its deceptions. Now, they're all facing off in bankruptcy court.

Global Crossing's assets received only two formal offers upon its bankruptcy declaration: from Hong Kong–based Hutchison Whampoa and from Singapore Technologies Telemedia. Both companies offered to invest $750 million for a 79 percent stake in the reorganized company. CEO John Legere claimed that sixty companies had signed confidentiality agreements in consideration of buying all or part of Global Crossing, but it became clear he was exaggerating because there were no other real offers. After an eight-month lapse, the two original bidders together bought a 61.5 percent stake in Global for only $250 million, or about 2.7 cents a share. Both Winnick and Cook stayed in the background throughout Global Crossing's demise, but Winnick still held onto 8 percent of the stock.

WINNICK'S HOUSE APPEARANCE

Winnick was called to testify before a congressional investigation in October 2002, nine months after Global Crossing declared bankruptcy and three months after he had declined a Senate invitation to attend a telecom crisis hearing in late July 2002. This time, the House Energy and Commerce Committee presented their request in the form of a subpoena.

Winnick, former general counsel Jim Gorton, CFO Dan Cohrs, former president and chief David Walsh, and executive vice president of finance Joseph Perrone assembled in front of the investigation subcommittee. There they deflected questions about shady capacity swap trades. Despite daily calls with then-CEO Tom Casey, Winnick maintained that he had no idea his company was in trouble when he exercised $124 million of stock options eight months before it declared bankruptcy and denied that he knew any details of capacity swaps.

Lenette Crumpler was a thirty-one-year Rochester Tel/Frontier veteran from well before the days when Global Crossing acquired Frontier and substituted its stock for Frontier's. She subsequently lost her entire 401(k) plan because of Global Crossing's bust. During her House Energy and Commerce Committee testimony in October 2002, she spoke of relentlessly deceptive e-mails during that time when Global Crossing's stock was falling and the *Wall Street Journal* was reporting massive company debt. She stated, "Tom Casey sent e-mails telling us the company was fully funded for two years and could weather the storm. Joe Clayton sent us an e-mail saying that the *Wall Street Journal* was wrong about Global Crossing's debt."[65] The company went bankrupt a year after those heartfelt e-mails were sent to employees.

Winnick, always the consummate salesman, sold himself as a model of corporate governance. In front of the House committee, in a perfectly executed "dodge and deflect" move, he pledged $25 million of his own money to all the employees who had lost theirs in Global Crossing stock because, he said, "It's not about the money, it's about the people." The audacity that propelled him to billionaire status came to the fore as he called on other CEOs to "step up and write a check" too.[66] His sales pitch scored with investigation subcommittee co-chairman Jim Greenwood, a Pennsylvania Republican who gushed that the gesture was "a shocking act of leadership," for which Winnick "could be very proud." Yet his pledge amounted to only a little over 3 percent of the $734 million Winnick stuffed into his own pockets during the five years of Global Crossing, and less than 10 percent of the $275 million that his 9,000 employees lost in their 401(k) plans when Global Crossing took over Frontier Communications in 1999 and replaced Frontier stock with Global Crossing stock. It was a tiny drop in the bucket compared to the $5.2 billion senior insiders and executives extracted.

At the time, Linda McGrath, president of CWA Local 1170 in Rochester, told me that she considered the gesture "a move to placate congressmen," stressing that Winnick's "shocking" leadership was certainly absent three years ago. As for the promised check, a spokeswoman for Representative Louise Slaughter (D-Rochester) told me several months later, "We have seen absolutely no evidence that any of the $25 million has surfaced."[67] Furthermore, legal sources claimed there were restrictions on that type of money transfer or guarantee. Despite Winnick's dramatic and well-publicized promises, former Global Crossing employees didn't receive a sudden windfall from their ex-employer.

In the end, Winnick got off free and filthy rich. He knew how to buy credibility and use it to his full advantage, and his friends helped him out when he was in trouble. Attorney General John Ashcroft threw out the case against Gary Winnick on Christmas Eve 2002, when he assumed the press wouldn't notice, which, for the most part, they didn't. The SEC dropped the ball as well, amid obvious evidence about the precarious nature of the Global Crossing empire and the suspicious timing of its executives' departures and cash-outs.

Despite numerous attempts to keep the investigation of the company's deception alive in Washington, its former employees lost hope quickly. Irene DiNolfo, former marketing manager for Frontier, who helped established an ex-employees solidarity group, told me, "It was frustrating to keep fighting. The only congressperson who helped us was Louise [Slaughter]. The bankruptcy court sided with Global Crossing every step of the way. I even wrote a number of letters to Senator Hillary Clinton and received no response."

Michael Nighan suspected the same lack of interest: "We're not Enron or WorldCom, so we got lost in the shuffle." In fact, there was greater public outcry and congressional interest for Enron and WorldCom than there ever was for Global Crossing.

Global Crossing wound up demonstrating the resilience of a corporate America that makes and breaks its own rules but rebounds healthier for it. Nighan's fears were well founded; in December 2003, almost two years after declaring bankruptcy, Global Crossing was back—it had shaved its debts in bankruptcy court from $11 billion to $200 million. Newly issued Global Crossing stock began trading on the NASDAQ again on January 22, 2004, at $33 a share. The company that couldn't stay afloat, even having invoked misleading accounting techniques, was back to business as usual. And not a cautioning sound was heard from federal regulators, Wall Street, or the mainstream media.

Winnick eventually contributed another $30 million to a $325 million settlement of a class-action lawsuit filed by investors and employees, settled in March 2004. His generosity was celebrated by his publicist, Howard Rubenstein, who said, "This settlement says a lot about Gary Winnick's character. Clearly he does feel badly about all those who were hurt by Global Crossing's collapse, both shareholders and employees. And he has proved it by his actions." Rubenstein neglected to mention that Winnick's share of the settlement was less than 5 percent of his personal stash. A month later with the lawsuit coast clear, Global Crossing announced a review of previously stand financials for 2002 and 2003.[68]

WORLDCOM

On July 21, 2002, WorldCom became the biggest corporate bankruptcy in the history of the world. With a nine-cent stock price and having committed the largest fraud, WorldCom filed for Chapter 11 protection from creditors, declaring over $107 billion in assets and $41 billion in total debt.[69] The timing came as a gift to Gary Winnick, diverting attention from Global Crossing and taking away his spotlight for presiding over what had been the largest telecom bankruptcy in U.S. history. The types of balance sheet deceptions that WorldCom perpetrated were not unique to them: they just got caught. Nor was their fraud limited to the upper echelons of the firm, though it certainly emanated from there. It saturated the entire company at every level.

A month before declaring bankruptcy, in June 2002, WorldCom announced it had overstated its earnings since the beginning of 2001. Instantly, everyone became familiar with the company's name as it was propelled to scandal status. But the most troubling aspect of WorldCom's admission was that WorldCom itself reported it, not the SEC, who was supposedly monitoring their books, not the accountants or bankers who helped manufacture its faux earnings, and not the Wall Street analysts who had been complicit in overstating its virtues. In fact, that June day while WorldCom stock hovered at $1.22 (off a high of $64), Jack Grubman, Salomon Brothers' telecom analyst, had it listed as a "must-own."

WorldCom is an excellent example of how the external power and control born of size can influence policy and create its own escape route from retribution while undermining the employees who questioned the "fuzzy numbers" along the way. Lack of regulatory oversight allowed WorldCom's fraud to flourish as it maintained an inaccurately rosy picture of its profitability for years. Its power over regulators, combined with the SEC and FCC's general lassitude, was so strong that neither regulatory body called any of its practices, mergers, or financial reports into question until March 2002. While the SEC completely failed to perform its oversight function, the FCC abetted WorldCom's acquisition schemes, acting as cheerleader for the Internet and broadband boom that aided its growth.

Complex mergers are the ultimate way to concentrate capital and open a channel for fudging numbers as they aggregated two companies into one. Through its string of acquisitions, it was obvious WorldCom was able to grow; but additionally, it was using balance sheet consolidation as a way to blur information reported in SEC filings and annual statements. Also, mergers bring about internal problems of integration, including system and culture clashes that destabilize day-to-day business. When WorldCom acquired MCI, the corporate culture clashes between the new-economy Internet company and the old-economy long-distance company exploded while productivity declined and revenues shrank. The overlapping of many duplicate departments at both firms produced instant layoffs. Accounting manipulation replaced actual growth as a way to meet quarterly earnings projections.

CULTURE OF CONTROL

By all accounts, WorldCom was a difficult place to work. Many employees felt they were shut out of the decision-making process, unable to have any effect on company policy, and overly scrutinized. As a result, many mentally gave up long before they resigned or were fired. Others complained they felt more like numbers than people, a major factor in a management-cultivated laissez-faire attitude that contributed to multilevel corruption.

The scrutiny included an elaborate review process in which, for about two months each year, employees filled out lengthy online questionnaires about each other. These were compiled for use as senior management saw fit, sometimes as background material for termination—and there were lots of terminations in 2001 as the markets headed south—and sometimes for promotions or bonuses.

Other employee clashes with management practices proved more painful, particularly between legacy (or pre-merger) MCI and WorldCom personnel. Seventeen-year MCI veteran Lesley Fish saw that the MCI WorldCom merger would literally flush her legacy company down the toilet just three months after the country's fourth-largest long-distance phone company acquired MCI, the second largest, in a $37 billion deal. One morning in December 1998, Lesley overheard two women from new CEO Bernie Ebbers's side engaged in an animated discussion.

"Oh, look at these things," said one of the women, in disgust.
"There's no way Bernie'll put up with them," said the other.
"Well, they'll just have to go. They're a complete waste of money," said the first.
"Yeah. They're gone next spring at the latest."

The location of this cost-saving exercise? The ladies' room. The culprit? Paper toilet seat covers. Lesley couldn't believe what she was hearing.

As she told me, "It was plain asinine and embarrassing. Before Ebbers took over the company, people had the freedom to get things done and the trust to do them. Then, all of a sudden, you were confronted with a senior management concerned with minutiae. It was demeaning." According to her, MCI was a much better place to work prior to the merger.

Other oversight mechanisms began to circulate throughout the firm, including a forty-one point cost-cutting memo that suggested savings like using the stairs instead of the elevator when possible and leaving one out of three overhead light bulbs darkened to save on electricity. There were meetings held to contemplate whether trash should be taken out two instead of five days a week. It remained at five for sanitary reasons, so trash removal became known as a small victory.

There was an elaborate computer system administered from corporate headquarters in Clinton, Mississippi, aimed at reducing travel costs. A special Web site was created for finding the absolute cheapest flights and hotels, no matter how many stopovers and connections were required or how far the hotel was from the employee's intended destination. The system wasn't really used for booking travel, though—it just served as a watchdog to ensure any travel booked fit its recommendations. Any deviations, even by a penny, automatically generated an exception report that was sent to everyone in an employee's management chain for review and/or action.

In a December 2002 conversation with me at the Hilton Hotel in Washington, D.C., Monica Didier, former vice president and director of executive product program management in the Virginia office and a seasoned traveler, described one business trip that entangled her in red tape for weeks. She had booked a $223 United Airlines trip from Washington, D.C., to Chicago, with three days' advance notice. Not a bad deal, she thought. But, after her trip, she was informed that Southwest Airlines provided the same route for only $218. Monica's name had shown up on an internal report, one of many the company compiled to keep track of employees. After several conversations, she had to summarize the reasons for her $5 negligence and submit them to her VP in writing. She ultimately had to get senior sign-off from her superior.

A former salesman in WorldCom's New York City office explained the nickel-and-dime mentality for me. "We'd be out of toner for weeks because we were supposed to stretch what we had. I'd shake lots of ink around to make the toner last. When it stopped, you just waited until whenever the orders came in." Meanwhile, WorldCom regularly invested millions of dollars in failed systems-integration projects, attempting to reconcile the systems of acquired companies with its own. Additionally, the new systems that were promised failed to improve upon the old ones. As Cara Alcantar, a laid-off customer service representative from Phoenix, Arizona, who later became an employee activist, explained to me, "We waited months for a new billing system to be completed, but the grand integration plans didn't work in practice and we were told to keep the old one, even though it was total crap."

Despite being a global Internet firm, WorldCom had many problems integrating its own technology after the merger with MCI. The Phoenix billing system was just one of seemingly endless failures to upgrade, an odd state of affairs for a technology-based company. Meanwhile, all major cost decisions were made at the Clinton headquarters. As a result, things were constantly bottlenecked. "Vendors wouldn't get paid for months, sometimes over a year, because items just got stacked on Bernie's desk," said Alcantar, and it was Ebbers who had to sign off on nearly every vendor payment no matter the amount.

Meanwhile, senior executives were making millions of dollars perpetuating this bureaucracy. The business press continually reported that top CEOs, CFOs, and other executives deserved the massive salaries and stock awards they were getting, doing their part to pump up executive compensation even higher.

EBBERS, THE TECHNOPHOBE

Just after the media reported that WorldCom had received a request for documents from the SEC, Bernie Ebbers sent an e-mail to all employees on March 13, 2002, stating that WorldCom chose to make the SEC request available on its Web site, because "the bottom line is we have absolutely nothing to hide."[70] WorldCom stock was trading at $7.39. But, aside from its inherent defensiveness, the e-mail itself was something of a departure for Ebbers, known as a technophobe whose few company-wide e-mails had been confined to glowing accolades about growth and profit. The fact that his e-mails were limited to fluff didn't really make him a technophobe, however, just wise about keeping incriminating information off an electronic and traceable medium. Insiders reported he generally tended to do most of his communication in person, a practice one employee considered "relic-like," but his antiquarian management style may have been a factor in keeping Ebbers out of jail. He left behind no electronic trail for investigators. Whatever can be said about Ebbers's general knowledge of or experience in the telecom industry, he was aware that e-mail was trackable. Unlike e-mail, face-to-face conversations behind closed office doors were recorded only in the memories of those present.

Ebbers's e-mail also stressed that "it is important to remember that WorldCom went through full SEC reviews during the MCI merger, our proposed merger with Sprint and just last summer when we launched the WorldCom group and MCI group tracking stocks." That was all true—yet, despite those supposed reviews, WorldCom still managed to conceive and execute a multibillion-dollar deception, made possible by a combination of highly misleading accounting and a less-than-questioning SEC. In hindsight, some employees considered the launch of those tracking stocks (shares issued by a company which pay a dividend based on the performance of a specific portion of the company) as a way to muddy the balance sheet after the attempted Sprint merger failed to take hold, a desperate innovation since there was no other new way to finagle numbers on the horizon. Perhaps the senior circle knew the game was almost over and the tracking stock idea was a way to enable WorldCom to spin off MCI at a later date; they could move debt or costs back to the MCI side while negotiating a sale.

By separating the stock of the two companies, it was easier to move numbers around the balance sheet. Former senior communications manager in Atlanta and CPA Kate Lee said, "If you didn't understand the numbers beforehand, the tracking stock division made it virtually impossible." As it turned out, there wasn't enough time or suitable conditions to ready MCI for sale as WorldCom was imploding. Tracking stocks were dismantled thirteen months after the division was conceived.

CASHING OUT, EBBERS STYLE

In contrast to the Global Crossing clan that cashed out over $1.5 billion in stock during their three-year shareholder-gouging spree, the takeout of Ebbers's circle of executives was relatively conservative.[71] Because he considered selling stock a sign of disloyalty, his inner circle kept most of their shares. But Ebbers explored other avenues to financial accumulation, some dependent upon complicity with banks, either via generous stock-based personal loans or special helpings of hot IPO stock. He extracted $77 million via ample compensation packages, in addition to an $11 million profit from the hot IPO shares presented to him by his favorite investment banker, Salomon Brothers.[72]

Still, some members of the WorldCom senior circle did manage to cash out stock. John Sidgmore, the former vice chairman who became CEO after Ebbers resigned, took out $87 million. He claimed those shares were overwhelmingly legacy UUNet, his former employer, which WorldCom had acquired in late 2000, and thus shares that had been converted to WorldCom shares, not actual WorldCom-issued shares, in order to pacify Ebbers's concept of loyalty.[73] Former chief financial officer Scott Sullivan, once hailed as one of the smartest CFOs in the business, cashed out stock worth more than $49 million, $35 million of it between 1999 and 2000. He built a palatial estate in Florida over three years between 1998 and 2002 consisting of a five-building compound with an eighteen-seat movie theater, a two-story boathouse, a domed exercise room, an art gallery, and a wine cellar.[74]

Sullivan was similar to former Enron CFO Andrew Fastow in many ways. They were both relatively young, aggressive men who, for the most part, didn't court the limelight but quietly manipulated bankers, balance sheets, internal accounting, and auditors behind the scenes. They were both excellent financial engineers who felt that accounting rules and following laws were beneath them. Sullivan graduated from the State University of New York–Oswego in 1983 with a business and accounting degree and joined KPMG, where he audited deals for giant merger-fanatic companies like General Electric. He joined WorldCom in 1992 when it acquired his then-employer, Advanced Telecommunications.[75] He was fired by the board in June 2002, just before WorldCom declared bankruptcy.

The loyalty—or fear—Ebbers instilled lasted well beyond his departure from WorldCom. Sullivan didn't implicate him in any of WorldCom's fraud until March 2, 2004. Finally, as part of a plea bargain, to avoid a twenty-five-year sentence on federal charges he agreed to testify against his former boss. Ebbers plead innocent to securities fraud and other charges the next day. His trial was set for November 9, 2004.

LEAVING THE FOLD

It is amazing how an organization, a management group, and a board of directors that collectively had so little regard for regulation and law could succeed so well, go on for so long, and ultimately implode, leaving its upper echelon very highly compensated. Even while an extensive WorldCom PR machine was in high gear extolling the virtues and false promises of the Internet era and WorldCom was winning industry awards, there were scores of employees who couldn't get out the door fast enough. Morale plummeted well before the stock did and long before news of the company's fraudulent accounting measures came out. In late 1999, the company was treading water to stay alive—not from a financial perspective, but from an operational standpoint, because so many people were leaving. By May 2000, during the height of the telecom boom, WorldCom resignations abounded. Senior management responded with a unique retention bonus plan, one of the few times that WorldCom offered cash, not stock, as a carrot: $400 million to lock in 400 executives for two years.[76] (Ebbers received $10 million of that.) Up-front cash was doled out in exchange for a signed agreement stating that any of the employees receiving the cash would have to return a prorated amount of that money back to WorldCom if they left before July 31, 2002. The year 2000 was the last time World-Com had any excess cash lying around.

Like other management initiatives, the retention bonus plan made it clear that rank and file employees were not particularly valued since the plan only extended to vice presidents and above. Line workers, network engineers, and systems designers weren't offered anything, although they were leaving just as fast as management. A former engineer explained to me "It was all about grade level; if you were at a certain grade level and above, you mattered; otherwise you had to feel lucky for whatever they gave you." As a result, these workers continued to stream out of the company.

"The plan was just part of an overall company culture that valued executive dictates over workers' labor," said Paul Adams during an interview with me in Kate Lee's kitchen. Adams had been a senior manager in media relations in the Atlanta office until he was laid off in July 2002. "WorldCom was the poster-child company for making employees feel like numbers, not people," Lee agreed. She recalled Ebbers's opening remarks at a national sales meeting in St. Louis during 2000. As he looked out over the crowded room, the first words that came out of his mouth were, "I've never seen so much overhead in one place." Such sentiments "kind of made you feel warm and fuzzy all over," she noted.

Ebbers was well known for making such callous remarks at internal meetings. His abrasiveness was one of the reasons why he was rarely allowed to speak during earnings announcement meetings with Wall Street analysts.

ACQUISITION EXPRESS

In order to understand how WorldCom was able to commit the fraud that it did, it's important to take a look at how it evolved. WorldCom was the result of a seventeen-year shopping spree engineered by Bernie Ebbers and his posse and aided by Wall Street. Ebbers and Sullivan were always said to be constructing the next takeover deal. (Ebbers even named his yacht the "Aquasition.") Every time a big acquisition occurred, it was a license to hide more items in the balance sheet, or shift numbers around. By design, it was virtually impossible to read WorldCom's SEC filings and find all the possible points where fraud could have taken place.

According to a 118-page report issued by U.S. attorney general Richard Thornburgh on November 5, 2002, over 400 items fed into balance sheet entries had been altered from 1999 to 2000, totaling $4.6 billion.[77] This was during a period in which WorldCom was supposedly doing well and the telecom sector was enjoying a heyday. The nip and tuck of each little item caused the overall misrepresentation of the firm's financial condition to grow substantially. Meanwhile, because the SEC wasn't closely examining the significant changes in WorldCom's filings—it wasn't looking at the company on either a macro or micro level—WorldCom was able to continue embellishing its profitability. The SEC didn't even begin looking beneath the surface of WorldCom's books until the Enron scandal broke and WorldCom itself admitted deception first.

The reported total of items on balance sheets, such as total assets and total liabilities, was able to differ dramatically from the actual sum of its components. It's a little like the game of Telephone: a phrase gets whispered from person to person and becomes almost unrecognizable by the time the last person in the chain hears it. The challenge in accounting, as in the game, is finding out exactly where the phrase started going wrong, and stopping it right there.

Like Enron, WorldCom the corporation grew from lowly roots in the mid-1980s. Neither company began to truly dominate their sector until the late 1990s. The pivotal point in WorldCom's growth was the 1996 telecom deregulation, which turned it from an old-economy long-distance company into a new-economy Internet conglomerate. (This was in stark contrast to the meteoric rise of Global Crossing and Qwest from zero to billions in stock market value during the second half of the 1990s.) From 1985 to 2001, WorldCom acquired over sixty companies, but most of these were very small firms. It wasn't until after the 1996 deregulation act that it started acquiring the chunky multibillion-dollar ones.[78] Most of those were purchased with company stock rather than cash, a signature move of the 1990s boom. Often these companies were acquired fairly nonsensically, had little to do with the target company's strengths or weaknesses, and were bought just because they were available and easy to get. Bagging the prize—getting that next acquisition away from a competitor and gaining the goodwill, or value associated with the brand name being acquired—was reason enough.

WorldCom's legacy began in 1983, just before the first major wave of telecom deregulation and the 1984 bust-up of AT&T occurred. Long Distance Discount Services (LDDS), a resale phone business, was dreamed up by Ebbers in a Jackson, Mississippi, coffee shop.[79] The idea was simple: buy long-distance phone services in bulk from a lot of different providers and resell them at slightly higher prices. In 1984, the company had $1 million of revenues. In 1985, Ebbers became the company's CEO while still operating a string of low-budget motels on the side through his other company, the Master Corporation.[80] By 1989, LDDS and its subsidiaries were providing long-distance telecommunications services in nine states.

One of the directors of Ebbers's motel business was Carl Aycock. Aycock was also put on the board of directors of LDDS, where he remained through its transition to WorldCom and until December 17, 2002, when most of Ebbers's inner-circle board member friends were forced to resign. LDDS went public in 1989 by merging with the communications company Advantage Companies Incorporated in an all-stock deal. The chairman of the board at Advantage, Stiles A. Kellett Jr., then hopped aboard the LDDS train, where he remained until resigning in October 2002 amid some fuss over his very generous perks and his role as head of the compensation committee that okayed over $1 billion in loans to Ebbers.

A group of slightly larger acquisitions followed. By late 1992, LDDS was providing telecom services to twenty-seven states with revenues of $948 million. In December 1992, LDDS acquired Advanced Telecommunications Corp (ATC) in an all-stock deal. It also got Scott Sullivan in the deal—the man who would become credited with and indicted for the biggest hand in WorldCom's fraud, and who would plead innocent. Sullivan was promoted to CFO of LDDS in 1994 and appointed to the board in 1996. A few more mostly stock deals occurred in the early to mid-1990s; Metromedia Communications Corp. and Resurgens Communications Group, Inc., were acquired in a $1.25 billion deal, and IDB Communications Group was acquired in a $936 million all-stock deal.[81] Then came the Williams Technology Group, purchased for $2.5 billion in cash in 1995. With the "Will-Tel" deal, LDDS also acquired an 11,000-mile fiber-optic cable and digital microwave facilities common carrier network, based in Tulsa, Oklahoma. LDDS added $2.6 billion of debt to its balance sheet to complete the deal.[82]

In 1995, LDDS changed its name to WorldCom to underscore its growing international telecom business. After the Telecommunications Act of 1996 was passed, WorldCom shifted into a higher gear. The open competition the act promised translated into a clear business strategy: buy what you can as quickly as you can. In a flurry of activity and Wall Street collusion, Worldcom went on a shopping spree. For $12 billion worth of stock, it bought MFS Communications Company, which operated local networks in many major U.S. and European cities, giving WorldCom both local and long-distance service status. UUNet was part of MFS Communications Company. It had gone public in May 1995 in an IPO managed by Goldman Sachs, when it was hailed as the fastest-rising Internet star.[83] According to an April 1997 *Business Week* article, "At one time, UUNet was trading over 50 times its sales, not profits, but sales." The most significant personnel acquisition from the UUNet deal was its CEO John Sidgmore, who became WorldCom's COO and briefly served as CEO after Ebbers's ousting.

WorldCom acquired CompuServe from AOL in January 1998, again with stock. As part of the deal, AOL bought CompuServe's interactive services division back from WorldCom for $175 million. At the same time, WorldCom acquired ANS Communications from AOL and entered into a five-year contract with AOL to provide network services for them. It also acquired Brooks Fiber the same month. In their annual report,

WorldCom described that deal with AOL as a key source of revenue, though it didn't turn out to be anything of the sort.[84]

THE MCI MERGER

Then came MCI. At the time of its announcement, MCI WorldCom was the largest merger in U.S. history (although it would later be surpassed by a slew of other technology-spurred mergers). On September 14, 1988, the FCC, under the leadership of chairman William Kennard, approved the merger.[85] Salomon Brothers acted as WorldCom's adviser. The transaction combined the second- and fourth-largest long-distance companies in a record $37 billion stock deal that a number of consumer advocates and union groups, including Ralph Nader, the Communications Workers of America, the Consumer Project on Technology, and the Gray Panthers, strongly opposed. Nonetheless, the FCC stated that "in particular, the commission found that WorldCom and MCI demonstrated that the merger is consistent with the 'pro-competitive, de-regulatory' framework of the Telecommunications Act of 1996 and may produce tangible benefits to consumers . . . in its public interest analysis, the FCC concludes that the merger may produce new choices and increased competitions that will benefit consumers, including residential customers."[86]

It was another all-stock deal, and WorldCom even muscled out United Kingdom competitor British Telecom to acquire MCI, offering BT some stock for BT's aborted attempted takeover in the process.[87] Such payments were a kind of corporate "kill fee" since the legal or contract work often had already been drawn for the original company to take over, and it could be easier to "buy them out" than go through courts. Looking back, it was unlikely the FCC would ever have approved a foreign entity's takeover of a major U.S. firm, especially one so active in government contracts; WorldCom's interest in MCI conveniently fulfilled U.S. protectionist aims.

By December 1998, WorldCom's debt of $21 billion exceeded its revenues of $17.6 billion. But WorldCom wasn't done yet. Like an addict, it needed that next big merger fix. In October 1999, WorldCom announced its intention to merge with Sprint, one of its key competitors.[88] The Department of Justice (DOJ) vetoed the merger. That was the beginning of the end of WorldCom's game. A few years later, it was disintegrating into bankruptcy. In June 1999, four months prior to the Sprint merger announcement, WorldCom's stock price hit its high of $64 and the company reached its top market value of $180 billion. At the end of 2002, its stock was trading at 14 cents and its market value had shrunk to half a billion dollars.[89]

WALL STREET AND WORLDCOM

Over the years, the series of entities from LDDS to WorldCom paid Wall Street approximately $400 million in fees, which were roughly spilt between merger and acquisition business and debt and equity offerings.[90] WorldCom went unnoticed by the Wall Street old guard until the CompuServe acquisition. Much of WorldCom's M&A business (totaling over $69 billion) occurred after the 1996 deregulation. During that time, it also took out a lot of corporate loans, 92 percent of which were syndicated by the Bank of America, which extended a number of personal loans backed by WorldCom stock to Bernie Ebbers. Reciprocally, the bank was also one of WorldCom's top corporate clients.

But it was WorldCom and Salomon Brothers that were linked most tightly at the hip, according to the media. Similarly joined were Bernie Ebbers and Salomon's telecom analyst, Jack Grubman, who was repeatedly invited to address WorldCom board meetings. It had been DLJ that handled most of WorldCom's pre-MCI acquisition business, acting as their adviser for the deals with Resurgens Communications Group, Inc., which LDDS had acquired alongside Metromedia Communications in 1993, creating the fourth-largest long-distance network in the United States, and CompuServe. Salomon Brothers didn't start its advisory work with World-Com until the MFS/UUNet merger in December 1996, although it had been involved in most of its debt and equity underwritings before then.

By the time WorldCom hit its post-1996 deregulation stride, Wall Street was praising WorldCom's stock at every possible juncture. Paul Adams said, "Wall Street earnings announcements were totally staged. Jack Grubman would ask some inane and planted question, Sullivan did most of the talking, and Ebbers got off the stage as quickly as possible—before anyone noticed he didn't know what he was talking about."[91] It was a carefully managed show, and WorldCom management wasn't interested in unexpected questions.

WorldCom used Wall Street not just to acquire new companies and pump up stock, but sometimes as a way to communicate with its own employees. WorldCom workers did not hear about their pay freezes from their managers, but discovered the news alongside Wall Street analysts and outside investors, which did not build loyalty among the employees. Legacy MCI employees went three years without salary increases during the height of the telecom boom. WorldCom's nonexecutive employees went two years without a raise during the same period of time.

WORLDCOM REVENUE GAMES

As its real profits declined throughout 2001, the WorldCom PR department worked harder on spin. Insiders started noticing all sorts of discrepancies in the numbers. One noted by Adams turned out to be quite telling. There was an odd jump in WorldCom's quarterly earnings press releases regarding WorldCom's revenues: for the fourth-quarter 2000 announcement, reported 2000 revenues were $35 billion; for the first-quarter 2001 announcement, the same 2000 revenues had suddenly increased to $40 billion; then, for the second- and third-quarter 2001 announcements, the 2000 revenues went back to $35 billion again. WorldCom's first restatement of earnings occurred a year after that discrepancy appeared.[92] The first $3.85 billion of accounting "misstatements" were attributed to capitalizing line costs (fees paid to other communications companies to use their networks); instead of treating line costs like expenses (which they were), WorldCom and its auditor, Arthur Andersen, counted them as fully capitalized—that is, already paid for and hence assets.

There are two main types of expenses. One is operating expenses, the costs involved in running a company day to day, like wages, electricity, insurance, and equipment rentals. These are reported on a company's income statement in the period in which these expenses are incurred. The second kind of expense is a capital expense, which results from an acquisition or upgrading of a company's assets. It reduces cash by the purchase amount and increases assets (such as real estate and equipment) by the same amount. This expense should be depreciated over a defined period of time (typically annually). Each year's depreciation expense is generally reported on that year's income statement. Once the depreciation is recorded, the value of the asset is reduced by that amount on the balance sheet until the asset is written down or sold.

Even though a line cost is an operating expense, WorldCom marked it as a capital expense, accounting for it like an asset they owned instead of an ongoing expense they paid. That resulted in an overstatement of its net income, which indirectly fed into inflated stock values. In its 1999 annual report, WorldCom listed line costs as 43 percent of its 1999 revenues. In its 2000 report, it claimed those same 1999 line costs as 41 percent of their 1999 revenues. In their 2001 report, they put down those same 1999 line costs as 40 percent of their revenues.

Aside from capital expenses that arise from acquisitions, a company can put goodwill on its balance sheet and count that as an asset. Goodwill is a value concocted from the estimated worth of an acquired company's brand name, representing some combination of that company's share values and its ability to make money off its reputation in the future. For example, McDonald's has a large brand-name value, which translates into large goodwill. If McDonald's suddenly has to stop selling hamburgers because nobody wants to buy them, the value of its name brand should decline—but, in practice, it is rare for goodwill to be re-valued downward on a corporate balance sheet.

WorldCom and the larger telecom and Internet-based technology companies acquired smaller companies and puffed up the goodwill estimates of those companies on their balance sheets in the process. When the values of the companies they acquired began plummeting in 2001, it didn't spur an immediate wave of goodwill write downs across the industry. If that had happened, the bubble growth would have been less extreme.

In 1999, WorldCom reported its goodwill as $45 billion after the MCI merger, and stated, "This figure is periodically assessed by management based on the current and expected future profitability of acquired companies."[93] In fact, the goodwill number was not reassessed again, even though the telecom industry was deteriorating, particularly in 2001. In its 2001 annual report, goodwill had even gone up to more than $50 billion. When WorldCom first acknowledged its line cost fraud, in a June 26, 2002, press conference, it also mentioned it might have to reduce goodwill, but never got around to it before declaring bankruptcy a couple weeks later.

WorldCom and other corporate frauds have so far not tempted regulators to take a closer look at goodwill figures. Though accounting standards were changed in July 2001 so that goodwill would have to be reassessed each quarter, such requirements are meaningful only if they're enforced by the SEC. But because the FASB creates the goodwill rules, and the SEC is responsible for ensuring the accuracy of financial statements in general, checking the accuracy of goodwill itself falls between the cracks. The SEC just accepts the goodwill entries as fact, even though companies have a lot of room for fiddling with goodwill, which can be a very subjective number. For instance, if WorldCom valued the goodwill it added by acquiring MCI high, and then the long-distance business tanked but WorldCom chose not to reevaluate goodwill downward, the SEC wouldn't bother to ask why.

WHY LINE COSTS?

Line costs were an easy place to fudge numbers on WorldCom's balance sheet. Only about 10 percent of the company's employees had access to the line cost reports. Plus, thanks to a rather controlling work environment, employees weren't likely to question pooled line costs anyway. The different departments would report their line figures to WorldCom headquarters in Clinton, Mississippi. Then aggregated reports would come back with alterations to those numbers, and it was impossible to figure out why they had changed.

Actually, it's unfair to say that no one questioned the numbers. Some did, but their questions were thwarted by controller David Myers or by Scott Sullivan. "Dealing with Scott Sullivan was plain scary; he had all sorts of reasons why the numbers were adjusted the way they were," Monica Didier told me. "Numbers definitely changed on the way back down from Clinton, but Scott always had an excuse, like different overhead factors or regional charges. No one would listen anyway, so you just opted to cut yourself off and wait until your retention bonus period was over."

Didier, who resigned from WorldCom in late June 2002, went on to say, "The fact is, nothing about the company made sense after awhile. Middle managers had lost so much control already." But this fact didn't keep the tanking company from desperately trying to coerce its middle managers into believing it would survive against all evidence to the contrary and making sure they attended the related "pep rallies." During a June 2002 meeting, just a few weeks before news of WorldCom's first accounting fraud broke, two mandatory managers' forums were held. Didier attended both, the first time because she had to and the second because her presence had not been recorded properly the first time and she was specifically summoned.

Another accounting trick WorldCom employed was reserves manipulation: the company moved cash from a reserve fund onto its balance sheet right before a quarterly earnings report and would move the money back after the report was issued. Reserves manipulation accounted for the second misstated earnings announcement of another $3.3 billion on August 8, 2002 (for 1999, 2000, 2001, and the first quarter of 2002).[94]

WORLDCOM CRIMES: THE FRAUD THAT WAS DISCLOSED

WorldCom's head of auditing, Cynthia Cooper, landed on the cover of *Time* as one of three women whistle-blowers who were chosen as 2002's "People of the Year." Cooper had been at WorldCom since the days of LDDS and was well respected within the company.

But another WorldCom whistle-blower had appeared on the scene a couple of years before Cooper's team disclosed its initial fraud statement: Kim Emigh. Emigh was fired from his position as an engineer in the Dallas office in March 2001 for his efforts.[95] His concerns over a number of corrupt practices started in 2000—including what he estimated could have been a $35 million labor misclassification, based on a directive made on December 12, 2000, at the request of chief technology officer Fred Briggs that all labor capital costs be expensed.

A May 16, 2002, *Fort Worth Weekly* cover story on Kim Emigh circulated around WorldCom a full year and half after Kim had voiced his initial concerns about accounting methodology within the company, and prompted the company's internal audit department to investigate the balance sheet more thoroughly. Once it did, the line-cost fraud was brought to the attention of the SEC. The issue confirmed the concerns that the Communication Workers Association (CWA) had voiced in opposition to the MCI WorldCom merger.

To gain approval, WorldCom had argued "synergies" made its merger with MCI procompetitive. This gelled with the entire concept of competition, a cornerstone argument behind the passage of the Telecommunications Act of 1996 that was often invoked during merger approval discussions with the FCC. The CWA published an excellent report based on data from WorldCom's September 1997 SEC filings and the January 22, 1998, proxy statements in March 1998, offering a detailed analysis as to why the statements made by WorldCom about business "synergies" were not financially realistic or sustainable. Specifically, the report addressed line costs and goodwill figures, and concluded, "The combined MCI-WorldCom will be less efficient in generating revenue and income off its asset base."[96] Furthermore, the CWA stated that "the combined MCI-WorldCom will have to realize draconian 'synergy' savings and reorient its business strategy to realize the profit margins promised to Wall Street. The combined company will be under financial pressure to impose these large cost-cutting 'synergies' in an effort to position the new company in the same sort of high-margin market that WorldCom is pursuing today."[97]

In contrast to the accolades bestowed upon the merger by Wall Street, the CWA had issued a publicly available reality check that investors, regulators, and the mainstream media chose not to acknowledge.

FRAUD AT EVERY LEVEL

When you're really boxed in, you look for any way out. That's how it was at WorldCom. It wasn't just the senior management trying to get away with tweaking a report here, a line cost there; the practice of manipulating facts pervaded the firm.

After numerous interviews with former WorldCom workers, I discovered two common themes. The first is that "discrepancies" abounded within many different departments. The second is that many layers of the company were involved.

For senior management, it was a matter of grand design: make the Wall Street quarterly earnings announcements rosy, flirt with the media covering your historic ascent, pump up your stock price, and pile on the cheap debt. For the lower layers of employees, it was a matter of survival: bend the rules to your advantage and keep your head down.

Sales representatives complained their commission figures were inflated to make certain products look like they were performing better than others. Sales figures for important corporate clients were duplicated throughout different reports, showing growth that didn't exist. In other words, division heads embellished their numbers to improve the overall balance sheet totals.

Commission payout structures were altered just before year-end payouts were due, so salespeople couldn't always track what they were owed. Sales rep accounts would suddenly lose sales credits to other rep accounts to manipulate results in targeted areas of the firm. In that way, WorldCom used its salespeople to boost certain sales revenues and customer-base numbers in key departments as well as overall figures. As it turned out, employees were taking advantage right back by finding ways to game WorldCom's system back in their favor.

Mike* was relieved of his position as account manager in the Madison Avenue WorldCom sales office a month before Christmas. At that office, a team of fast-talking, faster-spinning salespeople and their managers had used their midsized customer base as fodder for their commissions. Mike tried to explain the commission structure to me, but even I, a banker of fifteen years, had trouble following it. All commissions were booked through Clinton, Mississippi, on an ancient system from the LDDS days.

The account billing scheme was a result of WorldCom's failure to integrate the systems of companies it acquired. Original MCI customers were still billed on the old MCI system, not on the WorldCom system. So, the WorldCom sales force would sell them new circuits as if they were new customers as opposed to simply considering it an intercompany shift.

"We'd give them some pitch about how it was good for efficiency, whatever," said Mike. "Then, we'd port their old numbers over to the WorldCom system and bill them off that system, too. That way, you'd get paid commission twice, once for the old numbers on the MCI system and once on the WorldCom system."

A number of salespeople regularly engaged in "flipping circuits," and the practice neatly fit into WorldCom's desire to dominate market share. Every time a salesperson added a new account and didn't disconnect or close the old account for the same customer, he or she got double commission. More importantly, that salesperson made it look like WorldCom was increasing its customer base. The customers didn't necessarily see any differences on their aggregate bill, and mostly "they didn't look that closely at their bills anyway," said Mike.

A similar scam happened with new products. Each time a new product

*A pseudonym.

like voice mail or toll-free service was sold, a salesperson would open a new account. The customer got a tidy merged bill, and the salesperson got paid as if he or she had sold each product individually to a new client. These and other tricks made it seem like WorldCom was adding customers when, in fact, they were just counting the same ones multiple times. Meanwhile, WorldCom stock continued trading down and its real revenues were declining. To keep up appearances, salespeople received more commissions to open new accounts than to service existing ones, a fairly common practice throughout the telecom industry to make it look as if a company were growing in market share, or acquiring "new" clients, despite its troubles or falling stock.

According to Mike, the executives were aware of these practices. So were the vice presidents. All of them turned a blind eye, because it improved their department's numbers and made them look good too. Senior management introduced another scheme when revenues continued to fall. During 2002, sales quotas were no longer attained by actual sales revenues, but by "ERV" units. "ERV" was WorldCom's acronym for "estimated revenue value," and ERV units were like the loyalty points you get for shopping at the same grocery or drug store, but instead of going to customers, they were awarded to the salespeople who sold "value added products," which were mostly Internet-related products (WorldCom's domain) and not basic consumer telephone services (the old MCI's domain). High ERVs were rarely directly related to actual revenues—after all, they were merely "estimates"—that looked good on the monthly revenue reports that went up to Clinton. No one asked questions about whether the products depicted on the reports had ever truly been sold.

RETIREMENT FUNDS AND 401(K) PLANS

Employees were under immense pressure to buy and hold stock. They watched helplessly as their retirement money dwindled, while being subjected to internal rhetoric about future riches and the need for patience. In the end, WorldCom workers lost between $600 million and $1.8 billion from their 401(k) savings plans.[98]

As a result of the WorldCom MCI merger, shares of old MCI stock in workers' various savings plans had been replaced by shares of WorldCom stock which ultimately tanked. What did that mean for MCI's employees? If an employee had bought $1,000 worth of MCI shares that were converted to WorldCom shares on the merger date, the total investment would have been worth about $1.88 when WorldCom declared bankruptcy, a 99.8 percent loss.

In addition, the company forced its employees to do business with its favorite credit providers, a widespread practice throughout corporate America during the 1990s. For example, Salomon Brothers was the only brokerage firm that WorldCom employees could use to exercise their company options. And during the stock boom, people were taking advantage of options heavily: converting them to 49 million shares in 1998 and 61 million shares in 1999.[99]

At MCI, there had been over twenty-five different 401(k) plan investments available. At WorldCom, right after the merger, that number dwindled to just four. According to Didier, two of them were in WorldCom stock.

Ebbers's signature scrutiny extended both to stock sales and to the lower tier of his executives. When Didier decided to cash in some stock in order to purchase an apartment in Chicago in early 2000, her name came up on one of "Bernie's lists" and she was interrogated by one of her superiors about her sale. Other managers were pressured to buy more stock (when it was trading around $2), amid talk about tough times and the company turning around with everyone's support. At the time, Didier, against her better judgment, reinvested $10,000 in WorldCom stock in order to pacify her superiors after her earlier sale.

As WorldCom stock was tanking, the senior circle increased pressure on employees to continue to buy more to keep it artificially higher. Thus, Didier was "strongly encouraged" to make her subordinates invest as well.[100] In her team, all but one of the employees was already invested up to the maximum in WorldCom stock, and therefore had already lost around 95 percent of their initial investments. One woman was having financial difficulties in her personal life and had chosen not to contribute to the 401(k) plan at all. She simply couldn't afford the deductions from her paycheck. Didier was instructed to "talk to her, get her to invest." At that point, Didier drew the line. The Big Brother routine had long gotten old and she could no longer play the part. So she lied instead. She said she'd spoken to her employee and a payroll deduction was under consideration, though the conversation never happened.

SEVERANCE

WorldCom cut 5,100 employees during its first round of layoffs in June 2002. By the time it announced additional cuts of 17,000 workers in July, rumors abounded that it was headed toward bankruptcy court. Workers were cut from all levels of the company, rank and file through vice president, spanning St. Louis, Tulsa, Clinton, Colorado Springs, and Atlanta. The wireless divisions were particularly hard-hit. During the June cuts, many of the senior executives were safely attending a "conference" at a lavish Hawaiian resort. WorldCom's CEO at the time, John Sidgmore, explained those 17,000 cuts at a Senate hearing by saying, "You have to understand they aren't really people on the payroll, it's just a division we're closing."[101] It seemed that Sidgmore was attempting to smooth over the fact that 17,000 people would be losing their jobs, by couching the move in terms of something that sounded less personally offensive, as if a "division" was not actually comprised of real people.

The cuts came with greater losses than simply the jobs themselves. They offered another means for WorldCom to extort its workers by withholding severance pay and COBRA payments. WorldCom took advantage of arcane U.S. bankruptcy rules favoring corporations over employees. Under current U.S. bankruptcy code, when a corporation files for Chapter 11, any severance pay due to employees who were terminated prior to the filing can be (but doesn't have to be) capped at a total of $4,650. The figure is supposed to represent an inflation-adjusted amount that started as $1,600 in 1979 when Congress passed the original code. And just where did that original number come from? "Well," explained one bankruptcy lawyer, "the legislators at the time pulled it out of their ears."[102]

WorldCom lobbied the bankruptcy court to allow it to pay just the severance cap amount, even though many terminated workers were owed far more, according to their employment contracts, and WorldCom's financial reports showed they had enough money still in the coffers to pay them appropriately. But even after the bankruptcy court granted its request, it didn't make those smaller payments on time. For Dawn Harden, an ex–financial systems analyst from Atlanta and a single mother of three, that was hard to swallow: "I went from $50,000 to food stamps. They have the money. Why haven't they paid me my money and benefits like they promised?" That's a question that Kate Lee took to heart—and then took to the bankruptcy courts and finally to Congress. Lee created the

Ex–WorldCom Employees Assistance Fund with three other casualties of the June layoffs. The fund was modeled after another relief fund, established by former Enron employee Rebekah Rushing in January 2002 to provide ex-Enronites with financial assistance.

Lee is one of the few true heroes to emerge from the corporate scandals of the new millennium. She wasn't a whistle-blower and she didn't send any smoking gun e-mails during her tenure at WorldCom. But she fought back. Raised near Dunwoody, Georgia, Lee received a degree in economics at the University of Pennsylvania, where she ran for class president because she wanted to change things for the better on campus. In my interviews with her, held at her home, it was clear she possessed a solid "do what's right" backbone coupled with a warm, direct, and open personality.

After her termination from WorldCom, she became an unstoppable fighter for the rights of the laid-off. Employees who had questions about their treatment, both those who had been fired and those still inside WorldCom, continually turned to her first. She forged alliances with the AFL-CIO. She wrote letters to all of senior management at WorldCom urging them to do the right thing by their employees. She appeared on TV, and was interviewed extensively by newspapers.

"I never really considered myself an activist," she told me. "I'm just doing what I think is right." It's hard to talk to Lee, who is one of the most articulate, energetic, and memorable people I've ever met, and see her as anything but an activist, though.

In its first few months, the fund received 501(c)3 (nonprofit) status and raised over $190,000. Contributions flowed from organizations like the Democratic Congressional Campaign Committee and congressmen like Senator Jack Reed (D-RI), but not a single WorldCom executive chose to make a contribution.

In early July 2002, WorldCom owed 4,000 severed employees a total of $36 million. In October 2002, WorldCom went to bankruptcy court (supposedly on behalf of those workers) to confirm it would pay that amount. But the concerted pressure exerted by the AFL-CIO, its network of lawyers, and the former WorldCom employees had led to WorldCom's court appearance, not the goodness of its corporate heart.

When the court ordered WorldCom to pay its employees what it owed them, the WorldCom PR machine spread the news of its generosity wide. WorldCom attorney Marcia Goldstein testified the payments would allow WorldCom to "restore the confidence of its employees, whose cooperation and continued loyalty are essential."[103] Yet behind the scenes, WorldCom chose not to pay that severance in lump sums, which clearly would have been most beneficial to its former employees, but opted instead for biweekly payments. Some sources claimed that departments ranging from human resources to finance to the postbankruptcy novelty Restructuring Department had incentives to retain as much cash as possible to make the company's finances look "richer" as it navigated through bankruptcy.

Lee said the $36 million was "like a rounding error to them. . . . And yet, do you think just maybe they could do the right thing, after all the negative publicity, just once do the right thing by their workers?" Many who had counted on that money coming all at once were well behind in mortgage and medical bills and facing home foreclosures.

WorldCom also adjusted severance down by inserting unexplained numbers of vacation days taken. One ex-employee e-mailed Lee that, when he called WorldCom's severance dispute hot-line to find out why his vacation days used had doubled, he was greeted with an array of helpful responses like: "I don't know." "I'm not sure." "Perhaps." "Maybe." "I don't have information on that."

THE AFL-CIO LENDS A HAND

The AFL-CIO mobilized quickly to help WorldCom's laid-off workers retrieve due severance, providing support and legal assistance. Several levels of the union were involved, from lawyers to union activists to President John Sweeney. Associate general counsel for the AFL-CIO Damon Silvers explained to me: "We had just come off a bankruptcy court coup against Enron, getting $35 million in severance for 4,500 employees. We had built up the expertise in the courts and knew how to exert pressure to retrieve severance and other benefits. Then, bang. WorldCom happened. We knew what we had to do and went out and did it."

Both Enron and WorldCom were nonunion. WorldCom was particularly opposed to unions, something its "culture" had in common with MCI; both firms deterred even the possibility of unionizing by mass firings at sites that hinted at collective action, an easy move in the telecom industry, where a simple flip of a switch can move work from one location to another. WorldCom had most of its offices located in right-to-work states as an added precaution.

The AFL-CIO stepped in anyway, and demonstrated the power of co-ordinated action. AFL-CIO activists set up laid-off worker information Web sites. They leafleted WorldCom job sites and call centers to spread the word. John Sweeney committed the AFL-CIO's support to the WorldCom workers during a July 2002 Wall Street rally to raise corporate governance awareness. The result was an October 2002 court decision that granted full severance and other benefits to all laid-off WorldCom employees. "There's no way we could have gotten as far as we did without the help of the AFL-CIO," said Kate Lee. "We succeeded beyond our wildest dreams," added Silvers.[104]

FUDGING INTERNATIONAL FIGURES

Scott Sullivan had always maintained that growth would primarily come from the international customer base, and in fact, the only two positive growth areas in the 2001 annual report were the Internet and international groups—prior to the earnings restatements, that is.

Yet, true to form, the international line costs were being manipulated. Steven Brabbs, the director of international finance and control based outside of London, was in charge of consolidating accounting numbers for Europe. He noticed some odd occurrences concerning the numbers in early 2000. In March, after his staff had closed books and reported first-quarter 2000 numbers to the Clinton headquarters, a June 26 memo revealed improperly booked costs from as far back as 2000. First-quarter 2000 costs were mysteriously reduced by $33.6 million because they had been improperly booked the first time. Once the international subsidiary closed its books for the first quarter of 2000, the domestic accounting staff made a journal entry that cut line costs by $33.6 million; Brabbs was told the directive came from Scott Sullivan.[105] A month later, he had to explain that the entry had been changed in the United States. Brabbs also informed Arthur Andersen, the firm's UK accountant and auditor. At that point, management hit the roof. David Myers (who was later indicted for fraud) admonished Brabbs for raising the matter to Andersen without his knowledge. The U.S. office declined to discuss the matter with Brabbs any further.[106]

This brouhaha preceded a number of visits to the London office by Ebbers and Sullivan. Sources there confirm the office suffered an incredibly tense atmosphere fraught with fights and mounting suspicions. While line costs were being lowered and actual sales figures were declining, the overall reported revenue for the International business in WorldCom's 1999, 2000, and 2001 annual reports was consistently rising. Internally, according to a former WorldCom VP, Ebbers and Sullivan were complaining that there wasn't enough growth in the international customer base, contrary to the annual reports and press releases.

International revenues for 2000 were up 45.8 percent to $2.4 billion from 1999 and revenues in 2001 rose another 25.8 percent to almost $3 billion. WorldCom also used their purchase of Embratel for $2.3 billion in August 1998 as part of the MCI merger and their subsequent mid-2001 reconstruction of Embratel to account for swings in both overall line costs as a percentage of revenue and to adjust international sales revenues upward.[107] In July 2001, WorldCom began reporting Embratel's financial results separately, as they were dragging on WorldCom's performance. In 2002, Embratel stock fell 78 percent and was the worst performing stock on Brazil's stock market index, the Bovespa.

SCRAMBLING TO STAY AFLOAT

Mass panic flooded the corridors of WorldCom during 2002, before news of its implosion became public knowledge. Insiders noticed lawyers and other "suits" regularly coming in and out of the Clinton headquarters. "At first, you thought they were just discussing the hard times the company was going through, how they had to get back on track and stuff," said one former Clinton-based employee. But the suits were just the first sign that deeper problems at WorldCom would surface.

WorldCom was thrown a $2.65 billion lifeline by JP Morgan Chase and other sympathetic banks in April 2002, and then began negotiating to raise that amount to $5 billion because everyone was scared of impending bankruptcy. That was before news of $3.85 billion worth of "errors" went public on June 26, 2002. "Our senior management team is shocked by these discoveries," declared Sidgmore. "We are committed to operating WorldCom in accordance with the highest ethical standards."[108]

On April 29, 2002, in conjunction with Ebbers's resignation, World-Com consolidated its loan and guaranty arrangements into a single promissory note worth $408.2 million, repayable with accrued interest over five years. The principal included $198.7 million that WorldCom paid to Bank of America for Ebbers's personal debts, $36.5 million deposited to collateralize a letter of credit used to support financing to Mississippi College—Ebbers's alma mater—and the $165 million loaned to Ebbers.[109] Bank of America was the lead manager for the majority of the syndicated loans issued to WorldCom. Incest was a factor: the bank also happened to be one of WorldCom's biggest corporate customers. Ebbers used the proceeds of that consolidated loan to repay debt on his other, personal loans that were secured by shares of WorldCom stock, and for his private business purposes. In return for the loan, he pledged shares of both stock he already owned and stock that he would ultimately acquire when he exercised his stock options, plus the equity interest in some of his private businesses.

Ebbers resigned from all directorships, offices, and WorldCom positions under pressure in April 2002. Despite that, he was appointed to serve on the board of directors as "nonexecutive chairman emeritus." His severance package consisted of $1.5 million a year for life and $750,000 a year to his wife after his death. It also included lifetime medical and life insurance benefits at WorldCom's expense and unlimited use of company aircraft. All his remaining stock became fully vested and exercisable. When he resigned, he owned options to acquire 1.8 million shares of WorldCom group stock at $30.9 per share and options to acquire 9.5 million shares at $21.55 per share. John Sidgmore was appointed temporary replacement president and CEO and KPMG LLP replaced Arthur Andersen as the company's public accountants. WorldCom also postponed its annual shareholder meeting, moving it from May 23, 2002, to June 14, 2002.

PAC CONTRIBUTIONS

Even while it was under SEC and DOJ scrutiny and hit with a series of class-action suits, WorldCom maintained its standing as one of the top five telecom carrier political donors for the year 2002. WorldCom's and, before the merger, MCI's cozy relationship with key Bush administration members like Dick Cheney and Colin Powell only increased the merged company's political access, of course. All told, WorldCom spent $7.6 million in campaign contributions throughout and past the 1990s and until they declared bankruptcy in 2002, $4.3 million of it after 1996 deregulation. Some of that money consisted of lobbying expenses, which came to about $3 million per year for both 2000 and 2001.[110]

On May 6, 2002, after Ebbers's resignation, chief operating officer Ron Beaumont sent out an audacious PAC contribution e-mail requesting donations to WorldCom's own PAC. Stock was trading at $1.84, senior leadership had just been overhauled, the company was under SEC investigation, and reporters were circling overhead. Beaumont wanted to make sure employees were aware of what was truly important: keep Washington happy. Continued deregulation was still the biggest goal—even more so with the company in trouble. PAC contributions couldn't be easier for employees to make, thanks to a biweekly payroll deduction plan, and were closely monitored at WorldCom.

Beaumont wrote, "As both a company and a group of employees that share a common interest, we need to band together to influence the world around us. One of the ways that we have available to us is our federal and local Political Action Committees (PACs). . . . We can be a major voice to support the strategic direction of our company with Congress. . . . I encourage you to continue your contribution. . . . Thank you, and let's make things happen."[111]

WORLDCOM AND THE GOVERNMENT

After committing the world's largest fraud, WorldCom made the biggest getaway. Being the government's top telecommunications partner helped; government contracts provided a significant source of revenue to World-Com (though not enough to keep its poor and corrupt business model from bankruptcy). In 2001, WorldCom reported that $1.7 billion, or 8 percent of its revenue, came from state and federal government contracts.[112] Indeed, without an entrenched position providing Internet and other data services and systems to Washington, D.C., WorldCom would have received more severe penalties from regulators. Because the government used the company, they weren't particularly vigorous in prosecuting it. The government didn't even find replacement companies after the fraud broke, something that continues to astonish me.

The WorldCom Government Markets division is located in Vienna, Virginia, just outside the nation's capital, and is managed by well-connected senior vice president Jerry Edgerton. Prior to joining WorldCom, Edgerton directed the federal operations group at Tymnet/McDonnell Douglas Network Systems Company. The division's operation was shrouded in secrecy, according to other WorldCom workers. Insiders say that Ebbers mostly left it alone—he didn't spend a lot of time in Washington. It suffered no job cuts when WorldCom was scaling back its workforce.

It seemed like many Washington departments enjoyed some kind of relationship with WorldCom, but the Department of Defense tops the list. DOD contracts with WorldCom include a $400 million, nine-year agreement with the Defense Information System Agency (DISA) and a separate ten-year, $4 billion contract with the same agency to provide the federal government with circuits to carry information between the Asia-Pacific rim, South America, the Middle East, and the Caribbean.[113]

In addition, WorldCom was one of the principal partners in the Information Strike Force team that supports the Navy Marine Corp Intranet (NMCI) program, an eight-year contract valued at $6.9 billion. The Federal Aviation Administration (FAA) chose WorldCom to provide satellite services in a ten-year, $250 million contract, in addition to a $1 billion communication service contract for the nation's air traffic control system.[114] WorldCom also provides private line and Internet services for the House of Representatives, and it established and manages the U.S. Postal Service network via a five-year, $3 billion agreement.[115]

The government had a lot invested in WorldCom. *Washington Technology* ranked WorldCom number twelve in its top hundred list of federal contractors for 2002, up from twenty-eight the previous year. That year, Washington paid over half a billion dollars to WorldCom, which leaped to lead the telecommunications sector in government contracts.[116]

But, even after massive bankruptcy and fraud disclosures, relationships with the government flourished. In November 2002, the U.S. General Services Administration (GSA) extended its Federal Telecommunications Service (FTS) 2001 contract with WorldCom for another year.[117] FTS2001 is one of the largest federal government contracts, and WorldCom was one of only two U.S. telecom service providers initially awarded FTS2001 contracts by the GSA (the other went to Sprint); WorldCom got an eight-year multibillion-dollar contract.[118] The extension included a contract with the GSA to provide long-distance phone service for seventy-seven federal agencies, which earned the company $331 million in 2002.[119] At the same time, WorldCom won a contract to provide telecommunications services for veterans' hospitals. A month later, the government gave WorldCom yet another contract to provide domestic and international data communications services under the SPECTRUM agreement, worth $360 million over ten years. "It is a privilege for WorldCom to provide its highly secure and reliable data communications services to U.S. Department of State agencies through the SPECTRUM program," said Edgerton.[120]

DISCLOSURE AND BANKRUPTCY

On June 25, 2002, WorldCom announced its intention to restate its financial statements for 2001 and first-quarter 2002 as a result of $3.85 billion of transfers from line-cost expenses to capital accounts that were not made in accordance with generally accepted accounting principles (GAAP).[121] Six weeks later, on August 8, 2002, WorldCom disclosed an additional $3.3 billion in improperly reported earnings for 1999, 2000, 2001, and first-quarter 2002. As a result, WorldCom added it would additionally have to adjust financial statements for 2000 and that further write-offs of assets were expected.[122]

When WorldCom declared bankruptcy, it had three times as many pages in its bankruptcy filing for subsidiaries as did Enron—though, of course, Enron had those 3,000 offshore special-purpose vehicles that didn't fall under bankruptcy law protection. Leading WorldCom's creditor list was JP Morgan Trust with $17 billion, followed by Mellon Bank with $6.6 billion. Rounding out the list were the usual suspects: Citigroup, Bank of America, and JP Morgan Chase.[123]

THE SEC INJUNCTION

For its colossal frauds, WorldCom only received a permanent injunction (a pardon, in layman's terms) from the SEC on November 26, 2002, which got no front-page coverage anywhere at the time.[124] Michael Capellas, formerly of Hewlett Packard, took over all three top spots at the firm— president, chairman of the board, and CEO—just before that injunction was announced.

In all, the SEC's investigation into WorldCom's activities lasted just nine months, ending with the punishment that WorldCom had to promise not to do it again. The judgment, signed by U.S. District Judge Jed S. Rakoff of the Southern District of New York, settled part, but not all, of the SEC's actions against WorldCom. Along with the injunction, the commission ordered an extensive review of the company's internal accounting control structure and policies, something which should have already been under way.

In addition, the court asked WorldCom to train their employees in the field of ethics; the company responded by adding an ethics department populated with just two people. WorldCom consented to all of the SEC's demands without admitting or denying the allegations in the Commission's complaint. To put it another way, WorldCom management refused to admit it had done anything wrong as a corporation, and the government did not require them to admit to anything to settle.

Afterward, the SEC stressed that their investigation into matters related to WorldCom's financial fraud was ongoing, but, seven and a half months after the injunction, the SEC and bankruptcy court settled on a fine of $750 million. That left the case open to civil charges. But as the shock and media pressure surrounding the massive fraud recedes, it is unlikely that the SEC will pursue further investigation into WorldCom's crimes as a corporation. Thus, even though indictments, notably of Bernie Ebbers, were parceled out almost a year later, nothing was done to reform the corporation itself from a regulatory perspective beyond the blaming of a few top offenders.

WorldCom not only successfully erased its debts, laid off 28 percent of its staff, ate through over $180 billion in market value, and handed millions of dollars to its senior executives, but it also managed to spin its tale of "misfortune" into a story about the negative impacts of economic downturn and the competitive telecom industry. It managed to make itself a victim, despite the plethora of actual victims left in its wake.

In addition to the company getting off the hook, the four officers charged by the SEC with participating in the massive fraud got off fairly easily; all received permanent injunctions. Former accounting managers Betty Vinson and Troy Normand were barred from serving on officer or director boards and from practicing accounting.[125] Comptroller David Myers and former accounting director Buford Yates cannot be officers or directors either, at least not at public companies.[126] Everyone had to promise—were "enjoined," to put it into legalese—not to violate the law again.

MICHAEL CAPELLAS

The decision to award Michael Capellas all the top spots at WorldCom is an example of how little had really changed after Ebbers resigned in disgrace. The old board at WorldCom, like so many other corporate boards, never rejected a single proposal put on the table, because its chairman was the CEO.

Before claiming the concentration of power at the helm of World-Com, Michael Capellas was the beneficiary of many corporate executive entitlements at his past jobs. He bagged $45 million at Compaq even while its overall value was declining, and had $5 million of his corporate loans excused.[127] He got a $14.4 million golden parachute just for leaving Hewlett Packard, and WorldCom gave him a boatload of stock options and an $18 million stock guarantee as a signing bonus.[128] That means that Capellas will get his $18 million even if the stock stays at 20 cents (the price when he joined the company) the entire time he's there. Then he's free to go. It's not like the man has a history of sticking around companies for very long anyway. Prior to taking over WorldCom, he was chairman and CEO at Compaq for four years (1998–2002), at Oracle Corporation for less than two years (1997–1998), at SAP America for less than two years as well (1996–1997), and at Benchmarking Partners (1996) for barely a year.

Capellas was appointed CEO at WorldCom around the time that Bush's Office of Homeland Security package was signed into law. While still president of Hewlett Packard, he gave the opening address at the September 2002 Homeland Security Expo in Washington, D.C., an expo designed to "showcase hundreds of products and services with homeland security applications."[129] The event was hosted by the U.S. Department of Commerce, in association with the Office of Homeland Security. The dates are noteworthy because they give the appearance that perhaps one reason WorldCom hired Capellas was that he seemed well-positioned to get government homeland security contracts. On November 15, 2002, a WorldCom press release announced Capellas's takeover of the World-Com reins; on November 25, 2002, the homeland security bill was signed and Tom Ridge appointed the nation's first secretary of homeland security on November 25, 2002. The SEC issued its permanent injunction against WorldCom two days later.

In conjunction with the press release announcing his appointment,

Capellas, his predecessor John Sidgmore, and PR guru Brad Burns held a press conference entitled "Moving Forward."[130] Concluding the conference, Capellas gushed, "I am absolutely jazzed about really starting to get with the employees and make it fun again. And we will be a role model of governance, and I feel good about being here."[131]

Capellas's upbeat report elicited a very different kind of response from a WorldCom employee in a post on *DotcomScoop: As the WorldCom Turns*, an insider's look at the Internet, technology, telecommunications, media, and finance sectors run by Ben Silverman, a business news columnist for the *New York Post*:

> I am jazzed because of layoffs.
>
> I am jazzed because my benefits have been denied me.
>
> I am jazzed because I don't have a pension, 401(k), or any other plans for retirement besides being worked to death.
>
> I am jazzed because Bernie Ebbers and Scott Sullivan are not in jail even though they have ruined hundred of thousands of lives.
>
> I am jazzed because having WorldCom on my resume makes it impossible to find a job anywhere else.[132]

CLEANING THE DECKS

In conjunction with the SEC pardon, the appointment of Capellas, and the pre-Christmas layoffs of a few thousand more workers, WorldCom launched a rather tasteless $10 million advertising campaign, taking out full-page ads in the *New York Times*, the *Wall Street Journal*, and other similarly well-read papers. In the ads, it touted its $1 billion in cash on hand, patted itself on the back for routing out some of the old executive crooks, and glowingly reported—as always—that its customer base was growing. New government contracts aside, I couldn't find any salespeople at WorldCom who knew which new customers the advertisement was referring to.

On December 17, 2002, the last of the old WorldCom regime, at least those at the top, left.[133] Six WorldCom board members—all Bernie's boys—resigned simultaneously: Carl Aycock, Max Bobbitt, Francesco Galesi, Gordon Macklin (former president of the National Association of Securities Dealers, an independent regulatory company based near

Washington, D.C., and CEO of the NASDAQ from 1971 to 1986), Bert Roberts (who owns a company that was paid $405,000 by WorldCom to provide air-transportation services), and John Sidgmore.

Around the same time, Mississippi senator Trent Lott got the cold shoulder from Bush. He was forced to step down as Republican party majority leader in December 2002 after a firestorm of criticism in response to his support of former South Carolina senator Strom Thurmond's segregationist campaign in the 1948 presidential race.[134] Trent Lott had been one of WorldCom's biggest political contribution recipients, and Ebbers had paid $1 million to establish the Trent Lott Leadership Institute at the University of Mississippi just after Lott had appointed a WorldCom representative to a congressional panel weighing the tax implications of Internet purchases.[135] Lott and his protégé, Representative Chip Pickering, had been instrumental in pushing legislation that benefited WorldCom.[136]

WHEN THE DUST SETTLED

Even after all the pardons, the erasing of debts, and layoffs, WorldCom's interim reports to the bankruptcy courts continued to demonstrate severe weakness. Why? Because the WorldCom business model is a bad model for any company. WorldCom acquired too many companies it didn't integrate. It couldn't even make ends meet with its pick of government contracts. It still pays its top people too much. It's still on the hook for Ebbers's $408 million loan. The Internet still isn't growing as much as John Sidgmore promised it would. Broadband isn't growing as fast as FCC chairman Michael Powell promised it would.

WorldCom's fraud and bankruptcy failed to bring any meaningful penalties for its corrupt executives or any admissions of guilt, much less apologies to the victims of its actions. Instead, to distance itself from its crimes, WorldCom reinstated the old MCI moniker on April 14, 2003.[137]

Ultimately, WorldCom escaped its crimes with a $750 million fine in a settlement with the SEC and bankruptcy court on July 7, 2003. The size of the fine, equivalent to just two weeks of WorldCom revenue was an explicit signal that it was not only acceptable, but advantageous, for corporations to play outside the rules. WorldCom, as the renamed MCI, emerged from its bankruptcy effectively debt-free (or at least $41 billion of debt lighter) on April 20, 2004, yet another sign that corporate crime can be a very successful business strategy. Six weeks later, Ebbers's lawyer requested his November 9, 2004, trial date be postponed due to conflicting commitments representing Tyco's general counsel. On June 9, 2004, Scott Sullivan widened his guilty plea to include a securities fraud charge filed by the state of Mississippi.

In the accompanying press release, Michael Capellas said, "Our emergence is not the finish line, it's the beginning of a new race." It remains to be seen whether that new race ends like the old one.[138]

6

Examination and Reform?

*We're demanding that CEOs and CFOs swear that the numbers they've reported
in their financial reports are correct and that they've left nothing important out.*

—SEC press release, June 28, 2002

*The U.S. needs to crack down on corporate crime, fraud and abuse that have
just in the last four years looted and drained trillions of dollars from workers,
investors, pension holders and consumers.*

—Ralph Nader

INSPECTION AND COSMETIC REMEDIES

WHEN THE ENRON SCANDAL FIRST ERUPTED, IT WAS MET WITH INTENSE,
fear-induced scrambling on Capitol Hill. Enron became the instant poster
child for everything a company could do to deceive the public. Less obvious was the fact that it exemplified corporations' increased ability to manipulate the boundaries of regulatory and accounting rules. It immediately
leapt to the top of the U.S. corporate bankruptcy charts and took down one
of the Big Five accounting firms with it: Arthur Andersen, auditors to other
notable frauds like WorldCom, Global Crossing, Halliburton, and Qwest.
The Enron saga maintained a grip on front-page headlines for almost four
months straight, as every angle of fraud was drip-fed to the public and executive involvement in an enormous deception was exposed.

Politically, though, the Enron affair was perceived as a Republican
problem, a web of deceit emanating from George W. Bush's home state
of Texas. On closer inspection, though, it's clear that Enron, a trading
company masquerading as an energy company, was a problem that was
allowed to fester and grow as much because of energy and energy trading
deregulation, undertaken during the Clinton presidency, as Republican
enabling.

When Global Crossing's bankruptcy hit the radar screen a month and
a half after Enron, in late January 2002, despite strong Republican ties,

notably those of co-chairman Lodwrick Cook, it was viewed as more of a Democratic problem. Gary Winnick's ties to the Clinton administration were well known, after all. Both political parties entered a sort of stalemate over corporate governance.

Stemming from this political gridlock, the severity of the telecom meltdown—which, as an industry, produced the highest percentage of post-bubble bankruptcies—and WorldCom's burgeoning fraud didn't make the front pages until June 26, 2002. That was when WorldCom's initial $3.85 billion earnings restatement was announced.[1] This occurred on the same day that Adelphia, the cable company run by the Rigas family, declared bankruptcy.[2] Four weeks later, Adelphia founder John Rigas, his sons Michael and Timothy, former VP James Brown, and former treasurer Michael Mulcahey were arrested, handcuffed, and perp-walked in a public display of so-called justice.[3]

Once WorldCom hit the headlines, the two political parties renewed their assaults on each other. A slew of so-called reform remedies marked the under-fire reaction of Congress and the SEC, culminating in the passage of a quick-fix solution purported to stop corporate crime dead in its tracks: the Sarbanes-Oxley Act of 2002.

The act took aim at a key conflict highlighted by Enron, a common and longstanding practice by which a company uses the same firm both to take care of its accounting and audit its books. Sarbanes-Oxley created a public accounting oversight board to scrutinize the corporate system, but took a year to find an untarnished leader, William J. McDonough. Later that year, New York State attorney general Eliot Spitzer and the SEC presented a beautifully showcased settlement and claimed it would reform Wall Street.

Reform, Washington-style, consisted of a dramatic series of photoops and media sound bites; perp walks for the frequently indicted, yet rarely convicted executives; SEC and other regulatory agency settlements for fractions of the money the culprit corporations lost the public and their own employees; and Senate hearings televised only on C-SPAN.

Meanwhile, though both the investment bank and superbank contingents suffered when their customers underwent defaults, bankruptcies, and fraud lawsuits, they nonetheless managed to bounce back more quickly then their customers did because they can profit both from profit and from pain. After all, banks are the key to capital, whether by extending loans, accessing the markets for institutional lenders or investors, or picking up the pieces of broken firms in the form of cheap assets they can transform into revenue generating opportunities by selling them to other corporations.

CEO PARADE

The Sarbanes-Oxley Act required "CEOs and CFOs of public companies to personally certify that the reports their companies file with the Commission are both accurate and complete."[4] Leading up to the actual passage of the act was a pilgrimage of said CEOs and CFOs to Washington to validate their financial statements. On June 28, 2002, the SEC released a list of 947 of the largest U.S. public companies. The senior executives of those companies had to certify or swear to the integrity of their financial results, specifically focusing on their most recent 10Q (the quarterly report submitted by all public companies to the SEC in which firms are required to disclose relevant financial information) or 10K (the annual report required by the SEC that is a comprehensive summary of a company's performance) reports. Former SEC chairman Harvey Pitt called the procession an "unprecedented step to help restore investor confidence."[5]

This was all made to seem like a new practice, heralded with requisite reform-oriented fanfare. Lost in the self-congratulation was the fact that many of these people—particularly the CFOs—had already been signing their SEC filings for years. In fact, their signatures adorned the last page of many a fraudulent earnings statement that had to be restated later. In practice, the exercise had little meaning. The whole episode showed self-described reformers operating on the level of moral panic, reacting too quickly and failing to create anything more than a gesture. Given that the new rotation of CEOs and CFOs replacing the ones at the most fraudulent companies couldn't possibly attest to anything properly, vouchsafing financial reports couldn't be anything but meaningless. Still, the exercise was good public relations for corporate governance and Sarbanes-Oxley.

For example, WorldCom's prefraud disclosure quarterly report ended, as was customary "legalese," with the clause: "Pursuant to the requirements of the Securities Exchange Act of 1934, the registrant has duly caused this report on Form 10Q to be signed on its behalf by Scott D. Sullivan, thereunto duly authorized to sign on behalf of the registrant and as the principal financial officer thereof." This was on May 15, 2002, and WorldCom CFO Scott Sullivan did in fact sign that statement.[6] Two months later, World-Com's first of many multibillion-dollar "misstatements" was disclosed. John S. Dubel was appointed the new CFO of WorldCom on July 29, 2002, and he verified all reports on August 14, 2002, as per the SEC request. Though, he hadn't even been at the company for a month, as part of his verification, Dubel swore he had reviewed and could verify the veracity of WorldCom's financials, and also admitted (because it was splashed all over the newspapers) to $7 billion in accounting "discrepancies."[7] Dubel's validation did not curtail the admission of more WorldCom frauds, however. In mid-September another $2 billion "discrepancy" was found—and in early November, still another $1.8 billion.[8]

As for Enron, no one showed up in person to swear to the integrity of anything, though a copy of some sworn statements from acting chief executive officer Stephen Cooper, who had taken Ken Lay's place in January 2002 as part of Enron's restructuring plan, did make it to the SEC by August 14. In them, Cooper helpfully confessed that "a restatement of prior reported financial information is not feasible and will not be completed."[9] Fraud aside, Cooper wasn't even at the helm long enough to attest to the validity of the annual reports in question.

Qwest's newly appointed CEO, Richard Notebaert, also declared that things looked pretty good from where he stood. Yet the company later found another $1.1 billion in accounting discrepancies.[10] As for companies that were not under investigation or in the spotlight for violating some securities law at the time—or just not energy or telecom companies—their CEOs also made the Washington pilgrimage to testify under less than honest pretenses. For example, HealthSouth CEO Richard Scrushy signed a sworn statement confirming that all the company's numbers were accurate. Seven months later, in March 2003, the SEC charged HealthSouth with over $1.4 billion of fraud, and up to $2.5 billion in earnings misstatements. Scrushy was fired. Beforehand, he managed to cash out $93 million of stock in 1998, one of the years under investigation.[11] On October 29, 2003, Scrushy was indicted by a federal grand jury on eighty-five charges that he had falsified books, records and accounts at the company. His trial was delayed until September 2004, at the earliest.

Regardless of how successful or honest the SEC considered the balance sheet validation process, it still took almost a year (until May 23, 2003) for the SEC to vote to adopt CEO and CFO validation requirements and, additionally, to require executives to certify their companies had adequate controls to prevent and detect accounting fraud. Those rules were slated to take effect on or after June 2004, two and a half years after Enron went down.

THE SARBANES-OXLEY ACT

Enron's frauds were certainly not unique or even the first to come to light during the post-1990s boom and bust. Since 1997, one out of every ten public companies has had to restate their financial figures due to "accounting irregularities."[12] It's true the Sarbanes-Oxley Act was a dramatic attempt at reform—though, given the environment of media and public outcry at the time, it was arguably more show than substance. Senator Paul Sarbanes (D-MD) and Representative Michael Oxley (R-OH) authored the eleven-section act. It passed 97–0 in the Senate, basking in the afterglow Enron had luridly cast and fueled by the more recent news of World-Com. Designed to look like a significant step in fighting the battle against corporate corruption, it was rushed through Congress and signed into law by President Bush on July 30, 2002.

But it's doubtful that even the corporations it was designed to police considered it to be effective. In response to a March 2003 study by accounting giant PricewaterhouseCoopers (itself fined $5 million by the SEC in July 2002 to settle charges of violations of auditor independence rules from 1996 to 2001), 84 percent of executives surveyed reported that Sarbanes-Oxley had changed compliance practices to some degree in their company. But just 4 percent cited *significant* changes, while 53 percent said it merely formalized existing "good practice." Fifty percent of the executives said the law would have *no* impact on corporate confidence, and 19 percent were uncertain whether or not it would have an effect.[13]

A central provision of the Sarbanes-Oxley Act was the establishment of a Public Company Accounting Oversight Board (PCAOB), a private sector, nonprofit corporation that would oversee the auditing of public companies, establish new auditing rules, conduct investigations, and administer disciplinary action. The board would consist of five members "appointed among individuals of integrity," to be assembled within ninety days of the enactment of the Sabanes-Oxley Act. Like an instant sports replay, the PCAOB's charter appeared identical to that of its predecessor, the Public

Oversight Board (POB). The POB had similarly been created by the Senate in 1977 to oversee the programs of the SEC Practice Section, established the same year. That practice section was comprised of accounting firms, responsible for the auditing of the financial statements of 17,000 corporations. Its mandate was to ensure the integrity of the business or auditing practices of its member firms. Those member accounting firms were supposed to represent the public interest "on all matters that may affect public confidence in the integrity, reliability and credibility of the audit process."[14] As a mark of its supposed importance, the POB's charter (which had been monitoring auditing firms) was expanded in February 2001 to not only oversee their SEC practices, but also the more general auditing and independence standards of the accounting profession. Ten months later the Enron scandal broke. Soon afterward, Arthur Andersen went down in flames for highly unethical and unprofessional practices.

The POB's 2001 budget was $5.2 million; it was dissolved entirely in May 2002.[15] It was resurrected as the PCAOB in July 2002, as part of the Sarbanes-Oxley Act. That new board was given a budget of $75 million for 2003 and $103 million for 2004.[16] Three months after its establishment, SEC chairman Harvey Pitt appointed William Webster, former CIA and FBI chief, to run it. Webster also happened to have been head of the audit committee at U.S. Technologies Inc., a company sued by shareholders over accounting issues, not quite the best ethical choice. This poor selection on Pitt's part was met with an onslaught of charges against Webster's integrity, leading to his ouster three weeks later.[17]

In February 2003, it was unclear whether or not the board had actually accomplished anything beyond voting on its own members' compensation of $452,000 a year.[18] In early March 2003, the bureaucratic tangle of new reform initiatives had the SEC announcing that it had "adopted a process for conducting an intensive search to *promptly* select a chairperson for the Public Company Accounting Oversight Board."[19] In addition, there was to be a nomination process, a shortlist process, a preliminary voting process, and then interviews. A month later, new SEC head William Donaldson, said that the search for a PCAOB chairman was the agency's "number one priority." Given how long it was taking the SEC to complete that search, it didn't bode well for its propensity to review financial statements with any greater expediency.[20]

Two months later, on May 21, 2003, the SEC announced it had unanimously approved the appointment of New York Federal Reserve Bank official William J. McDonough as chairman of the PCAOB as of June 11, 2003, almost a full year after the post was created by Sarbanes-Oxley.[21] McDonough was, in fact, on the verge of retiring completely before Donaldson selected him.

CRISIS OF SEC RESPONSIBILITY

The SEC was inadequately equipped to handle the necessary level of corporate examination during the 1990s for various reasons. From its perspective, the single most important fraud preventative measure was rigorous filing examination. Yet the SEC cut back its review of filings from 18 percent in 1995 to 11.9 percent in 1998. The last time it even conducted a review of Enron at all was back in 1997, coincidentally the last time Enron paid any taxes. In 1995–1998, the size of the SEC budget and staff stayed constant with inflation even though company filings increased by 28 percent and investor complaints went up 70 percent.

Arthur Levitt, today a board member at boutique venture capital firm, the Carlyle Group, headed the SEC from 1993 to 2001, years fraught with heavy fraud and marked by rampant deregulation. While his successors Pitt and Donaldson were even less likely to reform the securities watchdog regulatory body than he had been, a significant degree of responsibility for the dramatic rise in the amount of corporate balance sheet fraud lies with his management of the organization—not necessarily because he was unaware of brewing problems, but because he was unwilling or unable to do anything about them.

Back during the height of the stock bubble, Levitt gave a speech in September 1998 at the dedication of the New York University Center for Law and Business in which he expressed his commitment to fighting fraud—except he didn't use the actual term "fraud." Instead, he used less damaging words like "hocus pocus."[22] The timing of that speech was notable because it occurred at the pinnacle of stock price levels, debt accumulation, and media cheerleading.

Though detailed and well delivered, that speech and so many others like it displayed a key characteristic of Levitt's leadership of the SEC. If you read or listened between the lines, the speech came across as just another excuse manufactured to deflect attention away from the SEC's passiveness in the face of corporate malfeasance. Levitt told the NYU crowd,

"I am also calling upon a broad spectrum of capital market participants, from corporate management to Wall Street analysts to investors, to stand together and reenergize the touchstone of our financial reporting system: transparency and comparability."[23] Levitt, the leader of the body established to police corporate crime, was irresponsibly asking the perpetrators to do the SEC's job themselves.

The boom in mergers provided ample opportunities for corporations to muddy their new consolidated balance sheets. Deceptive financial statements arose because the larger the statements, the more places there were to hide a bogus earning here, a real loss there. The most deregulated industries, such as telecoms, energy, and banking, fostered the most fraud, fired the most workers, and handed executives the largest cashouts. These industries began to bleed into one another as mergers led to diversified business entities with increasingly complicated balance sheets, more reason to hide new debt and losses, and greater desperation to meet quarterly earnings.

Levitt's generalities did reflect awareness of the accounting and earnings manipulations. But there was no way that he, as head of the nation's securities regulatory body, could actually have believed that Wall Street was about to shut off its fee taps and begin monitoring itself. On the one hand, he realized there was widespread financial malpractice (as evidenced by almost saying "fraud"); yet on the other, he had to know that the financial community would never do what he proposed. Levitt went on to say that the problem of corporate fraud was "a financial community problem" that "demands a financial community response." In other words, it couldn't be solved by government intervention. This is an amazing admission, not least because he *is* the government, and basically recused the SEC from its own responsibilities by telling the offending parties, "Go on, fix it yourselves!" So as not to offend the offenders, he was careful not to name names, though it is hard to believe he couldn't have come up with an example or two. Goldman Sachs CEO Hank Paulson also failed to name names in his June 2002 call for stricter corporate governance, lest he upset any Goldman clients.[24] Both the SEC and Goldman Sachs were protecting their friends, after all.

In effect, Levitt deftly shifted culpability for corporate governance away from the SEC and toward Wall Street, one of the entities the SEC was supposed to monitor. He outlined a number of accounting "illusions" in his speech. Five of the more popular ones that he discussed were "big-bath restructuring charges, creative acquisition accounting, cookie jar reserves, immaterial misapplications of accounting principles, and the premature recognition of revenue."[25] These modes of deception were later revealed to be rampant in many of the corporate documents that his commission rubberstamped. The WorldCom-MCI merger was a prime example. The SEC received WorldCom's filings regularly, but never saw cause for alarm bells during its thirteen-year lifespan as a public company. In 1998, when World-Com was trying to acquire MCI (after having acquired sixty smaller companies), the SEC received all merger-related documents for inspection, as was customary, including annual reports, the reasons for the merger, advantages of the "synergy" of the two corporations, and financial soundness opinions (conveniently provided by the investment banks that were advising the deal). After combing through all that material, the SEC saw no potential danger in the biggest merger in U.S. history, nor did the FCC or the Department of Justice, who examined the same documents.

After years of complacency, the SEC had two outstanding opportunities in 2003 to instill some reform and reconfirm its responsibility to protect the public—or, at the very least, to issue a strong message that corporations and their banks are liable for the consequences of their actions: the Wall Street settlement and the WorldCom settlement. Unfortunately, the SEC under William Donaldson failed to enforce strict accountability in the implementation of either settlement.

SPITZER AND THE WALL STREET SETTLEMENT

New York District Attorney Eliot Spitzer seized on a terrific opportunity to gain exposure for his political pursuits by attacking Wall Street analysts. The media didn't fail to fawn over him while he uncovered damning e-mails and documents up until the big settlement was announced in December 2002 and confirmed in April 2003. *Fortune* deemed him "The Enforcer" on a September 2002 cover. The *New York Times* ran a front-page article in November 2002 titled "Assault on Wall Street Misdeeds Raised Spitzer's Profile," calling him "the forerunner for governor in 2006." [26] The piece quoted former New York mayor Ed Koch saying, "Everybody in politics believes Eliot's aspiration is to be governor." Spitzer's style chafed regulators in Washington, who wanted to be seen as the ultimate corporate watchdogs when it was politically advantageous, but without assuming the risk real change brings.

While Spitzer was commanding the headlines, Oxley, chairman of the House Financial Services Committee, told the U.S. Chamber of Commerce that "by coercing large sums of money from brokerage firms, actions like those undertaken by the Attorney General will seriously weaken the ability of American companies to raise funds in the capital markets."[27] In other words, Oxley was acting as a congressional defender for the banking industry. Though he was a co-author of the Sarbanes-Oxley Act that was heralded for making huge strides to terminate corporate crime, Oxley didn't particularly want Wall Street's profits or reputation to suffer for its complicit role in perpetuating fraud with its corporate clients. Oxley's stand was no surprise to *New York Times* columnist Paul Krugman, who wrote that "if you knew anything about Michael Oxley's legislative career, [it was] as if Prohibition-era Chicago had passed a Ness-Capone clean government ordinance."[28] Oxley was really a convenient mouthpiece for banks. The financial industry had put him in power and given him 60 percent of his 2002 election cycle PAC money.[29]

The "global" Wall Street settlement, spearheaded by Spitzer with assistance from the SEC, was finalized on April 28, 2003. It levied $1.4 billion worth of fines and several reform requirements. The headlines that accompanied the finalization of that agreement were recycled from the announcement of the settlement on December 20, 2002, a Christmas present for the Street disguised as punishment. In it, the SEC, the National Association of Securities Dealers, the NYSE, and Spitzer agreed upon "enforcement actions" with ten top Wall Street banks—including Citigroup–Salomon Brothers, JP Morgan Chase, Goldman Sachs, Merrill Lynch, Morgan Stanley, and Credit Suisse First Boston—and two research analysts made famous during the boom, Henry Blodget and Jack Grubman. The first of the settlement's top three reforms consisted of insulating (sometimes referred to as "firewalling") research analysts from investment banking pressures by requiring senior management to set research budgets and analyst compensation without input from the investment banking department. The second reform required firms to provide independent research to their clients from external sources and make analyst opinions on companies publicly available ninety days after they are released to internal clients. Of course, ninety days can be an eternity in banking, rendering analyst opinions obsolete before they hit the public anyway. Last, firms had to ban the practice of hot IPO spinning. The remaining three reforms covered transparency of rating information, assigned independent monitors for each firm, and set up $80 million worth of investor education programs.

The process leading up to the settlement started in 2001, when Spitzer's office began investigating conflicts of interest on Wall Street. By April 2002, regulators at the SEC—not wishing to appear uninvolved—hopped onboard and initiated a joint investigation into what the SEC deemed the "undue influence of investment banking interest on securities research at brokerage firms."[30] Yet, while so doing, the SEC expressed public distaste for Spitzer's grandstanding methods. During a speech to the New York Financial Writers Association in New York City in the spring of 2002, Harvey Pitt thanked host and CNN commentator Myron Kandel by saying, "I especially appreciate your tact in not referring to me as 'the other guy who regulates analysts.'"[31]

According to Spitzer's official statement, the settlement implemented "far-reaching reforms that will radically change behavior on Wall Street."[32] But it really does nothing of the kind. Tellingly, no Wall Street bank complained about the settlement, and it was immediately clear why. Because deception and related attention were so widespread in Corporate America, it was in Wall Street's interest to wrap up investigations quickly and forge a settlement to avoid too much probing into their own role, which had combined misleading financial engineering with an outpouring of easy money. In fact, not a single item in the settlement posed a serious threat to status quo, except for the part that forbade analysts and investment bankers from joint golfing trips with their corporate clients. The public should take little comfort in the settlement.

RIPPING APART THE SETTLEMENT

There were many reform-oriented omissions in the settlement. First and foremost, the whole premise of the research analyst–focused settlement is false. It primarily faults analysts for their public role in extolling the virtues of their top client corporations, but it doesn't reform the more clandestine behavior of investment bankers and senior executives who created the deals they paid analysts to hype. It merely requires their exclusion from the analyst compensation process. In practice, this means there will be a severe reduction in e-mail trails, which may make it look to an outsider like investment banking isn't involved. In reality, conversations linking analysts' pay to profit and deals will continue unfettered, behind closed doors.

More firewalls, such as prohibiting investment bankers and analysts from sitting together in the same office, joint business trips with clients, or road shows on behalf of their deals, are cosmetic changes. Such interactions are easily resurrected in other forms. For example, savvy analysts who did a good job of convincing their clients to invest in particular companies are now shifting over to investment banking or sales. Since those jobs are not covered by so-called reform, the same people will be able to say whatever they want to corporate customers; it just won't be called research. Additionally, banks are only required to provide independent research for five years, not exactly a permanent fix.

However, the central problem with Wall Street and conflicts of interest is not former Citigroup–Salomon Brother's telecom analyst star Jack Grubman (fined $15 million), and it certainly isn't Merrill Lynch's Internet analyst Henry Blodget (fined $4 million). These people merely played their roles in the system exceedingly well, but the media demonized their stock cheerleading and isolated them as particularly ill-behaved examples compared to the executives who compensated them and the investment bankers who influenced their recommendations. Despite the settlement requirements, little has changed in the way of fee-linked bonuses. As one managing director at a fine-paying investment bank told me, "It's not like junior analysts in training are being told they'll get penalized for bringing in deals."

The settlement does nothing to change the deeply institutionalized incentive system (and culture) within financial firms, nor the heavily conflicted relationships of senior banking and corporate executives. All the senior bank executives in charge remain in their influential spots. In the fall of 2003, a highly publicized conflict of interest accusation hinged on how Jack Grubman supposedly had upgraded his AT&T rating right before Salomon Brothers led the AT&T wireless division IPO in exchange for Citibank boss Sandy Weill's $1 million contribution to the 92nd Street Y to get Grubman's twins into the Y's nursery school.

There's no doubt that Grubman was a "dangerous" man, although his danger was overpromoted by the media. But so were many others, including the bankers who created a state of debt-heavy and frankly unsustainable companies; the institutional salespeople who sold higher risk, higher commission products to state pension funds; the fund trustees who bent their own rules to purchase "hot" names; and the strategists, like me, who found analytical reasons to market higher risk, higher margin products as dictated by the internal codes of Wall Street. Also responsible were the brokers who were in direct daily contact with the millions of Americans who got fleeced.

Though the settlement supposedly prohibits investment bankers from deciding which analysts cover which companies, it does not keep those same bankers or senior executives from sitting on the boards of their clients, a prime conflict of interest. Citigroup's board hung Grubman out to dry but didn't even admonish Weill—despite the fact that AT&T CEO Michael Armstrong was on the board of Citigroup at the time and, reciprocally, Weill was on the board of AT&T. With or without Grubman, Armstrong's and Weill's relationship was pretty tight, but the settlement left both their wallets untouched. Blodget and Grubman knew their success was tied to *never* giving bad news, but the CEO or chairman actually running the companies would be a more accurate target for retribution.

Second, the fines themselves, totaling $1.4 billion, were a joke. They amounted to just 1.5 percent of the $62 billion the top ten Wall Street firms made from 1998 to 2002 in investment banking fees alone. That's not including the amount of additional revenues these banks made over the same period, which totaled over $1 *trillion*, or 1,075 times the fines. Plus, only $875 million of the settlement was cash fines, of which only $387.5 million was characterized as disgorgement (or giving back of profits made through illicit activity) for wronged investors. Besides that, the $512.5 million fine thrown in for banks to effectively self-fund reform of their investor research practices, came complete with suggestions for spurious investor research and education activities like distributing research to their clients from independent firms that the banks *select*.

The reported fines levied seemed high, mostly because they were grouped together, but per each of the ten paying banks, they were small even by other 1990s standards. Between 1993 and 1995, Prudential Securities alone paid $1.5 billion in fines for scam partnerships. For another comparison, consider Merrill Lynch's Orange County debacle. In 1994, the entire county declared bankruptcy after posting $1.6 billion in losses, largely due to a bad cocktail of interest-rate derivatives, taken under Merrill Lynch's suggestions. Merrill's 1998 settlement was $470 million.[33] Earlier,

Drexel Burnham Lambert's 1989 junk-bond scandal settlement was $650 million.[34]

It is unlikely individual investors will see much of the settlement money anytime soon. Spurred by class-action lawsuits, Spitzer et al established ten different distribution funds for customers whose claims are "deemed appropriate" by the U.S. District Court, Southern District of New York, at "some" future date. But with thousands of individual investors misled by their personal stockbrokers and represented in hundreds of class-action suits across the country, it will take years to divvy up that cash.

Third, prohibiting the spinning of hot IPOs in a dead stock market environment when nothing's hot anyway is meaningless; there is no such thing as a hot IPO in a bear market. Since hot IPO stock was generally given to the choicest, highest fee-paying clients, the ban was designed to keep CEOs from these bribe-for-fee-business helpings of stock. When IPOs become hot again, there will be a myriad of simple ways to get around the ban such as doling out derivatives linked to hot stocks to CEOs instead of the shares themselves.

Neither Spitzer nor the SEC got any bank to admit to the conflict of interest that allows Citigroup (via its investment bank arm, Salomon Brothers) to help create WorldCom, hype and fund WorldCom, and use its retail customer financial network to distribute WorldCom stock to individual investors (through the old Smith Barney brokerage division). The settlement did not even address loan tying, easily the most harmful factor in corporate deception and expansion. The exchange of cheap credit to corporate clients for higher-margin banking business like IPOs and mergers crippled the economy when corruption, defaults, and bankruptcies rose dramatically and pension contributions and jobs were cut as last-minute resorts to stave off financial ruin.

Ultimately, whether Eliot Spitzer turns out to have been good or bad for individual investors can only be ascertained after the next major prolonged stock rally—when rule-bending, grand-scale regulatory neglect, and starry-eyed euphoria will reign again. And it will happen. The market has a very poor memory, and unfortunately, so do investors. But, by negotiating a settlement that avoided corporate culpability, he effectively closed the door on deeper inspection. Spitzer merely scratched the surface. The deeper problem of the period lies beyond the persuasive powers of the analyst, whose influence pales in comparison to the investment bankers, banks, corporations, and legislators who created and maintained the poorly regulated environment.

The only thing that would reform the banking system would be the actual division of issuing from distribution activities. Only the type of clear distinction of roles, instilled in the 1930s with passage of the Glass-Steagall Act, would reduce banks' incentive to speculate with consumer money and use retail customers as fodder for the stock and bonds of favored corporate clients. Yet there has been no mention of bringing back the Glass-Steagall Act.

THE WORLDCOM-MCI SETTLEMENT

The aftermath of the 1990s made it clear that corporate crime pays. This was most apparent in the case of WorldCom. The number of critical issues embedded in the WorldCom settlement should not be underestimated. At $11 billion and counting, WorldCom committed the biggest fraud in world history. It was crucial that the SEC, the bankruptcy courts, and Congress take every step necessary to deal with it accordingly. However, the SEC and the bankruptcy courts initially decided to try for $500 million, the equivalent of less than one week's worth of WorldCom's revenue—pocket change compared to the $180 billion in market value that vaporized when WorldCom's stock value plummeted from a $64.50 high in 1999 to $.07 a share. That erasure included $4.4 billion in workers' state and local government pensions and the $1.8 billion loss in WorldCom employee 401(k) plans. State pension losses ranged from $351,000 in North Dakota to $1.2 billion in California; New York State alone lost $406 million, Ohio $398 million, and Alabama $275 million.

The treatment of WorldCom—in everything from not fining or convicting key executives to allowing a permanent injunction and a "not guilty" plea to approving a name change to trade on an integrity it had already destroyed—kept the company from having to assume any blame. At the same time, WorldCom's actions had a ripple effect, decreasing overall corporate confidence and further weakening the stock market. In the end, the bankruptcy judge involved in the case, Judge Jed S. Rakoff, did finally adjust that SEC $500-million fine—all the way up to a still measly $750 million.[35] WorldCom's kid-gloves treatment won't deter other corporations from cooking their books in the future; in fact, it showed how such financial creativity makes sound strategic, long-term business sense. It was also an affront to the people who lost money and jobs.

In the end, WorldCom, its current senior management, and its ousted senior management really lost very little. Via the bankruptcy process, it managed to shed the $41 billion of debt it had accumulated and some of its unprofitable businesses, all the while keeping on the good side of its largest customer, the U.S. government. During fiscal 2002, WorldCom bagged $772 million in federal technology contracts, a marked increase from the $507 million they had received in 2001, and a huge jump from the $201 million they got in 2000. That year, they leaped to eighth place in federal technology contractor rankings, breaking into the top ten for the first time; they had placed twelfth in 2001 and twenty-eighth in 2000. Their number eight rank only accounted for prime contracting; it didn't even factor in subcontracting awards.[36] The following year, the U.S. government not only stuck by WorldCom, but even threw more business their way, including a $45 million no-bid contract to rebuild "postwar" Iraq's mobile phone network awarded on May 20, 2003.

WorldCom was given every opportunity to emerge unscathed, without providing any solid indication that the practices leading to its book-bloating had been systematically eradicated. Such assurances should be mandatory before any settlement is confirmed or before the fraudulent company is allowed to come out of bankruptcy. Otherwise, these kinds of settlements merely confirm that malfeasance is good business.

ENERGY SECTOR REPERCUSSIONS

The power energy sector got off equally lightly in the fine department, despite their multi-state market manipulation and admitted wash trading practices. In November 2002, California attorney general Bill Lockyer reached a decent-sized $417-million settlement with the Tulsa-based Williams Company for three years of market manipulation.[37] But only $147 million of those fines had to be paid in cash. The remainder consisted of a $180-million reduction of long-term contracts with the State of California that was to coincide with furnishing $90 million of generating assets like power plants to San Diego and San Francisco, plus $15 million each to Oregon and Washington.

In general, actual *cash* fines from the entire industry through mid-2004 totaled only $309 million, although losses and trading scam costs ran approximately $85 billion. Those fines included an $18 million tab for Houston-based Reliant Resources, amounting to two-tenths of one percent of its 2001 revenues. Reliant had to pay $13.8 million to FERC in January 2003 for withholding power to drive up prices in California in 2000 and an additional $25 million cash by September 2006.[38] That $309 million also included Dynegy's September 2002 $5-million FERC fine as well as their $3-million SEC fine for roundtrip trades. Many power marketer firms have until 2010 to pay.

Houston-based El Paso ultimately agreed to pay California $1.6 billion in November 2003, for withholding natural gas supplies during the crisis. This was on top of the $15.5 million to the California Department of Water Resources' Electric Power Fund to settle market manipulation charges in an agreement reached with Lockyer in February 2003, plus another $8 million to FERC for intentionally shutting down power plants in California.[39] Among other violations and lawsuits, Charlotte-based Duke Energy was fined $28 million by the North Carolina Public Utility Commission for understating profits by $124 million from 1998 to 2001. Of that September 2003 fine, 60 percent was to be paid to the Commodity Futures Trading Commission for false price reporting. Its 1998 understatements, according to lawyers involved in suing them for fraud, cost ratepayers almost $1 billion. If Duke had stated its profits accurately, it would have prompted statewide rate reductions under state utility regulation guidelines. In early October 2003, Duke CEO Richard Priory announced his resignation, two months before Duke was slapped with a $2.5 million wash-trading fine by FERC. Even as disclosures of accounting misstatements keep surfacing, dozens of energy companies are still negotiating with regulators for reduced fines—and, largely, to be left alone and continue with business as usual.

SIDESTEPPING CHARGES AND ONGOING SCANDALS

It's scary—but necessary—to realize that it wasn't just one or two sections of American industry racking up fraud and bankruptcies. Misrepresenting earnings was a common practice in companies as blue-chip as IBM, and as non–new economy as HealthSouth. The following examples of deceptive practices range across a number of industries and household names. It's painful to go through the list and realize the situation is truly that widespread and will only worsen without the introduction of stringent governmental controls.

A slew of companies made fraud headlines but got off with little or no charges or penalties, including Lucent, Xerox, and ImClone (though ImClone CEO Sam Waksal did go to jail). Other significant fraud-related earnings restatements erupted in 2003, from such corporations as Health-South, Bristol Myers–Squibb, ING Groep, and AOL Time Warner. Even the solid and longstanding IBM announced in June 2003 that the SEC was investigating their revenue accounting for 2000 and 2001.

Lucent Technologies turned sidestepping accounting fraud into an art form. The SEC had undertaken a two-year investigation into a self-reported $700 million of improper accounting, but dismissed its probe in February 2003.[40] Because of over-leverage and poor management, Lucent's stock plummeted 97 percent from its 1999 high, losing 72 percent of its value in 2002 alone. Its rating was cut to junk status in 2001 and remains on rating agencies' watch lists for a potential future downgrade. Struggling to survive, it continues to ax its employees, even though over 70 percent of its early 2000 123,000 employee base has already been cut. Lucent's revenues still fell 42 percent to just over $2 billion for the final quarter of 2002. Despite massive losses over the preceding two years, its top three officers (including newly-appointed CEO Patricia Russo) still made around $30 million total in 2002.[41]

In October 2002, ImClone founder Sam Waksal pleaded guilty to six counts of fraud, including bank and securities fraud, conspiracy to obstruct justice, insider trading, and perjury.[42] As punishment, he received a seven-year, three-month prison term and an additional $4-million fine in June 2003.[43] Three months earlier, Waksal had reached a settlement with the SEC stemming from insider trading charges; he got fined $800,000 and was banned from serving as an executive of a public company for life. On June 4, 2003, Martha Stewart, homemaking maven and icon, was indicted on nine counts of fraud for selling ImClone stock on insider information, which had netted her a mere $45,000.[44] She was convicted of obstruction of justice by a jury in March 2004 and scheduled for a July sentencing, with little hope of a retrial.

It was Martha Stewart who somehow personified the application of "justice" following the corporate scandals. After all, she lied, yet she did not hurt the public or cost people their jobs or future retirement security; others who did still go unpunished. In stark contrast, Ken Lay and Gary Winnick both evaded criminal charges though they presided over companies where lying was a constant business strategy. Adding insult to Martha's injury, former Tyco CEO Dennis Kozlowski, after "looting" (as the SEC described it) $600 million from his company, received a mistrial in April 2004.

Xerox was another household name that had been cooking various parts of its books for years. Manipulating revenue in various ways, Xerox managed to boost equipment revenues by $2.8 billion, and its pretax earnings by $1.4 billion, from 1997 to 2000. The company also used a number of one-time accounting tricks to inflate its operating results by $1 billion. For their ingenuity, Xerox had to pay a $10 million fine to the SEC (without admitting any wrongdoing) and agreed to restate earnings from 1997 to 2000—helpful, considering the numbers had been fabricated.[45]

HealthSouth, the nation's largest operator of rehabilitation hospitals, became the second company in twenty-five years for which the SEC halted New York Stock Exchange trading on March 19, 2003. The SEC disclosed they were filing charges that the company had overstated profits by $2.5 billion from 1999 through 2002. The House Energy and Commerce Committee began their own investigation in September 2003 to look for additional HealthSouth violations. The allegations suggested senior executives and accounting officers at the Birmingham headquarters overstated earnings to meet or exceed Wall Street earnings expectations.[46] On that March 19 morning, the FBI raided HealthSouth's Alabama offices in an insider-trading probe of chairman Richard Scrushy—rather like the film *Boiler Room*. The following week, the company's ex-CFO pled guilty to securities fraud. Merrill Lynch analysts helpfully downgraded the stock from "neutral" to "sell" after the FBI raid; it had already fallen from a mid-1998 $30.56 high to $3.91.

The same day, Bristol Myers–Squibb, the sixth largest drug maker, announced it had misstated its earnings for four years (it had previously announced misstatements of only two years) by improperly booking $2.5 billion of revenue. Sales had been artificially inflated after the company encouraged wholesalers to overstock its drugs. Bristol Myers was also connected at the hip to ImClone, with whom they had an agreement in 2001 to pay $2 billion for the experimental cancer drug Erbitrux.

Outside of the corporate arena, bank goodwill write-downs continued throughout 2003. On March 17, 2003, Netherlands-based ING announced a huge 79 percent write-down of $14.2 billion.[47] ING owns the well-known American insurance companies Aetna Inc., Equitable Life, and ReliaStar Financial Corp. Two-thirds of the write-down was due to the 13.5-billion-euro acquisition of Aetna and ReliaStar.[48]

Despite the magnitude of that write-down, Aetna handed its chairman and CEO, Jack Rowe, a $9 million compensation package, including $5.2 million in cash, for his leadership in 2002. That was a reward for beating Wall Street's earnings expectations. It had taken Rowe two years to post those better-than-expected results, which made one wonder just how he suddenly managed to achieve them.

Because of existing discrepancies between U.S. and international accounting law, ING's U.S. write-down did not affect the 2002 annual results reported in its home country, the Netherlands. According to U.S. accounting rules, acquisitions are treated as investments and reported as assets on the consolidated balance sheet. A profit or loss resulting from the acquired company must be reported on the consolidated income statement. In the case of ING, the acquired company posted a loss. However, that loss only hit the U.S. side of ING's income statement, not the Dutch side. That is because under Dutch regulation, the loss on an acquisition can be charged against shareholder equity on the balance sheet, but not reported on the income statement. If ING had reported earnings under U.S. rules, it would have lost 9.6 billion euros in 2002. Instead, it reported a 4.5-billion-euro net profit under Dutch regulations. The whole thing was a complex international balance-sheet shell game.

In late January 2003, AOL Time Warner, the world's biggest Internet service provider and media conglomerate, reported a 2002 loss of $98.7 billion, the largest in U.S. corporate history, and subsequently announced that vice-chairman Ted Turner had resigned from the company.[49] The loss resulted from $99.2 billion in write-downs to reflect the falling value of assets acquired in the late 1990s, when optimism about the future of the Internet sent AOL shares soaring to a height of $94 in 1999.

AOL Time Warner was one of several firms that took to name-altering to mask fraud or failure, ultimately changing its name back to pre-merger Time Warner. Other corporations took to reinventing themselves by changing their names as well. In addition to WorldCom's switch to the plain old MCI moniker, something more reminiscent of old economy–style telephone service. Reliant Energy changed its name to Counter Point.

KPMG Consulting, who became the replacement auditor of choice for many firms that had once used Arthur Andersen, changed its name to Bearing Point.

PAID TO FAIL: GOLDEN PARACHUTING

Not only did corporate crime pay overall, but another troubling outcome of the fraud shakeout was that executives were paid to fail at the expense of their workers. Too often, after the culprit CEOs were ousted by their boards or quit, perhaps to get away from the shame of the limelight, they picked up generous golden parachutes, particularly at WorldCom, Hewlett Packard, Kmart, Qwest, Dynegy, and Global Crossing, among other companies.

Former WorldCom CEO Bernie Ebbers resigned from WorldCom on April 29, 2002, and was awarded a severance package on May 17, 2002 of $1.5 million a year for life and myriad benefits even though he owed WorldCom $408 million in loans. While there was some public debate about whether he should receive such a substantial golden parachute when WorldCom's fraud was announced on June 27, 2002, in the end it became another hollow outcry, and Ebbers gets to walk away with the money. In contrast, WorldCom fired over 20,000 workers during the first half of 2002, and thousands of them spent months fighting for their due severance in bankruptcy court.

Hewlett Packard CEO Michael Capellas had $7.5 million in loans excused by Hewlett Packard even though the stock dropped 44 percent and he cut 7,000 jobs. In a well-executed double coup, he received $14.4 million for leaving Hewlett Packard and $18 million for joining WorldCom. Kmart's Chuck Conaway received a $9 million severance package despite leading Kmart to bankruptcy, costing investors $4.6 billion, and laying off 22,000 workers. Former Qwest CEO Joe Nacchio received a $15-million severance package for presiding over Qwest's multi-billion dollar fraud and 92 percent stock decline. Dynegy's Chuck Watson received a $33-million severance package when he got tired of hanging around for the company's SEC investigation. Both Gary Winnick and 9,000 laid-off employees left Global Crossing without any severance, but only Winnick walked away worth over $735 million.

THE MEDIA'S ROLE

The mainstream media spent much of the 1990s extolling the virtues of all the rags-to-riches senior executives in cover stories and glossy photo shoots. Negative viewpoints were infrequent. After all the scandals broke, the media became slightly more cautious in their reporting of things like equity analyst views, though the economic recession gave them little choice over carrying negative news.

Toward the end of 2002, a lot of "it's all behind us now" sentiment surfaced in the press, buttressed by fresh optimism. In a *New York Times* op-ed, former *Industry Standard* editor and New Economy memoirist James Ledbetter wrote, "I'd like to believe that those of us who witnessed the tech bubble will be smart enough to prick the next bubble that comes along before too many investors get duped. Encouragingly, some improvements were made; CNBC began identifying whether analysts it was interviewing owned stock in or did business with the companies being discussed on the air."[50] However, it doesn't really matter whether they indicate that an analyst owns stock in a company, or whether a bank does business with that company. If an analyst covers a company, that's because the bank does business, did business, or wants to do business with that company. Until disclosure gets meaningful and quantifiable—like delineating how much a company pays a bank in fees, or specifying which bank executive sits on the company's board or visa versa—admitting the obvious, as new disclosures did that "We, BANK XYZ, *may* have a relationship with CLIENT ABC," is meaningless and ineffective.

In early January 2003, the *New York Times* asked five analysts for their predictions about a number of industries for 2003.[51] All five worked at major investment banks: Merrill Lynch, Goldman Sachs, Morgan Stanley, Salomon Brothers, and Bear Stearns. The *Times* did not ask for thoughts from any independent analyst, even though it had spent many an article and editorial on the call for independent voices. At the time, the newspaper included a disclaimer acknowledging that Salomon and Morgan Stanley did business with the companies the analysts were discussing.

But, by the middle of 2003, these types of disclaimers had all but disappeared from media. It was back to business, and business reporting, as usual. The media had assumed its familiar role of hyping new corporate opportunities. Corporations responded enthusiastically. For example, recently downtrodden telecom companies resumed using media like publication on CNN.com to proffer the latest optimism about how wireless technology would resurrect the sector by running articles like "Get Ready to Tune into Wireless Net."[52] In October 2003 *Business Week* ran articles praising energy service companies like San Diego–based Sempra, effectively advertising the company's need to raise $1.5 billion in capital— not for buying power plants, but for expanding into the next great energy opportunity, liquid natural gas.[53]

By early 2004, the *New York Times* was spinning mistrials as progress. In April 2004, responding to the rather significant mistrial call of Tyco's Dennis Kozlowski, it ran two "justice is being done articles" back to back. These were entitled: "Some Failures, But Far More White-Collar Crime Success" and "Despite 2 Mistrials, Prosecutors Rack Up White-Collar Victories." The fact was almost none of the intricate corporate crimes and their perpetrators were litigated successfully in court.

LINGERING ACCOUNTING PROBLEMS

Currently, the job of monitoring financial institutions' activities is shared among a host of organizations: the SEC, which was chartered to examine corporate public filings; the Federal Reserve; the Comptroller of the Currency; the Federal Deposit Insurance Corporation (FDIC); and the FASB, which sets accounting standards. Collectively, their ability to intervene on behalf of the public and police the corporations under their purview needs to be substantially greater. Requiring firms to ensure its external auditors and accountants are separate companies, as outlined in Sarbanes-Oxley, was a cosmetic first step toward enhancing the potential for more effective oversight. However, even that will only work if the abovementioned bodies take more proactive measures in ensuring compliance. At a minimum, the FASB and the SEC should be combined and strengthened with better funding. These agencies should also be run by independent leaders selected by Congress, not presidential appointees. The SEC also should make use of FASB accountants, who are better equipped to understand and uncover accounting schemes. Proposals to install yet another layer of bureaucracy, such as additional auditing committees or the fraud task force that President Bush offered as an alternative to corporate governance reform, are less important than ensuring the regulatory bodies already in place are doing their jobs.

Since 1986, the FASB has tried to make accounting laws more rigorous but has had little luck and no meaningful help from legislators. The problem with the FASB is that although it makes the rules, it has no enforcement power, which lies solely with the SEC. Despite sweeping general "reforms," accounting rule enforcement remains largely untouched. Many of the accounting games honed in the 1990s continue—including establishing offshore companies to hide losses, using stock options as compensation, inflating goodwill estimates, and booking profits upfront from contracts for goods or services that may never be honored.

The 2003 uptick in the market that occurred after all the messy scandal fallout served as an illusory mask for many manipulative practices. Disclosures of crimes were mildly reduced due to a tepid stock market, not a regulatory paradigm shift. And we shouldn't forget that it was the raging bull market that both hid and promoted widespread corporate abuse.

But, major issues remain. One such problem is the accounting treatment of special-purpose entities. When a company sells an asset to a special-purpose entity, it effectively eliminates the debt incurred by buying that asset. Not only does it thus understate its liabilities, but, through twofold deception, it can also inflate sales revenues. The balance sheet improves because it looks like the company owes less and made more. In the case of accounting for leasing, a company only shows small periodic payments to that special-purpose entity as an expense on its income statement and no associated long-term debt. Thus, for balance sheet purposes, large long-term debt is removed, giving the appearance of less debt overall. The main company, however, still controls the special-purpose entity, which does not appear on the consolidated balance sheet—hence the distortion. Airlines frequently did this in the early 1990s; they borrowed money to buy airplanes, "sold" the airplanes to a special-purpose entity owned by them, and then leased the planes back from the same entity. Enron, Global Crossing, and many other energy and telecom companies mastered various versions of this practice in the late 1990s.

Another central element of the financial scandals was seized upon by the media and became a political hot potato. This frequently-cited factor was the accounting treatment of stock options. Stock options provide the right to purchase or sell a specified number of shares of stock at specified prices and times, and were a key way of inflating executive compensations during the new Gilded Age. The FASB suggested a number of methods to change accounting methodology for stock options. However, without the support of an actual law making the failure to expense stock options illegal, the practice will be impossible to enforce. The FASB's measure was not scheduled for congressional debate in either 2002 or 2003.

Another remaining problem is the treatment of goodwill. Accounting for goodwill proved a vehicle for financial distortion during the 1990s. Given the heavy volume of acquisitions during the period, many companies chose to inflate their goodwill as a way to overstate their reported assets. A safeguard to avoid this type of manipulation that would give shareholders a more accurate understanding of a company's balance sheet is strict external controls over more frequent goodwill adjustments. For instance, this would eliminate the ability of company that sold acquired firms from booking the revenues while maintaining the original goodwill on its balance sheet.

Lastly, firms can choose whether or not to book revenue up front in expectation of future cash, and of course it looks better for their near-term earnings statements if they can book as much as possible up front. The SEC would have to look through all contracts of goods and services, all cash-flow statements, and all methods of evaluating those goods and services in every area of a firm to find out whether or not reported cash was ever actually received.

The way it stands, companies take a calculated risk. If they are "caught" recognizing unearned revenue as a cash receipt, for instance, they settle on fines less than the profits booked from the deceit. Of course, if they don't get caught, also much the better. Or else they do what Enron and others did, which was to monetize and record revenues from contracts or trading transactions just before they release quarterly or annual earnings, then reclassify them after the fact. In that way, annual reports can be kept artificially inflated and quarterly reports used for interim adjustments that boost figures ahead of earnings announcements.

Unfortunately, we've not seen the last of the 1990s fallout and more can be expected in the future. Already, 58 percent of companies involved in financial fraud cases in 2001 have had to restate earnings, up from 47 percent in 2000. Those individual restatement amounts have totaled hundreds of billions of dollars.[54] As of the writing of this book, the companies involved in 2002 fraud disclosures were next on the docket for massive earnings restatements.

CORPORATE TAX REBATES

Over 60 percent of U.S. corporations paid no federal taxes during the period of booming corporate profits from 1996 to 2000, according to a General Accounting Office study released in February 2004. Three months later, the Senate voted (92–5) to reward corporate America with a generous gift: $170 billion of fresh tax cuts. That aside, in an exceedingly audacious yet perfectly legal act, the most egregious fraud culprits pleaded for the return of some of the federal taxes they paid—precisely because they *had* committed fraud. These same companies had hidden their true worth from the start; when they got caught and had to restate their earnings downward, they felt perfectly justified and entitled to getting back some of the taxes they had paid on inflated profits. Legally, they can: those who overpay, no matter the reason, are entitled to refunds by law.[55]

WorldCom and Enron filed for tax refunds from the IRS based on the taxes they paid on fraudulently booked billions of dollars. World-Com received $300 million in tax refunds, almost half of the $750 million fine they needed to pay for their crimes. Fortunately, Enron didn't manage to accomplish that little maneuver.

Compare WorldCom's refund to the corporate penalty cap: a mere $500,000 for filing false tax returns—if they get caught, that is. Enron only paid $63 million in taxes between 1996 and 2001 (with a market value of $80 billion), but even while embroiled in investigations for accounting practices, it had no problem upping its demands for tax rebates from the IRS.[56]

THE PUBLIC REACTION

It is puzzling that there wasn't a louder public outcry against corporate fraud. Partly, the U.S. media is at fault for not splashing the front pages with as many headlines extolling the new emerging face of anticorporate activism, like winning key proxy votes in shareholder meetings, as they had used to praise corporate titans. Historically-minded journalists or economists might say that the relative complacency was due to the fact that things just didn't get so bad, or at least they didn't remain so for long enough. Therefore, it's not like in the 1930s, for instance, when the situation was so grim that FDR's government recognized the need for regulation and restraint to insure a dependable financial future for the country and wasn't afraid to act accordingly. Today, corporate contributions play a much larger role in shaping the policies that govern them.

Another reason for lack of a deafening shout for corporate justice is that, besides those involved in shareholder, investor, and other corporate governance activism, people have other overriding concerns in their day-to-day lives. Plus, the magnitude of the frauds involved and the amounts of money that executives cashed out, and corporations still have hidden in their books, is huge; the sheer enormity is almost incomprehensible. Indeed, the accumulated wealth executives secured during the late 1990s and early in the new millennium is astronomical—it may seem easier to turn thoughts toward the more tangible issues like jobs, the rising price of gasoline, declining retirement benefits and the increasing cost of health care. But it's critical to realize that all of these things relate to senior corporate executives and business strategies focused on short-term gains at the expense of slower, longer-term growth or stable business plans that would ensure long-term job security with adequate pensions and other benefits.

Today, over eight million people in the United States are unemployed, and almost three million of them lost their jobs after the Bush administration took office.[57] Every time a big merger happens, people lose their jobs, due to layoffs. Every time a company can't pay off its massive debts, people lose their jobs. Every time a company's stock reaches new lows, people lose their jobs. And every time a company goes bankrupt, people lose their jobs. Along the way, if they're lucky enough to hang onto their jobs, they either lose their benefits or have to pay more out of pocket for them.

FORCING TRANSFORMATION

Individual reforms, in and of themselves, will not magically change corporate behavior that has been buttressed by years of loose legislation and extreme feelings of entitlement. It's hard to say whether the streams of newly minted MBAs who may be the CEOs of Corporate America twenty years from now will act any differently from the ones who came through the same management programs in the early 1980s and wound up running companies that manipulated both their shareholders and employees—especially if the balance between financial incentives to deceive versus punitive retribution if caught cheating remain the same.

Still, universities, which are supported by huge endowments partially funded by those same CEOs, have been adding corporate governance courses to their curricula in reaction to the scandals. Harvard Business School was one of the first. Its prospective MBA students are now told that the admissions process uses finer moral criteria than practiced in the 1980s. But Harvard is careful not to depict an endemic corporate leadership crisis, and accordingly describes its "Ethics, Fairness, and Values in Decision Making" course by stating that "the premise for this new Executive Education program is that the number of intentional unethical individuals in organizations is small, but that every employee is biased in ways that can lead to flawed decisions."[58] The fact is, it's easy to preach ethics in a bear market, but it's a lot harder to rein in irresponsible, unethical behavior in a competitive bull market. With or without ethical training of MBA students, any future bull market offering opportunities to extract short-term profit at the expense of long-term strategy will result in more widespread deception and loss—unless we adopt adequate regulatory reform.

It's tempting to shrug off the systemic and embedded nature of these activities as business as usual, and accept the cosmetic modifications as adequate reform. But acceptance of status quo, particularly in the face of severe crisis, never changes anything. Additionally, the temptation to sit back and accept the way things are tends to work in a correlated fashion with the perceived state of the economy. The stock market bouncing back during 2003 renewed false hope in the free market's powers of self-correction, causing ordinary people to shrug off demand for deep reform and the media to deemphasize corporate malfeasance issues. In addition, it provided an excuse for regulators and the government to focus on other items, like the war in Iraq in 2003 and the presidential election in 2004.

IT'S NOT JUST BAD APPLES: DEMAND ACCOUNTABILITY!

On December 16, 2002, Kurt Eichenwald of the *New York Times* wrote a piece chalking up the spate of scandals to a normal and regular characteristic of capitalism, claiming that every boom is followed by a bunch of white-collar crime disclosures.[59] The cycle may hold true, but the danger of that theory is that it perpetuates the bad-apple syndrome. A few instances of fraud here and there, a few evil perpetrators properly scapegoated, and everything should be great for another ten or thirty years. Yet why should fraud be so appealing when the economy is already booming? Does fraud actually create the booms instead? Even though the immense fraud fallout began in late 2001 and continues to this day, fraud started years earlier and is still going on. Booms merely give it more space to flourish and money to play with. Plus, when things are running smoothly, it's easier for the politicians and the media to look the other way.

Unfortunately, the only players who have the power to overhaul the system are the ones who control that system, and they have too much to lose by changing it. In the meantime, the employees are paying the price for their inaction. Corporations didn't merely defraud shareholders; their own employees were the first to pay the price when their firms hit bad times, like bankruptcies or criminal investigations. Yet these corporations are protected by every level of the government, no matter which political party resides in the White House. The rhetoric of self-correction becomes a far easier, less costly form of corporate "governance." Without more independent or government regulatory intervention into corporate and financial industry behavior, there can be no real reform, just empty talk and toothless gestures.

Even after a complete meltdown of the deregulated telecommunications industry, a crisis of confidence that hammered the financial sector, and a wave of dysfunctional debt-laden and asset-devalued energy companies emerging from energy industry deregulation, Washington has offered no explicit solutions. There is no talk of reregulating the energy industry. In fact, on June 25, 2003, FERC rejected California's request to invalidate more than $13 billion in energy contracts signed at the height of the state's electricity crisis, even though it's clear that widespread manipulation drove up prices, now locked in by those contracts.[60] Rather than allowing California to negotiate new contracts at non-market-manipulated levels, FERC decided to honor the old contracts set up with corrupt energy companies. It claimed that California had failed to show adequate proof that those contracts were based on fraudulent premises and should therefore be redrawn, or not honored. The two commissioners who voted to uphold those contracts were Bush appointees.

Additionally, there is no talk of reregulating the telecom industry. In fact, on June 2, 2003, the FCC passed a measure 3–2 to further deregulate the media industry, opening the door wider for even more consolidation and increasing the likelihood of more all-stock mergers.[61] As for the financial sector, there is no debate about shredding the 1999 Financial

Services Modernization Act and returning to the less conflicted, more tightly regulated banking industry of the Glass-Steagall era. But banks were split up once before; it's possible to do it again and revisit the SEC/Spitzer/Wall Street settlement to create a new agreement with some real teeth. In the meantime, banks need to disclose their backup credit facilities and loans before actual write-downs occur. We also need better disclosure of investment bank fees, particularly for large loan agreements with corporations, so shareholders can draw their own conclusions about how those relationships affect banking practices.

Reregulating industries and reinvigorating responsible regulatory bodies are the most important steps toward creating a stable framework for financial growth that controls fraud and deception. Not only do employees and pensions benefit from solid companies and a rigorous regulatory climate, so do shareholders. The more stringent the rules governing corporate behavior and the more eyes monitoring it, the fewer opportunities and avenues for deceit. But real reform requires a complete revamping of the banks, corporations, and government regulation.

This isn't happening. Instead, lobbying and political donations continued to flow with the 2003–2004 election cycles. As of March 2004, contributions outpaced (on an annualized basis) the prior two cycle figures for the financial, telecommunications, and energy sectors, whose spending is going up faster than in other industries. Accounting, deception, and deregulation march on. Jobs keep getting cut to pay for all the bad debt that the most highly leveraged industries are accumulating.

Yet there are some interim adjustments to the structure of corporate America that can and should be implemented to curtail at least some of the deceptions. These include requiring (1) an admission of guilt by companies engaged in fraud, (2) independent boards of directors, (3) stricter financial and accounting regulation and enforcement, (4) balance sheet transparency, (5) accountability of CEOs and senior executives, and (6) tighter rules surrounding corporate trading operations.

Fines alone will never be an effective way to regulate corporate behavior because they will never be large enough and they always come with "no admission of guilt" clauses, a guaranteed part of any settlement that is a built-in reprieve from examination or reform. Once the fine is handed down, the opportunity to dig into the core practices that led to the crime ends. If corporations had to admit their guilt in perpetuating fraud and deception in a way that required them to isolate the practice and the related regulation they sidestepped to commit the crime, it would point the public, and hopefully the government, to a more specific reform target.

Restricting corporate board membership to people who are not appointed by the companies' CEOs and who are otherwise not engaged in business with that company would help establish stricter corporate oversight. Boards must accept their responsibilities and take their roles in monitoring companies' practices seriously. If a board fails to respond to proven fraud, it should result in heavy repercussions, such as total replacement of the board.

Korn Ferry International's Twenty-ninth Annual Board of Directors Study discovered "significant gaps" in board practices. The study found that 72.3 percent of directors surveyed said that individual directors should be given regular performance evaluations; however, "only 20.9 percent of boards currently conduct such evaluations, and only 41.4 percent of directors on those boards think that the evaluations are effective." Their survey also found that 78.5 percent of the directors said a former CEO shouldn't sit on the board, and 72.9 percent said the board should hold regular executive sessions without the CEO during board meetings, which is impossible if the chairman is the CEO.[62] Yet the chairman and CEO are one and the same in 392 of the Fortune 500 companies. That is clearly not a sign of board independence but it's an obvious and attainable step toward better corporate governance.

There are other measures that should be taken to break the ties linking Corporate America, Wall Street, and Washington. For one, bankers and bank executives shouldn't be allowed to sit on the boards of their corporate clients. The Corporate Library, an independent investment research firm providing corporate governance data, analysis, and risk assessment tools, listed board independence as their leading governance policy: "A majority of the Board shall be independent based on the independence standards of the New York Stock Exchange. The Board should not include professionals who provide material services to the Company (e.g. lawyers, commercial bankers) or any person who has a conflict of interest or a material relationship with the Company."[63] In practice, of course, this is clearly not the case—look at the investor relationship between Ford and Goldman Sachs as just one of hundreds of examples. Nor should corporate executives sit on the boards of banks that provide them services. AT&T CEO Michael Armstrong shouldn't be on Citigroup's board, for example.

Finally, CEOs and senior executives should truly be held accountable for their companies' bookkeeping. They should not be allowed to dodge culpability and emerge unscathed when their employees don't have accurate information and can't protect themselves. The fines that have been levied on individual corporate criminals and companies are hardly a sufficient deterrent against poor practice, nor are they a way to stamp out future corruption. True reform might start when a percentage of every CEO's cash-out is taken out and given back to the employee retirement funds destroyed by executive malfeasance. More legislative encouragement and support should be given to employees who want to speak out publicly on corrupt practices within their companies; they should be able to enjoy some assurance that their jobs, or at the very least their incomes, are secure. Whistle-blowers should be able to speak up before bad practices contaminate and destroy the entire company, its stock value, and its employees' pensions and jobs.[64]

FAIR ACCOUNTING TREATMENT OF PENSION FUNDS

Stricter financial reporting transparency would mitigate the ability of corporations to use pension fund evaluations in order to manipulate profit. Lack of transparency in how pensions are valued has contributed to inflated earnings in bull markets, followed by severe shortfalls and diminished benefits to retirees in market downturns.

Among the 1,729 pensions surveyed by Greenwich Associates between 2000 and 2002, estimated assets dropped from $6.1 trillion in 2000 to $5.1 trillion at the end of 2002, a 17 percent decrease. U.S. corporate pensions have declined 23 percent since 2000, and public pensions went down 18 percent.[65] The companies with the largest plans, including G.M., IBM, and Verizon, were hit the hardest during the postscandal economic decline; each of their pension funds lost an estimated $15 billion or more between the end of 2000 and the end of 2002.[66] Three years of steady, sharp declines in the stock market had a particularly devastating effect on G.M.'s pension fund assets, leading to a $19 billion-plus deficit at the end of 2002, compared to the $7 billion surplus the pension fund reported at the end of 2000.[67]

Additionally, 42 million Americans have 401(k) plans worth a total of $1.8 trillion. Often, these are disproportionately invested in company stock; in order to adequately protect employees from sudden downturns in stock value, it is important to have lower limits on the maximum percentage of company stock employees can own within their 401(k) plans. Yet many Fortune 500 companies do not offer employees this safeguard, or set the company stock cap so high as to be useless. For example, Pfizer caps employee exposure at a whopping 86 percent, Ford 57 percent, Glaxo 35 percent, and Lucent 17 percent. In May 2003, instead of recognizing the obvious conflict of interest, the House passed legislation allowing companies to provide employees with financial advice from the same mutual fund companies that comprise their 401(k) plans.[68] For example, Fidelity could advise GM employees to select Fidelity funds within their retirement plans. Despite the monumental 401(k) losses caused by banks and corporate deception, that bill secures the polar opposite of independent financial advice for corporate employees. As Representative George Miller (D-CA) asked rhetorically, "Does this make sense when many of the biggest investment houses in the nation . . . have just paid out nearly a billion and a half dollars for committing just these kind of abuses?"[69]

Around the time the Senate was raising the U.S. debt by $1 trillion in May 2003, there was a $300 billion pension shortfall for retiring workers. Additionally, health benefits for current retirees were declining precipitously, and companies were using the economic downturn as an excuse to further decimate corporate and government worker pension plans.

In contrast, during the bubble, optimistic return estimates on pension assets and low interest rates used to discount those assets to present value combined to balloon pension fund values overall on company balance sheets. Shareholder activists are trying to remove misleading pension estimates from earnings on a company-by-company basis by ensuring the matter is on the proxy voting agenda at annual board meetings. Verizon was one company that agreed, under pressure from its retiree organization, the Bell Tel Retirees, to exclude future surpluses from its balance sheet in early 2003. In 2000 and 2001, Verizon had booked over $5 billion in earnings from its pension fund surpluses.

FASB Statement No. 87, *Employers' Accounting for Pensions,* establishes standards of financial reporting and accounting for any employer that offers defined benefit pension plans to its employees. Specifically, the statement requires a sponsoring company to expense what is called the net periodic pension cost (NPPC). The NPPC represents the annual accrued costs of a pension plan minus the expected return on plan assets.

Although the expected return is merely an assumption, which often differs substantially from the realized rate of return, it is the one used to calculate NPPC. Effectively, companies can inflate their expected rate of return, thus minimizing the pension costs that must be expensed for the period, and overstating earnings in the process.

Congress has not mitigated employee pension risk, nor has it pushed for integrity in pension plan valuations; instead, it has increased its support for 401(k) plans, which put the investment risk on the employee instead of the corporation, unlike defined pension plans of old through which the company guaranteed a certain level of income to its retirees.

On July 7, 2003, in another Bush administration antiworker pension initiative, the government proposed that corporate pension liabilities should be calculated using characteristically greater corporate bond yields instead of treasury bond yields, which had always been used in the past. Pension liabilities help determine the future payouts to employees and are computed using a number of arbitrary calculations. One such calculation is the division of a total plan's assets by current interest rates to determine its present value. The pension amount that an employee receives is directly related to that present value in any given year. Dividing (or discounting) that full plan value by a higher corporate yield would ultimately result in a reduction of current employer contributions. Negligent or criminal corporate leadership has already depleted pension funds enough.

FIGHTING BACK

The Bush administration did a stellar job of diverting media attention away from corporate governance reform with the lead-up to the Iraq invasion in March 2003. No more press conferences with Treasury Secretary John Snow—now it was Defense Secretary Donald Rumsfeld, set on defending the nation. Politics of mass distraction obscured the causes of corporate crime and its trail of lost jobs, depleted pensions, and eroded consumer confidence.

The attitude was "If we ignore it, it will go away." Somehow, the NASDAQ would regain the 75 percent of market value it lost. The economy would magically generate the 2.8 million jobs it shed. Overcapacity would be eliminated, and all would be well. But the plain fact is that the Bush administration did nothing substantial to address corporate corruption or the deregulatory environment that enabled it. The 1990s exercise in executive entitlement and political manipulation led to a prolonged game of dodge-the-blame-and-ignore-the-consequences. The crisis of corporate America was followed by a crisis of legislative inaction.

That inertia transformed thousands of newly jobless citizens and millions of retirees, who were facing declining prospects, pensions, and health benefits, into an angry activist force ready to fight. In the wake of Washington's indifference, people joined forces to combat corporate malfeasance and executive-employee inequity. They are battling to overturn years of corrupt practices and inadequate laws that shafted working and retired people. The crusade gained grassroots momentum, driven by both the usual and the least likely of activists. The AFL-CIO and its affiliates have been increasingly vocal about corporate governance issues and active in assisting nonunion workers. Other union groups, ex-employees of bankrupt companies, shareholder activists, and retiree organizations, such as the National Retiree Legislative Network, are working together. The amount of money they control as shareholders or pensioners is enormous.

Twenty-first-century America has nothing like the overwhelming consolidation of labor and populist movements of the 1930s that provided the political climate that fostered FDR's New Deal and badly needed regulations, but the country's current need for fairness in business practices has steadily grown into a multifaceted corporate activist movement. Without this movement putting pressure on elected officials to adopt real change, the next bull market's bust will be even more devastating than the last one was.

Today's corporate activists consist of diverse groups of people, numbering in the millions. Some of these groups have been around for decades; some arose from the ashes of the latest wave of corruption. Groups of laid-off employees formed to help each other and fight for more favorable legislation for workers. The ex–WorldCom employees' fund, modeled after the fund started by former Enron employees, raised $190,000 to help workers pay their bills while searching for jobs. Enron's fund raised $466,000.

Additionally, ex-employee groups, unions, and others are lobbying for sweeping changes to U.S. bankruptcy code. Currently, the code allows creditor committees to retrieve money and assets from a failed company. Creditor committees, mostly representing Wall Street banks, simply do not consider employees' interests in their efforts to recoup assets. It makes no provisions for an employees' committee to form, let alone make its own claims, and thus sacrifices employee needs on behalf of Wall Street bank creditors. Current federal law hangs employees out to dry when companies go under. Without appropriate employee representation at the bankruptcy court table, workers will continue to pay a high price for corporate, fraud-induced bankruptcy.

SHAREHOLDER ACTIVISTS AND CORPORATE GOVERNANCE

During the period from 1980 to 2000, individual investors' stock investments grew from less than $1 trillion to $14 trillion. In January 2003, longtime consumer advocate and corporate activist Ralph Nader had added another grassroots activist group to his list of notable corporate fighters—U.S. Investors. The group pointed out that the size and concentrated financial clout of the individual investor class "has the capability to protect its own interests, but only if investors are organized!"[70]

A new voice in the fight for employee rights emerged from the 44-million-member retirement community. One example is Bill Jones, a former middle manager at Bell Atlantic Telephone who formed a retiree group with a colleague in late 1995. Under old company policy, pension benefits were supposed to increase every two years with inflation. They discovered that although pension fund surpluses at Bell Tel were increasing, as was executive compensation, payouts were not. After you've retired and your pension benefits start declining, you don't necessarily have extra pockets of money to make up the difference, and you're certainly not able to go out and find another job.

Over seven years, the Bell Tel Retirees, which encompasses retirees from what is now called Verizon, grew from a two-person operation to 165,000 members. Membership increased by 25 percent in 2002 alone. Today, the group is mixed, with 40 percent former union members and 60 percent former managers. Jones argues that "once you become a retiree, that's your label; it doesn't matter if you were management or union." Jones told me he considers himself and his fellow retirees "the new breed of corporate activists," and Bel Tel Retirees uses a Web site newsletter and PR firm to broadcast its work.

Other retiree organizations also formed in the mid-1990s, including many established by employees who had worked at predivestiture AT&T

and later at the various Bells—employees who remembered times when workers' security and benefits were taken seriously. As Nelson Phelps, founder of the growing Association of US West Retirees (AUSWR) told me during a phone conversation, "We realized that corporations couldn't be trusted and no one was going to protect our rights but us."

In April 2001, the retiree organizations decided to join together to form the National Retiree Legislative Network (NRLN) to consolidate the lobbying efforts of individual retiree associations at the federal level in fighting for pension, health care, and governance reforms. With two million dues-paying retirees, the NRLN's membership has exploded since the corporate scandal boom.

Founder and president Jim Norby, who came out of five years of total retirement to become an activist, told me, "We discovered we weren't going to win anything individually. As we were attending to our grandchildren, politicians were changing the ERISA [Employee Retirement Income Security Act] law of 1974." The NRLN is expanding to include older employees, those "too young to quit, but too old to find another job," as Norby described them. The group is growing exponentially, with members coming from the largest corporations in America, including retirees from AT&T, IBM, G.M., Lucent, and Boeing. The NRLN is fighting for legislation to guarantee maintenance of health care benefits and appropriate pension payouts. They are also fighting for stricter corporate governance measures. Their Web site states, "We can help anyone with a burning desire to keep predatory executives from running through your pension money or taking away promised healthcare benefits."[71]

The primary concerns of retiree shareholder activists include board independence, exclusion of pension fund surpluses from executive compensation equations, and review of golden parachutes. In advocating truly independent boards, they stress that boards must have limited or no representation from management ranks, which is key to establishing checks and balances within corporations. Some members of the retiree and union movements advocate employee or union leader representation on boards as well.

The removal of pension asset performance projections from company income statements is essential to giving shareholders and employees a more accurate view of a firm's performance. Additionally, broad shareholder reviews of golden parachute packages would serve to curtail out-of-control rewards to executives whose companies tanked and whose employees lost jobs, salaries, or pensions. All shareholders, and not just members of the firm's compensation committee (who have a vested interest in treating their bosses well as payback for getting appointed in the first place), should have the right to inspect—and reevaluate—whatever perks get handed to corporate executives when they walk out the door. Redistributing CEOs' multimillion-dollar parting gifts to current and former workers would be a good first step toward fairer treatment of the workforce.

CORPORATE GOVERNANCE VICTORIES AND THE FUTURE

There have been some important grassroots and shareholder victories against unchecked executive privilege. The AFL-CIO won a golden parachute advisory resolution from Tyco International. Amalgamated Bank, with ten years of shareholder-activist experience and almost $6 billion in union funds, pressured one of their investments, Norfolk Southern, into adopting a proposal for reviewing golden parachutes.

The Bell Tel Retirees are one of the first retiree organizations to use proxy votes to stimulate change. In 2001, Verizon would have had to record a net loss instead of a $1.85 billion gain if they hadn't used pension surpluses to boost earnings. In April 2003, Verizon agreed to adopt pension exclusion measures after the Bell Tel Retirees "defeated the telecommunication giant (with a 59 percent majority vote) in a shareholder vote to trim overly generous executive compensation packages and golden parachutes." Other shareholder victories included a vote to limit severance pay that passed by 51 percent at Hewlett Packard and by 63 percent at Sprint.[72]

Reform can never truly be complete without an examination of the myriad causes of malfeasance and a true willingness to do something about them. According to James Lynn, who coordinates U.S. Investors with Ralph Nader, "Reform is a constant project that must be worked on and can't be forgotten; it is a long-haul project."[73] It requires a tremendous amount of focus and energy and desire to address the causes and not gloss over them. All activist groups stressed that if changes don't come from Congress, they will come from workers and shareholders.[74]

Completely revamping a regulatory system is complicated and time-intensive. Any system is embedded in decades of institutional barriers and centuries of concentrated wealth and power ready to fight the commands of equity and economic stability. Nonetheless, it's a necessary process. It takes grassroots organizing and disabusing widespread public complacencies. It takes demonstrations, letters to Congress, knowing the facts, knowing what's achievable, knowing who the partners are in the fight. It takes the commitment to not stop.

In order to have a lasting impact, the groups and individuals that do believe a more secure, less corrupt corporate America is possible need to grow substantially larger and become part of a much-needed system of legislative checks and balances by forcing significant change at the federal level. Without those numbers and the votes they represent—and the wider attention of the American public—there will be no true change and no hope of a more stable economic system.

Behind the lavish corporate indulgence of the 1990s was one simple fact. Executives won big playing with other people's money while ordinary people lost out. Corporations came out of their fraud-induced bankruptcy periods unscathed, beyond some minor damage to their reputations. Worse, because they emerged with their debts erased in bankruptcy court and banks rushing in to pile more on, they demonstrated that corporate crime definitely pays. In fact, it's a competitive advantage.

In the 1930s, the Depression fostered a climate of social responsibility and corporate regulation that lasted for decades. Today, no such attitude prevails on Capitol Hill—quite the opposite, in fact, as even more deregulation has become the core of energy, communications, and banking policy. After the discoveries of widespread 1990s fraud, the politicians that created the legislation enabling it never shouldered any responsibility for the fallout. Regulatory agencies continue to bless mergers without proper examination of how consolidated balance sheets impact financial transparency, how combined companies eliminate jobs, and how the public is not served by fewer companies controlling vital consumer choice. The memory of the sheer magnitude of corporate excess at the expense of pensions and jobs may fade in time, but we must bear down and keep it from happening again. It takes not forgetting the consequences of lax oversight and unquestioned enthusiasm each time the market rallies. It takes change over status quo. It takes constant demand for real reform.

Notes

Please note that all references to "Thomson Financial" refer to data accessible only to subscribers of the Thomson Financial data service.

INTRODUCTION

1. Mark Gimein, "You Bought, They Sold," *Fortune*, August 11, 2002.
2. Paul Krugman, "For Richer," *New York Times*, October 20, 2002.
3. "Suggestions for Reform—Curb CEO Pay," *Citizens Works*, March 16, 2003, http:// www.citizenworks.org/corp/reforms.php#CEOpay.
4. Bankruptcydata.Com Research Center 2001, 2002, http://www. bankruptcydata.com/researchcenter2.htm.
5. Ien Cheng, "Survivors Who Laughed All the Way to the Bank," *Financial Times*, July 31, 2002.
6. Thomson Financial Data, Corporate Debt: Outstanding Bonds and Loans, 1990–2002.
7. Securities and Exchange Commission Mission Statement, http://www. sec.gov/about/whatwedo.shtml (accessed May 13, 2004).
8. Edward N. Wolff, "Recent Trends in Living Standards in the United States," New York University and the Jerome Levy Economics Institute, May 2002, http://www.econ.nyu.edu/user/wolffe/LevyLivingStandards May2002.pdf.
9. "Pension Benefit Guarantee Corporation," U.S. Department of Labor, http://www. dol.gov/_sec/budget/pbgc20001.htm (accessed May 13, 2004).
10. Wolff, "Recent Trends in Living Standards in the United States," 16–17.
11. "Trends in Telephone Service," Industry Analysis and Technology Division, Federal Communications Commission, May 22, 2002, http:// hraunfoss.fcc.gov/edocs_public/attachmatch/DOC-222737A1.pdf.
12. Doug Henwood, *Wall Street* (London: Verso Books, 1997).
13. "Long Distance Costs Are Soaring," Telecommunications Research and Action Center, May 30, 2000, www.trac.org.
14. "AOL Time Warner Posts Record $99 Billion Annual Loss," *PBS Online Newshour*, January 30, 2003.
15. Henry Paulson Jr., "Restoring Investor Confidence: Agenda for Change," speech to National Press Club, June 5, 2002.

16. William Harrison Jr., "Banks Were Victims in Fraud Cases, Not Accomplices," *Wall Street Journal*, September 18, 2002.

17. Bruce Sauer, "Free Advice from Enron's Freefall," *Primedia Business Magazines and Media, Inc.*, January 1, 2002, 20–23.

18. "Financial Collapse of Enron Corp.," transcript of hearing before the House Committee on Energy and Commerce, February 7, 2002.

19. "Some of the Top Executives at Enron," Associated Press, February 20, 2004.

20. "Capacity Swaps by Global Crossing and Qwest: Sham Transactions Designed to Boost Revenues?" Transcript of hearing before the House Committee on Energy and Commerce, October 1, 2002.

21. "The Wall Street Fix," *PBS Frontline*, May 8, 2003, http://www.pbs.org/wgbh/pages/frontline/shows/wallstreet/wcom/players.html.

22. Center for Responsive Politics, "Political Contributions: Who Gives 1998–2000," www.opensecrets.org.

23. Ibid.

24. Securities and Exchange Commission, "Fact Answers: Lawsuits and Investigations Question 21 of 42," October 3, 2002, http://sec.broaddaylight.com/sec/FAQ_19_1348.shtm.

25. Securities and Exchange Commission, "Fact Answers: Lawsuits and Investigations Question 3 of 42," September 26, 2002, http://sec.broaddaylight.com/sec/FAQ_19_204.shtm.

26. Thomson Financial Data, Wall Street Firms, SEC and NASD Fines, 1998–2002.

27. "DOD Announces Top Contractors for Fiscal 2002," Department of Defense press release, January 23, 2003, http://www.defenselink.mil/news/Jan2003/b01232003_bt034-03.html.

28. Ibid.

29. J. Cummings, J. Schlesinger, and M. Schroeder, "Bush Unleashes Scathing Rhetoric," *Wall Street Journal*, July 11, 2002.

30. Adam Entous, "Bush Readies Crackdown on Corporate Crime," Reuters, July 8, 2002.

CHAPTER 1: THE BANK WARS

1. Thomson Financial Data, Corporate Bond Issuance, 2001.

2. Ron Chernow, *The House of Morgan* (New York: Grove Press, 1990), 326.

3. Ibid.

4. Ibid., 352.

5. Ibid., 353.

6. Paul M. Sweezy, *The Present as History: Essays and Reviews on Capitalism*

and Socialism (New York: Monthly Review Press, 1953), 195–96.

7. Bryan Burrough and John Helyar, *Barbarians at the Gate* (New York: HarperCollins, 1990).

8. Jacob M. Schlesinger, "Did Washington Set the Stage for Current Business Turmoil?" *Wall Street Journal*, October 17, 2002.

9. Ibid.

10. William Tabb, *The Amoral Elephant* (New York: Monthly Review Press, 2001), 91.

11. Charles Gasparino, "Citigroup's Weill Withdraws Nomination to NYSE Board," *Wall Street Journal*, March 24, 2003.

12. Ibid.

13. "The Wall Street Connection," PBS *Frontline*, May 8, 2003.

14. Thomson Financial Data, Bank Mergers, 1995–2000.

15. "Testimony of Chairman Alan Greenspan," Federal Reserve Board hearing, June 17, 1998.

16. Center for Responsive Politics, Campaign Contribution Data, 1993–1998.

17. "Steve Friedman Joins Goldman Sachs' Board of Directors," Goldman Sachs press release, May 2, 2002.

18. "Friedman Named Director of National Economic Council," White House press release, December 12, 2002.

19. Randi F. Marshall, "Advisor Pushes Bush's Economic Plan," *Newsday*, February 22, 2003.

20. Ibid.

21. Monica Langley, *Tearing Down the Walls* (New York: Wall Street Journal Books/The Free Press, 2002), 341.

22. Ibid.

23. Ibid., 363.

24. Ibid., 342.

25. Ibid.

26. Joseph Kahn and Alessandra Stanley, "Rubin Relishes Role of Banker as Public Man," *New York Times*, February 11, 2002.

27. Langley, *Tearing Down the Walls*, 341.

28. Ibid.

29. "Inquiry Urged on Taking of Job by Former Treasury Secretary," *New York Times*, November 18, 1999.

30. Ethics of Government Act, 18 United States Code, Section 207.

31. Lisa Endlich, *Goldman Sachs: The Culture of Success* (New York: Touchstone, 1999), 46.

32. Ibid., 77.

33. Ibid., 79.

34. Ibid., 83.

35. Ibid., 124.

36. Kahn and Stanley, "Rubin Relishes Role of Banker as Public Man."
37. Ibid.
38. "Salomon's Former Telecom Analyst in Settlement That Also Bars Him from Securities Investigation," CNN *Money*, December 20, 2002.
39. David Teather, "Rubin Cleared of Enron Impropriety," *Guardian*, January 4, 2003.
40. Ibid.
41. "Citigroup Paid Executive More Than CEO," Bloomberg News, March 12, 2002.
42. Ibid.
43. Ibid.
44. U.S. Business Reporter, Data Dictionary Services, http://www.usbrn.com/datadict. asp?txtSrchWord=Banking (accessed May 13, 2004).
45. Ibid.
46. Federal Deposit Insurance Corporation, third quarter 2002 report.
47. Federal Deposit Insurance Corporation, annual report 2002.
48. William B. Harrison Jr., "Banks Were Victims in Fraud Cases, Not Accomplices," editorial, *Wall Street Journal*, September 18, 2002.
49. Henry Paulson, "Restoring Investor Confidence: An Agenda for Change," National Press Club speech, June 5, 2002.
50. Duncan Wood, "A Fair Fight," Erisk.com, October 21, 2000.
51. Federal Deposit Insurance Corporation, Statistics at a Glance: Industry Trends, March 31, 2003.
52. Ibid.
53. Tim Carvell, "Citi of Fear: What Are Citigroup's Weird Ads Really Saying?" *Slate*, July 31, 2002.
54. "The JPM Chase Watch Archive," *Inner City Press & Fair Finance Watch*, http:// www.innercitypress.org/jpmcmb1.html, November 8, 2002.
55. JP Morgan Chase 2001 annual report, March 1, 2002; SEC 10K filings, March 22, 2002.
56. Associated Press, "J.P. Morgan Sues Ex-Global Crossing Execs," December 11, 2003.
57. "Bank of America Asks FERC for Permission to Trade Wholesale Energy," FERC docket number ER02-2536, September 3, 2002, www.ferc.gov.
58. Prepared testimony of Mr. William H. Donaldson, Commissioner-Designate, SEC, U.S. Senate Committee on Banking, Housing, and Urban Affairs, February 5, 2003.
59. Scott Silvestre, "Bank One Wants Borrowers to Provide More Business—Or Else," Bloomberg News, March 21, 2001.
60. Ibid.
61. Julie Creswell, "Banks' Not So Secret Weapon," *Fortune Magazine*, October 1, 2002.

62. Goldman Sachs letter to the Financial Accounting Standards Board, April 6, 2001.

63. Duncan Wood, "Goldman Ups the Ante Over Competition," *ERisk News*, June 14, 2001.

64. Ibid.

65. "Goldman Sachs to Invest in Sumitomo Mitsui Financial Group: Firms Will Expand Relationship Through Cooperative Efforts," Goldman Sachs press release, January 15, 2003.

66. "Goldman Sachs Reports First Quarter Earnings per Share of $1.29," Goldman Sachs press release, March 20, 2003.

67. Goldman Sachs 8K SEC filings—2002 Executive Compensation.

68. "John Thornton Retiring as President and Co-COO of Goldman Sachs," Goldman Sachs press release, March 24, 2003.

69. "Swiss Banks Clinches $11.5 Billion U.S. Deal," *BBC News*, August 30, 2000.

70. Charles Gasparino and Randall Smith, "CSFB's Frank Quattrone Leaves Amid Probe," *Wall Street Journal*, March 5, 2003.

71. Chris O'Brien, "Tech IPO Star Charged with 'Spinning,'" *San Jose Mercury News*, March 6, 2003.

72. "Capital One CFO Resigns Amid Insider Trading Probe," *Dow Jones Business News*, March 3, 2003.

73. Sandy Weill, Chairman and CEO; Todd Thomson, EVP, Finance and Investments and CFO, Citigroup; presentation, Merrill Lynch Financial Services Conference, September 6, 2002.

74. Ibid.

75. Thomson Financial Data, Merger and Acquisition Data, 2001, 2002.

76. William Harrison, presentation, Salomon Financial Services conference, January 30, 2003.

77. Hank Paulson speech, Salomon Financial Services Conference, January 24, 2001, www.gs.com

78. Ibid.

79. "Morgan Stanley Announces Fourth Quarter Results," Morgan Stanley press release, December 19, 2002.

80. Patrick McGeehan and Landon Thomas Jr., "No Worry, Even Now at Morgan Stanley," *New York Times*, March 2, 2003.

CHAPTER 2: SCRATCHING BACKS

1. Primary market: the market for new *securities* issues, in which the security is purchased directly from the issuer. Secondary market: the market

in which an investor purchases a *security* from another investor rather than from the *issuer*.

2. Thomson Financial Data, Financial Industry Mergers and Acquisitions, 1996–2000.

3. Ibid.

4. Thomson Financial Data, Ford, GM Consolidated Outstanding Debt, September 30, 2002.

5. John Porrietto, "Ford's Credit Rating Lowered," Associated Press, October 26, 2002.

6. "Ford Motor Company Announces Revitalization Plan," Ford press release, January 11, 2002.

7. Bill Koenig, "Ford Revamps F-150 Pickup to Counter New Revivals," Bloomberg News, January 6, 2003.

8. Lisa Endlich, *Goldman Sachs: The Culture of Success* (New York: Touchstone, 2000), 55.

9. Landon Thomas Jr., "Ford and Goldman, So Cozy at the Top," *New York Times*, December 8, 2002.

10. Ibid.

11. David Kiley and Matt Krantz, "Firms Examine Ties to Goldman after IPO Scandal," *USA Today*, December 23, 2002.

12. Ibid.

13. Thomson Financial Data, Debt Issuance, 1998–2002.

14. Ibid.

15. Ibid.

16. Ibid.

17. Ibid.

18. Ibid.; "The Platinum Metals Report," *Johnson Matthey Precious Metal Marketing Report*, July 2003.

19. Thomas, "Ford and Goldman, So Cozy at the Top."

20. Scott Silvestre, "Bank One Wants Borrowers to Provide More Business— or Else," Bloomberg News, March 21, 2001.

21. John Dingell, letter to Federal Reserve Board, OCC, and the General Accounting Office re: Bank Tying, www.house.gov/commerce_democrats/press/107ltr187.htm, September 12, 2002.

22. Ibid.

23. Ibid.

24. George Stein, "Fed, Comptroller Probing Loan 'Tying' Practices," Bloomberg News, September 2002.

25. Carrick Mollenkamp, "Bank of America's Loans to Rich Executives Backfire," *Wall Street Journal*, November 25, 2002.

26. Margin call: a call from a *broker* to a customer or from a *clearinghouse* to a *clearing member* demanding the *deposit* of cash or marginable *securities*

to satisfy the *Regulation T* requirements and the house maintenance requirement for the purchase or *short sale* of securities or to cover an adverse price *movement*.

27. Gretchen Morgenson, "More Clouds Over Citigroup in its Dealings with Ebbers," *New York Times*, November 3, 2002.

28. "Ahold Announces Significantly Reduced Earnings Expected for 2002," Ahold press release, February 24, 2002.

29. "State Suit Seeks Repayment of IPO and Stock Option Profits of Corporate Executives," Office of New York State Attorney General Eliot Spitzer press release, September 30, 2002.

30. Ibid.

31. Ibid.

32. Ibid.

33. "SEC Charges JP Morgan Chase in Connection with Enron's Accounting Fraud," SEC press release, July 28, 2003.

34. Ibid.

35. Ibid.

36. Paul Beckett and Jathon Sapsford, "Energy Deals Made $200 Million in Fees for Citigroup, J.P. Morgan," *Wall Street Journal*, July 24, 2002.

37. Carrie Johnson, "Senate Panel Says Two Banks Helped Enron Hide Loans," *Washington Post*, July 24, 2002.

38. Ibid.

39. "Telecom Lenders—Standing in Line for What?" *Business Week Online*, February 11, 2002.

40. Ibid.

41. Justin Fox, "Earnings—Can We Trust Them Now?" *Fortune*, February 18, 2003.

42. Ibid; SEC Release No. 33-7,881, Final Rule: "Selective Disclosure and Insider Trading," August 15, 2000.

43. Ibid.

44. David Weidner, "Banner Day for Banks," *CBS Market Watch*, March 20, 2003.

45. "Profits Soar for Financial-Service Firms," Associated Press, December 18, 2003.

46. Gretchen Morgenson, "Requiem for an Honorable Profession on Wall Street," *New York Times*, May 5, 2002.

47. Ibid.

48. Patrick McGeehan, "An Unlikely Clarion for Change," *New York Times*, June 16, 2002.

49. Emily Thornton, "Wall Street's Lone Ranger," *Business Week*, March 4, 2002.

50. "Lawmakers Query SEC's Pitt on Goldman Meeting," Reuters, October 4, 2002.
51. "Pitt Meets with Another Wall Street Firm Under SEC Investigation," Office of U.S. Representative Ed Markey press release, October 4, 2002.
52. Ibid.
53. Jonathan Glater and Landon Thomas Jr., "Proposed Rules for Analysts Raise Ire of Publications," *New York Times*, November 23, 2002.
54. Ibid.
55. Ibid.
56. Bond Market Association, April 2001, www.bondmarkets.com/research.shtml.
57. Warren Buffett, "What Worries Warren," *Fortune*, March 3, 2003.
58. "Global Credit Derivatives—Risk Management or Risk?" Fitch Report special report, March 10, 2003.
59. Ibid.
60. Ibid.
61. Ari Weinberg, "The Great Derivatives Smackdown," *Forbes*, May 9, 2003.

CHAPTER 3: DEREGULATION AND CREATING INSTABILITY

1. "Deregulated," *Consumer Reports*, July 2002.
2. Ibid.
3. Ibid.
4. Ron Chernow, *The House of Morgan* (New York: Grove Press, 1990), 307.
5. www.investorwords.com (online financial glossary).
6. Chernow, *House of Morgan*, 318.
7. Ibid., 321.
8. Ibid., 349.
9. Ibid., 355.
10. Ibid., 356.
11. Ibid.
12. Frank Freidel, *Franklin D. Roosevelt: A Rendezvous with Destiny* (Boston: Little, Brown/Back Bay Books, 1990), 141.
13. Population Reference Bureau, 2003 World Population Data Sheet, (www.prb.org), December 19, 2003.
14. Clifton Leaf, "White-Collar Criminals: Enough Is Enough," *Fortune*, March 3, 2002.
15. Ibid.
16. Statement from Chairman Gramm on SEC fees, February 1, 1999.
17. About the FCC, www.fcc.gov (accessed May 13, 2004).
18. Ibid.

19. Thomson Financial Data, Political Contributions, 1990–2002.

20. R. A. Dyer and Todd Mason, "Texas Energy Chief had Lay's Backing," *Fort Worth Star-Telegram*, February 7, 2002.

21. Ibid.

22. Peter Kelley and Larry Shapiro, "Wall Street Wants PUHCA Repealed," Public Citizen, March 1998, http://www.citizen.org/cmep/energy_enviro_nuclear/electricity/ deregulation/puhca/articles.cfm?ID=4256.

23. "The Public Utility Holding Company Act," Public Citizen, September 2002, http://www.citizen.org/documents/cmeep15.pdf.

24. U.S. Senator Dianne Feinstein, "Energy Manipulation," statement delivered to U.S. Senate, February 24, 2003, http://feinstein.senate.gov/03Speeches/engcr1081b.htm.

25. "Senate Approves Gramm-Leach-Bliley Act," Senator Gramm Press Release, November 4, 1999.

26. FDIC Bank Holding Company Act—Law, Regulations, Related Acts, http://www.fdic.gov/regulations/laws/rules/6000-100.html, November 12, 1999.

27. Chernow, *The House of Morgan*, 362–57.

28. Dolf Olviederlag, "Breaking Down Long Distance Plans," www.long distancereporter.com, December 16, 2003.

29. Yahoo Finance, NAS/NMS TELECOMM (^IXUT) Historical Prices, December 16, 2003, http://finance.yahoo.com.

30. Ien Cheng, "Survivors Who Laughed All the Way to the Bank," *Financial Times*, July 31, 2002.

31. "Which Utilities Are Registered Holding Companies?" Public Citizen, www.citizen.org, August 14, 1998.

32. Energy Information Administration, February 2003, www.eia.doe. gov.

33. "Powering the U.S. Electric Power Industry," Nuclear Energy Institute, July 2000.

34. Mark Cooper, "U.S. Capitalism and the Public Interest: Restoring the Balance," Consumer Federation of America, August 2002, www.consumerfed.org/publicinterest082702.pdf.

35. "False Freedom," *Consumer Reports*, http://www.consumerreports.org/main/content/display_report.jsp?FOLDER%3C%3Efolder_id=348021 &ASSORTMENT%3C%3East_id=333153, July 2002.

36. "El Paso CEO to Retire," *American City Business Journals*, February 11, 2003.

37. Besides El Paso, those companies include Dynegy, Aquilla, Reliant, Mirant, Calpine, Duke Energy, CMS Energy, and Allegheny.

38. David Ho, "FCC Approves Comcast-AT&T Merger," Associated Press, November 13, 2002.

Chapter 4: Enron, Energy, and Entropy

1. Thomson Financial Data, Power Market Companies, 1996–2002.
2. "The CFTC was created by Congress in 1974 as an independent agency with the mandate to regulate commodity futures and option markets in the United States. The agency protects market participants against manipulation, abusive trade practices and fraud." From CFTC mission statement, www.cftc.gov.
3. "Blind Faith: How Deregulation and Enron's Influence over Government Looted Billions from Americans," Public Citizen, December 2001, http://www.citizen. org/documents/Blind_Faith.PDF.
4. Ibid.
5. Ibid.
6. Ibid.
7. Center for Responsive Politics, Political Campaign Contributions, 1989–2002, www.opensecrets.org.
8. S 3283, 106 Congress, Library of Congress, http://thomas.loc.gov.
9. John Dunbar, Robert Moore, and MaryJo Sylvester, "Enron Executives Who Dumped Stock Were Heavy Donors to Bush," Center for Public Integrity, January 9, 2002.
10. Interview with Sherron Watkins, *Corporate Crime Reporter*, April 7, 2003, http:// www.corporatecrimereporter.com/watkinsinterview.html.
11. Enron 1999 Annual Report, http://www.enron.com/corp/investors/annuals/annual99/pdf.html.
12. Jacob M. Schlesinger, "The Deregulators: Did Washington Help Set Stage for Current Business Turmoil?" *Wall Street Journal*, October 17, 2002, http://www.dowjones.com/Pulitzer/pulitzer_2003/scandal/ scandal4.html.
13. Ibid.
14. RR-2426: Letter from Robert Rubin, Alan Greenspan, and Arthur Levitt to Congress on legislative proposal on CFTC concept release, June 5, 1998.
15. Ibid.
16. Center for Responsive Politics, "Political Campaigns—Who Gives?" 2000 election cycle, www.opensecrets.org.
17. Ibid.
18. Testimony by Ken Lay before the House Commerce Committee's Subcommittee on Energy and Power, May 15, 1996.
19. Bankruptcy Data Research Center: Top 2002 Bankruptcies, www.bankrupcydata.com.
20. Andrew Wheat, "System Failure Deregulation, Political Corruption, Corporate Fraud and the Enron Debacle," *Multinational Monitor*, December 4, 2001, http:// multinationalmonitor.org/enron/enronwheat. html.

21. "Enron Reports First Quarter Earnings of $0.40 per Diluted Share," Enron press release, April 12, 2000.

22. Enron 10-Q filing with Securities Exchange Commission, May 15, 2001, http://www.enron.com/corp/investors/sec/2001/2001-05-15-10-q.pdf.

23. Associated Press, "Explaining the Enron Bankruptcy," January 13, 2002.

24. Enron 10-Q filing with Securities Exchange Commission, August 14, 2001, http://www.enron.com/corp/investors/sec/2001/2001-08-14-10-q.pdf.

25. Public Citizen, "Blind Faith," http://www.citizen.org/documents/Blind_Faith.PDF.

26. Bankruptcy Data Research Center: Top 2001 Bankruptcies, www.bankruptcydata.com.

27. Interview with Sherron Watkins, *Corporate Crime Reporter*.

28. Ibid.

29. "Our Values," Enron 1999 Annual Report.

30. "Enron's 'Smoking Guns' Memo," *CBS MarketWatch*, May 7, 2002.

31. Mark Martin, "USA: Internal Memos Connect Enron to California Energy," *San Francisco Chronicle*, May 7, 2002.

32. Richard A. Oppel Jr. and Jeff Gerth, "Enron Forced Up California Prices, Documents Show," *New York Times*, May 7, 2002.

33. Testimony of Loretta Lynch before U.S. Senate Committee on Commerce, Science, and Transportation, April 11, 2002, http://commerce.senate.gov/hearings/ 041102lynch.pdf.

34. Testimony of Robert McCullough before U.S. Senate Committee on Commerce, Science, and Transportation, April 11, 2002, http:// commerce.senate.gov/hearings/041102McCullough.pdf.

35. "Enron Timeline," *Houston Chronicle*, January 17, 2002.

36. Enron-issued investor information regarding financial statements, www.enron.com/ corp/sec/, December 2001.

37. Ibid.

38. Joshua Chaffin, "Enron—Investigation and Hearings," *Financial Times*, March 15, 2002.

39. Kurt Eichenwald, "Four at Merrill Accused of an Enron Fraud," *New York Times*, March 18, 2003.

40. "Merrill Bankers Charged over Enron," *BBC News World Edition*: Business, March 18, 2003.

41. "SEC Charges Merrill Lynch, Four Merrill Lynch Executives with Aiding and Abetting Enron Accounting Fraud," SEC press release 2003-32, March 17, 2003.

42. Ibid.

43. Ibid.
44. "Merrill Lynch finalizes agreement with Securities and Exchange Commission," Merrill Lynch press release, March 17, 2003.
45. Public Citizen, "Blind Faith."
46. Ibid.
47. "Phil Gramm joins UBS Warburg," *CNN Money*, October 7, 2002.
48. "UBS Warburg Successful Bidder for Enron's North American Energy Trading," UBS press release, January 11, 2002.
49. Brian J. Back, "Probe into Enron's Financial Dealings Intensifies," *Portland Business Journal*, November 1, 2002.
50. Louis Uchitelle, "The Rich Are Different. They Know When to Leave," *New York Times*, January 20, 2002.
51. "Dynegy to Buy Once Mighty Enron for $9 Billion," Reuters, November 10, 2001.
52. Ari Weinberg, "Rubin Cleared but Enron Smoke Lingers," *Forbes*, January 3, 2003.
53. Interview with Debra Perry, senior managing director for corporate finance–Americas, and U.S. public finance, Senate Committee on Governmental Affairs, Moody's Corporation, October 30, 2002 (hereinafter, Perry interview).
54. "Enron Files Voluntary Petitions for Chapter 11 Reorganization; Sues Dynegy for Breach of Contract, Seeking Damages of at Least $10 Billion," Enron press release, December 2, 2001.
55. "Enron, Dynegy Settle Lawsuit," *CNN Money*, August 22, 2002.
56. Ibid.
57. United States Bankruptcy Court Southern District of New York, Form B1, Voluntary Petition, December 2, 2001, www.enron.com/corp/ pressroom/chapter11/pdfs/ PBOGCorpVP.pdf.
58. Ibid.
59. "Robert Rubin Cleared in Enron Probe," Reuters, January 3, 2003.
60. "Enron Is Scrambling to File Chapter 11 and Avoid Liquidation of Its Business," *Wall Street Journal*, November 30, 2001.
61. Polaris Institute, Enron Corporate Profile, January 2002, http://www. polarisinstitute.org/corp_profiles/public_service_gats/corp_profile_ ps_enron.html.
62. Center for Responsive Politics, "Political Campaigns—Who Gives?" 2000 election cycle, www.opensecrets.org.
63. Derrick Wetherell, "The Bush 100: Center Releases Report on Bush's Top Appointees," Center for Public Integrity, January 14, 2002, http://www.publicintegrity.org/report.aspx?aid=190&sid=200.
64. Department of Commerce, Commerce Organization, March 31, 2004, http://www.commerce.gov/organization.html.

65. David Teather, "Memo Emerges to Haunt President," *Guardian*, November 2, 2002.

66. Ibid.

67. Ibid.

68. Stephen Pizzo, "Time to Exhume the Body? SEC Harken Investigation Under Fire," *Daily Enron*, July 8, 2002.

69. Knut Royce, "Bush Violated Securities Laws Four Times, SEC Report Says," Center for Public Integrity, October 4, 2000.

70. Pizzo, "Time to Exhume the Body?"

71. Ibid.

72. Ibid.

73. Nate Blakeslee, "Tricky Dick II," *Nation*, February 8, 2002.

74. Jeffrey H. Birnbaum, "Mr. CEO Goes to Washington," *Fortune*, May 24, 2001.

75. Robert Bryce, "The Candidate from Brown & Root," *Texas Observer*, October 6, 2000.

76. Ibid.

77. Halliburton SEC filing, 10Q for Fourth Quarter 2002, http://www. sec. gov/Archives/edgar/data/45012/000004501202000062/0000045012-02-000062.txt.

78. Birnbaum, "Mr. CEO Goes to Washington."

79. Ibid.

80. "Vice President Dick Cheney and Mrs. Cheney Release 2002 Income Tax Return," White House press release, April 11, 2003.

81. "Vice President and Mrs. Cheney Release 2001 Income Tax Return," White House press release, April 15, 2002.

82. "Cheney Gets 'Golden Parachute' from Halliburton Co.," Associated Press, August 12, 2000.

83. "Cheney Sold $35 Million in Halliburton in August," Reuters, September 12, 2000.

84. Greg Farrell, "SEC Sues KPMG over Xerox Records," *USA Today*, January 29, 2003.

85. "KPMG Said to Agree to Settle Lawsuit," Bloomberg News, March 10, 2003.

86. GAO, "About Us: What is GAO?" www.gao.gov (accessed May 13, 2004).

87. "Data Shows Industry Had Extensive Access to Cheney's Energy Task Force," Natural Resources Defense Council press release, May 21, 2001, http://www.nrdc.org/ media/pressreleases/020521.asp.

88. Jennifer Coleman, "Enron Memo Details Cheney Ties During California Crisis," Associated Press, January 31, 2002, http://radioleft.com/ article.php?sid=268.

89. Truthout Organization, "Boxer Calls on FERC to Provide List of All

Meetings and Phone Calls with Enron Executives," January 31, 2002, http://www.truthout.org/ docs_01/02.01B.Boxer.FERC.htm.

90. David Ivanovich, "Cheney Met Six Times with Enron Execs," *Houston Chronicle*, January 9, 2002.

91. Peter Brand and Alexander Bolton, "GOP Threats Halted GAO Cheney Suit," *The Hill*, February 19, 2003.

92. Paul Krugman, "Delusions of Power," *New York Times*, March 28, 2003.

93. Brand and Bolton, "GOP Threats."

94. Neil A. Lewis, "Court Blocks Effort to Protect Secret Cheney Files," *New York Times*, July 9, 2003.

95. Neil A. Lewis, "Federal Judge Orders Release of Documents of White House," *New York Times*, April 2, 2004.

96. "Memo Shows Enron Division Headed by Army Secretary Thomas White Manipulated California Electricity Market," Public Citizen press release, May 8, 2002, http://www.citizen.org/pressroom/release.cfm? ID=1106.

97. Ibid.

98. Ibid.

99. Ibid.

100. Ibid.

101. Ibid.

102. Alan Chernoff, "Former Enron Exec Dies in Apparent Suicide," CNN, January 26, 2002.

103. Ibid.

104. Brian Cruver, *Anatomy of Greed* (New York: Carroll & Graf Publishers, 2002), 305–7.

105. "El Paso Executive Dead," *CNN Money*, June 3, 2002.

106. Ibid.

107. Ibid.

108. "Bank of America Asks FERC for Permission to Trade Wholesale Electricity," Reuters, September 11, 2002.

109. Statement of Dianne Feinstein on energy manipulation, delivered to U.S. Senate, February 24, 2003.

110. "Bank America Asks FERC for Permission to Trade Wholesale Electricity," Reuters, September 11, 2002.

111. Thomson Financial Data, Merger Volume, 1990–2002.

112. James Dukart, "Chuck Watson," *Utility Business*, June 1, 2001.

113. Arleen Spangler, "Standard & Poor's Updates Refinancing Needs for the Energy Merchants Sector," Standard & Poor's press release, April 24, 2003.

114. Nomi Prins, "Energy's Moribund Tendencies," *Guardian Unlimited*, July 28, 2003.

115. Thomson Financial Data, Merger Volume, 1990–2002.

116. "Strategy and Financial Policy Bolster Five Investment-Grade Energy Companies," Standard & Poor's press release, July 2, 2003.

117. Creswell, "Energy Trading Power Failure."

118. Ibid.

119. Ibid.

120. Alexei Barrionuevo, "El Paso's Rating Is Cut by Moody's to Junk Status," *New York Times*, November 27, 2002.

121. Chris Baltimore, "Enron Client Gained on Soaring California Power Prices," Reuters, June 7, 2002.

122. Nomi Prins, "Electricity Companies Need Tighter Regulation," *Newsday*, August 6, 2003.

123. Eileen Moustakis, "Shaken Power Market May Face More Cuts," Reuters, November 9, 2002.

124. Ibid.

125. Ibid.

126. Ibid.

127. "Aquila Fails to Find Partner and Will Abandon Energy Trading," *Alexander's Gas and Oil Connections*, September 5, 2002.

128. "Dynegy CEO Resigns," *CNN Money*, May 28, 2002.

129. Bankruptcy Data Research Center: Top 2002 Bankruptcies, www.bankruptcydata.com.

130. "El Paso Announces CEO Transition Plan: William A. Wise to Retire by Close of 2003," El Paso press release, February 11, 2003.

131. "Attorney General Lockyer Announces $15.5 Million Settlement with El Paso Electric to Resolve Energy Market Manipulation Case," California Attorney General Bill Lockyer press release, February 13, 2003.

132. "Who Killed Montana Power?" CBS *60 Minutes*, August 10, 2003.

133. "Dynegy Timeline," *Houston Chronicle*, January 17, 2002.

134. "Broadwing Signs Agreement with El Paso Energy," *Cincinnati Bell Telephone*, July 17, 2000.

135. "Reliant Makes Equity Investment in Grande Communications," *San Antonio Business Journal*, September 28, 2000.

136. Enron 2000 Annual Report.

137. Ibid.

138. "Enron, Rice University Sign Broadband Services Agreement; Rice Receives $8 Million Grants from Enron, Lay Family," Enron press release, June 22, 2000.

139. "Enron Broadband Services LP Joins Affiliates in Chapter 11," Dow Jones News Service, January 17, 2002.

140. "Williams Prepared to Deal with Bankruptcy of Former Telecommunications Subsidiary," William Communications press release, April 22, 2002.

141. "FERC Investigations," *Platts Global Energy*, August 15, 2002, http://plattsweb1.platts.com/featlib.shtml.
142. Ibid.
143. Statement of Dianne Feinstein on Energy Manipulation.
144. Josef Hebert, "Feds Probe Bogus Energy Swaps," Associated Press, May 22, 2002.
145. "Reliant Resources Announces the Resignation of CEO Steve Ledbetter as Chairman and CEO," Reliant press release, April 13, 2003.
146. "Berger & Montague, P.C., Sues on Behalf of Investors Who Purchased CMS Energy Corporation Securities Between August 3, 2000 and May 10, 2002," Berger & Montague press release, July 8, 2002.
147. Creswell, "Energy Trading Power Failure"; Nancy Dunne and Julie Earle, "Federal Regulators 'Knew About Bogus Trades,' " *Financial Times*, May 15, 2002.
148. Eric Billingsley, "FERC Investigates the Potential Misconduct of El Paso Electric," *New Mexico Business Weekly*, August 16, 2002.
149. David Barboza, "A Big Victory by California in Energy Case," *New York Times*, November 12, 2002.
150. "Reliant Resources, Mirant Served Subpoenas Related to California Energy Trading," *Dow Jones Business News*, November 11, 2002.
151. Paul Thomasch, "Duke Admits to 23 Round-Trip Power Trades," Reuters Business Report, July 16, 2002.
152. Peter Larson, "Reliant Admits to Sham Transactions," *Financial Times*, July 8, 2002.
153. Christian Berthelsen and Mark Martin, "FERC Energy Probe Shifts from Enron to Reliant," *Houston Chronicle*, April 20, 2003.
154. Ibid.
155. Ibid.
156. Ibid.
157. "Commission Approves $13.8 Million Settlement with Reliant Energy over Physical Withholding in California Power Exchange," FERC press release, January 31, 2003.
158. David Barboza, "Complex El Paso Partnerships Puzzle," *New York Times*, July 23, 2002.
159. Ibid.
160. Ibid.
161. Ibid.
162. Ibid.
163. Ibid.
164. "Judge Says Utility Withheld Gas During California Crisis," Associated Press, July 24, 2002.

165. Ibid.
166. Ibid.
167. California Attorney General Lockyer press release, February 13, 2003.
168. Constance L. Hayes, "S.E.C. Investigates El Paso's Accounting," *New York Times*, October 6, 2003.
169. Ibid.
170. Statement by Senator Dianne Feinstein, "FERC's Refusal to Nullify California's Long-Term Energy Contracts Signed Amid Fraud and Manipulation by Energy Companies," June 25, 2002.
171. California Attorney General Lockyer press release, November 11, 2002.
172. FERC's Non-Public Appendix to Order Directing Williams Energy Marketing & Trading Company and AES Southland to Show Cause (Docket No. IN01-3-000), available at http://news.findlaw.com/ hdocs/ docs/ferc/williamsaes111502osc.pdf.
173. Statement of Dianne Feinstein on energy manipulation, delivered to U.S. Senate, February 24, 2003.
174. Ibid.
175. Feinstein, "FERC's Refusal to Nullify."
176. Feinstein, Energy manipulation statement.
177. Doyle McManus and Richard Simon, "Cheney Rejects Price Caps, Aid for California Power Crisis," *Los Angeles Times*, May 5, 2001.
178. Ibid.
179. Ibid.
180. Ibid.
181. Richard A. Oppel Jr., "Federal Regulators Uphold California Energy Contracts," *New York Times*, June 26, 2003.
182. Conversation with author, June 29, 2003.
183. Feinstein, "FERC's Refusal to Nullify."
184. "Montana Sues PGE, 11 Other Electric Companies," *American City Business Journals*, July 3, 2003.
185. Matt Daily, "Texas Power Market Hit by Price Spike, Gaming," Reuters, March 13, 2003.
186. "About FERC: Chairman Patrick Henry Wood III," http://www.ferc. gov/about/com-mem/wood.asp.
187. "Reliant Resources May Face Criminal Charges in California Case," Bloomberg News, March 8, 2004.
188. Mary Flood, "Enron's Skilling Indicted Today," *Houston Chronicle*, February 18, 2004.

CHAPTER 5: TELECOM IMPLOSION

1. Thomson Financial Data, Wall Street Fees, 1990–2000.
2. Julie Creswell, with Nomi Prins, "Global Crossing Emperor of Greed," *Fortune*, June 9, 2002.
3. Center for Responsive Politics, Telecommunications Industry: Political Lobbying 1997–2000, www.opensecrets.com.
4. 1999 Global Crossing annual report.
5. Ibid.
6. Thomas Easton, "The $20 Billion Crumb," *Forbes Global*, April 19, 1999.
7. SEC filings, Global Crossing.
8. Creswell, "Global Crossing Emperor of Greed."
9. Richard S. Dunham and Mike McNamee, "Bush Sr.'s Profitable Crossing," *Business Week*, March 4, 2002.
10. "Judicial Watch's Dirty Dozen: The 12 Most Corrupt Politicians, Lobbyists and Business Leaders of 2002," *Judicial Watch*, December 23, 2002.
11. Creswell, "Global Crossing Emperor of Greed."
12. Global Crossing, www.globalcrossing.com/xml/global/fact_sheet_ver1.xml (accessed on May 13, 2004).
13. John Roger Energy Law, Fact Sheet: www.cailaw.org/iel/rogers.html, (accessed on May 13, 2004).
14. "Bush's Ruling Class," 1992 investigation, *Common Cause*, April, May, June 1992.
15. Ibid.
16. Points of Light Foundation, www.pointsoflight.org/awards/corporate.cfm (accessed on May 13, 2004).
17. Litex Corporation, leadership biographies, litexcorp.com/about/cookbio.htm (accessed on May 13, 2004).
18. "Global Crossing Announces Framework Agreement to Supply NATO," Global Crossing press release, July 25, 2001.
19. "Global Crossing Awarded Contract to Provide Virtual Network Linking British Embassies Worldwide," Global Crossing press release, May 10, 2000.
20. Michael Scherer, "The Mother Jones 400—Communications," *Mother Jones*, March 5, 2001.
21. Ibid.
22. Ibid.
23. Ibid.
24. Ibid.
25. SEC filing, 10-Q June 1999.
26. SEC filing, 10-Q December 1999.
27. SEC filing, 10-Q March 2000.

28. SEC filing, 10-K annual 2000 report.
29. Richard Mullins, "Untangling the Frontier/Global Knot," *Democrat and Chronicle*, April 14, 2002.
30. "Leo Hindery Succeeds Bob Annunziata as CEO of Global Crossing," Global Crossing press release, May 2, 2000.
31. Global Crossing, leadership biographies, www.globalcrossing.com, (accessed on May 13, 2004).
32. Dennis Berman, "Hindery Asks Global Crossing to Fork Over Back Pay, Rent," *Wall Street Journal*, October 15, 2002.
33. James Cope, "Global Crossing finishes optical network project," http://CNN.com/SCI-TECH June 26, 2001.
34. Ibid.
35. "Global Crossing Picks IBM's Gary Cohen and Arthur Anderson's Joseph Perrone for Senior Management Posts," Global Crossing press release, May 1, 2000.
36. Geraldine Fabrikant with Saul Hansell, "At Global Crossing, Deals with Son of Executive Raise Questions," *New York Times*, February 18, 2000.
37. Ibid.
38. SEC filing 10-Q June 1999.
39. Mullins, "Untangling the Frontier/Global Knot."
40. SEC filing, 10-Q September 1999.
41. SEC filing, 10-Q March 2000.
42. Creswell, "Global Crossing Emperor of Greed."
43. "Asia Global Crossing Prices Initial Public Offering of 68 Million Common Shares at $7 per Share; Begin Trading on NASDAQ," Global Crossing press release, October 6, 2000.
44. Alphonso Myers, "Friends No More: Global Crossing Claims Fraud in $1 Billion Suit Against TSSL," Telephony.Online, May 29, 2000.
45. SEC filing, 10-Q March 2000.
46. "Documents Show Active Role by Global Crossing Chairman," Associated Press, October 1, 2002.
47. Simon Romero, "House Staff to Question Ex-Executive," *New York Times*, September 27, 2002.
48. Ibid.
49. "Global Crossing Wins Network Services Contract from U.S. Department of Defense Valued Up to $400 Million," Global Crossing press release, July 9, 2001.
50. "Former Joint Chief of Staff Becomes Global Crossing Vice President of Federal Programs," Global Crossing press release, November 5, 2001.
51. Testimony of Roy Olofson, House Committee on Energy and Commerce Investigations Subcommittee, September 24, 2002.
52. Ibid.

53. Ibid.
54. Ibid.
55. Ibid.
56. Ibid.
57. Ibid.
58. Ibid.
59. "Global Crossing Reports Solid Third Quarter Commercial Revenues, Led by 43% Annual Growth in Commercial Data Revenues," Global Crossing press release, November 13, 2001.
60. George Chidi, "Global Crossing Battles Accounting Controversy," InfoWorld, February 2, 2002.
61. SEC filing, 10-Q September 2001.
62. Bankruptcydata.com, Research: 2001 Bankruptcies.
63. Roy Olofson v. Gary C. Winnick, State of California Case Number RLOVGCW151483.
64. Creswell, "Global Crossing Emperor of Greed."
65. Testimony of Leonette Clumfer, House Committee on Energy and Commerce Investigations Subcommittee, October 1, 2002.
66. Testimony of Gary Winnick, House Committee on Energy and Commerce Investigations Subcommittee, October 1, 2002.
67. Nomi Prins, "Winnick Watch: Gary's Latest," Left Business Observer, December 2003.
68. U.S. Bankruptcy Court, Southern District of New York, Voluntary Petition from B1, July 21, 2002.
69. "Global Crossing Announces Review of Cost of Access Liability and Expected Restatement of Financial Statements," Global Crossing press release, April 27, 2004.
70. Internal e-mail from Bernard Ebbers, "Informal Inquiry," June 13, 2002.
71. Creswell, "Global Crossing Emperor of Greed."
72. Gretchen Morgenson, "Ebbers Made $11 Million on 21 Stock Offerings," New York Times, August 31, 2002.
73. Dennis K. Berman, "Before Telecom Bubble Burst, Some Insiders Sold Out Stakes," Wall Street Journal, August 11, 2002.
74. Jon Swartz, "Sullivan Estate Might Not Be Exempt," USA Today, August 12, 2002.
75. Scott Sullivan, "Master of the Mega Merger," Oswego Magazine, Spring 1999.
76. First Interim Report of Dick Thornburgh, Bankruptcy Court Examiner for WorldCom, November 4, 2002.
77. Ibid.
78. Ibid.
79. "The WorldCom–Wall Street Connection," PBS Frontline, May 8, 2003.

80. First Interim Report of Dick Thornburgh, November 2000.

81. Thomson Financial Data, WorldCom Merger and Acquisition History, 1990–2000.

82. First Interim Report of Dick Thornburgh.

83. Andrew P. Madden, "IPO Block Party: Profiles of the Top 50 Technology Companies of 1995," *Red Herring*, December 1999.

84. 1998 WorldCom annual report, 10K SEC filing.

85. FCC Archives, CC Docket No. 97-211.

86. "FCC Approves Merger of WorldCom and MCI," FCC press release, September 14, 1998.

87. 1999 WorldCom annual report, 10K SEC filing.

88. "MCI WorldCom and Sprint Create Preeminent Global Communications Company for 21st Century," WorldCom press release, October 5, 1999.

89. NASDAQ data, 2002 WorldCom statistics.

90. Thomson Financial Data, Wall Street Fees, 1990–2000.

91. Paul Adams, conversation with the author, December 2002.

92. "WorldCom Announces Additional Changes to Reported Income for Prior Periods," WorldCom press release, August 8, 2002.

93. 1999 WorldCom annual report, 10K SEC filing.

94. "WorldCom Announces Additional Changes to Reported Income for Prior Periods."

95. Gayle Reaves, "Accounting for Anguish," *Fort Worth Weekly*, May 16, 2002.

96. "Taking MCI Out of Local Competition," *CWA Report*, March 1998.

97. Ibid.

98. Ibid.

99. Gretchen Morgenson, "In a Broker's Notes, Trouble for Salomon," *New York Times*, September 22, 2002.

100. Monica Didier, conversation with author, October 2002.

101. Senate Hearing, Energy and Commerce Committee, July 30, 2002.

102. Nomi Prins, "Whose Jobs? Our Jobs!" *Dollars and Sense*, March/April 2003.

103. Christopher Stern, "Laid-Off WorldCom Workers Seek More Severance Pay," *Washington Post*, September 10, 2002.

104. "Judge Rules WorldCom Workers Will Get Full Severance and Other Benefits," AFL-CIO press release, October 1, 2002.

105. Internal e-mail from Steven Brabbs to Lucy Woods, forwarded to Cynthia Copper, June 26, 2002.

106. Ibid.

107. 2001 WorldCom annual report, 10K SEC filing.

108. "WorldCom President and CEO John Sidgmore Responds to U.S. President George Bush," WorldCom press release, June 26, 2002.

109. "Ebbers Out at WorldCom," *CNN Money*, April 30, 2002.

110. Center for Responsive Politics, WorldCom data, www.opensecrets.org.

111. Internal e-mail from Ron Beaumont on PAC contributions, May 6, 2002.

112. 2001 annual SEC 10K Filing, Government Contract Revenues.

113. WorldCom Government Contracts, WorldCom Web site, www.mci.com.

114. Ibid.

115. Ibid.

116. Washington Technology Contractor 2002 annual rankings, March 6, 2002.

117. "U.S. General Services Administration Extends FTS2001 Contract with WorldCom," WorldCom press release, November 13, 2002.

118. Ibid.

119. Ibid.

120. "U.S. Department of State Awards WorldCom 10-Year Global Telecommunications Contract," WorldCom press release, November 19, 2002.

121. "WorldCom Announces Intention to Restate 2001 and First Quarter 2002 Financial Statements," WorldCom press release, June 25, 2002.

122. "WorldCom Announces Additional Changes to Reported Income for Prior Period," WorldCom press release, August 8, 2002.

123. U.S. Court bankruptcy filing, July 21, 2002.

124. SEC injunction document, Litigation Release No. 17866, Accounting and Auditing Enforcement Release No. 1678, November 26, 2002.

125. SEC Litigation Release No. 17883; Accounting and Auditing Enforcement Release No. 1683, November 6, 2002.

126. SEC Litigation Release No. 17842, November 14, 2002.

127. "Final Approval of Michael Capellas' Amended Compensation Package," *The Corporate Library*, December 2002, www.thecorporatelibrary.com.

128. Dean Takahashi and Therese Poletti, "Capellas' Quick Exit from HP Raises Concerns," *San Jose Mercury News*, November 11, 2002.

129. "Commerce Secretary Evans and Governor Ridge to Lead National Homeland Security Expo," White House press release, August 19, 2002.

130. "Moving Forward," transcript, Federal News Service, November 15, 2002, 11:20 A.M. EST.

131. Brian Bergstein, "WorldCom CEO Vows to Improve Ethics," Associated Press, November 16, 2002.

132. Ben Silverman, "As the WorldCom Turns," Dotcom Scoop, November 19, 2002, www.dotcomscoop.com.

133. "WorldCom Board Members Offer Resignation to Chairman and CEO Michael Capellas," WorldCom press release, December 17, 2002.

134. "Lott Steps Down as Senate Majority Leader," CNN, December 20, 2002.

135. "Who Gives?" July 2002, www.opensecrets.org.

136. Ana Radelet, "Close Ties—Not a Surprise," *Mississippi Clarion-Ledger*, August 22, 2002.

137. "WorldCom Files Plan of Reorganization and Changes Brand Name to MCI," WorldCom press release, April 14, 2003.

138. "MCI Emerges from U.S. Chapter 11 Protection," MCI press release, April 20, 2004.

CHAPTER 6: EXAMINATION AND REFORM?

1. Simon Romero and Alex Berenson, "WorldCom Says It Hid Expenses, Inflating Cash Flow $3.8 Billion," *New York Times*, June 26, 2002.

2. Joseph B. Treaster, "Adelphia Files for Bankruptcy," *New York Times*, June 26, 2002.

3. Stephen Taub, "Adelphia CEO Arrested," *CFO.com*, July 25, 2002.

4. SEC Release 2002-119, August 2, 2002.

5. SEC press release, June 28, 2002.

6. SEC File Number 001-10415, form 10-Q, May 15, 2002.

7. Jared Sandberg and Susan Pulliam, "WorldCom Finds More Errors; Restatement Will Be $7.2 Billion," *Wall Street Journal*, August 9, 2002.

8. Susan Pulliam and Jared Sandberg, "New WorldCom Report to SEC Will Acknowledge More Flaws," *Wall Street Journal*, September 19, 2002; Christopher Stern, "SEC Case Against WorldCom Grows," *Washington Post*, November 6, 2002.

9. Stephen Taub, "Market Shrugs Off Certification Day," *CFO.com*, August 15, 2002.

10. Deborah Solomon, "Qwest's Recent Disclosure May Spark More Scrutiny," *Wall Street Journal*, July 30, 2002.

11. Richard Scrushy, "Still Uncharged Is Unfrozen," *Forbes*, May 8, 2003.

12. Financial Statement Restatements: Trends, Market Impacts, Regulatory Responses, and Remaining Challenges, GAO-03-138, October 4, 2002.

13. PriceWaterhouseCoopers management barometer, March 24, 2003.

14. POB Charter, February 2001.

15. "Resolution Passed by the Public Oversight Board," Public Oversight Board news release, May 1, 2002.

16. Frank C. Minter and Douglas L. Smith, "Sarbanes-Oxley: Who Gets the Bill?" *Strategic Financing*, March 2003.

17. Floyd Norris, "New Arbiters of Auditing," *New York Times*, October 28, 2002.

18. Associated Press, "Pitt Defends Oversight Board's Salaries," February 12, 2003.

19. SEC Release, 2003-28, March 3, 2003.

20. *CBS MarketWatch*, "SEC Chief: Governance Laws Are Working," April 8, 2003.

21. "Statement of the Commission Regarding the Selection of the Chairperson of the Public Company Accounting Oversight Board (PCAOB)," SEC press release, April 15, 2003.

22. *CPA Journal*, "The Numbers Game," December 1998.

23. Ibid.

24. Henry Paulson Jr., "Restoring Investor Confidence: An Agenda for Change," June 5, 2002, National Press Club, Washington, D.C.

25. *Big bath restructuring charge*: occurs when companies set up large charges associated with companies restructuring; these charges help companies "clean up" their balance sheet. *Creative acquisition accounting*: in the purchase price allocation procedures, companies classify a large portion of the acquisition price as "in-process" research and development, which can be written off in a "one-time" charge—removing any future earnings drag. *Cookie jar reserves*: using unrealistic assumptions to estimate liabilities for such items as sales returns, loan losses or warranty costs. Companies stash accruals in "cookie jars" during the good times and reach into them when needed in the bad times. *Immaterial misapplications of accounting principles*: intentionally recording errors within a defined percentage ceiling. *Premature recognition of revenue*: recognizing revenue before a sale is complete, before the product is delivered to a customer, or at a time when the customer still has options to terminate, void or delay the sale.

26. Richard Perez-Pena and Patrick McGeehan, "Assault on Wall St. Misdeeds Lifts Spitzer's U.S. Profile and Makes Enemies," *New York Times*, November 4, 2002.

27. Michael G. Oxley, speech at the U.S. Chamber of Commerce, Washington, D.C., May 22, 2002.

28. Paul Krugman, "Fool Me Once," *New York Times*, October 8, 2002.

29. Center for Responsive Politics, "Who Gets: 2002 Election Cycle," www.opensecrets.org.

30. "SEC, NY Attorney General, NASD, NASAA, NYSE, and State Regulators Announce Historic Agreement to Reform Investment Practice," SEC press release 2002-179, December 20, 2002.

31. Andy Serwer, "There's a Rumble Between Harvey Pitt and Eliot Spitzer. Is Wall Street Big Enough for the Both of Them?" *Fortune*, June 23, 2002.

32. "Statement by Attorney General Eliot Spitzer Regarding the "Global Resolution" of Wall Street Investigations," New York Attorney General press release, April 28, 2003.

33. "Orange County, Merrill Lynch Announce Settlement Lawsuit," Orange County Executive Office press release, June 2, 1998.

34. "Business Notes: Wall Street: The Junk Man Goeth," *Time*, February 6, 1989.
35. "Judge OKs $750M Fine Sparing WorldCom," Associated Press, July 8, 2003.
36. "WorldCom Lands Iraq Contract," *BBC News*, May 20, 2003.
37. "Williams Solidifies Long-Term Power Contract with California; Adds Gas Contract Under Broad Agreement," Williams press release, November 11, 2002.
38. "FERC Approves Settlement with Reliant in California Cases: Proceeds Could Total $50 Million," FERC press release, October 2, 2003.
39. Jennifer Coleman, "El Paso to Settle for $15.5 Million," Associated Press, February 14, 2003.
40. Associated Press, "Lucent to Settle SEC Investigation," February 27, 2003.
41. "Patricia Russo Named Chairman of Lucent Technologies; Henry Schacht Steps Down, but Will Remain a Member of the Board," Lucent Technologies press release, February 19, 2003.
42. Associated Press, "Former ImClone CEO Pleads Guilty," October 15, 2002.
43. "Martha Pal Gets 7-Year Jail Term," CBS, June 11, 2003.
44. "Lifestyles Guru Martha Stewart Resigns as CEO," ABC, June 4, 2003.
45. "Xerox Settles SEC Enforcement Action Charging Company with Fraud," SEC press release, April 11, 2002.
46. Matt Adrejczak, "HealthSouth and CEO Charged," *CBS MarketWatch*, March 19, 2003.
47. "ING Group 2002 Operational Profit Result Strong, Net Profit and Net Equity Not Affected by Goodwill Write Down," memo from Yvo Metzelaar, Managing Director and CEO, ING Vysya Life Insurance Company Pvt. Ltd., March 18, 2003, http://news.eians.com/wire/2003/03/18/18iz16.html.
48. "ING Group Closes Acquisition of ReliaStar," ING Group press archive, September 1, 2000; "ING Group Closes Acquisition of Aetna Financial Services and Aetna International," ING Group press archive, December 14, 2000.
49. Chris Isidore, "AOL Tumbles after Record Loss," *CNN Money*, January 30, 2003.
50. James Ledbetter, "The Boys in the Bubble," *New York Times*, January 2, 2002.
51. Landon Thomas Jr., "The Views from Wall Street; For Chastened Analysts, More Skepticism about Investing," *New York Times*, January 2, 2003.
52. Jeordan Legon, "Get Ready to Tune into Wireless Net," *CNN Money*, March 13, 2003.

53. Christopher Palmeri, "Sempra's Golden State," *Business Week*, October 20, 2003.

54. "Shareholders Take It to Judge," www.cfo.com, August 20, 2001.

55. Rebecca Blumenstein, Dennis K. Berman, and Evan Perez, "After Inflating Their Income, Companies Want IRS Refunds," *Wall Street Journal*, May 2, 2003.

56. "Power Play/Enron Timeline," *Houston Chronicle*, November 10, 2001.

57. Economic Policy Institute: Job Watch, February 6, 2004.

58. "Introduction to Ethics, Fairness, and Values in Decision Making" course, Harvard Business School, http://www.exed.hbs.edu/programs/efv/.

59. Kurt Eichenwald, "Economy & Business; After a Boom, There Will Be Scandal. Count on It," *New York Times*, December 16, 2002.

60. Richard A. Oppel Jr., "Federal Regulators Uphold California Energy Contracts," *New York Times*, June 25, 2003.

61. "FCC Sets Limits on Media Concentration," FCC press release, June 2, 2003.

62. "Korn Ferry's 29th Annual Board of Directors Study," Korn Ferry International press release, October 17, 2002.

63. "Baxter International Inc., Corporate Governance Guidelines," The Corporate Library, February 25, 2003, http://files.thecorporatelibrary.net/policies/gov_bax.htm.

64. U.S. Department of Labor, "Discrimination Against Employees Who Exercise Their Safety and Health Rights," www.osha.gov/as/opa/worker/whistle.html (accessed May 13, 2004).

65. Chris Sanders, "U.S. Pensions Lost $1 Trillion in Last 3 Years," Reuters, February 28, 2003.

66. Janice Revell, "Beware the Pension Monster," *Fortune*, December 3, 2002.

67. Danny Hakim with Jonathan Fuerbringer, "G.M. to Raise $10 Billion for Pension Gap," *New York Times*, June 21, 2003.

68. Leigh Strope, "House Bill Would Allow Advice from 401(k) Managers," Associated Press, May 15, 2003.

69. Ibid.

70. U.S. Investors, "III. Incubation," *Citizen's Works: Annual Report 2002*, www.usinvestors.org.

71. National Retiree Legislative Network Web site: Members, http://www.nrln.org/Members.htm.

72. Marc Gunther, "A Big Win for the Little Guys," *Fortune*, June 16, 2003.

73. Conversation with author, July 2003.

74. Nomi Prins, "Debate: Corporate Underdogs Bite Back," *Guardian*, April 7, 2003.

Index